D1329831

Political Settlements in Divided Societies

Political Settlements in Divided Societies

Consociationalism and Cyprus

Christalla Yakinthou

University of Western Australia
Bluestocking Institute for Global Peace and Justice

First published 2009 by
PALGRAVE MACMILLAN

Palgrave Macmillan in the UK is an imprint of Macmillan Publishers Limited, registered in England, company number 785998, of Houndmills, Basingstoke, Hampshire RG21 6XS.

Palgrave Macmillan in the US is a division of St Martin's Press LLC, 175 Fifth Avenue, New York, NY 10010.

Palgrave Macmillan is the global academic imprint of the above companies and has companies and representatives throughout the world.

Palgrave® and Macmillan® are registered trademarks in the United States, the United Kingdom, Europe and other countries.

ISBN-13: 978-0-230-22375-2   hardback

This book is printed on paper suitable for recycling and made from fully managed and sustained forest sources. Logging, pulping and manufacturing processes are expected to conform to the environmental regulations of the country of origin.

A catalogue record for this book is available from the British Library.

Library of Congress Cataloging-in-Publication Data

Yakinthou, Christalla, 1980–
  Political settlements in divided societies : consociationalism and Cyprus /
  Christalla Yakinthou.
      p. cm.
  Includes bibliographical references and index.
  ISBN 978-0-230-22375-2 (alk. paper)
  1. Conflict management—Cyprus. 2. Cyprus—Politics and government—
  1960–2004. 3. Cyprus—Politics and government—2004– 4. Cyprus—Ethnic
  relations—Political aspects. I. Title.
  DS54.9.Y35 2009
  956.9304—dc22   2009013638

Dedicated to my parents, Effie and Robin Yakinthou

Contents

Tables

Figure

Acknowledgements

There are a vast number of people to whom I must acknowledge a great debt. This book has been developed out of my doctoral dissertation, and as such I thank my PhD supervisors, Associate Professors Bruce Stone and Samina Yasmeen of the University of Western Australia, for their constant support and encouragement to see me over the line of submission. I have received quite a gift, I think, to be set on this path.

Thank you to Janina Burley, for holding the boat steady. I thank my friends Faize Akcaba, Filiz Naldoven, Kerstin Wittig, Burcu Barin, Özle and Cem Tamtunali, Ozgün and Emete Özkan, Cemal, Eleni and Michalis Konstantinides, and Michalis and Marro Polikarpou, who, in many ways, have facilitated my research, and who have filled Cyprus with such vibrancy and beauty for me. I am grateful to Professor John McGarry for his advice and suggestions for the development of this book. I thank Professor Oren Yiftachel for his comments on a number of my chapters, and Dr Narelle Miragliotta for her suggestions. Serhan Peksoylu has generously shared his knowledge of north Cyprus politics, and I thank Dr Altay Nevzat for taking the time to comment on Chapter 2. I thank Dr Andrekos Varnavas, for his speedy correspondences on all questions Cypriot, and for his, and Helen's, friendship.

Linley Hill of Political Science and International Relations, and the staff of the HSS Library's Scholars Centre at the University of Western Australia have always gone above and beyond the call of duty. I acknowledge the assistance provided to me by the university's honorary research fellowship.

Particular thanks to those friends who generously made time to proofread various parts of my work. I would especially like to extend thanks to Evan Stamatiou, who so painstakingly read and re-read drafts, and whose perceptivity and incisive comments have made my work much richer. *Je te dois une fière chandelle*. It is a pleasure to acknowledge the depth of gratitude I owe to several members of the discipline of Political Science and International Relations at UWA: Dr Kate Riddell, Dr Liza Beinart, Shae Garwood, and Sky Croeser. I am privileged to be part of such a circle of women; the world is warmer, smaller, brighter, and richer for it. Thank you to Costas Demetriades, for his many years of friendship. We may infrequently agree on matters of politics, but I have enjoyed our debates. I thank Francia Kinchington for her advice; Francia, you are the only woman I know who can combine in one conversation a Foucauldian analysis of the Cyprus conflict and a re-interpretation of Plato's form of beauty as applied to stiletto shoes. Thank you also to Theofanis Xydas, my neighbour and cousin who kept me company and taught me to play tavli between interviews. I am indebted to my family in Cyprus, who welcomed me so warmly every time I walked through their door. I am deeply grateful also for the many years of support and encouragement from my godparents, Nick and Dianne Tomazos, who nurtured my intellectual development and curiosity.

Θα ήθελα να εκφράσω ιδιαίτερες ευχαριστίες στη γιαγιά μου και στον παππού μου Σπύρο και Χρυστάλλα Χρήστου. Δεν υπάρχουν λόγια με τα οποία να σας ευχαριστήσω που μου γνωρίσατε την Κύπρο, και μου χαρίσατε τον ανεκτίμητο αυτό πολιτιστικό θησαυρό που κληρονόμησα με την καταγωγή μου. Χωρίς να το ξέρετε, με βοηθήσατε να αρχίσω και να ολοκληρώσω την εργασία αυτή που μου χάρισε τόσες όμορφες ψυχικές εμπειρίες, και μου άνοιξε μελλοντικους δρόμους που αδημονώ να διαβώ.

Most importantly, my deepest thanks to my parents and brothers, whose enormous faith and unwavering support made this project not only possible but also so much more comfortable than it could otherwise have been. I am very lucky to be loved by such pure-hearted people.

Finally, I thank everyone in and around Cyprus who so generously shared their time and knowledge with me, both officially and unofficially, especially at a time when they were running between negotiations and meetings. I am grateful for their time.

Abbreviations

ADIK	*Μαχητικό Δημοκρατικό Κίνημα*, Fighting Democratic Movement
AKEL	*Ανορθωτικό Κόμμα Εργαζόμενου Λαού*, Progressive Party of Working People
AKP	*Adalet ve Kalkınma Partisi, Justice and Development Party*
BNP	*Bi-Communal Development Programme*
CMP	*Committee for Missing Persons*
COE	*Council of Europe*
CTP/BG	*Cumhuriyetçi Türk Partisi/Birleşik Güçler, Republican Turkish Party/United Forces*
CUP	*İttihat ve Terakki Cemiyeti, Committee of Union and Progress*
DEV-İŞ	*Devrimci İşçi Sendikaları Federasyonu, Revolutionary Trade Unions Movement*
DIKO	*Δημοκρατικό Κόμμα*, Democratic Party
DISY	*Δημοκρατικός Συναγερμός*, Democratic Rally
DP	*Demokrat Parti, Democrat Party*
EC	*European Council*
EDEK	*Κίνημα Σοσιαλδημοκρατών*, Movement for Social Democracy
EDI	*Ένωμενοι Δημοκράτες*, United Democrats
EEC	*European Economic Community*
EOKA	*Εθνική Οργάνωσις Κυπρίων Αγωνιστών*, National Organisation of Cypriot Fighters
EU	*European Union*
EUPSO	*EU Programme Support Office*
EURO.KO	*Ευρωπαϊκό Κόμμα*, European Party
EURO.DI	*Ευρωπαϊκή Δημοκρατια*, European Democracy
IKME	*Ίδρυμα Κοινωνικοπολιτικών Μελετών*, Socio-Political Studies Institute
KAMU-SEN	*Kıbrıs Türk Kamu Görevlileri Sendikası, Civil Servants Trade Union*
KAP	*Kıbrıs Adalet Partisi, Cyprus Justice Party*
KEP	*Ελεύθεροι Πολίτες, Free Citizens' Movement*

KÖGEF	*Kıbrıslı Öğrenciler Gençlik Federasyonu, Turkish Cypriot Students Youth Federation*
ND	*Νέα Δημοκρατία, New Democracy Party*
PASOK	*Πανελλήνιο Σοσιαλιστικό Κίνημα, Panhellenic Socialist Movement*
PEO	*Παγκύπρια Εργατική Ομοσπονδία, Pancyprian Federation of Labour*
TKP	*Toplumcu Kurtuluş Partisi, Communal Liberation Party*
TMT	*Türk Mukavemet Teşkilatı, Turkish Resistance Organisation*
TRNC	*Kuzey Kıbrıs Türk Cumhuriyeti, Turkish Republic of Northern Cyprus*
UBP	*Ulusal Birlik Partisi, National Unity Party*
UCR	*United Cyprus Republic*
UN	*United Nations*
UNDP	*United Nations Development Programme*
UNDP-ACT	*United Nations Development Programme-Action for Co-operation and Trust*
UNFICYP	*United Nations Peacekeeping Force in Cyprus*
UNHCR	*United Nations High Commission for Refugees*
UNOPS	*United Nations Office for Programme Services*
YBH	*Yurtsever Birlik Hareketi, Patriotic Unity Movement*

Chronology of Key Events in Cyprus, 1571–2004

1571–1878	Ottoman conquest and rule of Cyprus
1878	British administration of Cyprus under Ottoman rule
1882	Establishment of Legislative Council as a partly elected body
1914	Britain annexes Cyprus *de facto*
1919	Paris Peace Conference: Greece does not press for *enosis*
1923	Turkey signs Treaty of Lausanne, recognising British rule over Cyprus
1931	October Revolt against the British, and subsequent abolition of the Legislative Council
1947	Winster Plan
1954	(July) Hopkinson Plan
1955	Birth of EOKA
1955	(August) London Tripartite Conference
1955–6	(October–March) Harding-Makarios Negotiations
1956	Birth of Volkan
1956	(December) Radcliffe Proposal
1957	Volkan superseded by TMT
1958	(January) Foot Plan
1958	(June) Macmillan Plan
1959	(19 February) Zurich and London Accords
1960	Foundation of the Republic of Cyprus
1963	(December) *Kanlı Noel*
1964	(January) Withdrawal of Turkish Cypriot representatives from Republic of Cyprus government
1964	Establishment of UNFICYP, and UN peacemaking mandate (Resolution 186)
1965	Galo Plaza Report on Cyprus
1967	(28 December) Establishment of the 'Provisional Turkish Cypriot Administration'
1974	(15 July) Attempted Greek *coup d'État* and overthrow of Makarios
1974	(20 July) Beginning of first Turkish military incursion
1974	(23 July) Collapse of *coup* in Cyprus; Glafkos Clerides becomes interim President of the Republic of Cyprus in Makarios' absence
1974	(25 July) Ceasefire and first Geneva talks
1974	(14 August) Second Turkish military incursion

1975	Declaration of the Turkish Federated State of Cyprus
1977	Makarios-Denktaş High Level Agreement
1977	Death of Archbishop Makarios
1979	Kyprianou-Denktaş 10 Point Agreement
1983	Unilateral declaration of independence of TRNC
1992	Ghali Set of Ideas
1993	Confidence Building Measures
1997	EU Luxemburg Summit (Decision to open negotiations with Republic of Cyprus, and to exclude Turkey from negotiations. Impacted on the Turkish Cypriot community and especially on rapprochement activities)
1999	(December) European Council Summit Meeting, Helsinki (decision to recommend Cyprus' accession irrespective of the conflict's resolution)
2002	European Council Meeting, Copenhagen (suspension of *acquis* in north in case of no resolution)
2003	(February) Presidential elections in Republic of Cyprus: election of Tassos Papadopoulos
2003	(16 April) Republic of Cyprus signs EU Accession Treaty
2003	(23 April) Partial lifting of restrictions of freedom of movement
2003	(December) Parliamentary elections in TRNC
2004	(24 April) Referendum for acceptance or rejection of Comprehensive Solution to the Cyprus Conflict
2004	(1 May) Accession of Republic of Cyprus to EU
2005	(April) Election of Mehmet Ali Talat as president of TRNC

Chronology of the Annan Plan

2000	(July) Alvaro de Soto's Preliminary Thoughts
2000	(November) 8 November Document
2002	(November) Submission of Comprehensive Settlement of the Cyprus Conflict (Annan I)
2002	(December) Submission of Annan II
2003	(February) Submission of Annan III
2004	(March) Submission of Annan IV
2004	(March) Submission of Annan V
2004	(April) Referendum for acceptance or rejection of Comprehensive Solution to the Cyprus Conflict (Annan V)

Introduction

> Ethnic conflicts do not just exist or come into being. They
> are the product of deliberate choices of people to pursue
> certain goals with violent means.[1]

Cyprus is a complex case of a conflict society. Armed conflict between the
Greek and Turkish Cypriot communities lasted, on and off, for 20 years:
from the mid-1950s when the Greek Cypriots founded anti-British and pro-
Greek EOKA[2] (Cyprus had been a British colony, gaining its independence
in 1960) until the country's *de facto* partition in 1974. The most significant
crises occurred in 1963–4, when the power-sharing government collapsed as
a result of political discord between the groups in government, leading to
constitutional crisis and the subsequent withdrawal of the Turkish Cypriot
representatives from government and of the community into enclaves to
protect themselves from violence, and the failed Greek *coup d'état* in 1974
which resulted in a military intervention and subsequent occupation by
Turkey. As a result of the 1974 war, the country has since been composed of
two geographically distinct ethnic zones, a Turkish Cypriot north, and a predominantly Greek Cypriot south.[3] There have been few officially acknowledged violent conflicts between the communities in the post-division years.
After the Turkish Cypriot community unilaterally declared its independence
in 1983, each community has built its own largely democratic state, which
functions independently of the other. The Republic of Cyprus, controlled by
the Greek Cypriots, is the state which is recognised as governing the whole
of Cyprus, though *de facto* it only controls the southern two-thirds of the
island. While neither side is content with the situation, there is a negative
peace in Cyprus.

But the conflict has been continued through other avenues. Not only is
there fierce diplomatic point-scoring in the international arena between
Greek and Turkish Cypriot political elites, the rhetoric of war is deeply
ingrained. Military service is compulsory for men on both sides of the

1

divide, and conscripts serve their time patrolling the 'green line' dividing Turkish north Cyprus (the Turkish Republic of Northern Cyprus, TRNC) from Greek south Cyprus (the Republic of Cyprus). There is a very real sense that the 'other' community is the enemy, and that the borders gained or lost by war are to be protected against the other side's military. Memories of the conflict's worst aspects are still present. The majority of mass graves from the 1964–7 and 1974 periods of war are only recently being exhumed by the United Nations' Committee for Missing Persons (CMP), and the issue of the missing people[4] is highly political and hyper-politicised in both communities. Restrictions on freedom of movement between north and south Cyprus have been partially lifted after the 2003 unilateral decision by then-president of the internationally unrecognised TRNC, Rauf Denktaş, to open two checkpoints, allowing Turkish and Greek Cypriots to cross to the other side for the first time since 1975. More checkpoints have been opened since then, facilitating a degree of freedom of movement over the island. Despite this, intercommunal friendships are the exception rather than the rule, and recent surveys have shown that crossings between communities are not breaking down psychological barriers.[5] Greek Cypriots tend to cross to the north for three main reasons: to go on pilgrimages to churches or other holy sites; to see their ancestral homes; and for shopping and entertainment.[6] Turkish Cypriots tend to cross either for work (there are some 6000 Turkish Cypriots employed in south Cyprus) or for shopping and entertainment.[7] Very few on either side cross to visit friends. Until very recently, children of both communities have been taught from very early ages at school that the 'other' is the enemy, whom one should fear and loathe. Commemoration of historical events which represent pain and loss for one community, and victory for the other, continues. In different ways, the conflict is lived every day.

Over the four decades since the breakdown of peace in Cyprus, there has been a great concentration of international political and financial resources to find a suitable resolution, primarily under the auspices of the United Nations (UN). Many UN proposals and plans have been created and abandoned, and the conflict has absorbed both the efforts and reputations of many international diplomats. Not only have all of these attempts ended without success, they have made very little impact on the domestic political situation in Cyprus.

That appeared to have changed with the Annan Plan, a federal and consociational blueprint for the reunification of Cyprus completed in March 2004 with the support of the UN and put to the Greek and Turkish Cypriot people in separate referendums on 24 April 2004. The Annan Plan was designed to unite the country prior to the admission of Cyprus to the EU on 1 May 2004. The UN architects of the plan worked in tandem with the Cypriot negotiators to craft institutions which met the demands and addressed the fears of each community, drawing on previous efforts to find a suitable form of government for Cyprus. Though the plan was approved by a majority of 65 per cent of the Turkish Cypriot population, it was rejected in the 2004 referendum by a 76 per cent majority of the Greek Cypriot population. Without the approval of a majority of both ethnic groups the plan could not be adopted. The Republic of Cyprus acceded to the EU in May 2004. In any case, the referendum proved to be a time of great change in both Cypriot societies. It solidified Turkish Cypriots together in support of the solution and against pro-secession conservative government forces. It also forced public discussion, for the first time, in both societies about the realities of a power-sharing solution.

Cyprus now exists as an EU member state. But it remains divided. Officially, the whole country has acceded to the Union. However, in accordance with protocol 10 of Cyprus' EU accession treaty, the EU recognises the Republic of Cyprus, which effectively controls only the south, as the sole legal government over the whole of the island; the *acquis communautaire*[8] is suspended in the northern part of Cyprus. Thus, only the south of Cyprus directly receives the benefits (and meets the obligations) of EU membership.[9] Not only must the EU manage an intractable conflict which has now become internal but it has also to manoeuvre around and often facilitate the various states of legal and political exception which have been created with the accession of an island of which one part, which has met all the Copenhagen criteria and operates in accordance with EU protocols and under Community law, does not communicate with the other part of the island, which does not. Further complicating the matter, while northern Cyprus functions largely independently, it survives under the political, military, and economic largesse of long-time on-again-off-again EU candidate Turkey, which is now occupying the territory of an EU member state. In addition, the Republic of Cyprus takes a highly legalistic approach to any direct contact between EU-member and third states and the TRNC. The EU has therefore found itself with a cold but deeply entrenched and highly politicised, but seemingly 'cold' conflict on its eastern Mediterranean border. Meanwhile, the island has settled back into its accustomed status as a divided polity and unresolved problem on the agenda of international politics.

Looking at the politics of adopting political settlements

The problem of how political settlements are to be adopted in divided or post-conflict polities is one which is receiving growing attention, as the international community increasingly views protracted intra-state conflicts as carrying transnational consequences. It is not only the *means* of adopting political settlements in these societies that is so problematic but also the question of *what kind* of political settlement is most appropriate. Cyprus provides an illuminating case study of these problems. This is so not only because the basis of its division, ethnicity, is shared with many other divided polities, but also because it has been the object of many years of scrutiny and multiple, sustained efforts at resolution of its division. Ongoing failure to reach a political settlement under such circumstances can reveal a good deal about what impedes and what assists progress towards a settlement. The experiences of Cyprus, therefore, can offer lessons to both practitioners working on political solutions for divided and post-conflict societies and to academics and others seeking to understand how conflicts become intractable, where the primary impediments lie to successful constitutional architecture, and how those impediments can be overcome.

The broadest goal of the book is therefore to throw light on the challenges of adopting political settlements in intractable conflicts and divided societies. It does this by focusing on this particular conflict, the resolution of which has for years been held up, arguably in large part by elite intransigence. The book consequently offers answers for why elites in Cyprus are so unwilling to adopt a power-sharing solution. In doing so it hopes to offer new material for the wider debate regarding constitutional design and adoption of peace plans in divided societies; on the politics of institutionalising peace.

Successive efforts to devise political institutions for Cyprus were examined to see what considerations have informed choice and, in particular, what has been learned from past Cypriot failures as well as from failures and successes elsewhere in the world. Particular attention is paid in the book to the recent Annan Plan, because this has come closest to providing an acceptable solution to the problem of institutional design thus far. The case study also seeks to determine what weight was given by those working on the Annan Plan to the need to identify and foster supportive political conditions in Cyprus.

Examined first is the idea that consociational democracy is able to provide a political settlement to the Cyprus conflict. Chapter 1 analyses consociational theory and the criticisms of that theory most relevant to the case of Cyprus. Its main aim is to establish whether the ideas being used for Cyprus' reunification are flawed. Chapter 2 examines the role of Cyprus' modern history to understand how particular aspects such as ethno-nationalism and divergent ideas of democracy and freedom have left their mark on current political elites, and in so doing, affected the nature and chances of a political settlement for Cyprus. Chapter 3 looks at the first consociational state in Cyprus, the 1960 Republic of Cyprus, to consider how, and to what extent, the reluctance of elites to enter into another power-sharing arrangement has been affected by institutional design and traumas carried from the Republic's breakdown. The task of Chapter 4 is to analyse the 2004 consociational state proposed in the Annan Plan. It examines whether the plan was able to meet each group's major needs to provide an adequate political settlement of the conflict. It also investigates the extent to which the legacies of history and difficulties of institutional design identified in previous chapters were overcome by the Annan Plan.

Chapters 5–7 examine the roles of particular factors which have been identified as central to the failure to adopt a consociational solution in 2004, and as especially important to encouraging elite co-operation. Chapter 5 examines in detail elite relations in the period surrounding the 2004 Annan Plan, looking for domestic incentives for compromise and any underlying patterns which could have supported elite co-operation. Chapter 6 examines whether external actors were able to offer incentives for domestic elites to co-operate and agree to adopt the plan. Chapter 7 analyses the 2004 referendum, as the site of the Annan Plan's ultimate rejection. It pays particular attention to the constitutional engineers' decision to remove the need for elite agreement on the plan and seek only its popular support as the mechanism of adoption. It finds that the engineers were neither able to secure the elites' support for the plan, nor neutralise their role. The referendum was consequently undermined by the political elites. Together, the chapters explain why, despite considerable progress having been made towards creating a political system which would facilitate a unified democratic Cyprus, elites remain unprepared to share power.

Literature and sources

There are multiple bodies of literature relevant to this work. The broadest utilised is that on the politics of devising political settlements for deeply divided and post-conflict polities. From the literature on power-sharing design and democracy, I draw upon studies of both successful and failed implementation of consociational democracies, as well as upon debates about conditions under which consociational engineering is most likely to succeed. There is a significant body of literature critical of consociational theory, upon which I also draw. Chapter 1 contains an extensive review of this literature, and it is also discussed in subsequent chapters as relevant. In examining the problems of designing constitutions and of getting those designs adopted, this book contributes to the literature on consociational constitutional design.

The literature on Cyprus informs the work's analysis of why the particular institutions have been chosen for Cyprus, and how. Though there is a vast literature on many aspects of the Cyprus conflict, there is an absence of debate over the application of power-sharing democracy to the problem of reunifying Cyprus. A major contribution of this work, therefore, is to bring together the bodies of literature on consociational theory and on the Cyprus conflict. Additionally, literature from a number of periods in Cyprus' history is drawn together, stretching back to the very early colonial years, and forward to the post-Annan period. The literature on Cyprus is also used thematically: Chapter 2 draws on ideas about ethno-nationalism in Cyprus' early modern history; Chapter 3 utilises the literature on constitutional engineering in Cyprus; Chapters 5 and 7 focus upon the literature which examines the importance of elites and party politics in Cyprus; and chapter 6 is informed by recent literature on the politics of Cyprus' accession to the EU. The book also contributes to the literature on constitutional development in Cyprus.

In addition to extensive use of secondary sources, a variety of primary source material has been used. This includes the published and unpublished reports of involved actors – United Nations Security Council Reports, statements and documents, as well as the reports of United Nations Secretary General, special envoys, and representatives to Cyprus. United Nations peace plans, agreements, proposals, Sets of Ideas and Bases for Settlement provide part of the primary database used to inform my hypothesis. Turkish and Greek Cypriot interlocutors and political parties have published numerous opinion pieces dealing with the most desirable form of government, as well as comments upon plans and reports suggested by third party negotiators. Relevant political actors have made a number of speeches and presentations which I have used.

Preparation also included extended periods of research in Cyprus, from February to July 2004, and from August to November 2006. Approximately 50 field interviews with parties involved in the negotiation process, as well as with lobby groups and civil justice organisations, were conducted in Cyprus. Additional interviews were conducted by correspondence or telephone in 2005.

A number of interviews contained sensitive information, and information for particular parts of some interviews was given to me on the condition that the source's identity be suppressed. As a result, the sources for some of the text are referred to as 'confidential'. In the reference, I have identified the organisation to which the interviewee belongs, and that the information is confidential. The interview date is also suppressed, to prevent identification of the source.

Among the interviewees involved in the crafting of the Annan Plan were members of the UN core negotiating team who drafted the Annan Plan, senior and other UN staff involved in other areas of the conflict, and representatives of the EU based in Cyprus. I interviewed a number of high-level diplomats based in Cyprus who represented countries with a specific interest in, and ability to offer incentives for, resolution of the conflict. I also interviewed Cypriot politicians across the spectrum and on both sides of the island. Mid-level officials from both communities who were involved at the committee-level, drafting domestic laws and international treaties were also consulted. I conducted a number of interviews and informal discussions with journalists who had been following, or were specialists on, particular aspects of the conflict, as well as with academics in the disciplines of political science and international relations, anthropology and sociology, international law, and history. I had extensive contact with Turkish and Greek Cypriot civil society groups, trade unions, and political representatives and attended many open political meetings and pro- and anti- reunification rallies. All primary source material is listed in the bibliography.

A note on language

In societies such as Cyprus, language is employed as a significant weapon in the battle for legal, moral, and political supremacy. This battle involves everyone who picks up a pen to write about any aspect of the conflict, for a political statement will be made with the choice of one phrase or another. To avoid entering into this conflict, to be 'neutral', is almost impossible. The difficulty of avoiding the appearance of partiality is particularly reflected in one's choice of terms when addressing the Greek and Turkish Cypriot states. UN resolution 541 and 550 have confirmed the illegality of the self-declared TRNC, and Turkey is the only country of political significance to have recognised the state. Therefore, the Republic of Cyprus is the only internationally recognised government on the island. As Chapter 5 will further enumerate, the standard protocol when addressing the TRNC or any of its offices of state is to underscore the state's illegality. If an author wishes to remove any stigma of pro-Turkish bias, they have two choices: to enclose the 'TRNC' within parenthesis, highlighting its pseudo-status; or to attach words like 'self-declared/illegal' to the term. One may further avoid reference to the Turkish Cypriot state apparatus at all by referring to the state's elected representatives as 'leaders of the Turkish Cypriot community', rather than 'President' or 'Prime Minister'. Often, when writing in the Republic of Cyprus about the Turkish Cypriot state, parentheses are placed around references by editors without the author's approval.

But bias is inherent in this choice also, and the use of this protocol provides support to one side in a history which is contested. The Republic of Cyprus was founded in 1960 as a bi-national state; government was shared between Greek and Turkish Cypriots, and each community formed a check against abuses of power by the other. Late in 1963, the Turkish Cypriot representatives left government in protest when their veto over the proposed budget was overruled. Since that point, the governing of the Republic of Cyprus is managed exclusively by Greek Cypriots, who are elected primarily by Greek Cypriots. Turkish Cypriot government positions, constitutionally protected, remain empty. As Chapter 3 will explain, attempts by Turkish Cypriot representatives to reclaim their seats in government were effectively blocked by Greek Cypriots, who, in the interim period had passed a number of constitutional changes which the Turkish Cypriot representatives believed to be unconstitutional. The Turkish Cypriot representatives could return to government *only if* they approved the interim changes. They felt they could not, and instead in 1967 created a temporary body to govern the Turkish Cypriot community.[10] At this point, different narratives apply to the same events, and 'History' is contested. The Republic of Cyprus continued to be recognised internationally as the legitimate government of Cyprus, despite Turkish Cypriot petitions that without the Turkish Cypriot community, the Republic of Cyprus was unconstitutional.

The interpretation of Cyprus' history again diverges in the post-1974 environment when the Greek and Turkish Cypriot communities were completely separated as a result of the Turkish intervention, and once more in 1983 with the founding of the self-declared TRNC. To follow protocol is to implicitly endorse the Greek Cypriot version of history, and especially the embedded assumptions about the legitimacy of the Republic of Cyprus and whom it represents. But to not follow protocol conversely implies endorsement of the Turkish Cypriot version of history and its assumption that the Republic of Cyprus is illegitimate. One therefore finds oneself being assigned a position on the conflict by choosing (and it is not much of a choice) how to refer to the two political entities. To be entirely neutral in this conflict is impossible.

This dilemma is replicated in other choices of language associated with the conflict. The 'line' which since 1975 has officially separated the Turkish Cypriot community from the rest of Cyprus has a number of names, each of which carries specific assumptions. In the official narrative of the TRNC, this separation marker is called the 'border'. The use of the term border is significant because it implies legal separation and the existence of two states. In the official narrative of the Republic of Cyprus, by contrast, it is called the 'Attila line'. Operation Attila was the code name given by the Turkish army to the invasion, but 'Attila' is also a term synonymous in Greek Cyprus for 'barbarian', one who commits great atrocities. It is therefore the line of the Turkish barbarian. It is sometimes also called the 'green line' in the diplomatic language of neutrality.

Similarly, one must choose how to refer to the events of July and August 1974, when Turkey landed in Cyprus, occupying some 37 per cent of the territory and ultimately precipitating the country's *de facto* partition. To the Greek Cypriot community, this event was an 'invasion',[11] perhaps triggered by the attempted Greek *coup d'état* against then-President of the Republic of Cyprus, Archbishop Makarios, and his government, but disproportionate in its response, bloody in its process, and ultimately a vicious land-grab in its outcome. This narrative has been endorsed by international law and the international community in UN resolutions 353, 360, 365, 367, and 3212. To the Turkish Cypriot community, however, the same events of 1974 are narrated as a 'peace operation',[12] an event which saved the Turkish Cypriot community from the terrors of the Greek coup, and from what they considered to be their imminent annihilation. To use the term 'invasion' denies the Turkish Cypriot historical narrative which emphasises their relief at the Turkish army's arrival in July 1974; but to use the term 'peace operation' denies the Greek Cypriot historical narrative (and international law) which emphasises the illegality of the Turkish army's actions, and certainly overlooks the illegality of the island's partition and subsequent events. Some scholars have attempted to avoid adopting the narrative of either side by referring to the events as the Turkish 'incursion', or 'intervention'. However, even this terminology leads to criticism that one is sympathising with the Turkish version of events and overlooking international law and conventions violated by Turkey in its aggression against Cyprus. The least loaded term seems to be the '1974 war'.

While Chapters 4 and 5 examine how international law and international forums have been used in the battle for legitimacy between the Greek and Turkish Cypriot historical narratives, these points are raised here to emphasise how the challenges one confronts when writing about conflicts such as Cyprus begin long before one analyses power-sharing and applying it in divided societies. It also highlights how the competing official narratives have affected socialisation in Greek and Turkish Cypriot societies, and how the lack of a shared narrative undermines efforts to construct a shared state: without even a common historical language, how will peace be built?

Definitions

Divided societies are here defined as 'societies in which there is no transcendent democratic principle that enables legitimate, collective decisions to be taken on anything like a consistent basis'.[13] In this study, the term *deeply divided society* is understood in the following way: 'deeply divided societies are composed of non-assimilating ethnic groups which occupy their historical (real or mythical) homeland'.[14] The word *consociational* or *consociationalism* is used to indicate the constitutional design which was defined by Arend Lijphart and subsequently developed by other scholars. In cases where the design predates the definition, the term is used to indicate continuity with the later classification. However, consociationalism is identified most frequently in Cyprus (and in much of the literature on Cyprus) as 'power-sharing', not an entirely accurate term, as consociationalism is a form of power-sharing. *Institutions* are defined as 'implicit or explicit principles, norms, rules, and decision-making procedures'[15] upon which a state is based.[16] *Intractable conflicts* are characterised by opposing demands for security, power, status, and territory, which are particularly intense.[17] A *mutually hurting stalemate* is a situation where all parties to a conflict recognise that no party will be able to prevail in the conflict.[18] The *Annan Plan* is the term commonly used when referring to the 'Comprehensive Settlement of the Cyprus Problem', offered in March 2004 as a solution to the Cyprus conflict. The state proposed by the Annan Plan was to have been called the *United Cyprus Republic*. There were five versions of the Annan Plan, and the book has occasion to refer to each specifically. Where no numeral reference is made, the allusion is to Annan V.

1
Consociationalism in Theory and Practice

> Consociationalists ... agree that it would be better if their
> polity had a 'normal' set of institutions for dividing and
> competing for power. But experience has taught them that
> deep and protracted conflicts between national, ethnic and
> religious communities requires that power be systemati-
> cally shared as well as divided subject to competition.[1]

Consociational democracy is both highly contested in the academic literature and widely used by constitutional engineers working to re-establish
democratic governance in deeply divided polities. This work seeks to understand why elites in Cyprus have been thus far unprepared to share power.
As a first step in this project, the present chapter will examine whether the
body of 'consociational' ideas, on which efforts at a political settlement
have drawn, can create a stable political system which promotes and rein-
forces co-operation, and is able to manage potential political conflict. There
are a number of important criticisms of consociational theory which are also
highlighted by the Cyprus case. These criticisms, described initially in this
chapter and examined further in later chapters, provide insight into why
political settlement has been so elusive in Cyprus.

It is argued in this chapter that one particular idea of early consociational theory, which has been heavily criticised in the literature, deserves more sustained
attention. This is the notion that it is possible to identify factors that indicate
the likelihood of successful adoption of consociational democracy. If constitutional engineers can approach a conflict armed with knowledge of the key
factors, and also with knowledge of the relative importance of the various factors in their application to individual cases, this would allow them to ascertain
which particular difficulties may be faced in implementing a consociational
solution. It would also assist them to strategise more effectively.

This chapter first outlines the characteristics and value of consociational
democracy. It subsequently reviews and analyses major criticisms of the theory which are relevant to this study. Finally, the chapter examines Lijphart's

conditions for the successful application of consociational democracy, and suggests the application of four particular factors to the case of Cyprus.

Evolution of consociational democracy

Consociationalism is a form of institutional engineering which maintains that ethnic or inter-group tension can be resolved democratically by the creation of a permanent multi-group coalition government. The theory was largely developed by a group of political scientists in the late 1960s who examined a number of Western European countries as anomalous cases of democratic stability and has been significantly developed since then.

Fitting broadly within the accommodationist family of managing ethno-cultural diversity,[2] consociationalists, like most accommodationists, believe that

> in certain contexts, national, ethnic, religious and linguistic divisions and identities are resilient, durable and hard, rather than malleable, fluid, soft or transformable. Political prudence and morality requires adaptation, adjustment, and consideration of the special interests, needs and fears of groups so that they may regard the state in question as fit for them.[3]

Consociational theory predicts that if, in a fractured society, a system of governance is created which shares governmental decision making between political representatives of the disputant groups, then the conflict can be contained and stable government continued or established.

McGarry, O'Leary, and Simeon distinguish between three primary types of consociation; 'complete', 'concurrent', and 'plurality'.[4] Consociational theorists generally outline a number of mechanisms by which to encourage elite co-operation and regulate conflict. 'The first and key conflict regulating mechanism in a consociation is a cross-community power-sharing executive, in which representative elites from different communities jointly prevent conflict'.[5] Other key mechanisms include community self-government, proportionality, and sometimes include a form of group veto. Its aim is to encourage inter-group trust by instilling a culture of co-operation which originates with political elites and 'trickles down' to the community level.

The idea of consociational democracy, as defined by its originator and leading advocate Arend Lijphart, arose from three different sources. The first was Lijphart's dissatisfaction with the pluralist theory of his mentor Gabriel Almond and what Lijphart perceived as the need to explore the relationship between pluralism and political stability. The second was what Lijphart calls the 'motivational' work of the economist Sir Arthur Lewis who highlighted the merits of consensus-building governance in parts of West Africa. The third was Lijphart's own analysis of the Netherlands as a deviant case of democracy.

In his original, 1968, analysis of Dutch democracy,[6] Lijphart sought to explain the 'paradox' of political stability in a society divided on class and religious grounds, indeed, 'characterized by an extraordinary degree of social cleavage'.[7] According to this study, the definitive cause of Dutch stability was the 'spirit of accommodation' among political elites, who put aside competitive political self-interest in order to lead the country away from disaster.[8] However, a number of other factors that provide for stable democracy in the face of severe division were also identified. Those factors are first presented in the 1968 study (with qualifiers) and later developed in an article he published in 1969 in *World Politics*.

From the Dutch study, Lijphart developed his definition of consociational democracy:[9] 'consociational democracy means government by elite cartel designed to turn a democracy with a fragmented culture into a stable democracy'.[10] In the same article, he characterised consociationalism as *'glidningspolitik'*, the 'politics of smoothness'.[11] This was a description of a certain kind of political and institutional structure,[12] which he saw to have practical implications for 'plural' and deeply divided societies throughout the world. When Lijphart re-classified Scandinavia and the Low Countries into a functional type of pluralist democracy, he also added Switzerland and Austria to the set. Their inclusion gave him a small set of cases from which he extracted the elements of a model of a consociational polity.

Lijphart's version of consociationalism is but one approach to democratic development in divided societies, emphasising elite co-operation. When the dimensions of consociational theory were first being explored, 'consociationalism' was not exclusively associated with elite co-operation. Other scholars in the same period were also exploring the possibilities of sustaining democracy in deeply divided societies. 'Tracing the genealogy of the consociational idea, McRae pointed to Gerhard Lehmbruch's 1967 and 1968 articles about "concordant democracy", W. T. Bluhm's 1968 article on "contractarian democracy" in Austria, Val Lorwin's 1962 article on "vertical pluralism", and his later work, based on a 1969 paper, on "segmented pluralism" in Holland, Belgium, Luxembourg, and Switzerland'.[13] Lorwin's sociological understanding of segmented pluralism and Daalder's emphasis upon historical traditions as generating the necessary support for consociational structures were both popular analyses; however, they were superseded by Lijphart's perspective.

In the broader field of institutional engineering in divided societies, Lijphart was among the first to provide 'a rationale for power-sharing[14] in divided societies'.[15] His work opened up a debate, which has since progressed considerably. McGarry and O'Leary have been at the centre of a new consociational 'school', which has sought to broaden the applicability of consociational democracy in several ways. New, or 'liberal', consociationalists have expanded the focus of consociational theory beyond specific concentration on the design of political institutions like the executive, legislative, and electoral systems, to include attention to elements such as 'the design of the police and security forces; the handling of paramilitary offenders; demilitarization of both state and paramilitary forces; the integration of former paramilitaries; transitional justice processes (e.g. truth commissions); the return of exiles and the management of refugees; new human rights protection mechanisms; economic reconstruction; and provisions for monitoring ceasefires'.[16]

O'Leary has argued that 'consociationalism alone may not be enough to overcome some types of divisions'.[17] Where conflicts involve already-formed national groups, solution 'may require recognition of their national identity in new political institutions and co-sovereign or confederal relationships'.[18] We will see that the 2004 Annan Plan for Cyprus follows this revised notion of consociationalism. In addition, where conventional consociationalism has focused significantly on the traditional sovereign state, McGarry and O'Leary have argued that insufficient attention is given to the role of external parties 'in both exacerbating and implementing agreements'.[19] Institutional links with international parties in resolution of a conflict is emphasised.[20] In addition, they maintain that traditional consociationalism focuses overtly on peaceful disputes. 'New' consociationalism, then, gives more attention to the transformation from war to peace.[21] Though always existing in the peacemaker's toolkit, versions of this form of political design have become an increasingly attractive option for the reconstruction of post-conflict societies over the last decade.

In an attempt to situate the theory more precisely, Ulrich Schneckener categorised consociationalism as a particular form of consensus democracy,[22] often 'linked to ethnically segmented societies, or, rather, to multinational polities, i.e. states or regions in which two or more ethno-national groups live'.[23] Esman argues that 'a generation of debate, empirical testing, and reflection have tended to devalue the specific rules and practices identified with the consociational strategy for conflict management'.[24] Multicultural citizenship theory develops an idea of ethnocultural group rights within a state.[25] There is significant potential in future work for the fusion of new consociationalism with Kymlicka's multicultural theories.

The popularity of consociationalism has waxed and waned over the years since its conception. Nonetheless, a large body of literature has grown around both the concept and its most famous proponent. It has frequently been proclaimed a 'dead' theory (particularly in the 1990s), but continues to be a subject of debate as well as a tool for constitutional engineers. Twenty-first-century efforts to pacify and 'democratise' deeply divided and post-conflict polities have led to a revival in the perceived value of consociationalism. Over this time, the definitions and criteria of consociational democracy have evolved, both as a result of the continuing development of Lijphart's ideas in light of trends in institutional engineering and in response to severe and protracted criticism.

Characteristics of consociational democracy

In his early work, Arend Lijphart identified five basic elements of consociationalism: proportionality, grand coalitions, cultural autonomy, minority
veto, and a plural society. He also posited four 'factors conducive to consociational democracy'. They were elites who are singularly concerned about
societal fragmentation, who are committed to the maintenance and cohesion of the system, who are co-operative with elites from other subcultures,
and who are able to negotiate solutions that will keep all parties happy.[26]
In addition, he highlighted nine factors that would help gauge the probability of continued success of current consociational democracies. These factors focused on 'the institutional arrangements and the operational code of
inter-elite accommodation'.[27] A changing number and combination of such
factors were subsequently developed by Lijphart to predict the chances of
successful adoption and maintenance of consociational democracy. In 1969
these were listed as

> [t]he length of time a consociational democracy has been in operation ...;
> the existence of external threats to the country ...; a multiple balance
> of power among the subcultures ...; a relatively low total load on the
> decision-making apparatus ...; distinct lines of cleavage ...; encapsulated
> cultural units ...; internal political cohesion of the subcultures ...; an
> adequate articulation of the interests of the subcultures ...; widespread
> approval of the principle of government by elite cartel.[28]

In more recent years, pinning Lijphart down on a specific list of factors
supporting the implementation or perpetuation of consociational democracy has been difficult. As he himself says (to the chagrin of critics), 'the
basic characteristics of consociational democracy are inherently stretchable:
they can assume a large number of different institutional forms'.[29] This
also means that the institutional components of consociationalism are not
clearly definable, because they are context-dependent; for each case, a different combination of institutions and mechanisms may be relevant.

Despite the difficulty of classifying a particular set of institutions as 'consociational', Lijphart and other theorists began to identify a model with
certain characteristics, useful for resolving deadlock in divided societies.
Over time, this model became a prescription for overcoming, through the
institutions of government, seemingly intractable ideological or ethnic division at the societal level.

Lijphart recently re-classified the four main characteristics of consociational democracy into the two primary characteristics of grand coalition and
group autonomy and the two secondary characteristics of mutual veto and
proportionality.[30] As we have seen above, there is broad agreement that
these are the key characteristics of consociational democracy. An altered

form of the 'favourable factors' has remained,[31] but Lijphart has frequently stated that these factors are 'helpful but neither indispensable nor sufficient in and of themselves to account for the success of consociational democracy'.[32]

Lijphart has identified a number of institutions which constitutional engineers should utilise in creating a consociational polity.[33] A proportional representation (PR) electoral system with a high degree of proportionality is recommended, because it is the 'optimal way' of 'ensuring the election of a broadly representative legislature'.[34] Second, he advocates a parliamentary over a presidential system of government for its greater potential to create a broad power-sharing executive. Third, he recommends a high level of power sharing in the parliamentary executive, which he argues can be accommodated without producing excessive instability in cabinet. Fourth, the head of state should be invested with no more than ceremonial powers. In the case where the head of state is a president, this limitation would avoid any temptation to become 'a more active political participant',[35] evolving the system towards semi-presidentialism. Fifth, decentralised federalisation should also be preferred, to protect the units from domination by the centre. Sixth, in the case that the disputant groups are not geographically concentrated, a high degree of non-territorial autonomy is advised. Finally, he places great importance on a flexible version of proportional representation for administrative, military, and judicial institutions, which, he argues, would ensure 'broad representation of all communal groups'.[36] Liberal consociational theorists are more flexible regarding the application of particular institutions.[37]

The rationale for applying this constitutional model in deeply divided societies is, firstly, to ease political and inter-communal tensions by dividing and sharing power between the major groups and institutionalising co-operation in the executive. The model does not seek to change societal structures or ignore power struggles between groups; rather, it works *with* the existing societal context, reducing friction in nations already fraught with dangerous cleavages. Secondly, it justifies its means by its ends: proponents of consociationalism argue that a culture of co-operation can be encouraged within deeply divided societies by implementing a system that allows each group to maintain maximum levels of autonomy and encouraging negotiation and compromise at the decision-making elite level. The ultimate goal is to create a 'trickle-down' effect. Trust between elites builds confidence at the lower community levels between groups, thus strengthening inter-communal ties, which reinforce faith in the institutions of government. The goal is to manage tension between groups, and the hope is that inter-group trust will slowly be built.

The case of Cyprus illustrates the difficulty of establishing a shared government between antagonistic groups. The Greek and Turkish Cypriot communities have been (independently of each other) operating broadly democratic political systems for at least 20 years. However, to get the groups to trust one another enough to share electoral, legislative, and bureaucratic institutions has proven impossible to date. If elites can be encouraged to work together, and trust can be built from the top down, then progress might be made towards a stable democracy.

Value of consociational democracy

The system's value for consociationalists lies in its ability to use political elites and particular institutional structures (involving an executive coalition and group autonomy) to harness (and for some, eventually dispel) ethnic or other very deep divisions, with the goal of implementing, restoring, or maintaining a form of democracy. Lijphart has argued that 'consociational democracy is not only the optimal form of democracy for deeply divided societies but also, for the most deeply divided countries, the only feasible solution'.[38] Therefore, the theory's value as a basis for political engineering cannot be overstated. According to McGarry and O'Leary, 'experience has taught [consociationalists] that deep and protracted conflicts between national, ethnic and religious communities requires that power be systematically shared as well as divided subject to competition'.[39] 'It is indeed hard to see', says Lijphart, 'how a positive future for the world's most deeply divided societies can be visualised except through some variation on the theme of power-sharing'.[40]

Consociationalism is a popular model on two levels. For constitutional engineers, it provides a flexible model that can be manipulated according to the demands and requirements of domestic political interlocutors. Within academic circles it has been a principal reference point for debates about how peace is to be served in deeply divided and post-conflict polities.

Lijphart and his critics

For the purposes of this work, criticisms of consociational theory can be grouped into five main categories:[41] (i) the democratic quality of consociational democracy; (ii) the value of Lijphart's favourable factors as predictors of consociational success; (iii) whether consociationalism is an effective tool for ethnically divided societies; (iv) criticisms concerning elite incentives; and (v) problems identified in the literature with Belgium and Switzerland, and implications for Cyprus.

(i)　The democratic quality of consociational democracy

Nordlinger[42] was among the first to question the democratic credentials of elite accommodation. At what stage, he asked, does the quest for political and social stability subordinate the principles of democratic organisation?

While elites are supposed to represent the interests of their groups, it is not clear how closely those interests are pursued. Belgium, for example, functions almost entirely without broad-level citizen participation, or even knowledge of the secret dealings and negotiations between representatives.[43] Austrian elites have been accused of creating serious levels of public discontent, due to public isolation from political decision making.[44] How do these cases fit with traditional conceptions of democracy, and are these types of government at all democratic? 'Specifically, at what point, based on practices of exclusion, control, closed decision-making, limits on majority influence, and other devices used by elite cartels, should a consociational system, however stable, be judged to no longer be democratic?'[45]

As shown earlier, consociationalism has progressed since Lijphart's early work on what is now known as 'corporate' consociationalism. While the system's democraticness still receives extended criticism, particularly from liberal integrationists and assimilationists, consociationalism has tended to shed much of the pre-determinism inherent in corporate consociationalism. The focus for consociationalists in conflict and post-conflict societies is that discord between the opposing groups be immediately contained and that a functioning government be established or reinstated. While deliberative democracy and multicultural theory might provide more philosophically robust approaches to building a lasting peace, consociational democracy is more immediately valuable to deeply divided societies because it claims to work under minimal political conditions. McGarry and O'Leary have argued that the three key conditions for the establishment of consociational democracy are elites who are prepared to regulate conflict, deferential segments that follow elites, and a multiple balance of power.[46] To sustain a more robust political system, a society would need a great number of stabilising factors, including and especially a basic level of inter-group trust, which, in many such societies, has been eroded.

There is an additional criticism that consociational democracy weakens political opposition and discourages open political debate because 'incentives are structured towards cooperation among the elites rather than presentation of opposing points of view'.[47] Jung and Shapiro[48] have argued[49] that there are few incentives to publicly criticise particular executive decisions because most political parties form part of the governing coalition. Therefore, very little genuine political debate is heard at the public level, and 'there are few incentives to inform the voter of misdeeds, of failures in policy, and of corruption'.[50]

Reynolds contests this claim by providing a number of examples of strong and extensive public and political debates in the first years of South Africa's multiparty democracy. Additionally, if consociationalism does encourage this kind of elite co-operation, it could be considered a strong benefit in societies in which relations between communities are poor. A highly critical opposition, though perhaps a characteristic of robust democracy, may be damaging in societies where coalitions and inter-communal trust is fragile.

(ii)   The value of Lijphart's favourable factors as predictors of consociational success

The predictive value of Lijphart's favourable factors and his account of the relationship between the presence of these factors and consociational success are significant objects of criticism and have been attacked on many fronts. Lijphart's later work is based upon the assumption that consociational democracy can be an effective form of governance in any divided polity, because it is designed to encourage compromise. He sometimes adds the proviso that this form of democracy is more likely to succeed when certain factors are present. The criticisms of Lijphart's favourable factors, which are outlined below, fall into two categories: questions about Lijphart's methodology and the implications of the favourable factors for consociational democracy.

Over the years, Lijphart has identified various factors which, he argues, improve chances of successful implementation and maintenance of consociationalism in divided societies.[51] Of these factors, only four have consistently remained on his list. They are segmental isolation, external threats, a balance of power between segments of similar size, and a small population.[52] Segmental isolation is held to be favourable because groups have fewer sources of tension if their interaction is limited. Lijphart argues that a threat to the nation from an external power serves to unite the disputing factions, giving them common cause against a mutual enemy and helping to forge a common identity.[53] A balance of power between the segments can facilitate the development of an atmosphere of negotiation, where both sides realise they will have to compromise in order to obtain some of the conditions they seek. In such cases, neither group is able to control the institutions of government alone. A small population is desirable because it makes each segment easier to manage.

It has been difficult to situate the favourable factors within Lijphart's conception of consociationalism because of Lijphart's oscillating view of the predictive quality of his favourable factors. Bogaards cites Lijphart's statement that '[b]oth the explanatory and predictive power of the consociational model can be improved ... by identifying the conditions that are conducive to overarching elite co-operation and stable non-elite support'.[54] However, as Bogaards observes, Lijphart has also said that 'even if most or all of the favourable factors are lacking, it is still possible to have a successful consociation'.[55] Bogaards questions the value of factors which, he argues, serve no serious function.[56]

The factors are also criticised on the basis that they are not reliably predictive. Van Schendelen condemns Lijphart's use of the factors on the grounds that they are 'empty', and valueless as aggregates[57] – one is unable to predict, on the basis of the number of factors present in a case, the chance of successful consociational governance.[58] Pappalardo supports this claim, arguing that 'the predictive power of the consociational model cannot be assessed without a rigorous analysis of the conditions that are conducive to overarching élite cooperation. However ... many of the conditions that [Lijphart and other scholars] identify often fail to satisfy one or more criteria that test their reliability'.[59] Such criticisms do not discount the relevance of favourable factors *per se*, but merely suggest that a convincing set has not yet been identified.

Lustick,[60] Steiner,[61] Barry,[62] van Schendelen,[63] and Nordlinger[64] have criticised the scientific rigour of Lijphart's method of analysis and prescription; they argue that his empirical method is 'impressionistic' and 'largely inductive',[65] thus casting doubt on the strength of the theory's underlying assumptions.[66] Lustick maintains that in *Power-Sharing in South Africa* Lijphart selectively shifts 'between impressionistic and precise uses of definition and evidence',[67] depending on the political repercussions of his arguments.

In reply to Bogaards and van Schendelen's criticisms of the value of his favourable factors, Lijphart counters that the critics 'can think only in terms of conditions that are both necessary and sufficient'.[68] He makes it clear that 'when I argue that a particular factor ... is favourable, all I am saying is that the presence of this factor makes successful consociationalism more probable and its absence makes it less probable'.[69] This is a convincing response, as social science typically deals in probabilistic, rather than necessary or sufficient, relationships. He has also differentiated between those factors which are necessary and those which are favourable.

Lijphart seems to have abandoned the favourable factors owing to protracted criticism that they are weak predictors. This is unfortunate. This book will show that certain of Lijphart's factors can help explain the politics of constitutional engineering in Cyprus.

(iii) Consociationalism: An effective tool for ethnically divided polities?

For Lustick, Barry, and van Schendelen, Lijphart's determination to prescribe consociational democracy for a wide range of real-world cases makes the stakes very high because they question proof of the system's ability to successfully manage conflict. Lustick argues that Lijphart has moved away 'from his early notion of consociationalism as ... an unusual constellation of practices and circumstances found in several small European democracies, and toward a much more expansive view of consociationalism as a formula to be applied in almost any country facing political instability stemming from intergroup conflict'.[70] This transition is of concern for these authors because they argue that Lijphart has not sufficiently proven that consociationalism is capable of such broad replication as he asserts. While the critics are correct in saying that consociational theory (like most social sciences) lacks the rigour of the natural sciences, it is almost the only viable approach in many real-world situations. The choice in many cases is not between consociational or another system, but what particular power-sharing design is to be used, when and how it should be introduced, and in association with what other peace-building strategies.

Brass[71] and Reynolds[72] have argued that consociational democracy is problematic because it freezes ethnic divisions, building political structures around a particular set of demographic and social conditions, and because of its rigidity, cannot reflect any changes over time in domestic dynamics. In a recent article assessing Burundi's failed power-sharing government, Sullivan similarly points to the desirability of a more integrative approach. He suggests that '[r]ather than reinforcing ethnic identity through the formation of separate institutions, the aim should be to reduce anxieties by avoiding interactions which produce political and ethnic minefields, while at the same time quietly encouraging other more potentially positive areas of interaction'.[73]

The idea that consociationalism freezes and replicates ethnic divisions in institutional structures, making positive change very difficult, is one of the most disturbing charges against the theory. McGarry and O'Leary have replied to this criticism by admitting that corporate consociationalism did pre-determine and privilege certain identities, and by distancing modern consociationalism from such mechanisms. They have argued that '[m]ost modern consociationalists eschew these devices and prefer liberal rules that protect equally whatever groups emerge in free elections'.[74] They also argue that 'successful consociation can be biodegradable'.[75]

The case of Cyprus supports their claim. Significant controversy surrounded the perceived inflexibility of ethnic quotas and identity in the constitution of the proposed United Cyprus Republic (UCR) in 2004. Critics of the plan argued that by making ethnicity the basis for electoral and legislative participation at both the federal and constituent state level, it guaranteed that ethnic division would be frozen into the institutional structure of the state, and thereby perpetuated. However, it will be shown that the political engineers working on Cyprus were aware of and anxious to avoid creating a constitution which would indefinitely immobilise power relations as they stood between the communities in 2004. To combat this, the Annan Plan's architects designed a relatively low threshold for constitutional change. Any article of the constitution[76] could be changed by a majority of voters in each of the two constituent states.[77] Through this provision, the engineers attempted to ensure that the institutions they designed were as flexible as possible.

Some critics also argue that deeply divided societies are less likely to exhibit those factors which increase the probability that consociational democracy will be successfully adopted and maintained. It is further argued that societies which *do* exhibit a great number of these factors are probably not classifiable as *deeply* divided, and so Lijphart's claim that consociational democracy is an effective governmental model for deeply divided societies is not plausible. Horowitz argues that a society which possesses many or all of Lijphart's favourable factors cannot be defined as deeply divided because the 'presence of such conditions suggests precisely that the cleavages are not so intense'.[78] For Horowitz, the favourable factors serve merely to highlight the circularity of consociational theory. Using 'overarching loyalties' (a factor sometimes cited by Lijphart) as an example of a factor which is said to facilitate consociational arrangements, Horowitz claims that overarching loyalties 'are said to moderate conflict'.[79] Therefore 'the proposition is that the emergence of consociation is facilitated by moderate levels of conflict'.[80]

However, McGarry and O'Leary argue that the adoption of the 1998 Good Friday Agreement in Northern Ireland disproves Horowitz's hypothesis that consociationalism is an unattainable goal for deeply divided societies, and that *only* societies which are moderately divided are able to take up consociational structures.[81] The recent formation[82] of a power-sharing government on the basis of the Good Friday Agreement has reinforced McGarry and O'Leary's point that deeply divided societies *can* (at least) adopt consociational democracy.

In addition, consociational states are classifiable into two main sorts, those which represent the paradigm cases and those for which the paradigms are considered instructive. On a similar note, Horowitz has claimed that 'the European conflicts are ... less ascriptive in character, less severe in intensity, less exclusive in their command of the loyalty of participants, and less preemptive of other forms of conflict'.[83] Countries in the second category include Lebanon,[84] Iraq, Israel, Cyprus, Northern Ireland, Fiji, South Africa, Nigeria, Burundi, and India. McGarry and O'Leary use Northern Ireland to refute Horowitz's assertion about the empirical distinction between continental European and other cases of division. They argue that in order to save his hypothesis, Horowitz must '*either* regard Northern Ireland as typical of moderately divided European societies ... *or* accept that his thesis is refuted'.[85] One may also add Bosnia and the Former Yugoslav Republic of Macedonia as other deeply divided European societies to which consociational democracy has been applied.

To the criticism that consociational democracy is easier to adopt in West European states, Lijphart argues that consensus-building is a more familiar political trait in *non*-Western societies, and therefore is *more*, rather than *less*, *likely* to succeed. He has also replied that in 'Lebanon, Malaysia, and Columbia ... power-sharing and autonomy were developed by indigenous leaders without external influence or assistance'.[86]

(iv)   Criticisms surrounding elite incentives

As consociational democracy rests upon elite co-operation, incentives for political and economic elites to form and maintain strong collaborative relationships are a central factor in the model's successful application and maintenance. However, there are a number of critics who argue that Lijphart's theory rests upon an unsound hypothesis about elite behaviour. They argue that the problematic role of elites is not sufficiently addressed in the literature on consociational democracy, especially given that it is a continual obstacle for constitutional engineers. Some of the criticisms of the conceptualisation of elite incentives in traditional consociational theory have particular relevance to the case of Cyprus. They are therefore further explored in this work.

The consociational *problématique* is centred on elite behaviour; the theory is built upon the conciliatory power of elite co-operation, but in many cases it is the elites who profit most from division. It is recognised in the literature that in situations where elites are more interested in perpetuating conflict than forging co-operation, consociational solutions are going to prove unpopular and difficult to implement. Cyprus is one of those situations.

The integrationist approach to political engineering in divided societies has been consociational theory's major rival, and its proponents are particularly critical of consociationalism's reliance on elite cartels to control conflict. Donald Horowitz and Benjamin Reilly are two of the most significant advocates of integrationism.[87] Horowitz has argued that consociationalism is a system which encourages elites to 'conspire against the electorate'.[88] For Horowitz, the consociational model is weak because it 'contains no mechanism'[89] to encourage elite co-operation. He argues that 'there is no reason to think that politicians – especially electorally minded politicians – will behave in accordance with [consociational theory's] rules and form such a cartel across ascriptive lines'.[90] For Horowitz, 'there are good reasons to think they will not'.[91] Much literature in the consociational tradition focuses on the 'implicit assumption that politicians are more easily motivated to act "cooperatively" than are their constituencies'.[92] However, 'there is abundant evidence that when confronted with institutional choices of redistributive nature, politicians are limited in their ability to support compromise and cooperation by the need to anticipate popular pressure and, most importantly, the entry of political challengers seeking to capitalize on such popular pressure or mobilize it'.[93] Integrationists emphasise that, in deeply divided societies, the freedom of political elites is particularly constrained. Consociational democracy rests upon the assumption that elites have enough freedom of choice to pursue 'consociational methods of decision-making'[94] to overcome the dangers associated with inter-group tension. However, for Horowitz, 'such freedom does not generally characterize conditions in severely divided societies'.[95]

A number of scholars have contested this claim, arguing that Horowitz is flawed in his reasoning that elites have few incentives to compromise. Lijphart argues that a basic assumption in political science is that political actors seek power:

> Based on this assumption, a further basic premise underlying virtually all coalition theories ever since the pioneering work of William H. Riker

(1962) is that, in multiparty systems, parties will want to enter and remain in coalition cabinets. ... Because the only way for ethnic or any other parties not just to enter but also to stay in the cabinet is to reach compromises with their coalition partners, they have a very strong incentive to compromise – political power! – instead of no such incentive as Horowitz mistakenly argues.[96]

Further, the point of Lijphart's detailed attention to necessary and conducive conditions was to stress that elites would not, or may not always be able to, co-operate.[97]

This book's central goal is to understand why, if Cypriot elites have in principle agreed to adopt a power-sharing solution, attempts at adoption collapse. Chapter 3 will show how in 1960s Cyprus, Greek and Turkish Cypriot elites perceived their incentives for non-co-operation to be greater than their incentives for co-operation and compromise. The chapter will argue that driven by historical memory and competing ethno-nationalisms, elites were unable to co-operate and the state collapsed. In 2004, Cypriots were again offered a chance at sharing political power in a Cypriot republic. But, as Chapter 5 will illustrate, only the Turkish Cypriot governing elite found sufficient incentives to endorse adoption of the proposed peace plan. Their primary incentive for co-operation was the attainment of international political legitimacy, the reinforcement of their domestic political legitimacy, and the stabilisation of their state. For the already-legitimate Greek Cypriot governing elite, the incentive to perpetuate the conflict was greater than the incentive for adopting a consociational solution.

Cyprus is an unusual case in terms of the acquisition of power being a motivating factor in political accommodation. Therefore, it may also shed light on the debate about the freedom of elites to compromise and to pursue consociational methods of decision making. Greek (and increasingly Turkish) Cypriot politics provides an excellent example of how, in cases where there are significant levels of ethnic nationalism and public xenophobia, centrifugal forces dominate, and it is very hard for elites to beget sub-elite and mass-level support for inter-group compromise. Conciliatory elites are deeply afraid of being punished at the ballot box in the next election, and fear of losing votes has been a considerable inhibitory force discouraging parties from recommending co-operation with elites from the 'other' community.[98]

On the other hand, consociational theorists are criticised for failing to recognise that co-operative behaviour between elites within a consociation is often caused by grassroots pressure rather than elite initiative. While Austria is considered among the strongest European examples of the power of consociational democracy to moderate inter-segment conflict, it has been suggested that the elites were forced to compromise by the public.[99] Barry has contended that it is difficult to be certain whether consociational democracy was the *only* necessary and sufficient condition for the success of the second Austrian Republic. He reversed the central tenet of consociational theory, which states that the elites form a restraining influence upon the warring masses. Instead, he suggested that it was the masses which formed a 'restraining influence on the elites'.[100] In a socialist critique of consociationalism, Kieve argued that in the case of the Netherlands, accommodatory politics was not a necessary condition for stable democracy. Rather, elite co-operation arose from the elite's desires to prevent the development of the labour movement into a significant competitor. For Kieve, key events Lijphart cites as having instigated accommodatory behaviour between elites were actually labour movement actions which stimulated defensive responses by elites.[101]

The idea of grassroots pressure instigating conciliatory behaviour by elites is one which has application to the case of Cyprus' 2004 attempt at reunification. Cyprus provides excellent contrasting examples of the role of grassroots pressure on elite intransigence. Conciliatory Turkish Cypriot elites – supportive of the federal, consociational model being proposed – were brought to power in north Cyprus primarily because public pressure in the Turkish Cypriot community coalesced with a change in the political environment in Turkey. However, for a number of reasons, public pressure for the conflict's resolution was notably absent in the Greek Cypriot community. The Cyprus case therefore, problematically, offers proof of two opposed arguments.

It is clear that if consociational democracy is to succeed, the society's elites must be willing to co-operate in order to bring the regime into existence and manage it. Elite co-operation cannot be assumed; instead, it should be viewed as a variable affecting the prospects for adoption or maintenance of a consociational regime. It is therefore critically important for constitutional engineers to accurately ascertain whether elites have sufficient incentives to overcome inter-group divisions and adopt or maintain consociational democracy. If this factor is absent, and constitutional engineers intend to build a consociational road for a particular divided society, then they should look for opportunities to influence elite incentives.

(v)   Problems identified in the literature with Belgium and Switzerland, and implications for Cyprus

Belgium and Switzerland are the two consociational states which have direct relevance to the case of Cyprus; the 2004 Annan Plan clearly states that the UCR constitution is partly based on the Swiss and Belgian structures.[102] Late in the negotiations, Greek Cypriot elites showed deep mistrust of the two models, raising concerns which have also been debated between theorists. They are therefore examined in this section to understand whether a problem with the power-sharing system underpinned elite reluctance to adopt this type of solution.

Arguably, the most vital point that consociational theorists make about the value of their model is that it stabilises unstable systems, and mediates conflicts. However, a number of scholars have argued that Belgium and Switzerland, as paradigm cases of successful consociational democracy, do not support the primary hypothesis of consociational theorists that the model is responsible for stabilising unstable systems and managing conflicts.[103] There are two broad areas of criticism. Regarding Belgium, it is argued that consociational democracy has not ameliorated any system-destabilising divisions; regarding Switzerland, it is argued that the institutions which are most responsible for stabilising the state are not classifiable as consociational institutions.

Belgium has developed highly territorialised consociationalism.[104] It has been suggested that sensitive issues which previously caused much tension are now resolvable because of the existence of a complex system of elite negotiation and bargaining between the segments in this highly pillarised society. However, in spite of its consociational design, the separation of Flanders and Wallonia into two independent nations is becoming a topic of increasing relevance in Belgium, and has elicited fierce debate. At the end of 2005, a 'Manifesto for an Independent Flanders Within Europe' was issued by 65 members of the Flemish academic and business community.

> The manifesto argues that Flanders and Wallonia have divergent needs and goals because of profound political, economic, social and cultural differences. It claims the present federal structure, with antimajoritarian restrictions, leads to bad compromises at the national level and 'exorbitant and inefficient' financial transfers from Flanders to Wallonia and Brussels.[105]

While most Flemings would probably not support the region's secession, '[p]olls suggest a substantial majority in Flanders would favor transferring still more authority to the regions; many would create a confederal state, with very limited powers at the national level'.[106] In December 2006, the French-language Belgian television station RTBF ran a hoax news bulletin announcing that the Flemish parliament had declared independence from Belgium. The report was designed to stimulate debate about what is seen by many in Belgium to be an inevitable event, the complete dissolution of the Belgian federal state.

Belgium's struggle to hold itself together may be a concern for consociational theorists, and should the state dissolve, may also provide a significant case study for sceptics. If consociationalism is unable to overcome domestic differences and facilitate the continuance of one of Lijphart's paradigm states, then what kind of effect will there be on the perception of the theory?

A number of the UCR's institutions of government were modelled on the Belgian system. Therefore, the Belgian struggle with secession has touched on a very real fear for the Greek Cypriot community, which suspects that a consociational structure will merely be a stepping-stone to the Turkish Cypriot community's internationally endorsed secession.

As Chapter 4 will show, central institutions of the UCR, such as the federal presidential council, were also inspired by the Swiss system of government. More generally, the broad relationship between the UCR's federal and constituent states is based upon the Swiss federal system. A significant criticism of the 2004 Annan Plan by some Greek Cypriots was that the Swiss institutions would be unworkable in a country like Cyprus, which has no tradition of elite co-operation, or even inter-group elite communication. In light of this use, it is worth exploring whether critics are correct when they argue that it is not the consociational elements of the Swiss system which maintain the state's stability. Steiner has postulated that Switzerland very infrequently uses consociational principles to guide decision making.[107] Barry used a number of examples provided by Steiner to support his hypothesis that the Swiss case is *both* one of 'amicable agreement among the elite ... [and] at the same time a pattern in which binding collective decisions may be taken on very small popular majorities',[108] and it is this balance which preserves the state's equilibrium.[109] Further, he argued that the Swiss tradition of direct democracy is in fact the antithesis of 'amicable agreement' by the elite. 'Amicable agreements' depend on a group of people 'who either trust one another or do not need to because they can apply sanctions against defaulters'.[110] It necessarily involves a small number of decision makers, who are continually involved in the decision-making process, and who are authorised to make deals. This allows for the cultivation of a culture of negotiation, concession, and reciprocal bargaining. Popular voting is the opposite of this culture – effectively undercutting its formation.

Turning his focus to the executive, Barry concluded that it does not uphold the principal elements of consociational democracy. The seven-person federal council is composed of representatives from the major parties; however, those who are voted into the federal council are not always party nominees. On the contrary, the composition of the Swiss federal council is the source of significant inter-party tension because the members, elected individually by the federal assembly rather than on a common ticket, are frequently *not* the parties' nominees. In addition, federal councillors are perceived as individuals acting as heads of departments, rather than 'party oligarchs reaching concordats binding on their followers'.[111] Additionally, members of the Council are frequently called to take decisions against the interests or values of their parties.[112]

Overall, Swiss institutions are quite strongly consociational, and more importantly in the case of divided societies, it is the consociational parts which have been most important for softening division in Switzerland.

Similarly, criticisms of the Belgian model centre mostly on the long-term consequences of consociational systems, particularly regarding the facilitation of separation rather than its ability to minimise violent conflict. Both Belgium and the 'velvet divorce' of the former Czechoslovakia seem to indicate that secession is not necessarily accompanied by violent conflict.

Those given the task of devising constitutional solutions for divided polities are typically very pragmatic in their use of models. The comments of Didier Pfirter, then-Legal Advisor to Alvaro de Soto, Special Representative to Cyprus of the United Nations Secretary General, highlight the way a constitutional engineer conceptualised the problem of Cyprus:

> I didn't really read many theoretical works, I looked more at existing models ... particularly for the way Cyprus would function within the EU, we turned to the Belgian model, but also because Belgium is more of a bi-national state than Switzerland is. But on the other hand in Belgium you always have a Flemish Prime Minister which is just accepted; whereas in Cyprus that would not be accepted by the Turkish Cypriots. But then again Belgium is easier because you can have a more or less fifty-fifty government in parliament, because the population is such that while the Flemish are the majority they are not the overwhelming majority, while in Cyprus you had the problem that the Turkish Cypriots are a clear minority. So, in terms of the composition of the population Cyprus is more similar to Switzerland than to Belgium.[113]

With few exceptions, the engineer will find a model which appears to be relevant, and adapt it to the case at hand. While they will not always seek consultation with experts for a system's design, there does seem to be an increased willingness to draw on their experience, with projects like the UN and Norwegian Refugee Council's UN Mediation Support Unit Project, which provides specialist experts in six fields available for instant deployment to conflict and post-conflict peace-building zones.[114] But engineers will on the whole continue to draw upon cases where they see comparable dimensions of conflict and institutions which appear to contain that conflict. It is for the bi-national dimensions of Belgium's conflict, as well as its functioning within the EU, and particularly for the Swiss executive's ability to solve the Cypriot dilemma over the practical and symbolic distribution of power between Greek and Turkish Cypriot elites that the two models were primarily chosen. For engineers like Pfirter, cases like Belgium and Switzerland are valuable because they provide institutional pieces to solve complex puzzles. As Chapter 4 will show, the Swiss institutions were not adopted wholesale, but modified to correct perceived weaknesses and to fit the Cypriot context.

Are there factors that can signal improved chances for the successful adoption of consociational democracy?

Lijphart's favourable factors were an attempt to create a bridge between what is essentially a description of successful conflict management structures in a handful of European societies, and his desire to prescribe this type of solution for other divided societies. However, due to extensive criticism of Lijphart's leap from explanation to prescription, and confusion surrounding the relevance and application of the various factors, consociational theorists have shied away from developing the role of these factors more seriously. Much literature discusses the application of one or another of Lijphart's lists to a particular situation,[115] but few authors have tried to concatenate a group of factors favourable to the process of constitutional design.

Because the factors have been the source of significant criticism, their potential to signal the likelihood of successful adoption of consociational democracy has been significantly undervalued. Bogaards points out that the literature on Lijphart's favourable factors is confused and lacking analytic rigour.[116] Lijphart provides clues within his work that highlight the important role that favourable factors can play in the adoption and implementation of consociational solutions. However, according to Lijphart, these factors are 'helpful' but not 'sufficient' for the success of consociational democracy. Given this, some important questions should be answered. If there are conditions for the successful application of a consociational model, how are they to be identified? Can they be used to increase the likelihood of the successful application of a consociational structure or to increase constitutional engineers' awareness about areas of vulnerability? Is there another way in which they can be used?

It is the intention of this work to draw from Lijphart's various discussions of factors to help explain why elites in Cyprus have been unwilling to share power. Four factors have been specifically chosen. *Segmental isolation* geographically underpins consociational theory's assumption that if intercommunal tension is contained, elites will be more free to co-operate and form alliances. *A tradition of elite accommodation* is vitally important. The system is designed with a very strong bias towards collaborative decision making among elites at the executive and legislative levels. No signals of, or trends towards, elite co-operation therefore indicate a greater probability that a consociational solution will not be accepted by elites. A *balance of power* between the disputant groups stabilises the consociational structure; if one group feels itself to be a majority, or to be significantly more powerful than the other group, they are less likely, and will probably have fewer incentives to support a constitution which painstakingly ensures the even sharing of power between groups. *The ability of the international community to offer incentives for compromise* has been increasingly recognised in the literature as a factor which can change the dynamics of elite willingness to engage with a power-sharing solution;[117] McGarry and O'Leary, for example, have argued that 'outside forces can *facilitate* consociation by benign rather than malign intervention, e.g. by mediation, or inducing or encouraging warring or potentially warring parties to reach agreement'.[118] Entwined with the role of historical memory, it will be shown that segmental isolation, the balance of power between the segments, no tradition of elite accommodation, and the inability of the international community to offer adequate incentives for compromise, all contributed to elite reluctance to adopt a consociational solution in Cyprus.

Key factors reviewed

There is a fair amount of common sense in the premise that there are key elements or factors which are potentially useful both as analytic tools and as guides for constitutional engineers. Constitutional engineers are likely to look for domestic elements which will aid or weaken the possibility of successfully reconciling a divided society. It is likely that they will be aware of the importance of factors which might undermine institutions of government because these also make the negotiation process, ahead of the establishment of such institutions, more difficult. In this work, the four factors described above are examined for their contribution to understanding the difficulties of brokering a political settlement to long-term divisions in Cyprus. If the factors can help explain such difficulties, they may also be able to assist in unlocking the Cyprus stalemate.

Segmental isolation

Lijphart has expressed the advantage of segmental isolation through a number of his lists of favourable factors. In 1968 and 1969, this was articulated as 'distinct lines of cleavage'[119] between subcultures, in 1977 as 'segmental isolation and federalism',[120] and in 1985 as the 'geographical concentration of segments'.[121] According to Lijphart, the physical separation of communities 'will prevent latent hostilities from turning into conflict, and segmental autonomy can have a firm basis by means of federalism and decentralization'.[122]

The term 'segmental isolation' is used in the literature on consociationalism to refer to the geographical separation of combatant communities. As will be shown in Chapters 3 and 4, how to distribute the Greek and Turkish Cypriot populations was an issue of concern in both 1960s and 2004 Cyprus, but one which has changed considerably between the two periods. In Cyprus for many years there has been complete segmental isolation in the fullest sense of the term. The Turkish and Greek Cypriot communities began to separate in late 1963 as a result of inter-communal tension, though mixed villages continued to exist, particularly in Kyrenia and Paphos. As a result of the 1974 war in Cyprus the Third Vienna Agreement in 1975 provided for a population exchange which effectively created a very clear demarcation between Greek and Turkish Cyprus. Greek and Turkish Cypriots lived in complete segmental isolation for almost 30 years until April 2003, when public crossing points were opened.[123] Most peace proposals since 1977 have maintained the communal separation in principle, and the 2004 Annan Plan proposed a limited refugee return structure, while maintaining the general ethnic separation by creating a Turkish Cypriot constituent state in the north and a Greek Cypriot constituent state in the south.[124]

Of the four key factors, the distribution of the ethnic groups has undergone the most dramatic change between the two periods of Cypriot history examined here. In 1960s Cyprus, and particularly as the political situation deteriorated after the state's breakdown in late 1963, the geographical interspersion of Turkish and Greek Cypriots contributed to inter-communal tension. Among both Greek and Turkish Cypriots who lived in mixed villages, or in towns near members of the other community in the period of, and preceding, the state's breakdown, memories of racist taunts, graffiti, vandalism, and low-level violence are relatively common.[125] By the Annan Plan's presentation in 2004, the situation had changed dramatically; geographic and electoral separation[126] of the two communities was a foundation of the plan. At the same time, it was also a significant cause of Greek Cypriot discontent, because the Annan Plan legitimated a geographical partition which had been caused by war.

Segmental isolation is both controversial and critically important. It is a dynamic element because borders are often contested and groups do not always stay in one geographic area. The idea of segmental isolation has been labelled an 'apartheid' strategy by academic and political critics, and the forced or artificial separation of groups is hardly recommended policy. However, in societies which are already separated, and where at least one of the segments fears geographical reintegration, segmental isolation can become an important factor assisting political reconstruction and affecting elite will to compromise. In Cyprus, Turkish Cypriots fear becoming an anonymous minority engulfed within a Greek Cypriot society. Their willingness to negotiate a solution for the Cyprus problem is predicated upon a level of communal separation. Greek Cypriots, while grudgingly accepting segmental division, resent the separation[127] and argue that the Turkish Cypriot community has nothing to fear in integration.

Segmental isolation is a key factor which also affects two of the three other factors. In communities that are numerically unequal, segmental isolation strengthens the hand of the minority segment(s) by giving their claim a territorial base. This assists in creating the second favourable factor, an equal balance of power between the segments. It also means that elites are interacting on an equal footing, which is an incentive for co-operation.

Within the issue of segmental isolation is packaged a number of the elements which make the Cyprus conflict so complex. Turkey created, protects, and effectively enforces the groups' geographical separation. The isolation has also been a significant source of conflict between Turkey and Greece and

Turkey and the rest of the world because of its numerous political and legal implications. Any resolution of the conflict needs to adequately address the Greek Cypriot traumas about land loss, while also balancing Turkish Cypriot fears of engulfment by the Greek Cypriot community. Therefore, segmental isolation carries with it the 'property issue' because the separation is founded on population exchange – and the population exchange itself is a deeply traumatic and highly controversial element of the conflict. Segmental isolation, in the shape of territorial federalism, has been a cornerstone aspect of the Cyprus conflict's solution since the 1977 and 1979 High Level Agreements.

Balance of power between the segments

A balance of power among the subcultures was included in Lijphart's 1968, 1969, and 1977 lists of favourable factors.[128] In 1977 Lijphart linked two factors: '(1) a balance, or an approximate equilibrium among the segments, and (2) the presence of at least three segments'.[129] In 1985, the factor became 'no majority segment plus segments of equal size',[130] and it remained the same in 1995.[131] The rationale for this factor is that it 'facilitates negotiations among segmental leaders'[132] and aids compromise. The version of this factor to which attention is paid in this book is the core idea of an approximate equilibrium between the segments. However, Lijphart has also noted that there are significant difficulties associated with the application of consociational democracy when there is only one main cleavage, between two segments. If there is a substantial inequality of power between the groups, there is a high risk that the elites of the majority will attempt to 'dominate rather than cooperate with the rival minority'.[133] But if there are only two, evenly matched, groups, 'the leaders of both may hope to achieve their aims by domination rather than cooperation'.[134]

Relatively equal power between the disputant groups is a key factor in the successful adoption of consociational democracy because it creates the necessary incentive for power-sharing. An unequal power relationship between the groups would create an incentive for the more powerful to try to defeat the less powerful, particularly in the case where there are only two groups vying for power. Therefore, a power-sharing government, based on an acknowledgement by the groups of a degree of equality between them, is more likely to be adopted and to survive if it is underpinned by a balance of communal power.

Power is the most basic struggle which underlies the majority of conflicts, and the Cyprus conflict has been particularly characterised by inter- and intra-segmental struggles for power. The internal balance of power changed when the Turkish Cypriot community gained significant territory after 1974 and the communities separated geographically. In this way, segmental isolation also directly affected the internal balance of power by linking geographical and communal rights. The acquisition of land also provided Turkish Cypriot elites with a significant bargaining chip in future negotiations.

The Greek Cypriot community has tried to counterbalance that power by pursuing the international non-recognition of the TRNC. When Cyprus' accession path to the EU was confirmed in 1999, the balance of power again shifted; the Turkish government's wish to join the EU gave the EU, the UN, and the Cypriot government a lever to exercise pressure on Turkey to support resolution of the Cyprus conflict. Turkey's military power in Cyprus was thereby neutralised by its need to make concessions on Cyprus and other issues, in order to meet its goal of joining the EU.

Tradition of accommodation

A tradition of accommodation among elites appears as a favourable factor in 1977, 1985, and 1995.[135] Elites must be able to both see and pursue the benefits of co-operation. For this, leaders must be flexible and moderate, and must have a sufficient level of autonomy to control their communities. Tied to flexible and autonomous leadership is the idea that communities are able to be persuaded of the benefits of co-operation. As it will be shown in Chapters 3 and 5, elite co-operation is a vital missing element in Cyprus; hamstrung for a number of important reasons, and is perhaps the single greatest obstacle to a political settlement along consociational lines.

The most frequently emphasised reason for the breakdown of the 1960 consociational state in Cyprus was a lack of inter-communal goodwill at the elite level. In interviews conducted by the author, current political elites in Cyprus maintain that in the 1960s there was no real co-operation between the Greek and Turkish Cypriot leadership, and that they had no common interest in preserving the state. Elites on both sides of Cyprus have established and nourished a host of taboos against inter-communal co-operation at both the elite and community levels. Elite interaction is still viewed as a zero-sum competition for power between the segments, and co-operation at any level is fought. Where elite co-operation is necessary, it is only grudgingly accepted. Assuming that Greek Cypriot elites had sufficient incentives to support resolution of the conflict, and to welcome inter-group co-operation, the engineers of the Annan Plan realised that the EU 'factor' significantly changed Turkish and Turkish Cypriot incentives to co-operate and to accept a power-sharing solution. They therefore used Cyprus' accession to the union to encourage and develop incentives for elite co-operation.

Ability of the international community to offer incentives for compromise

Conflict situations are frequently subject to international pressures inhibiting the promotion of peace and institution-building. Conflicts in the Balkans, the Middle East, and Africa have proven particularly difficult to resolve due to heightened international interest. Frequently, a conflictual relationship between domestic elites is supported financially or ideologically (or both) by surrounding states and other interested parties. However, sometimes international actors also play a significant role in the resolution of conflicts by changing the dimensions of the conflict or by offering incentives to overcome elite intransigence.

Intra-state conflicts are most frequently resolved by a community of international actors, who are used as both intermediaries and constitutional architects. In most of these conflicts *realpolitik* rules, and the parties that are most interested in dissolving the conflict are also those that are interested in the results of a resolution. Further, domestic actors will seek support where they can find it, and often solicit the assistance of sympathetic international players. Frequently, the involvement of external actors further complicates the situation and inhibits both domestic and other international actors in their efforts at promoting peace and new political institutions.

At the same time, domestic stalemates can sometimes *only* be broken by international players, which have the ability to offer incentives and change the power dynamics between interlocutors. Ireland's accession to the EU, for example, created a kind of 'political systems of scale' element, in the sense that when Northern Irish political parties began playing in a much larger field, it altered the scale of power available to them, and ultimately contributed to the creation of greater incentives for co-operation. But in the case of Bosnia-Herzegovina, the United States and the EU were able to offer sufficient incentives to the Serbian, Croatian, and Bosnian groups to secure their support for the 1995 Dayton Agreement.

Chapter 6 will show that in the case of Cyprus, the relationship between domestic elites and international actors has played a significant role in the conflict's intractability and has been something of a Gordian knot for constitutional engineers. A number of regional and supra-national bodies are closely entwined in the Cyprus conflict, and have shaped chances for the conflict's resolution by their actions and alliances. It was the change in Cyprus' relationship with a powerful international actor, the EU, which propelled Annan's efforts for the island's reunification. The chapter will also show that the split incentives created by Cyprus' guaranteed accession also contributed considerably to the plan's ultimate rejection.

Conclusion

The body of ideas upon which efforts at political settlement, or the design of governmental institutions in Cyprus is based, is consociational theory. This chapter has examined whether these efforts have failed because of flaws in those ideas. Several points may be drawn from the preceding discussion. Consociationalism, a particular form of power-sharing, has not been demonstrated to be fundamentally flawed as an approach to institution building in deeply divided polities. While it might be risky to extrapolate from the success of the Western European paradigm cases of consociationalism, there are examples of consociational institutions in

Europe and elsewhere which can plausibly be claimed to have made a contribution to political stability.

Thus, consociational ideas, despite their weaknesses, do not seem to be an obstacle to political settlement; the contrary is more likely to be true. One aspect of consociational theory that may play a vital role in resolving conflicts such as that in Cyprus has received particular attention in the chapter, namely Lijphart's early hypothesis that there is an identifiable set of factors which might predict the successful adoption of consociational government. While such factors are elusive, a number of factors described in this chapter seem plausible in the case of Cyprus. They will be explored for their ability to explain the unwillingness of elites in Cyprus to adopt a consociational solution to their conflict.

2
Cypriot History(ies) as the Foundation of Modern Reunification Politics

> The best method of investigation is to study things in the
> process of development from the beginning.[1]

This work examines why Greek and Turkish Cypriot elites have been unable to accept the constitutional principle of power-sharing. The chapter will use the insights of historical institutionalism to establish links between Cyprus' modern history, group memory, and major areas of friction which inhibit elite co-operation. It will show how agreement on a power-sharing solution in Cyprus has been inhibited by the development of a single major cleavage between majority and minority ethnic communities. It will also show how incompatible political aspirations as well as incompatible notions of democracy and political freedom have restrained the groups' ability to resolve the conflict. Reinforcing linkages with mainland powers Greece and Turkey are also shown to have dimmed incentives for Cypriot elites to agree on the principle of power-sharing.

Historical institutionalism argues that 'the policy choices made when an institution is being formed, or when a policy is initiated, will have a continuing and largely determinate influence over the policy for the future'.[2] The theory is based on the concept that ideas are the basic units underlying institutions, and institutions are the basic units 'in the production of order'.[3] It maintains that institutions are subject to path-dependency; there may be change, but 'the range of possibilities for that development will have been constrained by the formative period of the institution'.[4] Future decision making is therefore directed by the original institutional design choices. The theory may explain why particular institutional structures have been replicated through a number of constitutional designs for Cyprus, including both the 1960 state and the Annan Plan.

Genesis of Greek and Turkish ethno-nationalism in Cyprus

It is acknowledged that 'homeland' disputes make consociational settlements more difficult.[5] 'The homeland has ... been reconstructed as the sole possession of the core group, allowing it to appropriate the state apparatus and establish an ethnocratic regime or ethnocracy. This has often generated protracted ethnic conflicts'.[6] Connor defines the nation as 'a group of people who believe they are ancestrally related ... the largest group that can be aroused, stimulated to action, by appeals to common ancestors and to a blood-bond'.[7] Nationalism – henceforth referred to as *ethno-nationalism* – is understood in this chapter as 'both an ideology and a political movement which holds the nation ... to be crucial indwelling values, and which manages to mobilize the political will of a people or a large section of a population'.[8] The battle for ownership of the Cypriot homeland shapes the nationalist imaginings of the ethnic groups.

Cyprus became part of the Ottoman Empire in 1571 and remained so until the Congress of Berlin in 1878, when in exchange for the protection of their borders from the expanding Tsarist Russian Empire, the Ottomans turned over administration of Cyprus to Britain. From 1878 until Cyprus was annexed *de facto* in 1914 when the Ottoman Empire joined the Axis powers in the war against the Allies, Britain was administrator of Cyprus. In 1923, Turkey signed the Treaty of Lausanne, which recognised British rule over Cyprus, thus renouncing its claim to the island. Cyprus was formally declared a British Crown Colony in 1925, and became an independent republic in 1960.

In the official rhetoric of states, the retelling of the modern history of Cyprus depends significantly, and quite literally, upon the position in which one is standing. South of the Green Line, Cyprus' modern history has been seamlessly stitched to a glorious Greek past, where today's Cypriots are the firm descendents of Mycenaean ancestors who colonised the island in the fourteenth century BC. For these people, pure Greek blood runs through the veins of true Cypriots, who are, without question, *Greek* Cypriots. In this region, the officially endorsed modern history of Cyprus until the post-1974 period is therefore a solemn and heroic tale which emphasises the many thwarted attempts at political recognition of a spiritual and cultural fact, the Greekness of Cyprus.

North of the Green Line, however, Cyprus' history begins in 1571, the year that Cyprus became an Ottoman province, and the beginning of Turkic settlement on the island. According to this portrayal, the Turkic blood spilt in the conquest of Cyprus mixed with the island's soil to give birth to the Turkish *spirit* of Cyprus.[9] Purified by the blood of the martyrs, Cyprus has been Turkish for three-quarters of its modern history, and therefore remains to this day legitimately Turkish.[10] There is also a corner of nationalist storytelling that emphasises the common *Cypriot* history of the people on the island, and stresses a story of a shared past of Cypriots against, and divided by, foreign others. However, to date it has been a marginalised perspective, and the evolution of Greek and Turkish ethno-nationalism in Cyprus has both grown from, and reinforced, the historical truths of Cyprus' Greekness or Turkishness.

A number of interrelated elements have shaped Greek and Turkish nationalism in Cyprus. Late reforms of the Ottoman Empire culminated in Greek Cypriot[11] rejection of an Ottoman identity. The Greek Orthodox Church of Cyprus subsequently played a central role in introducing a Hellenistic rhetoric and encouraging ethnic politics. At the same time, Greek expansionism in the form of *η Μεγάλη Ιδέα*[12] dominated the politics of both mainland Greece and regional Greek-speaking communities in the late-nineteenth and early-twentieth centuries. The Turkish Cypriot community was significantly isolated by these developments, and Turkish nationalism in Cyprus grew, linked to both the Young Ottomans and later, the Young Turk revolution. Subsequently, militant calls for *enosis*[13] of Cyprus with Greece encouraged Turkish Cypriot counter-calls for *taksim*.[14] Finally, the allegedly divisive role of Great Britain is said to have played a significant role in the development of Greek and Turkish nationalism in Cyprus.

The development of a single significant ethnic cleavage began towards the end of Ottoman rule in Cyprus. According to Beratlı,[15] Orhonlu,[16] and other sources cited by Nevzat,[17] the original and early Turkic migrants to Cyprus included many Turkomen, exiled by the Ottoman authorities, and soldiers who had fought in Cyprus, and were consequently encouraged to stay.[18] These immigrants formed a core with a high latent potential for national self-awareness, which was not developed into an ethnic or national consciousness until the Ottoman Empire's fatigue in the late nineteenth century. Between 1839 and 1876 a series of reforms was initiated to modernise the Empire's administration by centralising it. First implemented by Sultan Abdülmecid, the reforms sought to bring successful European practices into the Empire and to save the Empire from growing discontent within its millets.[19] These Tanzimat reforms themselves contributed inadvertently to the development of an *ethnic* (as opposed to religious) identity among Christian Cypriots, which had flow-on effects for the Muslim Cypriot community. The Nationality Law of 1869 was an extension of the primary edict issued by Sultan Abdülmecid, creating 'a new egalitarian citizenship and concept of patriotism'[20] within the Empire by establishing a common Ottoman citizenship independent of ethnicity or religion.

This patriotism was supposed to be built upon an overarching *Ottoman* identity, but instead succeeded in promoting an ethnic identity among subgroups. In the reforms, educational, legal, and cultural responsibilities which were previously managed by the millet were now to be managed by the state so as to more easily replace sectarian identities with Ottomanism. However, by the time the state-based reforms were implemented, the Ottomans had 'inadvertently ... strengthen[ed] the individual Orthodox citizen's capacity to conceive of him, or herself, along ethnic lines'.[21]

Nevzat maintains that some Turkish Cypriots tried unsuccessfully to convince their Greek compatriots that the Ottoman identity encompassed both communities. However, by rejecting the Ottoman vision being promoted within the Empire, the Greek Cypriots were also excluding the Turkish Cypriot community from the historical map of Cyprus. With Greek Cypriot rejection of Ottoman nationalism, 'the island's Turks ... increasingly use[d] the banner of Ottomanism to represent the national aspirations of the island's Turks only'.[22] By the beginning of the twentieth century, this identification as 'Ottoman' had begun to develop into a form of Turkism, in a manner which excluded the Greek Cypriot community. At the same time, Young Turkism was becoming an increasingly influential ideology in Turkish Cypriot circles.[23] Nevzat maintains that the Young Turks saw Cyprus as a 'critical centre for its activities in the years leading up to the Revolution',[24] and provides evidence to support his assertion that Turkish Cypriot intellectuals subscribed to the Young Turk ideology, citing dissatisfaction with the Sultan and protection from the *enotist* aspirations of Greek Cypriots as motivating factors.[25] These developments suggest that by the first decade of the twentieth century the single ethnic cleavage between 'Greek' and 'Turkish' Cypriots, so disadvantageous to a power-sharing style of government, was becoming more solid.

Bryant[26] expands upon the thesis previously articulated by Rolandos Katsiaounis,[27] that the death of Archbishop of Cyprus, Sofronis, in 1900 and the subsequent decade-long battle between the Bishops of Kition and Kyrenia for his position was the tangible beginning of ethnic politics on the island.[28] Showing how the Bishop of Kition employed 'the discourse of race and regeneration' to unify Greek Cypriot support for his candidacy for Archbishop against his opponent the Bishop of Kyrenia, whom, he argued, was 'unhellenic', Bryant argues that the '"Oriental" Romeic [of Cypriot history and culture] had to be expunged, and ... only the glories of Hellenism could triumph'.[29] This involved the 'mobiliz[ation of] the dispossessed masses' by using ethnic consciousness and the idea of an eternal enemy, which was the Turks. In his (re)creation of an ethnicist ideology, the Bishop of Kition gathered the Greek Cypriot masses, 'who found in it the necessary concomitant of a Hellenic history that had been oppressed but not defeated'.[30] In this ideology, he emphasised that 'the redemption of the race meant, by necessity, the defeat of the Turks'.[31]

This rhetoric tapped into, and provided the initial links for later use of, ethno-nationalist discourse in Greek Cypriot rhetoric. It also marked the Church's entrance as a key player in Cypriot ethnic politics that continues to this day. Katsiaounis affirms that '[t]he widespread ferocity of the political conflict deeply divided Cypriot society and inaugurated the era of mass politics in the island'.[32]

According to Bryant, the tension caused by this developing discourse was at first ignored and later protested by members of the Turkish Cypriot community. Bryant argues that the Turkish Cypriot community objected most vehemently to the *way that* Greek Cypriots were articulating their *enotist* aspirations and greater Hellenic ideals, rather than to the aspirations themselves.[33] In contrast to Nevzat, Bryant maintains that a counter ethno-nationalism arose in the Turkish Cypriot community largely because of their exclusion by Greek Cypriots from the 'history' of Cyprus, both past and future.

Nevzat broadens this perspective somewhat by emphasising that the rejuvenation of Ottomanism in post-Ottoman Cyprus was an attempt to give structure to the Turkish Cypriot community. While the Orthodox Church became a central 'organisational apparatus' for the Greek Cypriot community and its search for *enosis*, the Turkish Cypriots had no such organisational structure.[34] Nevzat points out that the church 'was an organisation with branches in every quarter, every village; with plentiful funds, and with authority over the entire Greek Cypriot community'.[35] In contrast, when the Ottomans left Cyprus, Turkish Cypriots lost much of their central organisational apparatus, which existed hand-in-glove with Ottoman administrative structures. While the Evkaf[36] continued to function, the British had considerable control over it.[37] At the same time, the Turkish Cypriot community was becoming increasingly politicised. 'The decades preceding the Young Turk Revolution of 1908 were characterised by incremental changes in Turkish Cypriot political attitudes and by the gradual, albeit hesitant, spread of nationalist feelings'.[38]

The Greek Cypriot nationalist view that 'Cyprus is three thousand years Greek, and Turks are mere transient, and illegitimate, invaders'[39] became increasingly problematic in the context of growing political awareness among Turkish Cypriots. This attitude was later articulated by Greek Cypriot political leaders in a variety of contexts, and carried within it an implicit denial of Turkish Cypriot legitimacy which caused considerable tension with the Turkish Cypriot community. The following comment, made much later by Archbishop (and at the time President) Makarios, can be considered typical: 'Cyprus is Greek. Cyprus was Greek since the dawn of her history, and will remain Greek; Greek and undivided we have taken her over; Greek and undivided we shall preserve her; Greek and undivided we shall deliver her to Greece'.[40] The Turkish Cypriot community consequently began to register its discontent through official channels. Much later Turkish Cypriot insistence on being an equal partner to the Greek Cypriots in government stems from this early fear of being categorised as a silent, powerless minority. At the time, this growing tension and concern was underestimated by the British and ignored by Greek Cypriot nationalists, who, in their single-minded desire to pursue *enosis*, mistook the protest through official channels (mostly in the form of letters of concern and protestations to the British administration) as political silence.

This silence was, however, 'that of a group which saw itself inevitably losing ground numerically, economically, and politically, and did not know what to do about it'.[41] The *enosis* campaign was managed by the Greek Orthodox Church of Cyprus,[42] whose representatives were hardly polished diplomats. Regarding *enosis* as the highest embodiment of freedom,[43] they rejected several early British proposals which would have increased the autonomy of the Greek Cypriot community and led gradually to independence.[44]

According to Richmond and Bryant, Turkish Cypriot reaction to the exclusionary *enosis* campaign was to strengthen their counter-identity, which had an equal claim to nationhood and legitimacy.[45] 'Turkish Cypriots adopted the modernising framework, constructivist history, and future-oriented rhetoric of the new Turkish Republic, but they combined this with a belief in a powerful enemy that has been the hallmark of ethnic nationalism'.[46] The powerful enemy that united Turkish Cypriots under the nationalist banner of Turkey became both Greece and the Greek Cypriots, who by their *enotist* aims threatened to eradicate the Turkish Cypriot people. Thus, both Bryant and Richmond claim that a reactionary identity formed which set its foundations in a competitive struggle for power *against* the ambitions of the other main ethnic group on the island, the Greek Cypriots, who themselves espoused a zero-sum perception of Cypriot history and future.

Early regional conflicts also contributed to the formation of a single ethnic cleavage in Cyprus, and were a foundation for later difficulties in accepting the principle of power-sharing. Katsiaounis emphasises the role of the Cretan revolution in 1896 against Ottoman rule in solidifying enotist aspirations in Cyprus among proletarian Greek Cypriots and provoking serious concern among Turkish Cypriots. He argues that the largely labouring class Cypriot volunteers[47] who fought in Crete and returned to Cyprus formed 'something of a nationalist bloc within the Greek community',[48] able to 'influence the labouring populace in ways which were denied to upper class propagandists'.[49] Before this point, ethno-nationalist aspirations had been the exclusive domain of (elements of) the Cypriot nouveau bourgeoisie. The Cretan revolution was also perceived by the Turkish Cypriot community as a serious warning; it heard with alarm the violent treatment of the Cretan Turkish minority. One may further develop Katsiaounis' thesis. Because both Cypriot communities related to the circumstances in Crete, its struggle for union with Greece and the subsequent adoption of a mono-ethnic majoritarian government were held in the collective memory of both Cypriot groups. Therefore, some years later when discussions turned to the establishment of a power-sharing system of government, images of Crete inhibited acceptance of the principle of power-sharing in both communities.

The role of Britain in the development or exacerbation of an ethnic cleavage in Cyprus is contested in the literature. Much scholarship has supported the thesis that during the early years of British occupation, the British cultivated ethnic identification in order to promote division.[50] As such, the Cypriots have generally been cast as victims (with varying levels of passiveness), and have been placed into the following categories: Cypriots are the victims of 'international conspiracies, victims of British colonial policy, victims of the "mother countries", or victims of their own leaders',[51] as well as victims of each other. There are a number of competing interpretations of Cyprus' colonial past, which focus generally on removing responsibility for the conflict from the Cypriots themselves, thus permitting the lack of reflexivity in Cypriot self-analysis[52] that has, to some extent, been responsible for the conflict's perpetuation.[53]

Britain's role in the genesis of Turkish and Greek ethno-nationalism in Cyprus has recently been contested.[54] The point of contention is whether the fracture between the Turkish and Greek Cypriot groups existed independently of British involvement on the island. Revisionists argue that active British manipulation of one side against the other was not used as a tactic until during the EOKA[55] period,[56] when, for reasons that will be articulated below, Cyprus became more strategically important. Bryant argues that the initial change of Cypriot identity from communal to ethnic was due, in part, also to the modernisation that Cyprus undertook during the early years of British occupation. While 'villagers were still divided by religion and religion became ambiguously and increasingly frequently linked to ethnic nationalism during the British period, [t]his was not a strategy of the British but a seemingly inevitable result of Cyprus' entry into modernity'.[57] This is not to say that the British did not play a central role in the change, just that their role – during this period – should not be as emphasised as it has been.

Nevzat has also argued that the British were unlikely to have followed a *divide et imperia* policy, for the simple fact that they did not need to. 'After all', he says, 'there was in reality little likelihood of Greek and Turk combining to challenge the continuation of British sovereignty over the island so long as they did not share, and had little foreseeable prospect of sharing any common platform for espousing what might be brought in the place of British rule'.[58] Further, Nevzat highlights the lack of British uniformity regarding British policy towards Cyprus by providing significant documented evidence to show that in many cases, high-ranking individual British officials were unwilling to exploit the existing ethnic tensions for British gains.[59]

The Legislative Council and origins of particular disagreements

The Cypriot Legislative Council, established in 1882, had its roots in the Grand Council, instigated under the Ottomans in the late nineteenth century. It should be noted that Cyprus was among the first colonies in the

eastern Mediterranean to have constitutional institutions and limited suf-
frage.[60] A number of areas of conflict within the Council, as well as its overall structure and the dynamics of interaction between the Cypriot members,
were to set trends and foreshadow conflicts that would later contribute to
the breakdown of the 1960 state. Some themes would also find echoes in
the 2004 Annan negotiations.

Meeting weekly, the Ottoman Grand Council 'occupied itself with all
questions of public utility and general administration'.[61] Some months into
the British occupation, previous British Consul and Manager of the Imperial
Ottoman Bank in Larnaca, R. Hamilton Lang suggested '[s]ubstituting British
for the Turkish functionaries, who are *ex officio* members of the Council,
eliminating the ecclesiastical members, both Mohammedan and Christian,
and giving Mussulmans and Christians equal representation'.[62] This would
form the basis for a 'very desirable Council, containing a highly civilised element, in whose hands would be all the initiative, and a less advanced section,
possessing local knowledge and practical experience of the country'.[63] The
reformed 1882 Legislative Council was in some respects similar to Lang's
suggestions. The Council was composed of nine elected Greek Cypriot
members and three elected Turkish Cypriot members, as well as six official
(unelected) British members. The High Commissioner held a deciding vote
in the case of numerical deadlock. With the support of the Turkish Cypriot
members, the British representatives could outvote Greek Cypriot councillors. This also meant that the British, with Turkish Cypriot support, had the
potential to form a permanent majority in the Council.

Popular belief, and a significant amount of secondary literature, strongly
asserts that the British and Turkish Cypriot Council members maintained an
alliance against the Greek Cypriot members which introduced 'a tradition
in which the two communities took opposite sides in politics'.[64] However,
recent research has shown that Greek and Turkish Cypriots frequently voted
together in the Legislative Council against British interests; it was the British
who most often voted as a bloc.[65] So while 'the British were on average more
likely to rely on Turkish rather than Greek support in the Council ... this was
not guaranteed or unconditional',[66] and while the British did try to manipu-
late the ethnic division for their own purposes, this was *not* a dominant and
coherent strategy at this time. Perhaps the more accurate charge which can
be made about the British role in the development of ethno-nationalism in
Cyprus is that they 'did not educate them in partnership; they played on the
existing antagonism';[67] 'with the resources and power at their disposal they
surely could have tried more'.[68]

The question of whether to use single or communal electoral lists, and the
implications of electoral system design on incentives for inter-communal
elite co-operation, have plagued constitutional engineers in Cyprus for
many years. It had its first articulation in 1881, when the Earl of Kimberly
strongly supported 'indiscriminate' voting for the Council; after much

opposition, he grudgingly accepted the implementation of separate Greek and Turkish electoral rolls.[69] This decision set a trend that was followed in both the 1960 and the 2004[70] constitutions. The original question surrounding electoral lists continues to be salient in debate about resolution of the conflict today.[71]

Subject to the approval of legislation by the Secretary of State for the Colonies, the Legislative Council had the right to enact all laws, including the annual budget.[72] The 9:3 Greek/Turkish Cypriot ratio in the Council was the first time proportionality was institutionalised in Cyprus. It also marked the first expression of concern with proportionality by the Turkish Cypriots. For Nevzat, 'what they appeared to strongly resent and fear was the relative composition of the said Council, so much so that they threatened to boycott it'.[73] The implementation of this ratio was perceived as a significant institutional marginalisation of the Turkish Cypriot community, which, for the first time, was being categorised as a protected minority. The institutionalisation of the Turkish Cypriots as a separate, protected communal group in 1882 has been carried through in constitutional design to this day, and featured heavily in both the 1960 Republic of Cyprus and the 2004 Annan Plan.

While communal separation in the municipal councils was a factor contributing to the 1960 Cyprus Republic's breakdown, the issue of ethnic representation in municipal politics had long before been an area of tension. In the 1907 Council, Hami Bey suggested an amendment to the Municipalities Amendment Bill, recommending that elected municipal presidents 'shall be Moslems and Christians to hold office in alternate turns for a term of years proportionate to the numbers of Moslem and Christian members constituting the council. The Vice President shall be a Christian where President elected is a Moslem, and he shall be a Moslem where the President elected is a Christian'.[74] This proposal was rejected by both the British and Greek Cypriot Council members, but continued to come up from time to time.

Early conflicts over issues such as separate municipal representation, the ratio of Greek Cypriot to Turkish Cypriot representation in government, and communal electoral lists were precursors to more serious conflicts over the same issues in later years. Disagreement over mono-communal municipalities and proportional representation were contributing factors to the collapse of the 1960 Republic of Cyprus, and will be further examined in Chapter 3. The proposed electoral system and proportional representation also caused inter-communal discord in the development process of the Annan Plan, and will be considered in Chapter 4. Thus we can see how the early institutional legacy and fears caused by the development of ethno-nationalism had important implications for subsequent attempts at constitutional design.

As later chapters will show, differing Greek and Turkish Cypriot perceptions of Cyprus' future have inhibited relations between elites and efforts to reach agreement on a constitutional design. This tradition was established early. While the British did not foster a culture of co-operation, neither did the Cypriot elites themselves attempt to develop a common identity.[75] By the early 1920s, Greek Cypriots were calling for Cypriot self-rule under British administration, with *enosis* as the final goal. This idea of self-rule, and of uniting to remove governmental power from the British, had the potential to become a location for compromise between the two communities. However, Greek Cypriots continued to emphasise their *enotist* aspirations and Turkish Cypriots remained distrustful and therefore hesitant about co-operation.

It will be shown in later chapters that these early political and ideological movements underpin present-day anxieties in both societies. In contemporary Cyprus, neither *enosis* nor *taksim* are generally supported in mainstream society or elites. However, inter-communal levels of trust, eroded by these early *enosis/taksim* struggles and subsequent events which confirmed the fears of both communities, have not improved. One sometimes hears in current debates about the Cyprus issue one or another member of the Cypriot Orthodox hierarchy refer to Cyprus as 'having finally achieved *enosis*'[76] by acceding to the European Union.[77] This will often spark one or two Turkish Cypriot responses that 'the Greeks still seek *enosis*, how can we trust them?' Likewise, the European Union's efforts to implement direct trade with north Cyprus post-accession have reignited Greek Cypriot panic about the Turkish Cypriot state's potential secession from the theoretical future Cyprus partnership. Underlying these debates are anxieties created within both societies by political and ideological movements which began in the late nineteenth and early twentieth centuries.

The creation of a deeply divided polity[78]

The development of a linguistic nationalism and building of ethnic consciousness reflected political developments. During the early twentieth century, basic literacy was rising, and those children who went to school were increasingly being taught to identify 'high culture' with the 'pure' languages of the mainlands, *katharevousa* Greek[79] and Ottoman Turkish. This period also facilitated a change in Greek Cypriot school textbooks from the religious to the identifiably Greek; children were taught both ancient and modern Greek as well as Greek history.[80] Turkish textbooks were to follow in the 1920s, but did not become the dominant teaching tool until some time later.[81] In addition, there was a change in the handling of villagers' complaints to the authorities. While, during Ottoman times, village muhtars would handle villagers' complaints regardless of the religion of either, British bureaucracy brought the standardisation of petitions written by representatives in the villager's 'mother tongue', which was presupposed to be *katharevousa* Greek or Ottoman Turkish. Though most villagers did not speak these languages (instead speaking one of the two forms of *Cypriotic* which blended either *demotiki* Greek with a high number of Turkish, Arabic and Italian loan-words, or popular Turkish with Greek loan-words), they became increasingly dependent upon the 'high' written languages, and used the dialects for every day communication, leading to the institutionalisation of 'high' and 'common' languages.[82]

Over the first decades of the twentieth century, the relevance of ethnic identity increased, and identity became more rigid. This can be seen in the changing status of both *linobambaki* and inter-communal marriage. *Linobambaki*[83] were Cypriots who practised both Christian Orthodox and Muslim rituals. They were, according to Bryant, descendants of Orthodox Christian men who had converted to Islam and taken Muslim wives during Ottoman times.[84] They openly practised Orthodox rites, and were tolerated by both communities, but not highly esteemed by either. Their identity was based not on faith but on their communal networks and friendship ties. According to censuses and police reports, they numbered about 2500 people.[85] During the period when ethnic identity was being solidified, one's religious identity became a secondary marker to one's ethnicity. *Linobambaki* were forced to swear allegiance to one group or the other, to become either 'Turks' or 'Greeks' in addition to *either* Christian or Muslim. After this period, 'intercommunal marriages – and even attempts at intercommunal marriage – entirely disappeared from the record',[86] indicating a fixity of identity which was previously not the case.

While Greece and Turkey were not wholeheartedly behind the push to unite the islanders with their motherlands, this did not seem to dissuade the development of Greek and Turkish nationalism in Cyprus. The 1919 Paris Peace Conference, and the 1923 Treaty of Lausanne were equally disappointing for Greek and Turkish Cypriot elites who desired unification. At the Paris Conference, Greek Prime Minister Eleftheros Venizelos did not press for *enosis*, bitterly disappointing many Greek Cypriots who had expected *enosis* to be confirmed by the conference. Similarly, Turkish Cypriots felt 'abandoned and betrayed'[87] by the Turkish state. This sense of betrayal was largely directed towards İsmet İnönü, chief negotiator of the Turkish delegation at the Treaty of Lausanne, who refused to push for the return of Cyprus during negotiations of the Treaty.[88] Though these occasions could have catalysed the growth of a Cypriotist identity among Greek and Turkish Cypriots by dampening the enthusiasm of ethno-nationalists, no strong movement was forthcoming. Thus each group continued to develop its ethno-political goals.

By 1930, Greek and Turkish Cypriot nationalists were being voted into the Legislative Council. Nevertheless, at the same time, the mainland Greek-Turkish détente led to increased co-operation on the Council between the Turkish and Greek Cypriot members, who began to succeed in 'imposing modifications to the details of Government bills and even in jettisoning proposals repugnant to Cypriot opinion'.[89] However, 'the more moderate Greek political wing had failed to grasp this propitious opening, and left it to the radicals to take the initiative'.[90] As a result, the 1931 October Revolt against the British, which culminated in the burning down of Government House, cut short this co-operation. Turkish and Greek Cypriot participation in government was terminated. Repressive measures were subsequently implemented which affected the control of educational material, the use of Greek and Turkish national flags, and the teaching of 'national "culture and values"'[91] for both communities, and consequently put an end to almost all outward manifestations of nationalism.

Entrenchment of the ethnic cleavage and its implications

After the Second World War, Turkish and Greek ethno-nationalism was driving events in Cyprus that were to have serious consequences. Pressure on the British to relinquish Cyprus to Greece began to increase after the war, particularly in the late 1940s and early 1950s.[92] In 1955 a guerrilla organisation called EOKA was formed with the aim of overthrowing colonialism and establishing *enosis*. It was not until the establishment of EOKA that anti-colonialism and the corresponding ethno-nationalism were considered to be seriously threatening to the British government.

EOKA instigated its armed insurrection against the British[93] at almost the same time that Cyprus' strategic importance to Britain increased. During the period of Churchill's retirement from office in 1955, Britain joined Turkey and Iraq in the Baghdad Pact. The pact had a threefold importance for Britain: it was an attempt at forming an anti-Soviet alliance, a defensive move against the increasing likelihood of Nasser's termination of British rights to bases in the Suez Canal, and an attempt to preserve British power in the Middle East. After Britain's failure to maintain its position, and the embarrassing pull out from the Suez Canal Zone, Middle East headquarters were relocated to Cyprus and military bases were being established at the time that EOKA's bombs began to fall. Thus, an anti-colonial movement in Cyprus was considered highly inconvenient at a time when Britain was trying to maintain power in the Middle East region, and re-establish a zone of defence against the perceived Communist threat.[94] Britain's response was to begin offers to the Cypriots of very limited forms of self-government, while simultaneously trying to stamp out EOKA.

At this point in the mid-to-late 1950s, linkages between the Cypriot groups and Greece and Turkey were being reinforced, and international actors, which were later to play central roles in the many attempts to solve the conflict, were being introduced. As EOKA became increasingly unmanageable, the British began to react with both domestic and international measures. While the Greek Cypriots used the United Nations as the forum to reduce Britain's exclusive control over solution of the conflict by introducing other actors, the British initially denied that a 'Cyprus problem' existed.[95] In a later counter-manoeuvre, Britain welcomed Turkey into the diplomatic fray,[96] encouraging 'the mainland Turks to speak out more strongly for Turkish Cypriot minority rights, and consequently for rejection of *enosis*'.[97] By this time, the Turkish government was under considerable domestic pressure from Turkish nationalists and Turkish Cypriots living in Turkey who were lobbying for a stronger Turkish policy on Cyprus. Turkish involvement in Cyprus was therefore likely to have increased regardless of British strategy.[98]

What had begun half a century earlier as conflicting ambitions for the future of Cyprus culminated in the two Cypriot communities taking up arms against one another. Increasingly insistent Greek Cypriot calls for *enosis* were leading to higher levels of inter-communal violence and ethnic nationalism. At the same time, elements of the Turkish Cypriot elite began to call for *taksim* or partition. In retaliation for the killing of Turkish Cypriot police officers by EOKA guerrillas, and to protect Turkish Cypriots from Greek Cypriot terrorists, the Turkish Cypriot guerrilla group *Volkan* was established in 1956. EOKA and *Volkan* marked a new era in the development of ethno-nationalism in Cyprus. By this stage, 'low level ethnic-nationalism was mobilized through complex processes instigated by both administrations in order to prevent sub-group disunity, and provide maximum backup for their demands'.[99] *Volkan* was superseded in 1957 by an organisation called TMT.[100] Among the founders of TMT was Rauf Denktaş, then-political advisor to the Turkish Cypriot leader Fazıl Küçük.[101] TMT and EOKA solidified a division which had been crystallising for the last (at least) 50 years. These organisations were the inheritors and product of early Greek and Turkish nationalism, modernisation, and British bureaucracy. The path they chose was made possible by actions taken long before.

TMT's activities resulted in the active separation of Turkish and Greek Cypriots, made easier in ethnically mixed areas by the fact that Turkish Cypriots felt under serious threat by EOKA and the machismo that accompanied the *enosis* rhetoric. Any efforts at reconciliation between Greek and Turkish Cypriots were staunchly and often violently resisted by important elements within the Turkish Cypriot leadership, which was taking direction from Turkey, and by the Greek Cypriot armed forces, which were controlled by the Greek military. The groups had reached the stage where, 'EOKA had turned its guns on democrats and Leftists who opposed its tactics and its xenophobia. In like manner, TMT slew numerous Turkish Cypriots who favoured Graeco-Turkish cooperation'.[102]

While the partition of Cyprus between Greece and Turkey was the favoured solution of Turkish officials, divergent views existed within the British camp. There were a number of British peace plans which suggested bi- or tri-condominium partnerships between Greece, Turkey, and Britain. However, the complete exclusion of the British from the final Greek-Turkish negotiations for Cypriot independence in 1958[103] indicates level of co-operation between Greece and Turkey and highlights the superfluity of Britain in the negotiations.

At the same time, domestic pressures in Cyprus were cementing division between the two communities. While support for *enosis* remained predictably high within the Greek Cypriot community, and especially among the leadership, endorsement of *taksim* increased within the Turkish Cypriot community, as an alternative to *enosis*. It became clear during the late 1950s that the British administration of Cyprus would not long continue in its present vein, and in December 1956, Britain offered new proposals for self-government. These proposals were rejected by one or both sides.

In an attempt to combat the Greek Cypriot uprising, Britain exploited the growing antagonism between the two Cypriot groups, framing them more clearly within a zero-sum battle for power. At the same time, the Turkish Cypriot community became increasingly anxious in the face of escalating EOKA and Greek Cypriot chauvinism.

These events had an important effect on future constitutional design. While the idea of partition found little international support, the argument that Turkish and Greek Cypriots could not operate a functional unitary government together was accepted. This assumption was based primarily on the communities' historical inability to agree on the division of power, or form of governance for Cyprus, as well as soaring tension and plummeting inter-communal trust. Constitutional engineers began to cast around for a set of political institutions that would facilitate the political separation of Turkish and Greek Cypriots, while also preserving the unity of the state. 'Consociational' elements (to use a more modern term) thus began to enter many of the constitutional designs proposed for Cyprus. Therefore, constitutional proposals for Cyprus have been based upon a combination of exclusionary ethno-nationalism, institutional ideas carried over from the early colonial period, historical fears which have taken the form of communal memory, and the influence of colonial and regional powers. The reaction of elites to such proposals come from the same roots.

Notions of democracy and freedom in Cyprus

The concepts of democracy and freedom have played a continuous role in both communities' conceptualisation and articulation of the conflict,[104] as well as shaping their respective expectations of satisfactory constitutional design. Incompatible notions of democracy and political freedom have obstructed acceptance of the principle of power-sharing. Democracy is understood in Cyprus in ethnic terms, just as freedom is 'freedom *for* a particular group'.[105] Since the conflict's first modern expression in the late nineteenth and early twentieth centuries, Greek Cypriots have associated freedom with *positive liberty*; that is, freedom as autonomy, or to achieve particular ends. This has been expressed as the right to pursue *enosis*. The Turkish Cypriot concept of freedom, however, can be related to Isaiah Berlin's definition of *negative liberty*; that is 'the area within which the subject – a person or group of persons – is or should be left to do or be what he is able to do or be, without interference by other persons'.[106] They have focused on the consequences of Greek Cypriot monopolisation of power. Thus, each community's understanding of freedom denied the basis of the other's.

Similarly, two understandings of democracy have developed over time in Cyprus. For Greek Cypriots, whose perception of their place in Cyprus is that of its rightful heirs, democracy has a strictly majoritarian character. As a majority, they can afford to deny that ethnicity is a valid means of allocating rights or obligations. For Turkish Cypriots, whose perception of *their* place in Cyprus is that of a beleaguered communal group, democracy should recognise ethnically defined communities. In this view, democracy therefore means a form of consensus governance in which community groups share power.

The perceptions of both groups about freedom and democracy have become politically loaded and now feature in the dialogue (or dual monologues) on the conflict as politicised short-hand terms containing a century-long accumulation of how Cyprus should have been structured, politically. The groups' incompatible perceptions stymie debate between the communities at either the political or the intellectual level over what the term 'democracy' means to each. Opposing conceptions of democracy are entwined with the notion of freedom; the most favourable conception of democracy for each group is united with a compatible conception of freedom. For the Greek Cypriots, majoritarian democracy is the expression of a nation's freedom to make decisions unencumbered by constraints imposed by minorities. It is often heard in Greek Cypriot political debates that power-sharing is an 'unjust' concept. For the Turkish Cypriots, consensus democracy defends the freedom of minorities from the tyranny of the majority.

As the Cypriot conflict evolved, these conceptions became progressively more important and formed the ideological basis for each side's outline of a 'legitimate and just state'.[107] As the Greek Cypriots formulated increasingly politicised ideas about union with Greece, and the Turkish Cypriots became equally insistent upon its prevention, 'those imaginings of a true and just democratic ethnos [were brought] into conflict'.[108] Today's struggles over 'justice', 'democracy', 'freedom', and 'equality' in Cyprus, examined in Chapters 4 and 5, therefore have their roots in early conceptions of the same theme. Much of the reason Cypriot elites are so unwilling to share power today can be traced back to core interpretations of historical events and political principles that have continued in an unbroken line through generations of Cypriot politicians.

The effect of external actors on domestic elites

External actors and domestic factors also played a role in shaping solutions for Cyprus and defining relations between Cypriot elites. Any partition of Cyprus would have involved extensive ethnic cleansing to create 'pure' ethnic zones because villages and towns were either ethnically mixed[109] or else communal groups were in close proximity to each other.[110] While partition (with the retention of British areas), or tripartite condominium may have been seen by Great Britain as the most economical means of protecting British interests in the region and against the Communist threat, the primary interest of the United States and other NATO members was preventing war between Greece and Turkey, two important regional NATO allies. Therefore, there was significant international pressure on the British to solve the Cyprus conflict in a more delicate fashion.

By dealing with the leaders of EOKA and TMT, who were later to become elected members of their communities in the 1960 state, the British provided a group of extremist separatists with both domestic and international legitimacy. Because, over time, they represented the desires of their respective communities, it would have been hard to address the groups' concerns any other way. But the ultimate result was that those parties who were most antagonistic and inflammatory towards the other side were legitimated as political leaders. When the 1960 Republic broke down in 1963, civil war continued to varying degrees until Cyprus' *de facto* partition in 1974. Negotiations for a satisfactory solution have been in various states of progress since 1964, and continue, to some extent, to this day. Until very recently, leaders from both sides, with very few exceptions, have been the extremists of the past. It is therefore not surprising that they have frequently been accused of intransigence by both the other and the international community, and that they have been unwilling to enter into a power-sharing agreement.

If struggles between groups, and particularly between elites, are primarily struggles for power, then the aim of consociational democracy to share power between all significant parties involved in the conflict is appropriate. By guaranteeing extremist groups representation in a coalition government,[111] the need for violence (to gain power, legitimacy, or a form of representation) is removed and the groups are forced by the institutions of government to become more moderate. However, when, as in Cyprus, there are only two significant communities, those same extremist groups often are the only (or primary) parties negotiating for power *against* each other. Chapter 5 will show that if elites also have strong support within their ethnic groups[112] then there are few incentives for the kind of compromise which would allow a consociational constitution to be adopted.

To provide a snapshot of the political environment affecting Cyprus in the five years leading up to the implementation of the 1960 constitution, one must superimpose many images: the double minority deadlock – where Turkish Cypriots were a minority on the island, but formed part of a majority in the region, while Greek Cypriots were a majority in Cyprus, but a minority in the region; the involvement of the 'motherland' of each of the groups, widening and deepening the conflict; the continual Greek Cypriot insistence upon *enosis* rather than independence; increasing Turkish assertion that the island should not be left to the governance of Greek Cypriots; anti-Greek riots in Turkey; British and Turkish convergence of opinion; the continual Greek Cypriot rejection of constitutional proposals for the sake of *enosis*; and British attempts to preserve a role in governance, as evidenced by the many proposals to the Greek and Turkish governments that suggested tripartite rule of Cyprus. The combination of pressures from these sources contributed to the attitudes of constitutional engineers working on Cyprus and the choice of institutions for the people.

By the early 1920s, Greek Cypriots were calling for Cypriot self-rule under British administration, with *enosis* as the final goal. Anti-colonialism had the potential to create a common ambition between the two communities. However, Greek Cypriots continued to emphasise desires for *enosis*, and Turkish Cypriots remained distrustful, and therefore refrained from extensive co-operation. Initial discord in the Legislative Council over the level of Greek Cypriot to Turkish Cypriot representation in government, communal or single-list voting rolls, and separate municipal representation were early indicators of later high-stakes conflicts between the communities.

Conclusion

This chapter has argued that Cypriot history has been an obstacle to a political settlement in Cyprus. The most obvious point made is that the deep, ethnically based division in Cyprus is a product of action and reaction, fashioned into a pattern over time by human memory. History closes off certain possibilities, but it prompts others. In a society such as Cyprus, which is deeply divided along ethnic lines, power-sharing is the only possible basis for government. However, particular historical legacies have made progress towards this type of resolution very difficult. These include strong linkages with continental powers and the development of very strong ethno-nationalism in both communities. But perhaps most important is the fact that Cyprus has inherited a single, dominant, ethnically based cleavage, splitting the society into two unequally sized segments. A single division produces majority and minority groups, whereas multiple divisions are more likely to produce an outcome in which each group is a minority of the whole. In this latter situation, consensus democratic arrangements protecting minorities are in the interests of all, whereas in the former situation there is likely to be a fundamental conflict over the choice of majoritarian or consensus democracy. It has been argued in this chapter that, in Cyprus, there have indeed developed competing, ethnically based notions of democracy (and freedom) and competing institutional preferences which embody those notions.

3
The First Consociational State: Why Did it Fail?

The flag of the Republic of Cyprus is the best in the world, because it's the only one that no-one would die for.[1]

In February 1959, the treaties founding the Republic of Cyprus were signed, resulting in the establishment of the Republic in August 1960. The 1960 Republic of Cyprus was the culmination of efforts by Greece, Turkey, Britain, and the two Cypriot groups, stretching back more than ten years, to broker a compromise regarding governmental institutions for Cyprus. However, the state could not be translated into a workable system of government and collapsed three years after its inception. This chapter seeks to explain that failure. In so doing, it analyses whether particular features of institutional design were obstacles to successful adoption as well as examining evidence about extra-constitutional obstacles. Understanding the failure of the 1960 Republic is vital to an analysis of why the legacy of memory has so negatively affected elite relations and institution building.

The chapter is divided into two sections. The first explains the institutions of the Republic, and how and why the consociational structure was chosen. The second examines whether the key factors can help explain the pressures on the governmental structures which led to the state's collapse in late 1963. The overall goal is to understand how the events of the period between 1960 and 1963 has since affected elite willingness to share power in Cyprus.

The consociational constitution of 1960

Interestingly, it seems that the 1960 republic was designed on broadly the basis of what were later considered corporate consociational principles. This early attempt to address the unusual Cypriot context drew on the experience of Swiss experts, providing a familial link with a paradigmatic consociational state. Early consociational theory identified four basic elements – rigid proportionality, grand coalitions, cultural autonomy, and minority veto

– which form the foundations of consociational institutions. The institutions of the 1960 Republic of Cyprus can also be said to be based on these factors. The principle of proportionality was incorporated into the structures of the legislature, judiciary, and civil and military services. A form of grand coalition was established in the executive branch's Council of Ministers. Cultural autonomy was incorporated into separate municipalities and at the legislative level in the two national Communal Chambers. Minority veto was expressed through the veto powers of the vice-president, as well as through the legislative requirement of double majorities in taxation, municipal, and electoral laws.

The 1960 constitution of Cyprus had its roots in the Zurich and London Accords of 1959,[2] which served as its legal framework. The constitutional agreements consisted of four groups of provisions: 'Those that recognise to each of the two communities a separate existence';[3] 'Constitutional devices assuming the particulars of each community in the exercise of the functions of government',[4] assuring the administrative autonomy of each group and ensuring the protection of the minority against the tyranny of the majority; the guarantee of human rights and fundamental freedoms; and finally, 'a complex system of guarantees of the supremacy of the constitution'.[5]

In addition to the constitution, there were three important treaties negotiated during the Accords: the Treaties of Establishment, Guarantee, and Alliance. The Treaty of Establishment granted two Sovereign Base Areas to the British Government, which became British Dependant Territories, and as such were excluded from the territory of the Republic of Cyprus. The British insisted that these be 'large areas with access to the sea which could function even against the will of the Cypriots'.[6] The bases were strategically important for the British because they provided a military headquarters for the Middle East region.[7] The Treaty of Guarantee disqualified any union of the Cypriot state with any other country, as well as providing for British, Greek, and Turkish guarantees for the protection of the security, independence, and territorial integrity of the Republic of Cyprus. It was designed in part to allay Turkish Cypriot fears of Greek Cypriot domination. The Treaty of Alliance provided for the establishment of small Greek and Turkish military contingents on the island.[8]

The executive, legislative, and juridical arms of the constitution were thoroughly consociational. The state was crafted to be a presidential structure,[9] 'with a limited dual Executive system reflecting the bi-communal nature of the Cypriot society'.[10] All citizens, including members of minority groups, were required to declare themselves part of either the Greek Cypriot or Turkish Cypriot community, and the Greek and Turkish languages were given equal validity in law.

The executive was composed of the president, vice-president, and the Council of Ministers, which was made up of seven Greek Cypriot and three Turkish Cypriot ministers. The president of the Republic was to be a Greek

Cypriot and the vice-president a Turkish Cypriot. The executive powers of both offices were specifically laid out; presidential and vice-presidential vetoes included the fields of foreign affairs, defence, and security.[11] Both offices also had the right to return all decisions to the legislature for re-examination, and had veto rights over laws passed and decisions taken by the House of Representatives. The presidential and vice-presidential lists were almost identical, and certain powers were conjoint.[12] The president was the executive head of state, and in cases of absence, was to be deputised not by the vice-president, but by the president of the House of Representatives, who was a Greek Cypriot.[13] Both were directly elected by their own community to serve five-year terms.[14]

The major difference between the powers of president and vice-president involved their roles in the Council of Ministers. The president appointed the seven Greek Cypriot ministers, and the vice-president the three Turkish Cypriot ministers. They could each remove the ministers they had appointed,[15] and neither president nor vice-president had voting rights in the Council. The Council of Ministers was 'dependent upon the appointing authority'[16] and did not answer to the House of Representatives. The Council of Ministers held all executive power except that which was reserved for the president and vice-president, or issues that fell within the jurisdiction of the Communal Chambers. The legislative and executive powers of the Council were delegated by laws passed by the House of Representatives and Council decisions were 'based on absolute majority, except on matters concerning foreign affairs, defence and security, where the final veto of the President or Vice President [could] be exercised'.[17] A Turkish Cypriot minister had always to head one of the three vital posts of defence, finance, or foreign affairs.

The legislative branch of government included the House of Representatives, which possessed general legislative power and the Communal Chambers, which dealt with communal matters.[18] The House of Representatives was bi-communal, operating on the basis of proportional representation. The 50 representatives were split in a 70:30 ratio in favour of the Greek Cypriots.[19] The president of the House was to be a Greek Cypriot and the vice-president a Turkish Cypriot. The bi-communal nature of the House of Representatives was reinforced by the separate election of Greek Cypriot and Turkish Cypriot members by their respective communities.[20] Most House decisions were taken by simple majority,[21] with the exception of electoral, municipal, and taxation laws, which needed separate majorities of the Greek and Turkish Cypriot representatives.[22] While the House could only be dissolved upon its own resolution,[23] it was heavily constrained by the extensive veto rights of the president and vice-president.

The 1960 republic was effectively a non-territorial federation. In power-sharing designs that are not based on territorial separation, it is usual for the groups to be given control in areas normally reserved for regions or states. This principle was followed in the Cypriot constitution of 1960, where the Communal Councils exercised control over a range of matters. They were empowered to deal with religious, educational, cultural, and teaching issues; communal taxation; and most areas that singularly affected their community.[24] Communal courts were established to deal with judicial issues pertaining to these subjects.[25] 'Posts in the judiciary, civil service, police and gendarmerie were to be apportioned in a 7:3 ratio between the communities, while the army was to be formed in a ratio of 6:4'.[26] Separate ethnically based municipal councils were to be established in each of the five major towns.

The third arm of the Republic, the judiciary, comprised the Supreme Constitutional Court and the High Court of Justice. The jurisdictions of the Supreme Constitutional Court were the allocation of powers with regard to the legislature and the constitutionality of legislation.[27] It was composed of three judges: one Greek Cypriot, one Turkish Cypriot, and one 'neutral' judge who was the president of the Court and who was not a Cypriot citizen. They were appointed jointly by the president and vice-president of the state.[28] The Supreme Constitutional Court could return a legislative decision to the House of Representatives for reconsideration[29] and was empowered to decide whether the House of Representatives could continue to legislate after the expiration of its term.[30] It made the final decision on ethnic disputes in public service cases[31] and had jurisdiction to rule on constitutional ambiguity.[32]

The High Court of Justice held jurisdiction in trying treasonable offences, as well as 'offences against the constitution and the constitutional order'.[33] It was most frequently used as a court of appeal for cases referred from subordinate tribunals.[34] It was composed of two Greek Cypriots, one Turkish Cypriot, and one 'neutral' judge who was president of the court and who had two votes.[35] Appointment was made by the same methods as the Supreme Constitutional Court.[36] The composition of judges of the lower courts depended upon the ethnicity of the defendants.[37] The High Court determined the ethnic composition of the lower courts for cases in which parties belonged to different ethnic groups.

Many of the articles enumerated in the constitution were made basic and unalterable. Basic articles included 'the provisions relating to the executive final veto, the [double majority] ... in the House of Representatives, the seventy-thirty ratio in the House of Representatives and the Public Service, the sixty-forty ratio in the Army, and the *Treaty of Alliance*, as well as the *Treaty of Guarantee*'.[38]

What drove the choice of political system?

Constitutional genetics of the Republic of Cyprus

Historical institutionalism may suggest an important guiding mechanism underlying constitutional engineering for Cyprus and can complement the key factors in explaining the 1960 Republic of Cyprus' failure. If it is the case that the original designs which created the first Turkish-Greek Cypriot partnerships in government established a way of thinking for subsequent generations of constitutional designers, then it may also shed light on the state's breakdown. Both this chapter and Chapter 5 will show that Cypriot elites have internalised the struggles, fears, and suspicions of their predecessors, and that these elements have inhibited the potential settlement in Cyprus.

As noted in Chapter 2, there is an ancestral link between the 1882 Legislative Council and the 1960 state. It has been argued that the Greek Cypriots distrusted British offers for gradual constitutional liberation because of their experiences of the Legislative Council. The Council turned Greek Cypriots into a permanent opposition and gave them more limited powers than they had expected.[39] The Council's abolition in 1931 after the Greek Cypriot anti-colonial uprising, which resulted in the burning of Government House, also affected Greek Cypriot attitudes towards colonial constitutions.[40] What would be the point agreeing to self-governance under British rule if the institutions could so easily be taken away? Indeed, 'the majority of the Greek Cypriot leadership no longer believed in ... evolutionary processes, which in their view had only brought defeat and disappointments'.[41] Against this backdrop of memory it would be difficult for Greek Cypriots to accept many of the subsequent British proposals in the late forties and early- to mid-fifties. Hence, the Legislative Council and its subsequent neutralisation affected the Greek Cypriot perception of the choice of political system.

Ideas from preceding proposals

A number of the Republic of Cyprus' institutions reflected strong continuity with preceding, rejected, constitutional proposals for Cyprus. The idea of communal chambers and separate municipalities was first articulated in the Macmillan Plan. The composition of the Supreme Court and communal autonomy over religious and educational matters was patterned from the Radcliffe proposal. The idea of proportional representation originated in the first Legislative Council and echoed through a number of proposals. The main features of the proposals preceding the Republic of Cyprus are listed in Table 3.1. In addition, Chapter 4 will show how a number of these institutions continued in the proposed 2004 Annan Plan.

In late 1947, the British government began casting around for a solution to the 'Cyprus problem'. The Winster Plan was its first significant effort and proposed shared governance under the ultimate control of the Governor with 18 Greek Cypriot and four Turkish Cypriot members of a Legislative Council.[42] The 18:4 ratio in favour of Greek Cypriots corresponded to the 1882 ratio.[43] Jarstad describes the system of government as 'a colonial version of consociationalism'.[44] It was accepted by the Turkish Cypriot

Table 3.1 Constitutional proposals leading up to 1960 Republic of Cyprus

Date	Name of plan	Key elements
1947	Winster Plan	• Greek Cypriot legislative majority • 18:4 Greek Cypriot/Turkish Cypriot representation in Legislative Council • 5 representatives of Governor • Governor holds executive veto
July 1954	Hopkinson Plan	• Majority of British-appointed officials • 12 seats in Legislative Assembly to elected Greek Cypriot representatives • 3 seats to elected Turkish Cypriot representatives • 6 seats for British officials • 12 seats for Cypriot representatives appointed by Governor
August 1955	London Tripartite Conference	• assembly of elected majority • proportional quota of seats reserved for Turkish Cypriots • formula for ethnic power-sharing
October 1955–March 1956	Harding-Makarios Negotiations	• based on formula of self-determination
December 1956	Radcliffe Proposal	• 36-member Legislative Assembly • 24 Greek Cypriots • 6 Turkish Cypriots • 6 members nominated by Governor • Ministry for Turkish Affairs • Supreme Court composed of 1 Greek Cypriot, 1 Turkish Cypriot, and 1 'neutral', non-Cypriot Chief Justice
January 1958	Foot Plan	• 5–7 years limited self-government
June 1958	Macmillan Plan	• tripartite governance between Greece, Turkey, and UK • Maximisation of communal autonomy • Greek Cypriot and Turkish Cypriot communal legislative chambers • Partnership council composed of 4 Greek Cypriot and 2 Turkish Cypriot advisors to Governor

Source: Evanthis Hatzivassiliou, pp. 45–72; Dimitris Bitsios, *Cyprus: the Vulnerable Republic*, Thessaloniki, Institute for Balkan Studies, 1975 pp. 25–34; Diana Weston Markides, p. 72.

members of the consultative assembly, but rejected by the Greek Cypriots, under significant pressure by the ethnarchy, because although it gave Greek Cypriots a legislative majority, it did not offer *enosis*.[45]

The Hopkinson Plan followed in July 1954, proposing a government composed of a majority of officials (British representatives) in the legislature and a minority of ethnic Cypriots. This plan was also rejected by the Greek Cypriots, who were deeply unhappy with the idea that British-appointed members would form a majority.[46] It was followed in August 1955 by the London Tripartite Conference, attended by British, Greek, and Turkish representatives. The members of the conference proposed an assembly made up of an elected majority, with a proportional quota of seats reserved for Turkish Cypriots.[47] It included a formula for ethnic power-sharing, but failed as a result of both Greek and Turkish dissatisfaction.

By this time, the regional situation was transforming Cypriot attitudes towards a solution. Xydis[48] believed that the enthusiasm for *enosis* among Greek and Greek Cypriot negotiators was significantly dampened by the anti-Greek riots in Istanbul and Izmir at the end of the London Tripartite Conference. For Xydis, this event triggered their 'willingness to discuss self-government for Cyprus'[49] on the condition that self-determination remain a future goal.

Almost immediately after the London Conference's failure, the new British Governor, Sir John Harding, began direct negotiations with exiled Archbishop Makarios in October 1955. The negotiations were based loosely on the principle of self-determination[50] (as were the Tripartite Proposals) and lasted until March 1956 before ending in stalemate. In December of that same year, at the same time as the climax of the Suez crisis, the Radcliffe proposal was put forward, outlining a Legislative Assembly with 36 members: 24 Greek Cypriot, six Turkish Cypriot, and six members nominated by the Governor. It recommended the establishment of a Ministry for Turkish Affairs,[51] as well as a Supreme Court composed of three judges; one Greek Cypriot, one Turkish Cypriot, and one Chief Justice from outside Cyprus, who was thus considered 'neutral'. We find these last elements repeated in the eventual constitution of the Republic of Cyprus. This plan was rejected by Greece[52] and accepted by the Turkish Cypriots and Turkey. The Greek Cypriots refused to negotiate while Makarios was still in exile.

The next in the line of suggestions was the 1958 Foot Plan, which proposed five to seven years of limited self-government in the hope that the groups would learn to share government. This was followed several months later by the Macmillan Plan, which was developed by the British unilaterally and which recommended joint governance between Greece, Turkey, and the UK. Under this plan, communal autonomy was maximised and emphasised; another aspect echoed in 1960. There were two communal legislative chambers, one Greek Cypriot and one Turkish Cypriot, facilitating complete institutional separation between the communities. A 'partnership council' was also included, with four Greek Cypriot and two Turkish Cypriot advisors to the Governor.[53]

By October 1958, the three 'motherlands' were discussing the possibility of Cypriot independence and, from late December, Greece and Turkey's foreign ministers were participating in secret negotiations to that end. This led directly to a summit meeting in Zurich, Switzerland which was led by Prime Ministers Karamanlis of Greece and Menderes of Turkey. 'The negotiators apparently kept no official minutes and bargained for five days before reaching a comprehensive settlement. On February 11 1959, the Prime Ministers of Greece and Turkey signed an agreement for the establishment of the Republic of Cyprus. The outline of the settlement was then taken to London for final ratification'.[54] On 19 February, the prime ministers of Greece, Turkey, and Great Britain, as well as the leaders of the Turkish and Greek Cypriot communities signed the documents. The Zurich and London Accords[55] settled on a Presidential system of governance, with a 70:30 Greek Cypriot to Turkish Cypriot ratio in the Legislature. The extensive Turkish Cypriot veto rights were also worked out in these negotiations. The full constitutional details were to be completed subsequently by a Constitutional Commission[56] based in Nicosia.

Greek and Turkish Cypriot interests and attitudes

Commentators differ as to why such a system was chosen for this state, but there are four main reasons cited in the literature. The primary reason given most credence in this thesis was compromise, to control and appease opposing Greek Cypriot and Turkish Cypriot concepts of statehood. It was also a tool to limit the chances of conflict between the communities.

It does seem that the political institutions of the Republic of Cyprus were chosen as a compromise to meet as many as possible of the important needs of both communities on the island.[57] One of the plan's Greek architects has argued that the Greek team's main concern was to see that

> (a) Cyprus retained its territorial integrity and its unity as a political entity, (b) that the State machinery functioned efficiently, and (c) that the Cyprus Republic acquired the legal personality of an independent territory, so as to be internationally recognized as a sovereign State.[58]

These goals, he claims, were largely met during the Zurich and London processes.[59] It also seems that the initial architects of the plan, Zorlu and Averoff, had identified several areas likely to create or exacerbate conflict, but were unable to resolve them at those early stages.[60] These previously identified sources of tension became issues at both the Constitutional Commission and later, as friction increased, within the government. The failure to fill in all the legal details of the Republic of Cyprus at that early stage provided avenues for both sides to reinforce their advantage, and they actively infused such areas with the underlying power struggle. As it will be shown later in the chapter, contrasting interpretations of the constitution created the most significant areas of conflict between the communities in the Republic of Cyprus' infant years. This uncertainty was so problematic because the areas became opportunities for each group to project their national vision. This conflict ultimately prevented the constitution's translation into a working system of government.

The strength of the constitution was that it 'sought to overcome the suppression of the minority that could arise from a majoritarian approach';[61] but even in this the state's architects 'failed to successfully articulate the advantages to both sides for the preservation of the consociational state'.[62] Richmond argues that the crafters of the 1960 Cypriot state should have more carefully emphasised the constitution's mutual benefit 'the message that the new arrangement was a safeguard for the Turkish Cypriots against the Greek Cypriots and Greece, and for the Greek Cypriots vis-à-vis Turkey'.[63] Because this was not adequately emphasised, the Greek Cypriots perceived the 1960 state to be a betrayal of their rights and manoeuvred to remove the 'impositions' in late 1963. The Turkish Cypriots saw those moves as an attack on their rights and counter-manoeuvred to maintain them.

It is likely that conflicting Turkish and Greek Cypriot perspectives on the purpose of an independent Cypriot state was a significant factor driving the choice of institutions. The domestic institutions tried to neutralise the struggle between Greek Cypriot desires for a majoritarian system and Turkish Cypriot fears of suppression by the majority. The Greek Cypriots believed that the Turkish Cypriots stood in the way of self-determination. Since *enosis* was unachievable, majoritarian democracy would at least protect Greek Cypriot numerical superiority and translate that superiority into legislative power. Thus they were unwilling to preserve a system which they perceived as distorting the power dynamics of Cypriot society. The Turkish Cypriots believed that the Greek Cypriots wanted to subjugate them as a minority in a Greek state.[64] They therefore sought a constitution that would protect their communal rights and enhance their status from that of simply a minority to that of a partner in any future state. Thus they perceived the Zurich and London Accords to be significant achievements which protected and defended their status.[65] So while the constitution 'satisfied the Turkish Cypriot community, it did not go far enough for the nationalist Greek Cypriot leadership'.[66] While the constitution aimed to control inter-communal antipathy by protecting both communities against the other, those efforts were unsuccessful.

Furthermore 'the net result of this constitutional factionalism was to prevent the constitution from becoming a common symbol'.[67] However, the constitutional factionalism must be attributed in large part to the frustration of ethno-nationalist desires. While the institutions were a linear progression from the 1882 institutions, and from a number of subsequent proposed designs, they did not meet Greek Cypriot visions about how a democratic, or just state, should look. In light of that unfulfilled expectation, it is not surprising that the constitution did not become a common symbol.

International factors

Much of the literature considering the 1960 republic's design has argued that the state was designed primarily to meet the needs of the international community. McDonald has argued that 'the complex of associated treaties severely constrained the sovereignty of the state and did not so much end colonial status as spread it wider through the guarantee of three NATO nations [Greece, Turkey, and Britain]'.[68] According to this view, the primary purpose of resolving the Cyprus conflict was to facilitate peace in the broader Mediterranean region, and especially Greek-Turkish peace.[69] Constitutional scholar S. A de Smith encapsulates this position in his discussion of the Nicosia consociational model. His argument has consequently been used almost reflexively by supporters of this position to reaffirm their assertions:

> The Nicosia model will never attain enthusiastic emulators, but it must be judged as the only acceptable remedy for a desperate situation in which *the will of the local majority had to be subordinated to the interests of international peace.*[70]

However, while the interests of international (and particularly Greco-Turkish) peace should be considered as the important factors motivating the 1960 constitution's design, they cannot be considered the only or primary factors. Reputable sources, including former Republic of Cyprus President Glafkos Clerides, scholar Stephen Xydis, and former Greek Foreign Minister Dimitris Bitsios,[71] have argued that the Greek and Turkish foreign ministers and premiers negotiated the resolution at length, mindful of *both* the domestic and international pressures on their own countries as a result of the Cyprus conflict, as well as the concerns of the Cypriot groups.[72]

Breakdown of the consociational state: Why did it fail?

While the literature analysing the 1960 state's failure centres generally on weakness in the constitution, with consociationalism, or with elite incentives for compromise, this chapter argues that the attitudes of historically conditioned elites generated conflict over the political institutions, which was projected onto the political and social structures. The following section will examine the ways in which segmental isolation, a balance of power between the segments, a tradition of accommodation, and the international community's ability to offer incentives for compromise contributed to the state's breakdown.

Segmental isolation

Segmental isolation underpins consociational theory's assumption that elites will be freer to co-operate if inter-communal tension is contained. The crucial point regarding segmental isolation in 1960s Cyprus is its absence.

In 1960, the groups had come straight out of a violent conflict where the Greek Cypriots sought to obtain *enosis* and the Turkish Cypriots sought partition. Throwing two conflicting and geographically interspersed groups together at independence in a delicate power-sharing democracy was a recipe for escalation of inter-communal distrust.

Segmental isolation protects and complements communal autonomy in consociational democracy. In Cyprus, communal autonomy had a non-geographical foundation. Had there been segmental isolation, it is feasible that the idea of power-sharing might have been more easily legitimated. However, as it was, the majority and principal minority community on the island were geographically integrated, and there was significant resentment among Greek Cypriot elites over their perceived concession of power to a minority group that had no real territorial legitimacy. Anything that might have prompted a change in communal dynamics, such as the issue of segregated municipalities, triggered Greek Cypriot fears of *taksim*. At the same time, Turkish Cypriots were equally fearful of any development which would enhance Greek Cypriot political domination.

Conflicting Turkish and Greek Cypriot perspectives on segmental isolation were expressed in the municipality conflict, which, in turn, played a significant role in the state's breakdown. Unified municipalities existed in Cyprus until 1958 when, during the EOKA crisis, the Turkish Cypriot leaders sought and received permission from the British administrators to create temporary separate Turkish Cypriot municipalities.[73] The Greek Cypriot municipalities continued to operate under the previous law,[74] which provided for united municipalities. The 1960 constitution tried to overcome this discrepancy by ruling that each of the five major towns was to create ethnically separated municipalities. Article 173 (2) stated that

[t]he council of the Greek municipality in any such town shall be elected by the Greek electors of the town and the council of the Turkish municipality in such town shall be elected by the Turkish electors of the town.

The 1960 constitution granted a six-month extension of the existing municipal law (for unified municipalities, under which the Greek Cypriots were still operating) to provide the president and vice-president with time to iron out the details of the new law, particularly regarding municipal boundaries. However, the municipal issue became a major sticking point for both communities, and the carry-over colonial law was extended a number of times before the issue came to a head. The Greek Cypriots fiercely resisted implementing the new law. President Makarios was particularly averse to the idea of separated municipalities. 'Makarios didn't want to allow them to have the separate municipalities because, in his mind, that was the beginning of partition'.[75] He argued that it would be a logistical nightmare to create separate municipalities because 'although *de facto* boundaries existed segregating the recognised ethnic quarters within the towns, some Cypriots had integrated, especially in newer middle and upper class neighbourhoods'.[76] Thus, Greek Cypriot governing elites opposed any attempts to implement Article 173 of the constitution. The Turkish Cypriots on the other hand held tightly to the implementation of the provision, for the very reason that it gave them communal autonomy at the municipal level. This conflict is cited by some scholars as the key factor contributing to the state's breakdown.[77]

The inability of the executive to solve the municipal crisis caused the problem to progress through to the House of Representatives, where the issue remained unresolved. The temporary law finally expired on 31 December 1962 and Cyprus was left without municipal legislation. That same day, the Turkish Cypriot Communal Chamber passed a law legitimising the separate status of the Turkish Cypriot municipal councils.[78] Two days later, on 2 January 1963 the Council of Ministers, dominated by the Greek Cypriots, passed a law bringing the municipalities under unified control.[79] The problem snaked its way through the legislative arm of government unresolved, leaving in its wake an impotent and increasingly tense executive and legislature. The issue thus moved on to the judiciary, where each community contested the constitutionality of the other community's law in the Supreme Constitutional Court.

In the first judgement in the history of the Court that was not given unanimously, both laws were ruled unconstitutional by majority vote. Bi-communal division finally claimed the judiciary when the Greek Cypriot judge dissented from the decision taken against the Council of Ministers law, and the Turkish Cypriot judge dissented from the decision taken against the Turkish Cypriot Communal Chamber law. The municipal issue was the single most damaging set of cases heard by the Supreme Constitutional Court and brought the Court to its knees with the eventual resignation of its president, Justice Forsthoff as a result of communal pressure.

The geographical distribution of the two ethnic groups was also a factor which changed significantly over the course of the conflict. In the period leading up to 1960, and in the first three years of the Republic's life, Greek and Turkish Cypriot villages largely co-existed with mixed villages, and each town also had Turkish Cypriot quarters.[80] There was never full intermixing between groups, but neither was there full separation. As tension increased, the Turkish Cypriot community began to feel increasingly threatened and 'surrounded' by the Greek Cypriot community. This feeling of threat has been identified as a problematic factor by Lijphart, and is one reason he suggests that segmental isolation is advantageous in societies that exhibit significant levels of inter-communal tension.[81]

In this case, it seems that the groups' interspersion caused increasing conflict over the life of the Republic of Cyprus. But the conflict then initiated the two communities' separation, which caused a major change in the facts on the ground. Segmental isolation increasingly became the norm in the breakdown period. Between 1963 and 1967, a significant proportion of the Turkish Cypriot community was concentrated in enclaves in each of the major towns. But the community was still dependent on the (*de facto* Greek Cypriot) government for essential services and supplies, which were infrequently and only resentfully provided. Building and other basic materials were denied to the community on the rationale that these items could become weapons used against Greek Cypriots.

It will be shown in Chapter 4 that segmental isolation has played a significant role in the reunification politics of post-independence, and particularly post-war, Cyprus. However, that element was established in the breakdown[82] and post-breakdown[83] period of Cypriot history. Full segmental isolation was realised after the failed Greek coup and resultant Turkish occupation of 1974, which caused a clear ethnic demarcation – a Turkish Cypriot north and a Greek Cypriot south. This separation allowed the Turkish Cypriot community to feel safer and able to redress what was for them a disadvantageous balance of power. It has, however, become a disturbing element of the conflict for many Greek Cypriots, who maintain that the loss of their properties in northern Cyprus is a situation which must be remedied. When the facts on the ground changed with the two groups' separation, other factors (especially balance of power) were also altered. According to consociational theory, these changes should have made a solution more likely in 2004, but as Chapter 4 will show, this was not to be the case.

Ultimately, the lack of segmental isolation in Cyprus contributed significantly to the 1960 state's early demise, primarily because pressure over communal safety was transferred to the legislative and judicial arenas. Inter-communal distrust caused the Greek Cypriot elite to be suspicious of constitutional provisions for communal autonomy and corresponding defensiveness among the Turkish Cypriot elite. The clear causal link between battles over provisions which reinforced communal autonomy through segmental isolation, such as the municipal law, and the state's breakdown, encourages recognition of a strong relationship between segmental isolation and a desire or ability among elites to compromise.

Balance of power between the segments

Balance of power is defined here as approximate equality of communal power. It is a valuable factor because it encourages negotiation between segmental elites and aids compromise. Chapter 1 argued that relatively equal power between the disputant groups creates the necessary incentive for power-sharing. An unequal power relationship between the groups creates an incentive for the more powerful to try to defeat the less powerful, particularly in a situation where there are only two groups vying for control. Thus, a power-sharing government, based on an acknowledgement by the groups of a degree of equality between them, is more likely to be adopted and to survive if it is underpinned by a balance of communal power.

Cyprus in 1960 suffered from the 'problem of two'; a significant majority disenchanted with the division of power, and a minority highly protective of its constitutional advantages. While the involvement of Greece and Turkey in a sense balanced the scales of communal power in Cyprus, their presence in the background was not sufficient to relieve this problem; on the contrary, they often complicated the perception of internal power distribution.

Lijphart argues that a balance of power between multiple segments aids reciprocal bargaining and compromise, but power is divided in Cyprus only between the two major communities, creating an intensely competitive relationship between them.[84] This has been clearly identified by Lijphart as a disadvantage to successful consociationalism: '[t]he problem of a duality is that ... it entails either a hegemony or a precarious balance'.[85] He has argued that the 'dual imbalance of power constituted the crucially unfavourable factor' in the 1960 Cypriot state.[86]

When the Republic of Cyprus was established in 1960, a broad balance of power between the two communities was created primarily by the relationship between Greece and Turkey. While the Greek Cypriots, at 80 percent of the population, had a significant numerical superiority, the advantage was levelled by external factors. At the time of the Zurich and London Accords, Britain was heading towards a Cypriot constitution which would have made the island's division between Greece and Turkey a distinct possibility. The Macmillan Plan was a tripartite condominium which would have significantly curtailed Cypriot decision-making capacity and involved Turkey in Cypriot governance.[87] Knowing they were negotiating from a weakened position, Greek officials worked quickly to bring about an alternative solution. The Greek-Turkish détente, in effect, changed the distribution of power between the Cypriot communities. The constitution was an extension of this equilibrium; its adoption should have been smoothed by the détente.

The establishment of a partnership government equalised Greek and Turkish Cypriot social and political power. However, this was perceived as an injustice by the Greek Cypriot elite, who resented the inflation of Turkish Cypriot power in the Republic of Cyprus. As soon as the balance of power became contestable, it lost its influence as a facilitative factor for compromise and as a stabilising mechanism. From this case we may infer that not only is a balance of power important to elite willingness to share power, but so also is the *acceptance* of this balance by all groups. The apparent balance achieved in 1960 turned out to be hollow because in every instance thereafter where compromise was necessary, conflict ensued.

The taxation issue exemplifies how an inadequate balance contributed considerable strain to the consociational structure, ultimately leading to its collapse. Section II of Article 78 of the Constitution stated that 'any law imposing duties or taxes shall require a separate simple majority of the representatives elected by the Greek and Turkish communities respectively taking part in the vote'.[88] Disagreement on the passage of a new tax law meant that the new Republic was not authorised to collect taxes. The colonial tax provision was extended until March 1961, with the intention of providing more time to legislate an acceptable law. However, by that time the mutual veto was being used to bind progress on the implementation of taxation laws to the full execution of the 70:30 Civil Service provision and the establishment of separate municipalities. Attempts by each community to implement new taxation laws in the House of Representatives were voted down by the other:

> In order to have a new income tax law, we needed separate majorities of the Greek and Turkish [Cypriot] members of parliament. The issue was complicated by the issue of the Turkish [Cypriot] demand to have separate municipalities as provided by the constitution ... but [Makarios disputed the need for separate municipalities]. And because of that the [Turkish Cypriots] retaliated and they did not vote for the income tax law changes ... so, [the state] was threatened with collapse, and in order to avoid collapse various other measures were taken.[89]

Eventually both groups turned to their respective Communal Chambers to raise revenue. The effect of this conflict was to enhance the role of the Communal Chambers in the Republic's running because it impelled both communities to legislate different sets of laws. It also substantially increased resentment among both communities' elites, who were learning to use the legislative mechanisms in a negative fashion to thwart each other's objectives.

Because there was no acknowledged balance of power, a destructive struggle for dominance ensued. In December 1963, Makarios sought to redress what he considered the 'dysfunctional' elements of the constitution by suggesting 13 constitutional amendments.[90] His proposals were immediately rejected by the Turkish government and subsequently also by the Turkish Cypriot ministers. At the same time, serious inter-communal fighting and Makarios' proposals precipitated the withdrawal from the executive and legislature of the Turkish Cypriot representatives. Consequently, after 1963, when the Turkish Cypriot community had lost its legislative representation, the Greek Cypriots found themselves in complete control of a state no longer consociational. From that point of advantage, they moved to reshape the Republic of Cyprus along majoritarian lines. In the decade until 1974, Greek Cypriot control of the government machinery and the increasing economic disparity between the Greek and Turkish Cypriot communities prevented the realisation of a power-sharing state. The failed Greek coup and subsequent Turkish incursion in July and August 1974 signalled the complete failure of the 1960 consociational state.

The lack of a balance of power destabilised the 1960 state. Greek Cypriot elites were resentful about sharing power with a significant numerical minority, and Turkish Cypriot elite were highly protective of their communal autonomy. The groups' disagreement over the power balance underpinning the consociational state caused continual friction between elites and discouraged a culture of bargaining and co-operation vital to the success of consociational democracy. The 1960 state's end is stark evidence of this factor's importance. Had there been an accepted or genuine balance of power, Makarios would not have sought to amend the constitution so extensively in the way that he did, and the Turkish Cypriot elites would not have responded with such a radical move.

A tradition of accommodation

From the beginning, Cypriot consociationalism had neither inter-group elite co-operation nor elite support for the new state and its constitution. Both the Greek and Turkish Cypriots went into the negotiations that brought about the 1960 Republic of Cyprus hoping for something different, and consociationalism was the second-best option for both sides. The leaderships' incompatible intentions were quickly revealed in the many lines of tension within the state. Constitutional friction in Cyprus 'was bi-communal in all spheres of governmental activity; namely Executive, Legislative, Judicial and Administrative ... thus there developed an intricate system of frictional crises which set the two communities in constitutional factionalism'.[91]

The incentive for Greek Cypriot elites to compromise was the threat of partition. However, once that threat was overcome, the incentive for compromise was dulled. The Macmillan Plan's speedy completion and presentation 'had convinced Makarios that partition was imminent and prompted him, against the wishes of EOKA, to allow that he would accept independence in lieu of self-determination'.[92] Küçük and Denktaş were concerned with protecting the rights of the Turkish Cypriot community and the interests of Turkey in Cyprus.

Political inexperience may also explain elite reluctance to share power in the first consociational state. Loizos maintains[93] that part of the reason for the collapse of the 1960 state was that political leaders from both sides 'found themselves in power before they had matured'.[94] They did not have the chance to learn conciliation, nor had they the opportunity to learn other aspects of the art of governance. Used to pursuing the goals of their respective communities, sometimes at the expense of the other, their tools were violence and confrontation. These people, who had risen to prominence because of their ability to promote particular interests, and who, in order to maintain their existence, had to be extreme, uncompromising and single-minded, now found themselves leaders of communities which needed to compromise in order to survive. Archbishop Makarios and Dr Fazil Küçük were each the embodiment of rival movements. So, when the state was formed, the president and vice-president each personified a different and mutually antagonistic symbol to the Greek and Turkish Cypriot populations. This clearly constrained their ability to work together in government.

Consociational theorists argue that the promise of gaining and maintaining political power should go some way to enticing political elites to co-operate. Indeed, the 1960 state depended upon a generous interpretation of the basic articles by the political representatives and a high level of co-operation in the executive between president and vice-president. However, there was no tradition of accommodation upon which they could build; their personal reputations meant that they were constantly under great pressure to maintain the extreme positions held in the pre-independence period. In addition, powerful extremist forces were operating against the leadership;[95] and with all of that, these new national leaders were being asked to represent their state in the particularly volatile politics of the Middle East region. Such a task was far beyond their experience.[96] There were important problems: they had no experience at all of running a democratic (and especially a divided) nation; and the two communities which had previously been encouraged to view their relationship as a zero-sum game now had to be reassured that their representatives would work to protect their interests. However, historical antecedents including no tradition of accommodation, surrounding pressures, and the lack of electoral incentives to take the hard edges off their policy platforms inhibited elite co-operation from the beginning.[97]

Further to this problem was the person of the president, who as the head of the Orthodox Church of Cyprus could not easily gain the confidence of the Turkish Cypriot population.[98] As a symbol of Greek nationalism, Makarios was under enormous pressure from right-wing Greek Cypriot factions to push for *enosis*. His frequent speeches supporting Cypriot Hellenism may have been an attempt to appease Greek nationalists and thus pacify intra-communal tension. But they inflamed Turkish Cypriot fears of domination and made the vice-president especially vulnerable to the attacks of Turkish Cypriot nationalists who accused him of being a pawn on Makarios' chessboard.

The lack of Greek Cypriot co-operation in the 1960 state is frequently put down to the foisting of an unfavourable constitution upon Makarios and his colleagues by Greek negotiators[99] during the Zurich process.[100] This argument is based on a common misconception in the Greek Cypriot community about Cyprus' constitutional history. Thus it is claimed that Greek Cypriot elites were not sympathetic to the 1960 constitution *because* they were not involved in its creation and therefore had no control over the quality of its provisions. However, this position is contradicted by convincing sources: Glafkos Clerides[101] and Rauf Denktaş,[102] as well as detailed notes taken by Averoff,[103] and also recorded by Xydis,[104] show that Makarios was consulted throughout the talks, as was Küçük.[105] Clerides emphasises that 'it must be stated clearly that the Zurich Agreements were concluded with Makarios fully informed and concurring with all of their provisions ... [but] he concurred because he believed stark necessity dictated their acceptance if a worse solution were to be avoided'.[106] In order to later justify the Greek Cypriot elites' lack of support for the original constitution, history was tweaked slightly.[107]

Ability of the international community to offer incentives for compromise

This book has posited that the international community can influence elite willingness to enter into power-sharing systems of government when there are few domestic incentives for elite compromise. A positive relationship between domestic elites and key international players can stabilise the environment surrounding a conflict. It can also broaden the scope of play and change incentives for co-operation. In both the birth and breakdown of the 1960 Cypriot state, key international actors significantly influenced events. They were not, however, able to offer sufficient incentives to encourage prolonged elite co-operation.

Intra-state conflicts are most frequently resolved by a community of international actors, who are used as both intermediaries and constitutional engineers. In most of these conflicts *realpolitik* rules, and the parties that are most interested in dissolving the conflict are also those which are interested in the results of a resolution. It has frequently been argued that the Zurich and London Agreements were primarily vehicles for Greek, Turkish, or (and sometimes all three) British domestic and regional requirements. In any case, Greece and Turkey played central roles in the development of Cypriot independence. The détente between them created an environment in which a solution could be found, and indeed, Greek and Turkish diplomats conducted the main negotiations which produced the 1960 Republic of Cyprus.

In the pre-adoption stage, the Turkish negotiators worked closely with Turkish Cypriot elites to press for a favourable solution for the Turkish Cypriot community. As discussed above, the Greek negotiators also consulted with the Greek Cypriot leadership. The relationship between Greek and Greek Cypriot elites illustrates how international elites are able to bring pressure to bear on their domestic counterparts to encourage a conflict's solution. It has been frequently stated that while Makarios had initially supported the Zurich Agreements, he then reneged on the eve of signing in London. The story goes that Greek Prime Minister Constantine Karamanlis warned Makarios that night that if the Greek Cypriot leadership rejected the Zurich-London Accords, then they would receive no further support from Greece.[108] Makarios subsequently supported the Agreements.[109]

However, while international actors were able to bring a constitutional settlement to Cyprus, they were not subsequently able to carry that influence through to ensure the constitution's successful functioning. Insofar as international actors *did* have a number of levers to exert pressure for Cypriot co-operation, they were themselves operating in a dense web of domestic and international pressures: the strain of Greek-Turkish relations in an unstable region, post-colonialism, and significant Cold War tension. Greek, Turkish, British, and UN interests were by no means aligned. Assuming that the international community had a shared interest in the Cypriot state's stable functioning, it would still have been very difficult to co-ordinate levers to ensure Greek and Turkish Cypriot co-operation for the Republic of Cyprus' smooth operation.

This web of international factors affected the ability of international players to offer incentives for domestic elites to co-operate. It also affected their ability to stabilise the regional environment. Both Cypriot communities have suffered from a poor relationship with regional powers – Turkish Cypriots fear Greek Cyprus' relationship with Greece and Greek Cypriots fear Turkish Cyprus' relationship with Turkey, as well as feeling threatened by Turkey's military presence on Cyprus. 1960s Cyprus was only the forerunner to greater tensions in that arena. Complicating the issue, domestic elites of both communities have resented the roles of their motherlands in Cyprus. In addition, the relationship between Cypriot political leaders and the United Kingdom, the United States and the (then) Soviet Republic has had a multilayered influence on the state's failure.

Regional actors were able, by their influence, to shape the domestic environment. According to the hypotheses of Markides, McDonald, and others, the 'Greekness' and 'Turkishness' of Cypriots and their relationships to their 'motherlands' was reinforced at the expense of efforts to develop Cypriot loyalty (of which there was little at the time). Thus they somewhat simplistically argue that the treaties upon which the constitution was based were designed to reaffirm national ties and ensure Cypriot dependence on Greece and Turkey. Weston-Markides argues that 'the Zurich agreements had been designed to ensure that the Cypriots' political rights as citizens derived from their communal allegiance and, indeed, to prohibit the already remote possibility of the emergence of any concept of Cypriot nationhood'.[110] Kyriakides is more descriptive in his explanation, arguing that 'the ability of each Communal Chamber to receive direct assistance from Greece and Turkey respectively, on the one hand, tended to strengthen the ties of the two communities to these two countries, and, on the other hand, to undermine the authority of the government of the Republic'.[111]

The international environment also played a significantly inhibitive role in the Cypriot state's success. O'Malley and Craig argue that during the Republic of Cyprus' genesis, Britain was particularly anxious to ensure several basic objectives: the alliance of the Republic of Cyprus with Great Britain, Turkey, and Greece to form a barrier against communism and protection of the Baghdad Pact; the development of economic institutions with pro-West leanings; the protection of the British Sovereign Base Areas from Cypriot revocation and the maintenance of United States communication facilities on the island.[112] A note from a British Colonial Office paper in 1957 states that

> [i]t is of great strategic importance that Cyprus should not come under the control of a government which was favourably disposed towards the USSR. The presence of a Soviet base in the rear of NATO forces, and close to the Turkish mainland would be liable to have a most seriously undermining effect on the stability of the right flank of NATO and upon the Baghdad Pact.[113]

British and Turkish thinking seemed to be that if Turkish Cypriots could be given extensive veto powers in a shared government, they would naturally side with Turkey on issues of foreign and domestic policy and could therefore be used to both veto unfavourable economic policy and counteract any communist leanings, which were significant in the Greek Cypriot community.

Therefore, the role of regional elites also played a negative role in the Cypriot state. It has been argued in this chapter that domestic and regional pressures contributed to hardening the behaviour of the president and vice-president instead of facilitating their co-operation. Such pressure meant that on the occasions when the president and vice-president exhibited moderate and conciliatory behaviour they were actively discouraged on several fronts; by internal opposition from political competitors who were dissatisfied with the resolution,[114] or with their positions as a result of the resolution, and by Greek and Turkish nationalists on the 'mainlands' who wanted to maintain and deepen the inter-communal divide to protect their own interest on the island.

1960s Cyprus suggests that this, the fourth, key factor is primarily facilitative; in cases where a consociational settlement is being negotiated and there is minimal elite co-operation or balance of power between the segments, the ability of international actors to offer and sustain incentives for compromise is vital. While the 1960 case suggests that the capacity of international actors to offer incentives for domestic elites to compromise, or to alter the domestic environment, is important to the success of consociational democracy, the factor was not strong enough in Cyprus to facilitate the state's full operationalisation.

Conclusion

This chapter has argued that the 1960 consociational state was chosen to meet a number of requirements. Elements of the design represented significant continuity with the colonial Legislative Council and previous constitutional plans first suggested by the British. Elements of the plan also gave considerable rights to Greece, Turkey, and Britain, reflecting the close interests of international actors in the design of the plan. But the plan was most strongly shaped by the need to control and appease opposing Greek and Turkish Cypriot concepts of statehood. The 1960 state tried to find a compromise between the Greek Cypriot desire for a majoritarian system of governance and Turkish Cypriot fears of suppression by the majority. However, the state's breakdown indicates that the compromise was not truly accepted by the Cypriot political elites.

In this chapter it has been shown that the absence of a number of the key factors helped to cause the state's failure. Most obviously, a disagreement over the power balance underpinning the consociational state significantly inhibited elite co-operation, which was the immediate cause of the state's breakdown. The lack of segmental isolation and no history of accommodation between elites exacerbated tensions and affected elite relations. Without strong incentives for compromise, which could only be offered by international actors, the state collapsed. The chapter has shown how particular features of institutional design became obstacles to the successful adoption of a consociational state, primarily because the extra-constitutional elements, articulated here as four key factors, were absent.

The failure of the original state also had great political and social consequences. The state's failure, and its effects, have become deeply lodged in the group memory of both communities and, in a number of ways that will be explored in subsequent chapters, has further complicated efforts to resolve the conflict by inhibiting elite preparedness to share power in Cyprus. In addition, the breakdown of the 1960 state has shaped significant parts of the constitution proposed by the UN in 2004.

4
Getting the Institutions Right: Making Plans for Cyprus

there is nothing more permanent than the temporary

This chapter examines the most significant post-breakdown attempt to craft a comprehensive political solution to the Cyprus conflict. Drawing extensively upon information from interviews with involved parties, reports, and other primary sources, the chapter argues that the Annan Plan was carefully and methodically constructed to create a state which addressed both groups' primary concerns and fears as well as their most important demands. Much of the Annan Plan was shaped by experiences of the failed 1960 state. Thus the constitutional engineers were keen not to replicate the flaws of the 1960 constitution. At the same time, domestic elites have internalised communal history and memories, which have become friction points in peace negotiations. Therefore, many of the plan's provisions were designed to overcome particular communal fears caused by the 1960 state's breakdown. This chapter has two main sections, the first outlines the proposed federal and constituent state structures and the second analyses the Annan Plan's development in order to understand whether the plan itself inhibited elite willingness to share power.

The 2004 Annan Plan

The United Cyprus Republic (UCR), as the engineers of the Annan Plan titled the proposed new state of Cyprus, was to comprise a set of institutions inspired by consociational models drawn from European states. Throughout the crafting of the Annan Plan, the engineers took great pains to explain their institutional choices. This is evidenced by the UN Secretary General's Reports on Cyprus[1] which discuss at length the choice of institutions in the context of each side's interests, and in the context of lessons from the 1960 Republic of Cyprus. The decision to use consociational institutions was effectively made for the UN by the fact that little else would have been acceptable to both sides, and the solution's broad outline had been long established.

Both the Swiss and Belgian models of governance were suggested by Turkish Cypriot interlocutors, and despite late Greek Cypriot complaints, in the Secretary General's 2003 Report on Cyprus,[2] Annan suggests that the model of Switzerland provides an acceptable and functional compromise in relation to the motivations and needs of both sides.[3] Prima facie, this also seems to support traditional (corporatist) consociational claims for the transferability of the flagship consociational state structures.

This section will outline the format of the proposed resolution for Cyprus, in order to later compare the institutions chosen with those sought by the interlocutors, and with those the engineers considered most desirable. Both the proposed federal and constituent state constitutions, which each have a different structure to the federal, are discussed here.

In mid-2000, UN Special Representative to Cyprus, Alvaro de Soto, began constructing a team of experts to resume work on the long-stalemated negotiations, with an eye to resolving the conflict before Cyprus' likely entry into the EU.[4] It quickly became clear to the UN team that, if left to the interlocutors, the talks would remain indefinitely at the pre-negotiation stage. To progress the situation towards tangible negotiations, the UN began to work on the outline of a comprehensive solution to the Cyprus conflict. The first of the UN's documents was submitted on 12 July 2000. Called 'Preliminary Thoughts', it was a bland document, designed to 'sound out' the groups.[5] It was followed on 8 November 2000 by a second document which advanced the negotiations by suggesting that a single negotiating text should be the basis of further negotiations.[6] Soon after, Denktaş terminated the negotiations; halting them for a year on the basis that the negotiations to date had insufficiently dealt with the issue of Turkish Cypriot sovereignty. The first Annan Plan (Annan I) called the 'Comprehensive Settlement of the Cyprus Problem', was submitted to the Greek and Turkish Cypriot communities in November 2002. The second revised plan (Annan II) was submitted one month later on 10 December. Annan III was submitted in February 2003. In the same month, presidential elections in south Cyprus brought into power conservative party DIKO in an ideologically unusual ruling alliance with communist party AKEL. The president-elect was DIKO leader Tassos Papadopoulos, who replaced outgoing president Glafkos Clerides as chief negotiator for the Greek Cypriot community. When Annan IV was submitted in March 2004, the leadership dimension had changed, significantly affecting the negotiating dynamics. By this time, parliamentary elections in north Cyprus saw CTP leader Mehmet Ali Talat become prime minister of north Cyprus. As the first left-wing prime minister, his election was a significant break from the past. His election reflected the pro-settlement and anti–status quo public sentiment which had been building for some time in north Cyprus. It also marked a tangible changing point in Turkish Cypriot negotiating dynamics, replacing Denktaş' combativeness and intransigence with a negotiating party which co-operated with the UN team, providing a clear list of negotiating goals and compromises.[7] This changed dynamic was carried through to Annan V.

The UCR was designed on the whole as a federal, liberal consociational state. The new state of affairs in Cyprus was devised to be an indissoluble partnership between the federal government and two equal constituent states, called the Greek Cypriot Constituent State and the Turkish Cypriot Constituent State. Following consociational principles, the constitution specified the powers and functions vested in the federal government, devolving the bulk of powers (including the day-to-day functioning of the states) to the constituent states. Each constituent state was to exercise powers related to the administration of justice at the state level; law and order; criminal, company and family law; public safety; industry and commerce; social security and labour; environmental protection; tourism; fisheries and agriculture; zoning and planning; sports; education; and health. Each constituent state would have also had corresponding executive, legislative, and judicial offices to that outlined for the federal level.

The federal state

The federal state envisaged in the Annan Plan was comprised of an executive (which included a Presidential Council, a Federal Administration, and Federal Police), a legislature (Senate and Chamber of Deputies), a judiciary (the Supreme Court), and independent institutions (Central Bank, Office of the Attorney General, Office of the Auditor General). The powers to be exercised by the federal government included external relations; relations with the EU; operation of the Central Bank; federal finances; natural resources; aviation, navigation, and territorial waters of the UCR; communications; Cypriot citizenship; amnesties and pardons; antiquities; and intellectual property. In addition, its authority was to extend over federal administration; elections and referendums; offences against federal laws; and federal property. There was to be no hierarchy between federal and constituent state laws.

The powers of the federal legislature included the approval of international treaties for ratification; the election of the Presidential Council; the adoption of the federal budget; and, by special majority, the referral of serious crimes by members of the Presidential Council and the independent institutions to the Supreme Court.

The Senate was to be composed of 24 senators from each constituent state, elected 'on a proportional basis by the citizens of Cyprus, voting separately as Greek Cypriots and Turkish Cypriots'.[8] Ordinary decisions were to be taken by a simple majority of its members, which included one quarter of present and voting senators from each constituent state. For the approval of the federal budget, Presidential Council elections, and matters deemed as being of critical interest to the constituent states, a special majority would be needed to pass decisions. This would require at least two-fifths of sitting senators from each constituent state (ten) to support the bill.[9]

The Chamber of Deputies was to be composed proportionally, according to the population of each constituent state[10] and the number of people holding citizenship in each constituent state. A maximum of 75 per cent of the deputies were to hold the internal citizenship of the Greek Cypriot State and a minimum of 25 per cent that of the Turkish Cypriot State. Deputies were to be elected for five years on the basis of proportional representation (PR), and all decisions were to be taken by a simple majority of members present and voting.

The Presidential Council, the executive, was to contain nine members elected from a single list with the endorsement of a clear majority (a minimum of 40 per cent) of senators from each constituent state. The Council's composition was intended to reflect the country's population ratio; however, at least two members were required to come from each constituent state. Were the plan to come into force over the next few years, while relative populations remained as at present, it was required that six members would come from the Greek Cypriot state and three from the Turkish Cypriot state.[11] The President of the Council was to represent the country as both the head of state and the head of government. The offices of president and vice-president of the Council would rotate on a 20-month basis from a member of the Greek Cypriot state to a member of the Turkish Cypriot state.[12] The president and vice-president were required to come from different constituent states, and the president was to be deputised by the vice-president.

Presidential Council members were each to head a department, as decided by the Council. The Presidential Council would also appoint members of the judiciary and independent offices. Decisions were to be taken by consensus, or by simple majority of voting members. A minimum of one voting member from each constituent state would need to have voted in favour of a decision in order for it to be passed, and neither the president nor the vice-president was to have a deciding vote. During the first ten years after entry into force of the Foundation Agreement, the heads of government of the constituent states would be invited to participate, on a non-voting basis, in meetings of the Council of Ministers (which would later become the Presidential Council).[13]

The federal administration and judiciary specified in the Annan Plan also followed consociational principles. Staffing of the public service was to be in accordance with the relative populations of the constituent states.[14] The federal police was to be composed of an equal number of staff from each constituent state, and the head and deputy head of the federal police would not be permitted to come from the same constituent state.

The Supreme Court was to be comprised of an equal number of judges from each constituent state and three non-Cypriot judges.[15] All Supreme Court judges[16] were to be appointed by the Presidential Council. Decisions were to be taken by consensus, or by simple majority of the Cypriot judges.

If there were no majority among the Cypriot judges,[17] the non-Cypriot judges would participate in the decision of the court to cast a single vote. The Supreme Court was to have exclusive jurisdiction over the following matters: disputes among components of the UCR; the validity of constituent state and/or federal laws and questions of precedence of laws; challenges to, interpretations of, and allegations of violations of the Foundation Agreement, the Constitution, and treaties signed by the United Cyprus Republic;[18] and resolution of deadlocks in federal institutions if the deadlock was retarding decision making.[19]

The Annan Plan also provided detailed procedural guidance on all aspects of the country's reunification. Reunification would involve extensive reshuffling of populations as disputed territory claims are settled[20] and the geographical boundary of each constituent state is reshaped according to negotiated agreements between the sides. Citizenship, similarly, has double relevance as individuals would, in accordance with the Plan, be identified both as members of the United Cyprus Republic and of the constituent state upon which their ethnic identity is based. Internal constituent state citizenship would be important because the Plan envisaged limitations being placed on the freedom to establish permanent residence within the state in which the citizen does not hold constituent state citizenship. These limitations were to be removed upon Turkey's entry into the EU or upon agreement by representatives of both constituent states.

The Turkish Cypriot constituent state

The Greek and Turkish Cypriot constituent states were to have different political structures, both to each other, and to the federal state. The Turkish Cypriots chose a semi-presidential model of governance. The executive of the Turkish Cypriot constituent state was to comprise a popularly elected president, who was to be the head of state, and was to serve a five-year term; and a prime minister and his or her Council of Ministers. The president would preside over the Turkish Cypriot Council of Ministers if s/he considered it to be necessary,[21] and would 'exercise any ... powers and ... perform any other duties entrusted to him by this Constitution and the laws, by the Constitution of the United Cyprus Republic'.[22] The prime minister would function as the head of the Council of Ministers, and be appointed by the president from among the deputies of the Assembly.[23] The prime minister's term of office was linked to the term of the Assembly. S/he was to be responsible for the formation of the Council of Ministers[24] and 'to the Assembly ... for the programme of the Council of Ministers'.[25]

The primary legislative body was to be the Assembly of the Turkish Cypriot State, composed of 50 popularly-elected deputies responsible for the debating and passing of legislation in the areas previously identified as being within the jurisdiction of the constituent states.[26] The Presidential Council of the Turkish Cypriot Assembly was to be drawn from the deputies of the Assembly, as were the president and vice-president of the Assembly. The Council was to be 'constituted proportionately with the number of members of the groups in the Assembly'.[27]

The Greek Cypriot constituent state

The executive of the Greek Cypriot state was to consist of a president, as head of government, and a Council of Ministers consisting of up to 14 members who would each head a ministry. The president was to be elected by popular vote and would have the power to appoint and dismiss the Council of Ministers. The Council was to hold all executive powers of the Greek Cypriot state not already reserved for the president.[28]

The legislative power of the Greek Cypriot state was to be exercised by the House of Representatives.[29] Legislative competence would extend 'over all matters not covered by the exclusive competences of the United Cyprus Republic'.[30] The House of Representatives would have comprised 60 members,[31] serving a five-year term.

Consociationalism and the Annan Plan

Consociational models are designed to absorb and diffuse societal tensions within a country. Liberal consociationalism's repertoire involves four basic institutional devices and principles: proportionality, cross-community executive power-sharing, cultural autonomy, and veto rights.[32] In crafting the UCR, the constitutional engineers utilised each of these devices.

Proportional representation was used in the construction of the Presidential Council, the Chamber of Deputies, the federal administration, and the federal police. The election and function of the Presidential Council can be said to encourage compromise and the building of inter-group coalitions. In the first instance, the Presidential Council's election on a common list meant that the candidates would need to build alliances with parties from the other community to create that common list. In the second instance, moderate political behaviour among those who would wish to be candidates would also have been encouraged by the need for bi-communal endorsement of the list in parliament. Cultural autonomy is a central tenet of the plan and underlies the construction of the Republic as it stands. It is most obviously represented in the autonomy of the constituent states vis-à-vis each other and the federal state; constituent state power over educational, cultural, and religious matters, as well as holding residual powers; the depoliticisation of issues at the federal level by devolving powers over most matters likely to be controversial to the constituent states or to the EU; voting for federal Senators on the basis of mother tongue, and voting generally according to internal constituent state status; the allocation of citizenship according to mother tongue; and limitations on the right of primary residence within the 'other' constituent state.

For reasons discussed in earlier chapters, the principle of communal veto is emotionally and historically charged in Cyprus. It was therefore integrated into the institutional structure in a subtle way. In the plan, it is allied with the principle of co-operation and is somewhat diffused by being embedded within the federal structure so that 'the companion concepts that no decision could be taken by persons from one constituent state alone and that no single person could veto decisions or block the running of the state run like a golden thread throughout the plan'.[33] A form of veto is intrinsic to the plan; but the veto is institutionalised in the senate level, and a series of complex deadlock-breaking mechanisms means that the veto does not reach the executive, therefore quelling Greek Cypriot fear that minority veto will again cause the paralysis of the state.

Consociational theorists subscribe to the maxim that the ends justify the means: high levels of autonomy and limited interaction between disputant groups at the popular level (segmental isolation) is intended to encourage compromise and negotiation at the elite level of decision-making. It should therefore facilitate a culture of co-operation, through a 'trickling down' of toleration from elite to mass society, eventually rendering consociational institutions obsolete in some cases. The plan attempted to ensure that issues likely to cause friction were encased within the legislative jurisdiction of each constituent state. The reunification of the two societies was intended to be gradual, facilitated by a sanitised political agenda at the federal level. The election of the members of the Presidential Council on a single ticket, and the requirement that they obtain at least 40 per cent of votes from senators representing each constituent state, would necessitate compromise and negotiation within the executive. In addition, the condition of special majority voting for the passing of certain types of legislation[34] is designed to encourage negotiation and a culture of exchange, as one group should be encouraged to support the other with an eye to its own future legislative requirements.

Consociational theorists primarily recommend a multi-person, or collegial, executive. A form of the collegial system is often used, whereby all or part of the cabinet is elected by parliament and executive decisions are taken by the collective group. The design of the UCR executive was thoroughly consociational, with a multi-person council chosen on a proportional basis, linked to the population of each constituent state. In addition, the EU would have contributed another consociational principle to the executive's functioning by removing much decision-making responsibility from the executive. EU membership would have left the UCR Presidential Council a rather innocuous, ceremonial machine whose importance lay primarily in the symbol it presents of communal representation and inter-communal co-operation at the head of government.

Unable, or unwilling, to undertake the monumental task of reconstructing the psyches of Greek and Turkish Cypriot society, the negotiators – working in concord with Turkish and Greek Cypriot elites – opted for a constitutional construct which allowed both sides to retain many of their respective visions of statehood and selfhood, while providing for the political reunification of the country. The underpinning philosophy, in line with consociational theory, is that if one begins with appropriate institutions, a reshaping of consciousness will follow.

The Annan Plan's development

The plan was built from information gleaned from previous years of negotiations, rather than as a document negotiated from scratch between the Cypriot interlocutors. There were two reasons for this: the first was that over the course of the plan's four-year development there were considerable periods where one or both sides were not providing the UN with various negotiating positions required for the construction of a compromise solution. '[Sometimes] the team of the Secretary-General simply were hearing views on various subjects and they tried to visualise what would have been an acceptable compromise between sides that were not really talking to each other with a view to settle'.[35] As a result, 'the UN team under de Soto was driven *faute de mieux* to draw up the first Annan Plan based on drafts and concepts that had been in circulation for years and in some instances for decades'.[36] A core member of the UN negotiating team maintained that there was 'very little engagement in [the] negotiations' by either side, and that the interlocutors were 'more willing to discuss options' in one-on-one shuttle talks than they were during face-to-face negotiations.[37] This is reflected in the high number of proximity and shuttle talks as measured against face-to-face discussions. During the Annan negotiations there were only 72 face-to-face meetings between the leaders as compared to 150 bilateral meetings between de Soto and each leader separately and 54 meetings in the proximity phase.

Second, almost 40 years of negotiations, policy papers and high-level agreements had established a set of guidelines that were accepted by and acceptable to both groups. 'What we came up with was something which built on past plans. It was not a creation out of nothing, but a consideration of previous negotiation processes, ideas, maps, and plans'.[38] This was reinforced by US Ambassador to Cyprus Michael Klosson:

> The plan itself has a long pedigree in UN proposals. Many of its provisions were borrowed from earlier proposals. It includes ideas that have been supported by leaders of one or *both* communities at various times. For example, under the Annan Plan, the Turkish Cypriot State would control slightly more than 29 percent of the island's territory. This number was not pulled out of a hat. It was discussed extensively as far back as 1985, when the Turkish Cypriot side accepted it at a UN summit. At the talks in 1992, the Turkish Cypriot side agreed to the eventual demilitarisation

of Cyprus, the desirability of a single sovereignty and single citizenship, and the importance of freedom of movement and settlement. All of these are reflected in the Annan Plan.[39]

Cypriot political leaders have themselves suggested various power-sharing models, and, as it will be seen, the institutional structure of the UCR was dictated by the ideological positions of the interlocutors. These ideologies were closely intertwined with (and often stemmed from) the fears and concerns each group had for its survival and its position in a reunified Cyprus. As Chapter 5 will show, a complicating factor over the years of the Cyprus conflict has been each side's use of international norms and laws about conflict within (or between, depending on the perspective) states. Both communities have made much use of their differing interpretations of concepts such as sovereignty, freedom, democracy, and group rights. They have both brought with them into negotiations their definitions of these terms, around which are folded their visions of both the spirit and the practicalities of a 'viable' solution.

The UN engineers identified the groups' opposing conceptualisations of the conflict and its solution as a major obstacle. In constructing the Comprehensive Settlement of the Cyprus Problem, Kofi Annan and his team sought to 'allow each side to maintain its position on how the new state of affairs would come into being'.[40] In his 2003 report on the situation in Cyprus, Annan articulated that he was driven by the 'need to find a form of government which (a) reflected and guaranteed the political equality of Greek Cypriots and Turkish Cypriots but also reflected in a democratic manner the significantly larger numbers of Greek Cypriot citizens; and (b) carried cast-iron guarantees against domination while ensuring that the government would function effectively'.[41] In other words, his intention was to balance power between the communities in a way which both guaranteed the existence of each and reflected population differences between them.

The influence of the 1960 constitution: Institutional learning

The experience of the 1960 Republic of Cyprus significantly informed the Annan Plan. The 2004 system's design was consciously affected by certain elements of the 1960 constitution which were considered positive or negative by either the interlocutors or the engineers.

At several points, the authors of the Annan Plan sought to address deficiencies of the 1960 constitution that either they, or the interlocutors, identified. When asked in interviews to identify weak or 'dangerous' elements of the 1960 constitution, UN negotiators singled out a number of perceived institutional flaws. They identified a danger in creating separate electorates for the election of president and vice-president 'because both were playing to antagonistic audiences, and likely to run on nationalist platforms'.[42] Much emphasis was placed on the point that without institutional encouragement of pre-election elite co-operation, candidates would be most likely to run on populist, nationalist platforms. There are echoes of the integrationist strategy of promoting pre-election elite co-operation in the engineers' concern. They also highlighted the dangers of what was effectively a dual presidency in the 1960 system, which created a significant need for consensus between the president and vice-president without a correspondingly strong incentive for their co-operation. In addition, it was frequently emphasised that the 1960 constitution was a compromise that 'no-one really wanted'.[43] The engineers attempted to apply these 'lessons' to the 2004 plan.

Negotiators from both communities also often used the 1960 constitution as an example to highlight both satisfactory and unsatisfactory proposals for the plan under negotiation. 'Each side would use the 1960 constitution as an example to highlight certain points, positive or negative: [they would say] "we want X, like the 1960 constitution, but it's obvious that Y didn't work well in 1960, so it shouldn't be included"'.[44]

Greek Cypriot negotiators had a significant desire to avoid repeating what they perceived as being the destructive ambiguities which caused the contesting and delayed implementation of the 1960 constitution's laws.[45] This was emphasised by then-head of the Greek Cypriot delegation to the Committee on Laws, and Attorney General of the Republic of Cyprus, Alecos Markides: 'Having the experience of Zurich in 1960, we suggested in October 2002, in New York ... that all the laws needed by the federation should be operational on the very first day of the new arrangement'.[46] Their concern was that there should be no obvious gaps or uncertainties which might lead both communities to feel that the other would seize an advantage, as was the case in the 1960 Republic. The UN engineers clearly agreed with this hypothesis: 'we were convinced that ambiguity was very much the seed for the next conflict, and for failure'.[47]

This Greek Cypriot fear of constitutional ambiguity stemmed primarily from the destructive effect of the 1961 taxation crisis and was also linked to the dispute over separated municipalities. As explained in Chapter 3, the provisional colonial taxation laws eventually expired the year after the birth of the Republic of Cyprus. Communal disagreement on the development of a new tax law left the Republic without the authority to collect taxes, and each community's attempts to implement new laws regarding taxation were opposed by the other community. The issue of whether or not to create ethnically separated municipalities eventually paralysed the Supreme Constitutional Court.

The UN was therefore set the task of creating a highly detailed blueprint of institutional and political reunification which would leave no unanswered questions. Its goal was to address all contentious issues and 'propose a crystal-clear solution'.[48] The complexity and importance of this task was compounded by the situation's fragility: the architects of the Annan

Plan had to reconstruct reality for mutually suspicious communities that had lived entirely without each other – refusing to acknowledge even the existence of the other as a political entity – for a generation. To avoid clashing interpretations of its provisions, the Annan Plan was remarkably thorough in its detail. This point was highlighted by Alvaro de Soto: 'if you look around in the last few years, at the different peace agreements that have been signed, a lot of them are very jerry-built essentially and have raised enormous questions that create for somewhat chaotic situations. Whereas here it is all spelled out.[49] In this way, a significant cause of conflict between elites in 1960s Cyprus was removed in the 2004 Annan Plan.

Every element of the federal state had to be fully fleshed out. By the fifth plan:

> The one hundred and ten laws became one hundred and forty laws, and those draft laws were to be in operation from the very first day, that is to say that the federation would have a taxation law, a budget, everything in place from the very first day. There was a provision that if by reason of the complexity of the system you fail to amend a particular law, it continues as it is, unless amended.[50]

This vast task involved 300 Cypriots and some 50 UN experts working in 14 technical committees. It was labelled by one UN engineer as an almost 'super-human' effort by those involved.[51] The resulting plan in its entirety ran to some 9000 pages.

Constitutional design often involves balancing conflicting considerations. In this case, the ability of the federal government to function immediately provided several concerns for Turkish Cypriot negotiators, who felt that they would need more time to come into line with the proposed federal economic and EU laws. 'To this end, a federal law was introduced suspending the application in the Turkish Cypriot State of certain federal laws which transposed provisions of the *acquis communautaire*'.[52] In such ways, the negotiators succeeded in their attempt to balance the fears and desires of each community.[53]

The UCR Presidential Council may be used as an example of the engineers' efforts to address Greek and Turkish Cypriot fears caused by the 1960 state's breakdown. Turkish Cypriot concerns about preventing Greek Cypriot domination of government stemmed primarily from the 1960s legislative struggles between the Greek Cypriot-dominated Council of Ministers and the Turkish Cypriot Communal Chambers. Particular emphasis was placed on the taxation battle highlighted in Chapter 3 and Makarios' subsequent attempts to modify the 1960 constitution against Turkish Cypriot wishes.[54] The Presidential Council was therefore designed to meet the Turkish Cypriot desire to 'underline political equality and prevent any domination',[55] while also addressing Greek Cypriot worries about executive functionality. These Greek Cypriot concerns were also acknowledged by the UN Secretary General in his 2003 Report on Cyprus, when he made a point of noting that '[t]he Greek Cypriot side, concerned with the workability of the government, wished to eliminate the veto (which it considered to be a major ingredient in the deadlocks and conflict that arose in the early years of the Republic's existence) and separate electorates (which it thought tended to affect workability and promoted division)'.[56]

In the context of EU membership and significant constituent state powers, the Presidential Council's main function was to 'guarantee the harmony of Cyprus, and not really to have decisive government action ... it was going to guarantee proper representation'.[57] Three primary models were canvassed by the engineers. Options were the French semi-presidential dual executive, election of the president and vice-president by an electoral college on a single ticket, and the Swiss system of an executive council with rotation of the head of state around the executive council over its fixed term. There was also some examination of the Indian executive, where the president is drawn from the minority community and the prime minister, whose position holds more power, is drawn from within the majority community. However, Turkish Cypriot resistance to mixed electorates meant that power-sharing options with a rotational head of state were the main options explored.[58]

In the end, the Presidential Council of the United Cyprus Republic was modelled upon the seven-person Swiss Federal Council, with some adjustments. Unlike the Swiss system, the Cypriot Presidential Council would be elected by the legislature from a single, closed list. Election of the Presidential Council required separate majorities of Turkish and Greek Cypriot members of parliament.[59] This would 'ensure that those elected would have clear support from their own constituent state (a Turkish Cypriot concern) and from both constituent states (a Greek Cypriot concern)'.[60] Thus there was an institutional encouragement for moderation; if one wanted to play a role in national politics, s/he would have to be at least marginally acceptable to the other side. 'The system presupposed politicians from the Greek Cypriot and Turkish Cypriot side to come together and to have a common programme of government, and be elected by parliament to govern'.[61]

The rotating presidency was designed to reinforce political equality and replaced the 1960 condition, common to corporate consociational systems, that only a Greek Cypriot could hold the position of president and a Turkish Cypriot only hold the position of vice-president. Rotation was highlighted as positive by several sources on both sides, and even, in some cases, by the plan's detractors. Prominent Turkish Cypriot journalist and political activist Şener Levent was vociferously opposed to the Annan Plan in favour of reinstating the 1960 constitution but he supported rotational presidency.[62]

Both the 1960 Cypriot constitution and subsequent UN proposals employed what was in many ways a dual head of state, with a Greek Cypriot president and Turkish Cypriot vice-president, each elected by their particular community, and each enjoying veto rights over certain issues. According to the 2004 Annan Plan's main architect, the plan's substitution of a rotating presidency was a significant improvement on the 1960 system, and an incentive for moderation.[63] The mechanism, whereby decisions in the Council were to be taken in the first instance by consensus and then if consensus proved impossible by simple majority,[64] was also designed to combat the Greek Cypriot fear, mentioned above, of executive paralysis brought on by veto.

Removal of the 1960 constitution's executive veto highlights the determination of the interlocutors and the UN engineers to ensure that significant weaknesses of the 1960 design would not be copied into the Annan Plan. By minimising federal executive powers and maximising both communities' decision-making autonomy, the engineers consciously controlled the risk of causing deadlock in a critical area of government.

> To have a veto power like the Vice President had in the context of the 1960 constitution is one thing. To require a consensus, to require the participation of at least one Turkish member of government in the formation of the [decision] of the federal government is quite another thing. Why? Because [in the 1960s] the veto paralysed the particular function of the whole state. Whereas the lack of one vote from a Turkish member of government would only paralyse the particular function of the federal government, which however, has very minimal powers. This was not a haphazard choice.[65]

The design's comparison to, and advantage over, the 1960 system was also emphasised by another Greek Cypriot diplomatic source. He maintained that removal of 'the right of veto for the representatives of either community' was a positive element, because '[it] means that the state can function more effectively than the previous constitution'.[66] This is confirmed by Didier Pfirter, legal advisor to the Secretary General's Special Advisor, 'the government envisaged in the plan is designed to be lean and efficient, with only a small number of members. Unlike the 1960 constitution, this plan also does not allow any single person to veto any decision, and no separate majorities are required for any decision'.[67] As this statement makes equally clear, the UN engineers were cognisant of the need to show tangible improvements upon the 1960 constitution, and to stress to the Cypriot public that their plan would not contain the weaknesses of 1960.

The construction of the legislature also reflects the engineers' efforts to address both groups' concerns about the 1960 state's weaknesses. A bicameral parliament was proposed in order to address the concerns of each side. The 50-50 composition of the Senate was designed to reflect the Turkish Cypriot need for the political equality of each constituent state, while the construction of the Chamber of Deputies met the Greek Cypriot desire for representation by population size.

The negotiating process provides an example of the influence of 1960 institutional experiences on the process of engineering. It has been previously stated that the overriding Greek Cypriot concern was that the UCR's structure be *functional*. On the other hand, the overriding Turkish Cypriot concern was for *equality of influence* in the decision-making mechanisms. These concerns stemmed from each community's desire to protect against what they saw to be the primary reason for the 1960 state's breakdown.

A struggle between 'efficiency' and 'equality' occurred during discussions within the Committee on Laws during Annan I–III. The committee was established to draft the basic laws which would enter into force on the first day of the new state. During discussions about the structure of the UCR's public service, Turkish Cypriot negotiators suggested that heads of department be divided evenly on an ethnic basis. This proposal was considered unreasonable by both the Greek Cypriot committee members and the UN. Turkish Cypriot committee members subsequently suggested instead that the head of department would have two deputies; that one of the three positions (head of department and two deputies) would have to be filled by a Turkish Cypriot; and that every decision taken must include the Turkish Cypriot representative. By way of compromise, it was eventually agreed that a single person would take the required decision, but that if the decision were contested, *then* a committee of three people would review the decision and a Turkish Cypriot would always be present in that committee.[68]

Great attention was paid in the Annan Plan to the effective design of conflict-breaking mechanisms. This was a direct consequence of the failure of the 1960 Supreme Constitutional Court to moderate conflict. Repeated reference was made during the negotiations to the Supreme Constitutional Court's contribution in 1963 to the breakdown of the Republic of Cyprus. This is supported by consociational theory, which recommends the implementation of a very strong system of conflict mediation, generally encompassing the juridical and political realms. As a result of the legal equality of federal and constituent state laws, the Supreme Court in the Annan Plan was designed to be a final deadlock-breaking mechanism. It was quickly agreed that an equal number of Turkish Cypriot and Greek Cypriot judges should preside over the Supreme Court. Despite this, the engineers saw the most effective conflict-breaking mechanism as being the inclusion of non-Cypriot judges in cases where the court's decision was divided along ethnic lines, and disagreement would cause paralysis in a function of the state.

Annan's team drew on the experience of the 1960 state's breakdown in deciding to 'allow for the sharing of the burden of possible regular exercise of the casting vote ... [by including] three such [neutral] judges'.[69] This provision, suggested by the advisory team from Greece,[70] was ill-received by both sides, and was only 'reluctantly' agreed upon in January 2003.[71] As a result, provision was made for the federal parliament to remove from the constitution (by qualified parliamentary majority) the need for neutral judges when trust was sufficiently high between the groups. The unorthodox concept of using the Supreme Court as an emergency device to overcome deadlock in institutional or legislative arenas was considered an incentive for compromise. That the deadlock could be broken by the Supreme Court should have become motivation for compromise by the parties to the conflict, because their intransigence would run the risk of returning a Supreme Court decision which may have been less favourable than a compromise solution worked out by the parties themselves. 'It would have been a big incentive for politicians to find compromises in order to avoid ... the ruling of the three neutral judges whose decision would be good for nobody'.[72]

The influence of post-1963 Cypriot history

The events, detailed in previous chapters, which resulted in the 1960 state's breakdown, and the breakdown itself, created a history whose memory must be overcome if a viable solution is to be found in Cyprus. The Annan Plan's engineers were clearly aware that history had raised a number of design issues, which they needed to solve. The most significant of these is the issue of sovereignty. The 'Turkish Federated State of North Cyprus' was declared in 1975, very soon after the Turkish Cypriot community's re-establishment in northern Cyprus. In 1983, the TRNC was unilaterally declared, against significant Greek Cypriot and international opposition.[73] Since that time, there has been a cold war over recognition between the communities, where the Turkish Cypriot side has made significant efforts to garner international support for its breakaway status, and the Greek Cypriot side has made equally significant efforts to block that recognition.

The issue has frequently become a deal-breaker during negotiations for peace. Ex-president of the TRNC Rauf Denktaş has habitually insisted that resolution of the conflict be based upon the idea of two sovereign states (the TRNC and the Republic of Cyprus) coming together to form a loosely confederal state. He has frequently stalled negotiations by insisting that Greek Cypriot negotiators recognise the TRNC's sovereignty – an abhorrent idea for the Greek Cypriot community. Since the 1977 High Level Agreement, when Makarios agreed to a federal solution, Greek Cypriot negotiators have reluctantly accepted a federal arrangement – a compromise linked in the Greek Cypriot mind with the surrender of a degree of sovereignty to the Turkish Cypriot community.[74] But the issue of sovereignty has remained highly contentious.

British Special Representative to Cyprus, Lord David Hannay, has commented extensively on the UN's concern that Denktaş' sovereignty preoccupation would hamper the negotiations. He noted that Denktaş 'continued to harp on these [status and sovereignty] at every meeting he had with Annan and de Soto ... virtually to the exclusion of everything else. This began to worry de Soto, who was concerned that it might bring the whole negotiation to a halt'.[75] De Soto's concern was justified; the Annan negotiations were frozen for a year between November 2000 and 2001 by Denktaş' refusal to proceed without recognition of the TRNC's existence. Following a meeting with the Turkish government, Denktaş stated publicly that 'co-existence of two states, two peoples, two sovereignties and two democracies'[76] was the only acceptable foundation of any resolution, and that proximity talks were 'a waste of time as long as our parameters are not accepted. They are being run on the basis that the Greek Cypriots are the sole legitimate government on the island'.[77]

It can be argued that Denktaş' fixation on the sovereignty issue stems directly from two stages in modern Cypriot history. The first is the post-1963 environment, when the Greek Cypriots unilaterally amended the 1960 constitution[78] after the Turkish Cypriot representatives walked out of government in protest when their veto of the proposed budget was overruled. The Turkish Cypriot representatives found themselves unable to return to government unless they approved the constitution's amendments,[79] which removed a number of provisions they considered to be communal safeguards against Greek Cypriot domination, but whose removal the Greek Cypriot representatives considered necessary to ensure the smooth operation of government.

The Turkish Cypriots subsequently lobbied the international community to refuse recognition to the Republic of Cyprus government without Turkish Cypriot representation. The international community responded that Cyprus was a *sovereign* country, and any interference in its internal affairs was outside the international community's jurisdiction. This response catalysed the Turkish Cypriot fixation on sovereignty.

This assumption was compounded in the post-1974 environment, when the Greek Cypriots were able to use the Republic of Cyprus as a vehicle to legitimise their protests against the Turkish occupation. The Republic of Cyprus, which was originally a *bi*-communal state, became an exclusively Greek Cypriot instrument, especially important at international forums. From this vantage point, the Greek Cypriots gained the international community's tacit support, a significant advantage in the diplomatic war. Equally, because the Turkish Cypriots lacked international standing, they were denied a voice in international forums to articulate their own version of a just solution to the conflict.

There are two primary consequences of that situation for efforts to create peace in Cyprus. The first is that, until very recently, the only forum in which the Turkish Cypriot leadership has had international standing, enabling its perspective on the conflict to be legitimated, is at the negotiating table. As a result, there has been every incentive at the elite level to continue the negotiations indefinitely. Second, insistence on the recognition of Turkish Cypriot sovereignty has both stalled negotiations and influenced the shape of the 2004 resolution. It has been recognised as a key factor for both communities by the engineers, publicly in the Secretary General's reports[80] and in private interviews.

The text of the Annan Plan itself is a delicate attempt to appease both communities' demands about sovereignty. During interviews, particular members of the UN core team showed a nuanced understanding of the Greek Cypriot emphasis on protecting their own sovereignty and legitimacy:

> The Turkish Cypriots had the arms on the ground and the Turkish soldiers on the ground and the Greek Cypriots had international legality on their side. So that's why the Greek Cypriots are excessively touchy about anything that could imply even a scratch on this thing that *they* are the government of Cyprus and the others are a nothing. One cannot have any contact with them or anything that could imply a little bit of recognition of the Turkish Cypriots; it had to be fought against strongly because it could diminish what was the main asset that the Greek Cypriots had.[81]

As the above statement shows, Greek Cypriots have been equally sensitive over the sovereignty issue. Legally, the Greek Cypriot argument against even unofficial acknowledgement of the TRNC centres on the potential or capacity of non-state actors implicitly to bestow recognition upon an invalid state.[82] International law maintains that only *states*, represented by *governments*, can give or withdraw recognition of other states or governments. However, a second strand, the 'law of implied recognition' asserts that unofficial contacts by non-state or state actors may imply recognition of the other state, *even when* state authorities have explicitly rejected claims of statehood; this is known as recognition through the 'backdoor'.[83] Strong international legal precedents have, however, affirmed that if the other side *formally* and *clearly* denies (or withdraws) recognition, then there is no possibility for the piecemeal application of the law of implied recognition by any number of individual contacts. Therefore, recognition of the TRNC is not within the legal capacity of non-state actors.

The constitutional engineers have acknowledged the close relationship between each side's concerns on this matter, and its negotiating ideals:

> A breakdown of the new state of affairs followed by secession of a sovereign Turkish Cypriot state and the consequent partition of Cyprus could be described as the Greek Cypriot nightmare ... a breakdown of the new state of affairs followed by the larger Greek Cypriot population alone exercising the sovereignty of the state could be described as the Turkish Cypriot nightmare.[84]

Unable to find a middle ground, the engineers for a time worked around the issue of sovereignty by very carefully withholding use of the term. However, the Secretary General ultimately decided that remaining silent on the issue would 'leave unanswered questions and not put the nightmares to rest'.[85]

The Belgian model was useful in solving this problem. In order to satisfy Greek Cypriot concerns, the plan states that the United Cyprus Republic 'has a single international legal personality and sovereignty, and partition or secession are expressly prohibited'.[86] To meet Turkish Cypriot concerns, the plan 'provides that the constituent states sovereignly exercise all powers not vested in the federal government, organising themselves freely under their own constitutions consistent with the overall agreement, as well as providing (as in Belgium) for no hierarchy between federal and constituent state laws'.[87]

Recent history has also played a role in the way the UCR has structured electoral participation and citizenship. A significant criticism of consociationalism, as expressed in Chapter 1, is that it is a structure which freezes ethnic relations as they stand at the period of highest tension. It is argued that the system builds political structures around a particular set of demographic and social conditions and, because of its rigidity, cannot reflect any changes over time in domestic dynamics. Considerable controversy surrounded particular elements of the Annan Plan which linked citizenship, electoral participation, and right of residence to one's ethnicity. All federal political rights but one were to be exercised on the basis of internal constituent state citizenship status. However, a provision was inserted into the fifth version of the plan that voting for federal senators would be determined by mother tongue, rather than internal citizenship status.[88] This was designed to meet Turkish Cypriot concerns of 'being undermined in the long term by Greek Cypriots establishing residency in the north and seeking Turkish Cypriot internal constituent state citizenship status'.[89] The Turkish Cypriots feared that the more populous Greek Cypriots might come with time to dominate both the northern and southern constituent states. If voting and citizenship rights were not tied to ethnicity, then what would stop Greek Cypriots becoming citizens of the Turkish Cypriot state and electing Greek Cypriot representatives, leaving the Turkish Cypriot community voiceless again? This fear has clear roots in the 1960 constitution's perceived failure to protect Turkish Cypriot communal rights and the ease with which Greek Cypriots became the dominant voice in government after 1963.

Finally, citizenship was (and remains) a highly controversial issue, and as with all concepts which have been identified as central to a solution of the conflict, was very closely intertwined with each side's philosophic and national vision. Greek Cypriot concern with the issue of who is to receive Cypriot citizenship stems partly from the fear that Turkey has had a long-running policy to populate north Cyprus with Turkish nationals, who would outnumber Turkish Cypriots and thus have a controlling influence on the political decisions of the Republic of Cyprus (or any future Cypriot state). This fear is articulated in the Greek Cypriot rhetoric as Turkey's wish to 'finish what she started with the invasion'. They consequently insisted that Turkish nationals with TRNC citizenship should not be granted citizenship of the UCR. The citizenship issue consequently touches a very deep Greek Cypriot fear of being controlled by the Republic of Turkey, either through military or other means. This was reflected in their persistence on the recognition of 1960 citizenship rolls, noted in the Secretary General's 2004 Report on Cyprus.[90]

> The Greek Cypriot side was of the view that there should be a single Cypriot citizenship and that it should be held only by people who were citizens of the Republic of Cyprus in 1960 and their descendants (and by persons who have since acquired such citizenship in accordance with the law of the Republic). In particular ... [they] considered that Turks who had migrated to northern Cyprus since 1974 should not be given citizenship.[91]

The official Turkish Cypriot position was that all citizens of the TRNC should also become citizens of the UCR, regardless of their ethnicity. This is also noted in the Secretary General's report:

> The Turkish Cypriot position, based on the approach of two pre-existing states coming together, demanded blanket recognition of existing citizenship rolls and dual citizenships for the future, that is, the allocation of constituent state citizenship by constituent state authorities, which would automatically entail citizenship of the United Cyprus Republic.[92]

However, at the public level, Turkish Cypriot attitudes to this issue is not uniform. A number of Turkish Cypriots agree with aspects of the Greek Cypriot position. There is a firm belief among many Turkish Cypriots that the cultural and political attitudes of Turkish Cypriots differ substantially to those of Turkish nationals living in Cyprus. Accordingly, a very significant Turkish Cypriot concern is of being overrun by Turkish nationals and becoming a minority within their own state. This concern is deepened by the increased rate of Turkish Cypriot emigration from Cyprus, especially within the younger generations.

> In Cyprus, people were being pulled out of their jobs because they were Turkish Cypriot, and they were being replaced with people coming from Turkey. Thousands of people were unemployed, hopeless, and that's when people started to emigrate to Canada, England, Australia ... soon there will not be a 'Turkish Cypriot youth', and when all the politicians realise this it will be too late.[93]

This concern was also expressed by several Turkish Cypriot parliamentarians, who speak of a permanent economic crisis in the north leading to a sense of desperation within the community. They fear that Turkish

Cypriots – especially the youth – will either permanently cross to the south or continue to emigrate from Cyprus, thus altering the demographic and cultural landscape of the north and making the TRNC almost entirely Turkish.[94] National and cultural identity and issues of belonging are very closely entwined with the issue of citizenship, regardless of ethnicity. One's understanding of how citizenship is to be issued in a reunified Cyprus relies upon where one draw's Cyprus' cultural and national borders.

But immigrants from Turkey have also become an active and prominent part of the social and cultural landscape of northern Cyprus, and any attempts to force their return to Turkey would be unsupportable. The situation is not nearly as simple as is often portrayed by Greek Cypriots. Many Turkish immigrants have lived in Cyprus for decades, integrating into the community, and consequently consider Cyprus to be home. A clash between different understandings of both international law and humanitarian norms are built into this aspect of the conflict.[95]

Over the Annan Plan's five versions, the engineers tried to address each community's concerns regarding Turkish immigration. In a private meeting with de Soto and Clerides, Denktaş had made a throwaway comment that there were 'only 30,000' Turkish migrants in north Cyprus.[96] Clerides, whose government estimated that there were in excess of 100,000 Turkish migrants in north Cyprus, immediately agreed to accept all those migrants if they did not exceed 30,000. However, the numbers proved to be somewhat in excess of that figure.[97] In Annan I, Turkish migrants to north Cyprus were separated into three categories: those who were born and raised in Cyprus, those who had married Turkish Cypriots, and those who were living in Cyprus and had been given citizenship of the TRNC.[98] Children born in Cyprus and the spouses of Turkish Cypriots were not included in the original number of 30,000 migrants allowed by the plan to stay in Cyprus. By Annan II, the categories had been removed, and a single figure was listed.[99] The idea of a single, inclusive figure to be included on the UCR citizenship roll was carried through to Annan V.[100] It also capped future migration to Cyprus from Turkish (and Greek) nationals at five per cent of the number of Cypriot citizens of the Turkish Cypriot (or Greek Cypriot) constituent states.[101] Providing UCR citizenship to the large number of Turkish nationals met Turkish Cypriot negotiators' concerns, while limiting future migration met the concerns of Greek Cypriot negotiators.

The Annan plan and future political development

Opponents of the Annan Plan argued that the provisions which linked ethnicity to electoral participation, citizenship, and right of residence immortalised the ethnic divide between Greek and Turkish Cypriots by tying ethnicity to a number of important aspects of a citizen's life. They argued that to make ethnicity the common vehicle of electoral and legislative participation at both the federal and constituent state level would guarantee that rigid segmental isolation on the basis of ethnicity would continue indefinitely.

Another important issue that caused deep fears in both communities was the distribution of powers between the constituent and federal states. Greek Cypriots feared that the constituent states would be so powerful as to render the federal state meaningless, creating a *de facto* partition of Cyprus. The opposing Turkish Cypriot concern was that the federal government would be imbued with powers that would strip the Turkish Cypriot constituent state of its ability to make major decisions concerning the welfare of its population.[102] This raised the Turkish Cypriot fear of being dominated again by the Greek Cypriots. Consequently, powers in the plan were distributed along consociational lines; the federal government was given a certain number of important functions, but none which were likely to cause inter-ethnic tension and the constituent states were largely left to govern themselves.

The engineers displayed awareness and significant concern about the idea that the Annan Plan's structure might leave the communities saddled in a calmer future with unnecessary provisions. To overcome what they saw as the structure's necessary rigidity, they implemented a relatively low threshold for constitutional change. 'We tried to make it easy for the Cypriots to eventually shape [the constitution] in the way that they want it, but to provide them with something that works and it works forever if they cannot agree to change it'.[103] To change any article in the constitution,[104] a simple majority of one quarter of senators present and voting from each constituent state is required.[105] The change must then be approved by the people of both constituent states by referendum.[106]

However, critics argued that with this kind of structure, it would be impossible to overcome ethnic separation. Therefore, path dependency would ensure the perpetuation of an ethnically divided society. Consociational theorists and the engineers of the Annan Plan would counter that the very reason that such rigid institutions would be implemented in a situation like Cyprus is because ethnic identity is so deeply entrenched at the time of engineering. Therefore, it is the most appropriate basis upon which to restructure a state in internal conflict.

Conclusion

This chapter has argued that the Annan Plan, in both the broad strokes and the particulars, reflected the engineers' determination to avoid the 1960 state's flaws. The constitutional engineers' careful construction of the Annan Plan showed a nuanced understanding of the way history and memory must be addressed when crafting the political structures which will underpin a post-conflict state. The engineers' painstaking approach created a plan which would minimise inter-communal conflict, avoid deadlock, and meet both communities' primary needs. The central government's structure and minimal responsibility, and the high degree of group autonomy are examples of ways the engineers sought to reduce the chances of conflict. The Supreme Court had the power to break executive deadlocks, and, because of the complexity of the system, if particular laws were the subject of disagreement, they would continue to function until such time as an amendment could be agreed upon. The Turkish Cypriot fear of being dominated by the Greek Cypriot community was assuaged by the high level of group autonomy mentioned above, proportional representation in the public service and the rotating presidency. The Greek Cypriot need for validation of their majority status was reinforced by their greater representation in the Chamber of Deputies and in the Presidential Council.

In creating such structures, the constitutional engineers seemed to have succeeded in overcoming the 1960 constitution's most significant weaknesses, and other institutional problems, which have been identified in the chapter. To the extent that the plan had weaknesses, these were also guided by the engineers' need to incorporate into the solution a number of protections against strong inter-communal fears. At the same time, the engineers showed awareness of the system's shortcomings and tried to incorporate provisions which could create a more dynamic constitution, as elite co-operation and inter-group trust grew.

The engineers did not appreciate, however, that those same group memories of history, which they tried to appease in the plan, would trigger very strong negative responses to the plan itself. The next chapter will show how Cypriot elites were both trapped by, and utilised, those memories. In the Turkish Cypriot community, elites used the Annan Plan to assure the public that their experiences from the 1960s would not be repeated. However, Greek Cypriot elites used the plan to trigger Greek Cypriot vulnerabilities and fears of Turkish domination; fears which, for obvious reasons, had not been put to rest in the post-war years. This suggests that a pre-existing reluctance on the part of central Greek Cypriot political elites to enter into a power-sharing agreement with the Turkish Cypriot community surfaced during the Annan period. The next chapter will explain why this could have been the case.

5
How Close Were They, Really? Elite Support of a Power-Sharing Solution

> Identity of interests is the surest of guarantees, whether between states or individuals[1]

The Annan Plan entered the annals of history as the most recent and most thoroughly constructed attempt to create a political solution for the Cyprus conflict, but it was an attempt which failed to receive sufficient cross-communal elite and public support. While Chapter 7 will analyse causes of the plan's rejection by the Greek Cypriots in the April 2004 referendum, we must first understand the ability of elites to accept the plan, and to co-operate, given the course of Cypriot history. Each of the next three chapters explains a different layer of the 2004 plan's rejection. Chapters 5 and 6 look at elite behaviour from the perspective of domestic and international incentives. They lead to Chapter 7, which explains the final rejection of the solution so carefully designed by Annan's architects.

Literature on consociationalism posits elites as a vehicle through which a democratic society is (re)established in cases of internal division. While constitutional engineers have utilised elites as a supportive mechanism to underpin the Cyprus conflict's institutional resolution, the use of elites as conflict breakers has also proven to be an Achilles heel in Cypriot constitutional design. Political elites in Cyprus have historically been deeply entwined in the conflict as ethnic entrepreneurs; it is recognised in literature on Cyprus that 'early on the Cyprus conflict became elite-driven, with belligerent leaders emerging who saw their role as energising the populace'.[2] Given this tension, it is possible that Cyprus' inability to adopt a consociational solution is due in part to insufficient elite incentives to form co-operative relationships.

Elite incentives for co-operation are monumentally important for resolution of the Cyprus conflict because politics is deeply personalised. On both sides in Cyprus significant authority has been placed in the hands of a small number of political elites who have built their kingdoms on their roles as interlocutors of the Cyprus conflict. To protect these kingdoms, they have established relationships with their electorates which reinforce the latter's dependence upon them for both explanation and resolution of the conflict.

Incentives for elites to support the adoption of a solution

In the case of Cyprus, dissimilar domestic conditions created different motivations for each community's elites to support the solution's adoption. This is reflected in the contradictory consequences of elite behaviour in the pre- and post-referendum periods. In the north, adequate domestic incentives existed to encourage conciliatory behaviour by elites, while in the south, the same conditions did not exist, leading to elite encouragement that the Greek Cypriot community reject the Annan Plan.

North Cyprus

North Cyprus is an interesting study of how the 'kingdom' can be shattered when elites no longer receive public support for traditional positions of non-co-operation. North Cyprus shows that grassroots pressure can create electoral incentives for compromise. In the north, Rauf Denktaş served four consecutive five-year terms as president of the TRNC, albeit in a number of governing alliances with parties from across the ideological spectrum. As the founder of the Turkish Cypriot state, and a key figure in the anti-*enosis* struggles between 1955 and 1974, Denktaş is an important figure to both Greek and Turkish Cypriots. For many years, he formed a link between Turkey and Cyprus, always ensuring that Turkish policy on Cyprus safeguarded his state. He was also a protective figure to the Turkish Cypriot community, against the memory of Greek Cypriot threats. He, along with figures like Clerides and Papadopoulos represent an institutional memory of the modern Cyprus conflict.[3] Famous for his aversion to reunification of Cyprus,[4] Denktaş led a group of political elites who saw very few incentives for compromise and co-operation with the Greek Cypriots.

Lacher and Kaymak[5] argue that a significant portion of the political and socio-economic elite in the north had strong reason to protect the status quo beyond their ideological aversion to union with the Greek Cypriots. 'Political connections allow a socio-economic elite to enjoy relative wealth and privilege, of which landed property is the single most important source'.[6] Wealth gained from importing monopolies and the transference of Greek Cypriot property offered serious financial disincentives for support of reunification. Favour of the status quo was reflected at the electoral level. Pro-secession parties consistently received over 60 per cent of the popular vote in elections since 1974 and received the support of two-thirds of the electorate in the May 1998 general election.[7]

However, a significant change in Turkish Cypriot public sentiment over the early period of the Annan negotiations brought to power, in December 2003, a government mandated to end the status quo.[8] According to Lacher and Kaymak, 'it is precisely the exhaustion of the distributive capacities of the North Cypriot state, and its diminishing ability to integrate society beyond the elite groups mentioned ... that is at the heart of this transformation'.[9]

A strong tradition of political pluralism within the Turkish Cypriot community was for a long time suppressed by dominant political and military forces in northern Cyprus,[10] but it continued to exist.[11] Direction as to the future of the Cyprus problem was strongly debated, both during and between election periods. As Figure 5.1 below shows, over the last six years, and especially since the introduction of the Annan Plan as a basis for resolution in 2002, north Cyprus has seen a swing from centre-right coalitions forming government to a left-centre right coalition which currently holds power.

With the change in government, elite incentives to support adoption of the Annan Plan also dramatically increased. While traditional Turkish Cypriot political elites tangibly benefited from perpetuation of the *status quo*, then-Prime Minister Talat (now president) and his party rose to power *as a result of* public discontent with the situation in north Cyprus. Therefore, his political legitimacy rested on resolution of the conflict. For this reason, the Turkish Cypriot governmental elite had the strongest incentive to support the Annan Plan's adoption.

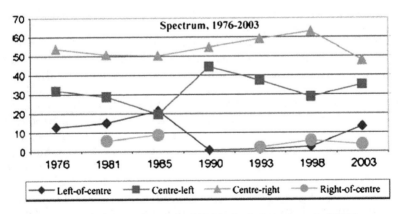

Figure 5.1 Electoral support along left-right ideological spectrum in TRNC
Source: Ali Çarkoğlu and Ahmet Sozen, 'The Turkish Cypriot General Elections of December 2003: Setting the Stage for Resolving the Cyprus Conflict?', *South European Society and Politics*, vol. 9, no. 3, Winter 2004, p. 129.

The promise of democratisation and increased government transparency was arguably the most important incentive for those Turkish Cypriot political parties which were then in opposition (and now have formed government). In this they were staunchly supported by a significant proportion of the Turkish Cypriot public. It was frequently stated to the author by a number of Turkish Cypriot politicians that the Annan Plan would enable Turkish Cypriots to establish a state of their own 'which would be genuinely democratic'.[12] 'The Turkish Cypriot state is at the moment so fluid and corrupted – there is one set of rules for "friends" of the state, and another for those who are not "friends" of the state. The Annan Plan will give us tangible rights as citizens'.[13] The security and rights that stem from a stable democratic state provided an enormous incentive at the public level (and in the opposition parties) for resolution.

The power shift in northern Cypriot politics occurred as a result of both international and domestic factors. The hope of entry into the EU as part of a broader Cypriot state provided Turkish Cypriot elites and society with an incentive for resolution of the conflict. It also gave them a common incentive to overthrow the rejectionist Denktaş government. At the European Council summit in Helsinki in December 1999, the decision was taken to allow the Republic of Cyprus into the EU regardless of the conflict's resolution. In practical terms, this meant so long as Greek Cypriot elites were constructive in their efforts to solve the conflict, the Republic of Cyprus was going to join the EU and receive the benefits membership entailed. However, in the case of the conflict's continuation, the Turkish Cypriot north would have to wait for Turkey's entry (a long-term possibility), and then would still not be guaranteed entry.

But the EU incentive took some time to be realised. Prior to 2001, the EU was viewed with suspicion and negativity by Turkish Cypriots. As a result of a number of factors this suspicion was lifted. British diplomatic sources emphasised the importance of several intensive seminars explaining the EU and its organs. The seminars were co-ordinated by the British Council and the British High Commission, and targeted the political leadership of northern Cyprus. A broad group of the political elite (outside of government) began to find economic, societal, and political benefits in EU membership.[14] According to these sources, the seminars 'helped quite a lot in giving a broad group of people a shared desire to be in Europe'.[15] They also triggered the realisation that 'the only way into Europe was through a settlement'.[16] Regardless of the possible British overestimation of their contribution to this changed perspective, awareness of the benefits of European membership for the north of Cyprus increased the (non-government) elite's desire for membership, which motivated the creation of a broad-based coalition to challenge Denktaş for leadership, and which insisted on resolution of the conflict under the auspices of the Annan Plan. This coalition, with its knowledge of the working of the EU, was able to build enough momentum to obtain a majority in the December 2003 parliamentary elections. With the momentum created by victory, the CTP and other allied parties were able to play a leading role in the resolution negotiations.

There were also significant domestic incentives for Turkish Cypriot elites to support a solution. An international policy of non-recognition of the TRNC has disabled Turkish Cypriots on many levels.[17] Without recognition, trade with most countries is very difficult. This has created a heavy reliance on Turkey for economic aid, and has also led to economic depression.[18] While since 2004 the Turkish Cypriot community has been able to export its goods over the green line[19] and via Greek Cypriot ports to European markets, the situation is politicised.[20] The employment market is restricted; 'exceedingly low entry requirements have ... drawn a huge percentage of Turkish Cypriots aged between 17 to 23 into the universities. Since the late 1990s increasing numbers of university graduates have been pushing into a very limited job market'.[21] High unemployment means that there is enormous competition for jobs, and a highly educated populace both increases the level of competition and adds to a 'brain drain' to the south, or out of Cyprus. Most travel outside of Turkey or the UK requires a Turkish passport, which consequently brings visa complications.[22] As studies have shown, the implications of non-recognition extend beyond the economic; there are significant social and psychological effects.[23]

At the same time, public trust in elites in the north has declined considerably in the last decade, particularly after a banking crisis in 2000 which robbed many of their savings. As a result, '[s]upport for the opposition galvanized particularly around the appearance of impropriety on the part of politically well-connected bank owners and managers who were let off lightly in court'.[24] In addition, the 2001 financial crisis in Turkey had serious consequences and knock-on effects in north Cyprus. Both elements contributed to the financial disenfranchisement of many Turkish Cypriots. This facilitated a turnover in political leadership, but at the same time, ensured low levels of trust in political figures.

As a result of these conditions, and coupled with a growing Cypriotist identity in north Cyprus at the time, there was a much greater groundswell for resolution in the lead-up to the negotiations for the Annan Plan. This, in turn, placed more pressure on Turkish Cypriot politicians to seek a solution. The Annan Plan was considered a means of escaping domestic and international restrictions on the Turkish Cypriot community. It was seen as a way of lifting the community out of a permanent economic crisis, as well as removing psychological barriers of feeling 'under siege', loosening trade and travel restrictions, stimulating employment, halting inflation (with the removal of the Turkish lira), and reversing Turkish Cypriot emigration.[25] For all of these reasons, the Turkish Cypriot community supported the diplomatic efforts for reunification, giving Turkish Cypriot governing elites a very real set of incentives to support the plan's adoption.[26] All these factors have contributed to Turkish Cypriot support of the 2004 solution.

South Cyprus

In the south, hard-line Greek Cypriot elites with a history of involvement in the Cyprus problem have generally been elected president,[27] indicating Greek Cypriot willingness to defer to traditional authorities on matters relating to the Cyprus conflict. By and large, they seem to have been elected on two bases: first, they 'understood' the Cyprus conflict because of their long involvement; and second, they were considered strong negotiators who would bring the Greek Cypriot community back to a position of advantage.

To properly examine incentives for elites to support resolution, one must understand the role of party politics, and particularly the role of the president. The current Republic of Cyprus is a modified version of the 1960 state. Designed to be a presidential system with very strong vice-presidential powers, when the Turkish Cypriot representatives withdrew from government in late 1963, the counterbalance against the president's powers was also removed. Absence of a vice-presidential 'check' on presidential powers has effectively meant that the state has a very strong presidential system. Hannay's summary of the president's powers emphasises how wide-ranging they are:

> The president was elected for five years; there was no limit on the number of times he could be re-elected; he had no vice-president ...; he had no prime minister and appointed all the ministers (who did not need to be elected members of the legislature); it was the norm to rule without a majority in the Assembly; he was the negotiator for the Cyprus problem.[28]

Parties serve an important function in Cyprus politics, 'decisively influence[ing] the choice of candidates for and election of the President of the Republic'.[29] The two largest parties, on opposite ends of the political spectrum, are communist AKEL and centre-right DISY.[30] Between them, they have shared up to 69 per cent of the electorate.[31] However, due to their steadfast refusal to work together,[32] both parties are at the mercy of more minor parties in the formation of multiparty coalition governments. As a result, relatively minor parties have had bargaining power in coalition governments that is disproportionate to their electoral support.

High levels of voter loyalty mean that each party can expect a significant proportion of their identifiers to vote for the party-endorsed candidate in presidential elections. Therefore, cross-party alliances for presidential elections can generally expect to garner votes in approximate proportion to their support in parliamentary elections. In the 2001 parliamentary

Table 5.1 2003 Republic of Cyprus presidential election results

Candidates	Party affiliation	Votes	Percentage
Tassos Papadopoulos	DIKO	213, 353	51.51
Glafkos Clerides	DISY	160, 724	38.80
Alecos Markides	Independent	27, 404	06.62
Others		12, 712	03.07
Total		414, 193	100.00

Source: Republic of Cyprus Press and Information Office.

elections, AKEL won 34.7 per cent of the vote (see Appendix 3). In the subsequent 2003 presidential elections, AKEL formed a three-way alliance with centre-right DIKO and centre-left EDEK, which received 14.8 and 6.5 per cent of the parliamentary vote respectively. The alliance supported DIKO leader Tassos Papadopoulos as its presidential candidate. As Table 5.1 above shows, Papadopoulos won with a 51.51 per cent majority in the first round, and AKEL entered a government coalition for the first time.

In the lead up to the December 2003 election, President Glafkos Clerides based his re-election platform on acceptance of the Annan Plan, which was in limbo at the time. His request was that Greek Cypriots elect him for a further 16 months so that he could see through the negotiations. As the second-largest political party, DISY could be sure of approximately 30 per cent of the vote. As the strongest political party, AKEL could count on just over 30 per cent. Clerides therefore offered AKEL a number of important ministries in exchange for formal endorsement of his candidature.[33] If accepted, this would have been an almost revolutionary alliance between two historically opposed parties. Clerides' request was founded in good strategy. Throughout his negotiation of the Annan Plan, Clerides had struggled with significant internal party opposition to his approach. Needing cross-spectrum political support, Clerides calculated that in order to have a sufficient foundation to maintain legitimacy and negotiating power, and to have a positive result returned for the referendum, he would need the backing of two important groups in Cyprus politics. With the support of AKEL – the party which has founded itself on the philosophy of a *Cypriot* Cyprus and with the strongest history of bi-communal support, as well as the strongest voter loyalty – and of the majority of refugees, Clerides calculated that the Annan Plan would have sufficient support at a referendum. As a result, Clerides made it clear to the UN that he would need, as a minimum requirement, to ensure a substantial measure of refugee return, territorial adjustment, and property restitution. He also maintained strong channels of communication with the AKEL leadership during the negotiation of Annan I–III, and authorised the UN negotiators to also communicate frequently with particular AKEL representatives. So the subsequent offer of a formal

DISY-AKEL coalition during the December 2003 presidential campaign was not without foundation.

However, AKEL rejected the alliance. While AKEL's reputation has been built on Turkish–Greek Cypriot co-operation, in 2003 it surprised analysts and supporters alike by forming a government with two parties known for their hard-line positions on the Cyprus conflict, during the most likely time to resolve the conflict. Even more surprising was AKEL's support of hard line Papadopoulos for president. But AKEL supporters and party members had been significantly isolated and disgruntled in the DISY government's decade-long clientelistic power-network. Emphatically unwilling to accept the government coalition offered by Clerides and DISY, an alliance with DIKO offered AKEL legitimate governmental power for the first time. It is an open but speculative secret that DIKO and Papadopoulos offered AKEL a two-term partnership which read like a Faustian pact. AKEL's support of a DIKO member for president of the Republic would serve both groups by providing AKEL with its governmental bonafides and giving DIKO the reigns of power.[34] In the second term, the coalition would continue, but DIKO would support a candidate chosen by AKEL for president. In two terms, therefore, AKEL would go from the largest party never to have held any real governmental power to holding the Republic's presidency.

So by the time CTP had reached power in the north, the now-conciliatory Clerides had been ousted from power on his side of the island. In the February 2003 Greek Cypriot presidential elections, Glafkos Clerides and DISY were voted out of office, replaced by DIKO's Tassos Papadopoulos. Historically, DIKO has been a hawkish party on the Cyprus issue; while Papadopoulos seemed to have succeeded in convincing AKEL elites that he had a genuine interest in supporting Annan's efforts for reunification of Cyprus; his personal history should have been sufficient to have provoked alarm. A militant, foundation member of EOKA and one architect of the notorious Akritas plan,[35] Papadopoulos gained an early reputation for being zealously devoted to the union of Cyprus to Greece. In London in 1959, he was part of the Greek Cypriot contingent which voted *against* acceptance of the Zurich-London Accords, and has been circumstantially linked to a number of early attempts to assassinate then-President Makarios in order to bring about *enosis*. He subsequently played a decisive role in Makarios' rejection of the 1973 peace proposal, in which Turkish Cypriots renounced their controversial veto rights in exchange for having separate municipalities in the five largest towns, as well as Makarios' 1976 post-invasion rejection of a federal solution to the recent division. By the 1980s he had melted into relative political obscurity, only to reappear in 1990 as leader of DIKO. Though it is more likely that figures like Papadopoulos utilise historical memory as a vehicle for the pursuit of power, one may speculate that Papadopoulos could also illustrate the way historical memory can decisively shape elite behaviour; this type of political elite continuously acts out an unfulfilled historical memory which defines them, in order to attain the unachieved goals of a previous era and 'set the past right'.

The development and fabric of Greek Cypriot society has shaped the incentives of Greek Cypriot political elites to support the adoption of a consociational solution. As a result of strong economic growth in the south since the *de facto* partition, and a flourishing 'Europeanised' society, there has been very little pressure on elites to bring home a solution, and thus unlike in north Cyprus, no price for failure to do so. And because the Greek Cypriot state enjoys internal and international legitimacy and meets the needs of its citizens, its elites also enjoy a high degree of public loyalty. Therefore, political loyalty can also become a hindrance to implementation. It can provide political elites with a *carte blanche* for non-co-operation, safe in the knowledge that they will have internal public support. Tassos Papadopoulos' call for Greek Cypriot rejection of the Annan Plan in 2004 is an example of such behaviour.

Elite accommodation

It is fair to say that in deeply divided polities, the presence of the following three main factors indicates elite commitment to a lasting political resolution. First, there should be a burgeoning culture of co-operation between elites; second, they must show their respective publics that the conflict has truly ended; and, third, they must publicly express that, in accepting a resolution, both communities have obtained their core negotiating needs.[36] The elites must show their electorates with certainty that the proposed solution is *permanent*. The first element, a burgeoning culture of co-operation, is important because it provides signals to the public that the 'other' can be trusted. It is also important for the obvious reason that a consociational system is more likely to succeed if the political elites are showing a willingness to co-operate. The second and third each, in a different way, lay to rest the battles of history, and clearly indicate a change in the purpose of the nation; when elites express unequivocally that the conflict is over, traditional ideas and historical 'truths' are no longer being protected, and society is free to change its path. According to the ideas of historical institutionalists, successful institutional change is more likely to follow a change in ideas about the value and function of the state.[37]

Co-operation at the adoption stage is the most difficult task elites will undertake, because it involves breaking a long-standing culture of hostile zero-sum ethnic politics. It 'requires new forms of political engagement that run contrary to the antagonism which shapes the prevailing mode of antagonistic relationship'.[38] Necessarily, 'the decision to end antagonism always involves a step outside the ritualised known'.[39] To overcome inter-communal conflict, the leadership is required to emphasise its new co-operative culture at a number of levels, 'not just that of negotiating a power-sharing agreement, but of demonstrating to one's electorate that the new world of cooperation is indeed safe'.[40]

This section examines the three requirements identified above in the context of Cyprus during the period of the Annan negotiations to show that there was a significant lack of accommodation between elites during this critical period, which contributed to the country's inability to adopt a solution. Elite behaviour in the post-Annan environment is also used to show how patterns of elite behaviour were carried beyond the referendum period. Because any need by the parties to appear conciliatory and accommodating under the international spotlight was removed, the post-referendum environment sometimes shows more stark evidence of elite attitudes. We are also able to extrapolate, since the 2007 change of government in south Cyprus, whether attitudes have evolved, and the implications of any such changes.

Culture of co-operation among elites

Until recently, both communities' governing elites have been content with the perpetuation of the negotiation process, each group blaming the other for intransigence. Elites in Cyprus have not been known as *conflict breakers*, so much as *ethnic entrepreneurs*, perpetuating the conflict in order to protect their personal power-bases.

It seems that a combination of historical memory and electoral pressure have inhibited the development of a culture of co-operation among elites. Combatant attitudes of the 1960s continued into the post-war environment, where the ethnic groups very clearly defined each other as enemies. This trend has affected the modern negotiating climate to the present, primarily because neither the conditions nor the actors have changed significantly.

Maximalist political rhetoric regarding solution of the conflict has significantly inhibited the ability of elites to forge a culture of co-operation. After Makarios' death in office in 1977, the conflict became a political 'bank' from which Greek Cypriot politicians could draw at election time.[41] The public heard a constant stream of ethnocentric rhetoric such as that 'our borders are in Kyrenia',[42] 'we will not rest until all refugees are returned to their homes', while at the same time the political elite, who understood the improbability of such outcomes, were negotiating for a bi-zonal resolution, in full understanding that not all refugees would return to their previous homes.[43]

Consequently, for many years Greek Cypriot refugee and diaspora groups, and some political parties, have placed great weight on the idea that all Greek Cypriot internally displaced people[44] will return to their former residences. This idea is embodied in the political slogan 'all refugees to return home'.[45] For these parties, the '3R's' (return of all refugees, removal of all Turkish troops, and repatriation of all settlers) form the basis of any discussions about the conflict's solution. The following slogans are representative of the platform bases of many Greek Cypriot lobby groups: 'peace and restoration of human rights for all Cypriots, [and] the removal of the 40,000 Turkish troops and 114,000 Turkish colonists';[46] 'Greek lawful inhabitants NEVER FORGET, and wait for the holy day of RETURN';[47] 'we will continue to campaign until all Turkish troops are out of Cyprus, all refugees have the right to return to their homes and all colonists have been repatriated. We will never accept a settlement which compromises these principles'.[48] These slogans have also found resonance in the domestic Greek Cypriot political rhetoric, stated by political elites as the ends towards which they strive in peace negotiations.

Integrationists argue that consociationalism does not adequately address electoral pressures on elites against compromise. Horowitz has argued that politicians negotiating peace in deeply divided societies are hamstrung by a need to guard against their more radical competitors, who will use a 'conservative' electorate against the government.[49] Negotiating elites cannot be seen to be 'weak' in particular areas, because maximalist demands from radical parties carry significant weight. When Glafkos Clerides was negotiating Annan I, II, and III, it was clearly understood by the engineers that the plan would need to be favourable to Greek Cypriot refugee groups in order for Clerides to gain public support for his efforts.[50] In point of fact, as we will see in Chapter 7, the plan was attacked by then-President, Papadopoulos, then-President of the House of Representatives and now President of the Republic of Cyprus, Demetris Christofias, and a number of Greek Cypriot political parties on the basis that it did not meet the '3R's'. Intra-group pressure and electoral incentives to debunk a conciliatory approach to the negotiating process can therefore pose a significant problem.

Prior to 2003, elite co-operation took place on two levels: the entirely official, or negotiation level between elites; and the unofficial, where political, trade union, and community elites would meet for conferences, seminars, and conflict resolution events internationally or (rarely) locally.[51] Historical patterns of left-wing Turkish and Greek Cypriot conciliation contributed to their greater willingness to co-operate. Therefore, over the years of separation, the left-wing of politics had forged a stronger culture of co-operation than had the right-wing. The checkpoint openings of 2003 facilitated a greater degree of freedom for unofficial elite relationships by reducing the burden of organising meetings abroad or at particular 'neutral zones' on the island. Suddenly, network-building was made much easier. However, in the single year between the initial euphoria that accompanied the ability to cross more freely between north and south Cyprus, and the referendum, few of the burgeoning networks created between Greek and Turkish Cypriot elites had time to evolve into a pattern of co-operation. There was certainly not enough time to create a 'culture' of co-operation.

The zero-sum approach expressed by the negotiating elites during the Annan Plan's evolution was highlighted in the previous chapter. The negotiating procedure and outcome represent the absence of trust between elites.

Particularly during the last phase of negotiations (Annan IV and V), elite interaction showed a lack of understanding by each group of the other's physical and psychological security. Intra-group pressures, a lack of understanding for the pressure the 'other' was under, no serious tradition of compromise or co-operation between elites all help explain why elites – particularly Greek Cypriot elites – were unwilling to endorse a power-sharing solution in 2004.

Elsewhere, a culture of co-operation among elites has been established through small non-controversial acts which both build a rapport between elites and symbolise in the public mind a shift away from a zero-sum relationship. However, in Cyprus, the conflict defines the relationship between elites of all types. Because the governments have been in a perpetual state of negotiation for 30 years, the ability of Greek Cypriot non-government elites to forge relationships with their Turkish Cypriot colleagues has been hamstrung by the need to be seen to support the negotiating position of Greek Cypriot governments. Bases for co-operation with Turkish Cypriot opposition groups were limited, and most groups in the south were reluctant to put in the effort required to forge close co-operative relationships.

That said, political alliances were formed between the two ideologically-left parties, AKEL (in the south) and CTP (in the north), and their corresponding unions (PEO and DEV-İŞ) and youth organisations.[52] Co-operative networks have been formed over the years between the unions and youth organisations affiliated with AKEL and CTP. The trade unions, PEO and DEV-İŞ, worked together on the sourcing and distribution of Turkish Cypriot wages and superannuation left unpaid after the *de facto* division in 1974. However, most other projects are clearly marked as conditional upon reunification. President of DEV-İŞ, Ali Gulle, emphasised that solving the conflict is a precursor to, not a result of, inter-group co-operation. 'Our fist aim is to solve the Cyprus problem. We cannot think of anything else at the moment until the Cyprus problem is solved. The only thing we are planning now is the solution of the Cyprus problem and from there on of course we will work with PEO for the future'.[53]

In an interview with the author, Ali Seylani, Member of Parliament in the TRNC[54] and president of KAMU-SEN, the Civil Servants Trade Union, highlighted how co-operation was conceptualised in the pre-Annan period. When asked about establishing networks of co-operation with Greek Cypriot trade unions and political parties, he answered:

[T]he main problem was how to find a solution ... we aimed to be EU members as a united country. These were our targets. The working class problems were the second side of our focus: no discrimination with [regard to] nationality, religion, colour, etc. We discussed, for example, social security in the north and the south, how we can make a united system, how does it work in the EU? Can we learn from them? For example, what are the differences in salary and other issues between the civil sectors in the north and the south? But the main issue was always Cyprus, because our first aim was always to get more people to come together and organise a good relationship.[55]

When pressed about the best way to 'get more people to come together', Seylani emphasised that solving the conflict had to come first, and networks would necessarily arise after a solution.

Deputy leader of DISY, Averoff Neophytou, made a similar comment when asked about a different aspect of the conflict. Neophytou was asked whether the militant way Cypriot history was taught in Greek Cypriot schools was deterring support for a solution. While he recognised the importance of changing the hostile perception of modern Cypriot history in the Greek Cypriot community to chances of solution, Neophytou maintained that 'if we don't reach a solution it will be very hard to change the perceptions'.[56] Asked by the interviewer 'if it would not be better for the chances of a solution actually to try and change perceptions beforehand, he said: "That's the chicken and egg situation"'.[57] It seems that elites along the spectrum agree that co-operation is contingent upon solution of the conflict, rather than the conflict's solution being dependent upon elite co-operation.

External actors, aware of this problem, have been unable to alter elite preconceptions about co-operation. Historically, small-scale trust building exercises have consistently been put aside in favour of working on the 'big problem'. Even when concerted effort has been given to developing a co-operative culture between elites, it has largely been engulfed by bickering and petty politicking. In 1994, the UN tried to improve inter-group trust with a set of Confidence Building Measures (CBMs).[58] The package included 12 proposals for co-operation in the fields of journalism, commerce, education, sport, culture, environment, and health. They also included six provisions regarding the opening of the fenced town of Varosha and Nicosia Airport. However, the CBMs were deadlocked at the discussion stage, over disagreement on a number of symbolic issues primarily regarding sovereignty.[59] The UN tried several times more to apply trust-building exercises between elites, without success.

The negative atmosphere surrounding elite co-operation has constrained the few elites who have tried to build relationships between parties. In the pre-referendum period, there was talk about a political union between Alpay Durduran's Patriotic Union Party (YBH) and George Vassiliou's United Democrats as a potential federal party.[60] After the referendums, any talk of alliance was silenced by European parliamentary election campaigns in south Cyprus and subsequent attempts by both parties to recapture support in their respective electorates over several election periods. As hope for reunification slipped away, so did the parties' enthusiasm for establishing networks.

Between the Annan Plan's rejection and the 2008 election of AKEL's Demetris Christofias to the Republic of Cyprus presidency, there was significant, sustained pressure on elites who attempted to co-operate. In January 2006, a televised discussion hosting the leaders of CTP and DISY was interrupted by bomb threats; when the attendees left the television station their car tyres had been slashed.[61] In early 2005, Christofias cancelled an invitation to dinner with Turkish Cypriot president, Mehmet Ali Talat, due to allegations that he was 'fraternising with the enemy'. In this regard, the election of Christofias was important on two levels. First, it caused a considerable change in the official response to inter-group trust-building and more general bi-communal interaction. And second, the election of a historically and openly conciliatory figure as president also signalled a break in Greek Cypriot public attitudes to the conflict and its resolution. Though hesitant, networks at both the elite and public level, since Christofias' election, are slowly being rebuilt.

But the road ahead will not be strewn with roses. The affiliation between DISY and CTP illustrates the difficulty of establishing a co-operative relationship between Turkish and Greek Cypriot parties. As the two largest parties which supported the Annan Plan, they have been quietly building networks in the post-Annan period, but they have encountered a number of problems.[62] Inter-communal elite co-operation has been unpopular with the electorate of both sides, and even in the Christofias-Talat period, the public level is largely agnostic on this topic. Consequently, during election campaigns between 2004 and 2007, contact between the parties was limited. Parliamentary and municipal elections in both communities during that period delayed the strengthening of inter-party relations. The election campaign for the 2008 presidential election in the south also made Greek Cypriot parties very cautious about appearing too conciliatory. More generally, this example indicates that elite co-operation is also dependent upon supportive electorates, and offers initial support to integrationists' arguments that elites are sometimes hamstrung by an unsupportive public.

A clear opportunity existed in 2003, with the opening of checkpoints, for Greek and Turkish Cypriot elites to make a strong public display that the conflict between the communities was ending. However, the Papadopoulos government's cagey reaction to the 2003 checkpoint openings indicated a disinclination to transcend the rhetoric of conflict.[63] The unconstructive behaviour of both sides' governing elites regarding the opening of further checkpoints post-Annan also suggests that a culture of inter-group compromise at the elite level had not existed earlier, in the critical negotiation period. Most inter-group elite interaction at the official level has assumed a tit-for-tat quality, and is frequently shaped into a points-scoring exercise. The opening of the Astromeritis-Zodia checkpoint in the west of Cyprus on 31 August 2005 could have been used as a confidence-building or rapprochement exercise by elites of both sides to show co-operation. However, it was interpreted by both leaderships as an opportunity to blame the other for lack of good will.[64] When new checkpoint openings were being discussed, the Greek Cypriot side mocked Turkish Cypriot leader Mehmet Ali Talat by claiming that he barely had authority to open a checkpoint, let alone negotiate a settlement without Turkish consent. Later, both sides blamed the other for the delays in opening new checkpoints. Northern officials declared that work would be complete on the northern side in time for a 31 August 2005 checkpoint opening in Zodia, and that any further delays were the result of Greek Cypriot intransigence. Southern officials then panicked, first saying that it would take up to three months to make the checkpoint ready 'because we do things thoroughly', then finishing construction in ten days to avoid the embarrassment of having Talat claim that the south was obstructing freedom of movement. This charade has been repeated during work for the opening of the Kato Pyrgos and Ledra Street crossing in the centre of divided Nicosia, which eventually opened in early 2008.[65]

A culture of co-operation among Greek and Turkish Cypriot elites has been significantly retarded by historical memory and electoral pressure. On the whole, co-operation has been conceptualised by elites as contingent upon a solution, rather than a factor upon which a solution is contingent. As a result of this perception, the political and public environment has tended to inhibit the behaviour of the few elites who have tried to build a culture of co-operation.

Public displays by elites that the conflict has ended

There is overwhelming evidence that the Cypriot conflict has continued as a cold war through diplomatic channels. Consequently, the few public gestures by elites that the inter-communal conflict has ended are contradicted at several levels. Hostile non-recognition of the TRNC by the south and of the Republic of Cyprus by the north, the commemoration and celebration of historical events which are symbols of sorrow or loss to the other community, the perpetuation of compulsory military service by both communities, and the constant comments by political elites about where blame lies for non-resolution of the conflict all signal to Greek and Turkish Cypriots that the 'other' community is still the enemy. It is unsurprising, therefore, that a consociational solution has not been successfully adopted. The tension exhibited in north and south Cyprus is reflective of elite unwillingness (or inability) to render obsolete the zero-sum battle for supremacy.

The object of this work is to understand why elites have been unable to overcome such barriers and adopt a power-sharing solution in Cyprus that they have *prima facie* endorsed. Historical institutionalism argues that a change in political institutions must be precipitated by a change in ideas about the nation's primary function. Protection of traditional ethno-nationalist ideas and traumatic communal memory will inhibit change. Until recently, political elites have been able to perpetuate their respective ethno-nationalist interpretations of Cyprus' modern history.

The way a country's history is narrated to its youth is an important indicator of the society's values. Children will grow into future leaders, and their interpretation of their country's history – framed by current elites – will influence the way they see their own future. The vision of current elites can therefore continue to dominate ideas about a solution long after the elites themselves are gone.

Seen in this light, the 2004 Education Commission on the Revision of School Textbooks in north Cyprus was a significant event. Until recently, both societies have avoided re-evaluating their militant pasts, allowing political elites to perpetuate their selective reconstruction of Cyprus' recent history. Between January and September 2004, the Commission made extensive changes to the history textbooks taught to primary and secondary school students.[66] The books were a tangible signal from the Turkish Cypriot elite to both the Turkish and Greek Cypriot publics that the elite considered the conflict to be over. They were rewritten with a focus on the concepts of empathy and multi-perspectivity, and moved away from the traditional stark 'victim and aggressor' approach to Cypriot history. 'Starting from the 1960 events, [we showed] that ok, yes, Turkish Cypriots suffered a lot, but Greek Cypriots suffered also. It's not a one-sided thing. And we wanted to get rid of blood from the history textbooks'.[67]

These changes to the Turkish Cypriot history textbooks exemplify how elites can play an instigating role in preparing a conflict-ridden society to adopt a solution. The textbook changes were authorised by the incoming CTP government in light of anticipated reunification and Cypriot accession to the EU. The changes were clearly a political affair and included criticisms of previous north Cyprus governments and policies. In addition, the changes to the Turkish Cypriot history books paralleled and perhaps sought to legitimise the broader public sentiment at the time of reclaiming the Turkish Cypriot community's history. Previous Turkish Cypriot history books reinforced an official narrative which glorified Turkey's role in the establishment and protection of the TRNC; telling a story of Turkish might against Greek and Greek Cypriot transgressions. The Turkish Cypriot community was portrayed in both the books and the official narrative as voiceless: visible only in its victimhood.[68] Thus, the new textbooks tapped a broader public current, becoming the symbol of a significant change in the Turkish Cypriot community's self-portrayal.[69]

Equally telling was the prohibitive role played by Greek Cypriot political elites in similar efforts to change Greek Cypriot textbooks. In this case, Greek Cypriot elites gave a definite signal to the public that the conflict still lived. In early 2007 a dispute about Greek Cypriot history books ballooned into a political debate, when the acting Republic of Cyprus Minister of Education commented that Cypriot history books distributed to primary schools were inaccurate. Minister Silikiotis argued that the textbooks, written in Greece, downplayed the significance of the Cyprus conflict, as well as making inadequate reference to refugees from the 1974 war and the people still listed as missing from that conflict.[70] In a public statement, the minister argued that properly emphasising these aspects of the conflict was so important because '[w]e have an obligation towards the current and the younger generations to give them an objective and complete view of our history'.[71] In other words, books which did not follow the official version of history were 'subjective' and 'incomplete'. Other efforts by Cypriot educators and teachers to revise the history curriculum taught to school students have been quashed by the Greek Cypriot government and public outcries. Though a committee has twice been formed to examine the revision of the textbooks, it has so far done little. Demetriou has suggested that the difference between each community's ability to change its books is partly a matter of bureaucracy.[72] The formal changes the EU requires of the Republic of Cyprus education system are far-reaching and require deep systemic, long-term changes. This takes time, and at the moment is only at the committee-level of discussion.

The opacity surrounding inter-communal killings also represents a serious example of how Cypriot elites perpetuate the conflict. An open wound has been maintained in both societies regarding the whereabouts and cause of death of the approximately 2000 missing persons. There is ample proof that the whereabouts of a number of 'missing people' from both communities killed during inter-communal fighting are known by political representatives of both communities, as well as UN officials. The issue was handed over reluctantly to an investigative commission called the Committee for Missing Persons (CMP) in 1981. The CMP's powers are effectively weakened by both governments, and both the issue and the organisation itself are highly political, and significantly politicised. The CMP's mandate from the UN has been to establish the deaths of the missing, and has quite pointedly *not* been about establishing the cause of death. Until recently, the exhumation of these remains has had a number of political consequences, which neither side has wanted. Consequently, the CMP has been in a state of stalemate for 20 years. However, since late 2003 there has been significant impetus on the part of both leaderships to resolve the issue.[73]

Each society has taken a different strategic approach to the case of the missing people. The Turkish Cypriot government declared all the Turkish Cypriots missing to be dead, and consequently families of the victims were, to some extent, able to mourn the passing of their loved ones.[74] In the south, however, few of the Greek Cypriot missing have been declared dead. Instead, they remain *missing* and therefore possibly alive.[75] The unsolved nature of the case has allowed numerous Greek Cypriot governments to chastise Turkey in international forums, linking human rights and Turkish violence in Cyprus to a number of other Turkish human rights violations in Turkey and surrounding areas. Keeping the issue of the missing open and unresolved also serves the domestic function of reminding the public that the conflict is not over and perpetuating the concept of Greek Cypriot victimhood.[76]

During the period of the Annan negotiations, the CMP began making progress. To date, it has unearthed approximately 450 bodies in several locations, and just over 130 have been returned to their families.[77] However, advancement is heavily governed by strategy. On the Turkish side, the encouragement of progress is said to be linked to pressure from the EU to resolve outstanding issues. Resolution of the case of the missing in Cyprus is therefore Turkey's answer to EU pressure in several other areas identified as requiring reform.[78] On the Greek Cypriot side, progress on the issue allows elites to argue to both domestic and international audiences that they are actively proceeding towards resolving the conflict and building inter-communal trust.

The continued strategic use of moral rhetoric and international law by each society against the other is a significant indicator that elites are presently unable to facilitate a consociational solution in Cyprus. Their efforts to discredit the other community reinforce the image of a continuing conflict. As highlighted in Chapter 4, the Republic of Cyprus maintains that association with any Turkish Cypriot organisation which makes use of the TRNC name or insignia is tantamount to recognition of the state. The issue of recognition of the TRNC is linked to the broader inter-communal battle over sovereignty analysed in the previous chapter.

Recognition of the TRNC has grown into one of the most significant taboo-myths Greek Cypriot elites have perpetuated in their society. It has two distinct phases: the first was born in 1983 with the Turkish Cypriot state's proclamation; the second grew out of the first, and was born in 2003 when partial free movement between communities was permitted. Freer movement between the communities meant Greek Cypriots increasingly linked their personal actions (the choice to cross or not cross) to the increased possibility of the TRNC's recognition.

The Greek Cypriot conceptualisation of the TRNC's existence blurs questions of legality and morality. In this rhetoric, to cross to the north is immoral because it implies tacit support of the TRNC, which was created by an illegal invasion. Therefore, the taboo against crossing fosters the myth that to cross to the north is to 'support the invaders' and risk legitimising the breakaway state. This taboo-myth has impeded both inter-communal contact and the development of Turkish Cypriot contact with the international community. While the international community adheres to non-recognition of any northern Cypriot entity, non-recognition also disables any attempts at sporting or cultural contact between the two sides, important for breaking down the negative image of the 'other' and in building a working-level of trust.[79] More recently, Republic of Cyprus officials have continuously blocked any attempts by the EU to open trade or avenues of direct transport between north Cyprus and EU countries. Republic of Cyprus officials insist that any direct connections or relationships with the TRNC implies recognition of the state, and therefore will disincline Turkish Cypriot elites to engage in reunification efforts. However, by maintaining this approach, Greek Cypriot elites are simultaneously providing very strong signals that the conflict continues.

As highlighted by Constantinou and Papadakis (among others), the projection and internalisation of this policy is not an exclusive Greek Cypriot domain. TRNC documents and officials exclusively refer to the 'Greek Cypriot administration', 'Greek Cypriot leader', and so on. The Republic of Cyprus is only referred to in the context of its original bi-communal shape; as a historical referent, or to emphasise that the only legitimate Republic of Cyprus ended with the 1963 communal separation. And despite considerable diplomatic pressure, and Greek Cypriot anxiety, temporary visas are still issued by the TRNC to all individuals crossing between north and south. Pressure against inter-communal co-operation exists in the north as well as in the south, preventing the development of trade relations and partnerships between communities. On 31 March 2006, 22 tons of citrus fruits were to be transported from north Cyprus across the green line and shipped to an EU member state via Lemesos port (which is in south Cyprus). However, the consignment was cancelled by the Turkish Cypriot trader on 29 March after protests of truck drivers and dockers at Famagusta port in north Cyprus, and at the checkpoint where the fruit would cross. The trader complained of experiencing significant pressure within the Turkish Cypriot community,[80] at both the community and government level.

The conflict, which is articulated in Greek as τo $\kappa \upsilon \pi \rho \iota \alpha \kappa \acute{o}$,[81] and in Turkish as *Kıbrıs sorunu*[82] is perceived by both communities as a problem to be negotiated by the elites, something with which the public has no direct interaction. The Greek Cypriot government has asserted (and then retracted the claim) that non-state actors can bestow recognition upon a non-recognised state. Greek Cypriot elites use threats about implied recognition, caused by inter-communal contact, as a tool to control the conflict's perpetuation. Many Greek Cypriots feel genuine fear that their personal actions and behaviour will contribute to recognition of the TRNC and therefore to the permanent partition of Cyprus.[83]

The deep fear in the Greek Cypriot community that by their personal actions they can thwart the national negotiating strategy is evident in the treatment by public actors of any of the official labels of the Turkish Cypriot state. In an article exploring this aspect of the conflict, Constantinou and Papadakis note that 'the recognition discourse has become less reflective of a legal or political dispute and more illuminating of strategies of control and governance'.[84] The authors show that both communities have been keenly aware of the possibility of implied recognition.

> This has extended to almost any imaginable activity of an international nature, from trade to the landing of civilian company planes in the north, from sports meetings to academic conferences, including meetings or events devoid of any explicit political content. Turkish Cypriots, with equal insistence, have been officially encouraged to participate in such events, often feeling that through them they can also gain some international standing which can then be exploited by the authorities in the north for domestic consumption or to foster recognition. In general, the Turkish Cypriot official aim in international meetings is not so much to block completely the participation of Greek Cypriot individuals or groups (which is not feasible due to the international stance on the issue) but rather to take part alongside the Greek Cypriot organizations. Consequently, if a Greek Cypriot organization or individuals encounter a Turkish Cypriot group trying to join such events, they frequently protest and try to disqualify its participation and more often than not they are successful; if not, then the Greek Cypriots withdraw. In other words, most Greek and Turkish Cypriots joining international events abroad customarily consider it their patriotic duty to protect or promote their respective state recognitions.[85]

There is a strong convention among Greek Cypriot academics and journalists writing about the conflict to enclose reference to the TRNC and its offices within quotation marks. Mehmet Ali Talat, for example, is the 'President' of the 'TRNC'. The same rule follows for all officialdom. In Greek, the overwhelming trend is to preface any reference to institutions or titles of the state with the adjective 'ψευδο', meaning pseudo, or false. Talat is referred to as the 'pseudo-president'; the state is the 'pseudo-state', and so on. Northern Cyprus is very infrequently referred to in Greek as 'Βόρεια Κύπρος'(North Cyprus). It is almost exclusively labelled 'τα κατεχόμενα', meaning 'the occupied territory' (though the noun 'territory' remains assumed in most cases). Those who dare refer to this territory as 'northern Cyprus' flirt with the label 'υποστηρικτής του ψευδοκράτος', supporter of the pseudo-state, akin to being labelled a traitor.[86]

A week after the 2003 checkpoint openings, the government machine in the south began filtering through a number of mixed messages regarding the legitimacy and legal implications of citizen crossings. Presented with the opportunity to encourage inter-communal trust by responding positively to the openings, the recently formed Papadopoulos government instead promoted confusion among Greek Cypriots about the 'sovereignty' consequences of crossing to north Cyprus.[87] Underlying this seeming confusion was an unwillingness on the part of the Greek Cypriot government to welcome the 'other' and to foster partnership between the communities.[88]

So hung up on the issue of sovereignty was the Greek Cypriot government that it was either unable or unwilling to use this unparalleled opportunity to encourage understanding between the communities. A number of contradictory messages were therefore passed on to the Greek Cypriot public. One day before the opening, news agencies were reporting that 'the Cyprus government says it will oppose [the opening] because of Turkish Cypriot demands that those crossing present a passport, suggesting recognition of the Turkish Cypriot side as separate state'.[89] On the very first day that checkpoint openings were announced, the government spokesman for the Republic of Cyprus, Kypros Chrysostomides, issued a statement (quoted below by Xinhua news agency) that the decision to open the checkpoints was '"illegal" as the Turkish Cypriot regime is not internationally recognized. If the intention of Turkish Cypriot leader Rauf Denktash was "to give the impression of a separate sovereignty, the existence of borders and two state entities, this does not reflect the legal or political framework of efforts to solve the Cyprus problem"'.[90]

At no time did the Greek Cypriot government say that the new situation could be seen as a move towards peace. A week after the opening, Chrysostomides was still expressing cynicism. He is quoted by the BBC as saying

> that the policy of Rauf Denktas and his son, Serdar, 'does not seem to have been altered or changed', adding that 'what they insist on is the continuous upgrading of the occupation regime and their fundamental positions for separate sovereignty, borders and the exploitation of the arrangements made in the meantime, such as showing passports and issuing "visas" and the continuous effort to reduce the negative impressions from their intransigent stance so far' in the peace effort.[91]

The Greek Cypriot government's comments remained opaque, but were always tinged with unease. Around the same time as the comment above, Chrysostomides acknowledged the illegitimacy of concerns surrounding implied recognition when he 'dismissed fears that the display of passports by Greek-Cypriots in order to pass through checkpoints could be construed as recognition of the illegal regime and stressed that no private individual was in a position to "recognise" an illegal structure'.[92] In the second week, the Greek Cypriot president 'called on all Greek Cypriots to be extra careful during their movement in the occupied areas not just because of the possible "arrests" but also because of the existence of land mines and other dangers, which might undermine their personal safety'.[93] This cautious message, of doubtful validity (the mines are not in areas that people are likely to go), reinforced an early comment by Chrysostomides that 'the government cannot vouch for safe and secure travel in the occupied areas',[94] nevertheless adding that 'we will not prevent anybody from doing so'.[95] While the political consequences of Denktaş' decision to open the checkpoints was weighing on the Greek Cypriot government's mind, and while it could not be seen to be openly condemning the move, the leadership was clearly unwilling to capitalise on the development.

Supporting the government's unwillingness to capitalise in a positive way on the checkpoint openings was the powerful Cypriot Orthodox Church. The Church's disapproval of Greek Cypriots who travel north for 'pleasure' was reported within three weeks of the openings:

> 'We express our regret over cases of unacceptable behaviour on the part of a few of our compatriots', said a church statement issued after a Holy Synod meeting. ... The church leadership is concerned about the consequences of the Turkish Cypriot authorities allowing overnight stays at hotels in the north, many of which were previously owned by Greek Cypriot businessmen. ... 'During their visit to our occupied lands, they (visitors) commit acts which are unacceptable as Greeks and Christians, indulging in pleasure-seeking and staying overnight in illegal hotels', the statement added.[96]

With such strong language, Greek Cypriots were given the message that the conflict was not over.[97] These antagonistic elite attitudes have affected public attitudes to crossing. Recent polls show that some 40 per cent of Greek Cypriots have not crossed to the north. Of those who have, only ten per cent cross with any frequency.[98] Ninety per cent of Turkish Cypriots and 87 per cent of Greek Cypriots claim to have no meaningful contact with the other community.[99] Thus the checkpoint openings have paradoxically evolved into a barrier to the breaking down of mistrust between communities. Over the years, elites have passed onto the public a heavy burden to protect the Republic of Cyprus' legitimacy. This burden has been internalised by the high number of Greek Cypriots who do not want to cross to the north because showing identification is perceived as an act of recognition of the TRNC. Only ten per cent of Turkish Cypriots and 13 per cent of Greek Cypriots have any contact with individuals from the other group, reflecting 50 years of mutual mistrust. Four years of checkpoint openings have only just begun to scratch the surface of the mistrust built by history and reinforced by a generation of antagonistic elites.

A second consequence of the way the conflict has been set up is that its boundaries and definitions cannot be challenged or redefined at any level other than the elite. This breeds a popular myth that *only* the political elite is capable of resolving the conflict. But in addition, citizens have taken on the responsibility for protecting their state's honour against defilement by the other. So while only elites can resolve the conflict, highly defensive populations (especially in the south) stand guard at the conflict's conceptual gates. All of this means that unless there is a decisive breakdown in public trust of elites, as there was in north Cyprus in the lead-up to 2004, political elites will have a stranglehold on public perception of the conflict. If the elites themselves are motivated by the fulfilment of group historical ambitions, of personal power gains, or of a deep belief that they are protecting their community from ruin, then motivation for resolution of the conflict will be absent. This book has argued so far that all of the above motivations have coalesced in different periods in both communities to prevent elites compromising. And because elites hold significant power in Cyprus, they also hold the capacity to frame, resolve, or perpetuate the conflict because it is only they who have the authoritative voice.

At the symbolic level, both Greek and Turkish Cypriot elites perpetuate ethno-nationalist history. With the commemoration of a number of events, both the Greek and Turkish Cypriot political elite have indicated to their respective nations that the conflict is far from over, and that the 'other' cannot be trusted as partners in a federal state. While the elites may be negotiating a solution, they are simultaneously discouraging a co-operative atmosphere from which a consociational partnership must evolve.

The commemoration of events and organisations which perpetuate antagonism between the communities has been encouraged by the leaders of both sides, who continued their support of these 'national anniversaries' during the years the Annan Plan was being negotiated. The beginning of the EOKA struggle on 1 April is a solemn day, officially accompanied by significant displays of nationalism and militarism by Greek Cypriots, as are two particular Greek national holidays: the anniversary of the declaration of the start of Greek War of Independence from the Ottoman Empire, on 25 March 1821; and 28 October, known as *ο επέτειος του ÓXI,* or 'ochi day'[100] marking Greece's refusal to bow to Italian fascism in the Second World War, and which in Cyprus is also used to express protest against the Turkish invasion. All three occasions are offensive to the Turkish Cypriot community, but the commemoration of the EOKA struggle is a particular trigger for inter-communal mistrust. In north Cyprus, 13–20 July is commemorated by Turkish Cypriots as the 'week of thanksgiving to Turkey'. 20 July marks the celebration of Peace and Freedom, the beginning of the 1974 'peace operation'. It is a significant day of mourning for Greek Cypriots, who also hold commemorative events on that day to mark the Turkish invasion. The 21 December anniversary of the 1963 'Kanlı Noel' (Bloody Christmas) is commemorated by Turkish Cypriots as the 'week of remembrance' and the 'martyrs struggle of 1963–1974'. 15 November is celebrated as TRNC Independence Day, and is marked by protests in the south. Without exception, these days are characterised by military parades and shows of military power. They are generally attended by political elites of most stripes,[101] and also function as a show of solidarity between Greece and Greek Cyprus, and Turkey and Turkish Cyprus, as high-ranking government and military officials from the 'motherlands' almost always attend, and Greek or Turkish national flags abound.

The few public gestures by Greek and Turkish Cypriot elites in the lead-up to the referendum that might have signalled an end to the conflict were contradicted by the mass of actions which reinforced the conflict mentality. In the Turkish Cypriot community, changes to the history textbooks showed the central role elites can play in facilitating and legitimising[102] transformation of the community's conflict mentality. However, Greek Cypriot elites overwhelmingly resisted similar change to their own textbooks, strongly signalling that the conflict was still an important defining element of the Greek Cypriot psyche. The behaviour of both Greek and Turkish Cypriot elites at a number of junctures where they had the opportunity to signal an end to the conflict, and to encourage co-operation, leads one to conclude quite emphatically that there were very few effective efforts by elites at public displays of the conflict's end.

'The solution is fair and permanent'

In an elite-driven society like Cyprus, the public generally looks to its leaders for confirmation that a solution is fair and safe, and that it will last. Without this confirmation, it is very difficult to gain public acceptance of a solution. While Turkish Cypriot political and societal elites campaigned extensively for some time to ensure public support of the plan, Greek Cypriot elites remained largely muted in their response until only weeks before the referendums.

Immediately prior to the referendum, the Annan Plan was characterised by Greek Cypriot governing elites as 'all gain' for the Turkish Cypriots, and 'all loss' for the Greek Cypriots. Extensive commentary by then-president Papadopoulos in his pre-referendum address to the nation strongly characterised the plan as unbalanced and unjust. The following comments can be considered typical. 'The Turkish Cypriot community gains all the basic demands it made, from the first day of the implementation of the solution. To be exact, 24 hours after the holding of the referenda. ... In contrast, everything that the Greek Cypriot community is aspiring to achieve, even from a bad and painful solution, is postponed without guarantees'.[103]

A number of Greek Cypriot elites maintained the position that the Annan Plan was neither fair nor permanent long after the plan's rejection. In an interview with the author about the possibility of new negotiations two years after the referendum, a spokesman for the president of the House of Representatives in south Cyprus perfectly summarised the sentiments of the Greek Cypriot political class. 'If the Turkish Cypriot side doesn't want to discuss anything else, it means that they liked the plan perfectly!! If they don't agree to discuss anything else, it means they like it so much. Now if they like it so much, it means we won't like it'.[104]

A more positive attitude among Turkish Cypriot elites towards both the process and the result of the Annan Plan[105] significantly contributed to a higher level of public ownership of the solution in north Cyprus. Initial Turkish Cypriot reactions to the plan were largely unenthusiastic,[106] but extensive campaigning by the platforms 'Common Vision' (Ortak Visyon) and 'This Country is Ours' platform (Bu Memleket Bizimdir Platformu)[107] over the course of the negotiations resulted in Turkish Cypriot popular support of the plan, demonstrated during several rallies held in the north for reunification in 2003 and 2004. Between the Annan Plan's first presentation in November 2002, and its final incarnation as Annan V in March 2004, the plan was extensively canvassed in a number of public forums. In 2004, president of the Turkish Cypriot trade union DEV-İŞ, Ali Gulle, compared the period leading up to the referendum in both communities:

> You see there has been about a year and a half since the Annan Plan was first presented; and since then it has been on Turkish Cypriot radio and televisions every night for this whole time. It's not like on the other side. On the other side they are not very interested. They know they are in the European community and they don't bother too much. But on this side, because people don't know what their future is, they're listening and they're asking, every night, five or six channels, they're asking questions and they're on the point.[108]

Through television, radio, and public presentations, Turkish Cypriot legal experts and political commentators formed discussion groups to explain the plan to the wider community, and debate the plan's merits. A number of these forums were interactive, and members of the public would often call in with questions or criticisms. Public support for the Annan Plan grew in proportion to awareness, directly as a result of elite efforts to emphasise the plan's strengths. Elites emphasised that gains made in each plan were hard fought victories, and that the sacrifices were necessary to achieve peace.

While Greek Cypriot society is not necessarily more politically conservative, different socio-economic conditions have nurtured an unbroken relationship of trust in political elites, as a general rule. Until the presentation of the Annan Plan, years of secret, closed-door negotiations between Greek Cypriot and Turkish Cypriot elites have been consistently presented in the south as *a step towards* solution, rather than the foundation of a solution. By portraying the agreements or concessions made in the negotiating arena as temporary deviations from an ultimate goal, elites prevented any serious discussion of the value or necessity of such concessions, at the same time protecting themselves from public backlash. While political elites do tend to acknowledge that the elements of a solution are all present in Cyprus, and that 'the details of the solution have been worked out by the UN a long time ago',[109] no public debate has taken place on the details of such work.

Though opinion polls show that the Greek Cypriot populace largely accepts a power-sharing solution,[110] for the reasons noted above, before the final Annan Plan few attempts had been made to explain to the public the parameters of such a design.[111] There are two related reasons for this situation. Until the political schism caused by the 2004 referendum in the south, political elites were reluctant to explain the details of the resolutions accepted, fearing the wrath of an unaccepting public.[112] In comparison to the Turkish Cypriot community, the Greek Cypriot public explored the Annan Plan very late. A close examination of the term 'bi-zonal' did not take place within Greek Cypriot society until the completion of the Annan Plan in the weeks before the 2004 referendums, when public and televised discussions increased and published analyses of the plan which had been in circulation for some months[113] were examined more carefully. It was finally realised that 'bi-zonal' would mean a significant geographic space within Cyprus would be under legitimate Turkish Cypriot control. A public backlash resulted,[114] and a sense of betrayal permeated the Greek Cypriot community.

Until the referendum, the concept of a federation was only loosely understood in south Cyprus; it would be a form of government with two geographical sections and with two communities (bizonal and bicommunal). The thought that this bicommunal federal framework would entail a Turkish Cypriot ethnic majority on the northern side of Cyprus was not seriously considered. The acceptance of a federal structure lived side by side with the maximalist belief that all refugees would return immediately to their homes, that the Turkish army would withdraw from Cyprus immediately, and that all Turkish nationals living in northern Cyprus would go back to Turkey.

Greek Cypriot elites who argued that the Annan Plan was a fair solution were largely sidelined by hard line anti-plan elites who emphasised the dire consequences which would result from the plan's acceptance. It is therefore unsurprising that 76 per cent of the Greek Cypriot population voted against the plan. But in the north, there was strong public support for the plan which cut across ideological barriers. The referendum result in north Cyprus was 64 per cent support of the plan's adoption.

Conclusion

Consociationalism is a form of political resolution which places great emphasis on elites to foster co-operation in divided polities. This requires elites to have an interest in co-operation. However, in the case of Cyprus, that vital interest was not present, as incentives were not strong enough to entice both sides into endorsing the resolution on offer. This chapter has argued that there were unequal incentives for Greek and Turkish Cypriot elites to co-operate, which significantly inhibited development of the co-operative relationship necessary for the adoption of a consociational solution. In the north, grassroots pressure supported domestic political elites who were mandated to seek change. As the next chapter will show, Cyprus' accession to the EU buttressed domestic incentives for political change in north Cyprus. However, in south Cyprus, guaranteed EU membership served to reinforce domestic dissatisfaction, leading, as Chapter 7 will show, to the plan's rejection.

It has recently been said that 'in the determination of which forces will predominate the Cypriot political elites of the two communities respectively have a greater role, than they did in the past'.[115] One must be forgiven for disagreeing with this statement. Elites in Cyprus have *always* played a supreme role in the determination of the conflict's future. That they are so vital to the direction of Cyprus' future today is merely a product of the control they have had in the past.

The chapter has argued that elite co-operation was constricted by the burden of history, and that, particularly in the south, both the elites and the public were guided in their choices by attempts to fulfil goals of the past. Conciliatory Greek Cypriot political elites who supported the 2004 plan found themselves in a catch-22 situation. Partly because over the years negotiations infrequently progressed very far, and partly because there was high political risk and little electoral payoff, there was little effort pre-Annan to unpack the concepts of federalism and power-sharing. It follows, therefore, that one of the key reasons that in 2004 Greek Cypriot political elites were unable to endorse the proposed power-sharing solution is that those who were inclined to support the plan had been trapped by years of maximalist political rhetoric; their electoral support bases were simply not prepared to make such a leap.

6
UN and EU: Offering Incentives for Resolution

The peacemaker needs power and leverage to be effective.[1]

Consociational theory is predicated upon elite co-operation, but given a restrictive and competitive domestic environment such as Cyprus, where both the public and the elites are locked into a zero-sum rhetoric, peace plans have typically come from outside. Where elite co-operation is minimal, the ability of the international community to offer incentives for compromise becomes crucial.[2] In Cyprus, the UN and the EU were the primary actors which tried to change the domestic dynamics by taking on particular roles; the UN as engineer, and the EU as catalyst for a solution. However, these actors were unable to offer sufficient incentives to encourage both Greek and Turkish Cypriot acceptance of the UN's plan for reunification. The chapter explains constraints on the UN's ability to resolve the conflict, and examines Cyprus' EU accession as a lever for compromise and resolution.

UN involvement in Cyprus

The UN has clear legitimacy for preventing and resolving intra- and inter-state conflicts,[3] though its power is often heavily constrained by the reluctance of member states to enforce Security Council resolutions, by the broad nature of the resolutions themselves, and by structural conflicts between organs of the UN.[4] UN member states pledged to strengthen the UN's effectiveness in this area in the UN Millennium Declaration[5] and in Security Council Resolution 1318 (2000). The UN's strength lies primarily in its political legitimacy and 'soft power', which, despite recent crises,[6] remain significant. Its fiscal and military weakness dampen its role as a strong moderator.[7] For example, on this Rothchild observes that 'because of the UN's organisational and resource problems, it lacks leverage and cannot provide effective packages of positive or negative incentives to alter the preferences of leaders engaged in civil war'.[8] External leverage is particularly important in situations like Cyprus where parties make 'non-negotiable demands and ... shun compromise and credible commitment'.[9] It has also been identified, both here and elsewhere, as a key factor in the adoption of consociational democracy.

Certainly, the UN has played a central role in the many attempts to overcome the Cyprus deadlock.[10] The UN operation in Cyprus was established under Resolution 186 (1964),[11] which 'tried to provide a comprehensive peace-keeping, peace-making and peacebuilding structure in order to bring peace to the island'.[12] The linked goals of finding a constitutional settlement and controlling the outbreak of war in Cyprus were identified as missions for UN peacemaking and peacekeeping respectively, and endorsed in the 1964 resolution. The years 1999–2004 mark the UN's most robust post-war attempt to resolve the conflict.[13] Thus, the UN's involvement in the conflict has been extensive.

As each of the chapters have shown in different ways, the role of elites in this conflict's perpetuation is significant. In the Cyprus case, the UN's capacity to persuade parties on the ground to accept a solution has been curtailed and undermined in no small part by the parties' interpretations of the UN's role: elite incentives to perpetuate the conflict have consequently clouded the relationship between peacekeeping and peacemaking in Cyprus. Alvaro de Soto noted that the selective, strategic support of the UN's mandate by combatant groups 'is actually common to deeply entrenched longstanding – 'frozen' – conflicts everywhere, including e.g. the Western Sahara, the Middle East and Georgia-Abkhazia, in which one party bases its case on existing Security Council resolutions or other legal foundations which it believes will be undermined if it cedes even a millimetre'.[14]

Under Resolution 186, the Secretary General was authorised to appoint a mediator, who was mandated to assist in the promotion of a 'peaceful solution and *agreed settlement*'[15] of the increasingly volatile situation.[16] In concert with these efforts the UN foresaw the need for a peacekeeping operation that would provide the conditions of security under which the negotiations could proceed. Resolution 186 therefore also mandated the United Nations Force in Cyprus (UNFICYP) to aid the return to 'normal' conditions (i.e. the 1960 constitution).[17] Richmond has argued that the foundation of UNFICYP's establishment and the mediator's mandate within Resolution 186 appeared contradictory, and allowed each group to claim that the UN supported their respective perspective of the conflict, and its resolution, deepening the zero-sum mentality of the combatants.[18] The UN Security Council (and thus the mediator) appeared to support the Greek Cypriot position of searching for a new solution, while UNFICYP seemed to support the Turkish Cypriot position of returning to the 1960 treaties.[19]

The mediator's instructions thus appeared to support the Greek Cypriot position that the 1960 Constitution needed reform, contributing to Turkish

Cypriot fears that their constitutionally guaranteed position of security would be lost.[20] Furthermore, because there were no Turkish Cypriots left in the government of the Republic of Cyprus, they were frozen out of the decision-making body which advised on the choice of mediator. The UN, cornered by circumstance, contributed to the disenfranchisement and isolation of the Turkish Cypriot community by naming Greece, Turkey, Great Britain, and the Republic of Cyprus official partners in the negotiations. The Turkish Cypriot community was only acknowledged insofar as it was a disputant in the conflict. This made the community vulnerable on two fronts: becoming increasingly and exclusively reliant upon Turkey for representation and necessarily being denied a legitimate voice in the dispute. These separate, but intertwined, factors also meant that the only legitimacy the Turkish Cypriot elites would receive was at the negotiating table.[21]

On the other hand, the Greek Cypriot community enjoyed full recognition as, *de facto*, it controlled the internationally recognised Republic of Cyprus. The consequent international recognition provided the Greek Cypriots with the moral authority to speak as the sole legitimate Cypriot voice in the UN and in other forums,[22] establishing a pattern that was to allow them to blur the line between 'Cypriot' and 'Greek Cypriot' interests. This became a major factor producing intransigence in the Greek Cypriot community, culminating in its rejection of a compromise solution in April 2004. According to Richmond, the UN thus became a 'victim of the conflict itself',[23] and these initial blocks became the foundations of the problem's intractability. As will be shown below, legitimisation of the Greek Cypriot voice at the expense of the Turkish Cypriot legitimacy also carried over to shape the EU's interaction with each side.

UN interests have shifted over time, affecting its peacemaking capacity in Cyprus. The UN had a strong early involvement in Cyprus, shaping proposed solutions to the conflict. In the immediate post-breakdown period, the UN attempted dynamic forms of direct intervention that combined both peacekeeping and peacemaking. In early 1964, former Ecuadorian President Galo Plaza was appointed by the UN Secretary General to the position of Mediator on Cyprus, to promote 'a peaceful solution and an agreed settlement of the problem confronting Cyprus, in accordance with the Charter of the United Nations'.[24] The Galo Plaza Report attempted to create inroads towards a solution to the problem, but it instead increased tension significantly.[25] After Plaza's resignation, which resulted from Turkish and Turkish Cypriot dissatisfaction with his report and claims of prejudice, 'the most crucial aspect of the Secretary General's mission of good offices which replaced direct mediation were his endeavours to avoid alienating either side, or compromising what remained of the integrity of the UN involvement in terms of peace-making'.[26] The resignation of Plaza under claims of partiality precipitated a self-protective move by the UN and catalysed the watering down of subsequent UN peacemaking attempts, also shaping the content of subsequent peace plans.

Subsequently, the UN's oscillating efforts in Cyprus have reflected internal UN, domestic Cypriot, and international pressures.[27] Both UN involvement and international attention has, over the years, been directed towards controlling intercommunal tension, rather than towards solving the problem. This is a reflection of the international community's goal of preventing the conflict from sparking a Greek/Turkish war which would have damaged the south-east wing of NATO, affecting the balance of the Cold War. The UN was therefore not free to pursue effective methods of peacemaking, trapped, as it has been, by regional instability and power shifts between Greece and Turkey,[28] which also affected stability and power relations within Cyprus.

This stale and tense atmosphere has been interrupted only by the 1977 Framework Agreements between Makarios and Denktaş, the 1977 Kyprianou-Denktaş Communiqué (10 Point Agreement), and again with the 1992 Boutros Boutros Ghali Set of Ideas, which was a brief respite from the tradition of passiveness built by UN peacemaking since 1964. Ghali took a more active role in Cyprus than had previously been the case, weaving the role of mediation into the framework of good offices and holding the threat of the UNFICYP's withdrawal over the heads of the interlocutors to pressure them to negotiate genuinely.[29] The dynamism exhibited by Ghali was, however, short-lived, and by 1996 the UN had again fallen into what Richmond has described as a 'sterile and apathetic' role, and was overtaken by peacemaking efforts of the US, UK, and EU, operating under Security Council and General Assembly resolutions on Cyprus.[30]

The period between the submission and subsequent collapse of Ghali's 'Confidence Building Measures' in 1994 and the appointment of Kofi Annan to the position of UN Secretary General in 1998 was marked by high levels of tension, elevated by the Imia/Kardak crisis[31] in January 1996, three Greek Cypriot deaths on the island in the same year,[32] and an averted missile crisis in 1997.[33] The atmosphere again darkened in December 1997 at the EU Luxembourg Summit when the decision was taken to open accession negotiations with the Republic of Cyprus, while at the same time the EU remained silent regarding Turkey's candidacy. As a direct result of the Luxembourg decision, Turkey and the Turkish Cypriot government had moved their 'bottom line' negotiating basis from federalism to confederalism by early 1998. The move was a significant signal that negotiations would not progress, because Greek Cypriot negotiators had long been clear that confederation was not an option for Cyprus. But by 1998 the UN had resumed its role as primary peacemaker, and Annan began the process of incremental, negotiated change one more time. These efforts culminated in the 2004 Annan Plan.

The lack of extended violent conflict, and irregular contact between Cypriot political elites also affected the UN's involvement in Cyprus.

Additionally, the lack of protracted violent conflict has dulled incentives for Cypriot elites to compromise. Cyprus provides an unusual situation with regard to peacemaking because there has been no hurting stalemate which so often precipitates resolution of such conflicts. There have been three periods in which one side, but not both, has had an incentive to seek the conflict's resolution: between 1963 and 1967 (the Turkish Cypriot community); in the immediate post-1974 period (the Greek Cypriots); and again in the period before the 2004 referendum (the Turkish Cypriot community). In these situations, however, there had been no shared incentive to promote change in both communities. For most of the conflict's history, elite-level negotiators of both sides have expressed the desire for a solution, but both have seemed more comfortable in their entrenched positions. For example, some authors have argued that the comparative safety provided by the continued presence of UNFICYP prevents a hurting stalemate that might lead more quickly to solution; meaning that the Greek Cypriots would be more willing to compromise if they did not have the psychological security of UNFICYP against the 35,000 strong Turkish army stationed on the island. Similarly, the significant negotiating power created by the overwhelming physical presence of the Turkish army in Cyprus has significantly dulled Turkish/Turkish Cypriot incentives for compromise.

UN efforts to overcome constraints

The team of the Secretary General working on the Annan Plan had, at the outset of the negotiation process, identified the EU as the party in the strongest position to offer incentives to break the status quo.[34] The UN negotiating team therefore very carefully aligned its negotiating strategy to Cyprus' EU accession process.[35]

UN engineers, aware they were working in a highly constrained environment, utilised several tactics to overcome these impediments.[36] For example, the UN relied on the influence and motivation of regional and major powers – particularly the US and the UK in a two-pronged role[37] – to provide Cypriot elites with incentives to support the Annan Plan. At the international level, they were central to what one UN diplomat described as 'taking care of the environment in which we were working'.[38] They were particularly active in providing support in the Security Council and in exercising pressure on Cypriot and regional powers. Much of that pressure was directed towards Turkey, and particularly towards Denktaş, between Annan I (2002) and III (2003) to be more conciliatory.[39] Core UN negotiators have labelled American and British influence as significant insofar as it enabled progress in areas which would otherwise have remained stalemated.

In trying to connect with the community, and to overcome constraints placed upon them by Cypriot government elites, the negotiators had repeated unofficial contact with leaders of minority communities, NGOs,

Cypriot academics from both communities, economists, journalists, former politicians, leaders of political parties not included in the negotiating teams, and business and community leaders. They also actively monitored press reports and public responses in the press. Living on the island during the negotiation period was considered by the negotiators to be an advantage in understanding the society and the political attitudes. However, there are also shortcomings of implementing power-sharing solutions in real-world scenarios: while unofficial advice was central to the design of particular aspects of the plan, contact with the groups mentioned above did not necessarily equal societal input into the proposed constitution simply because 'it was hard to incorporate their ideas if they were going to be vetoed by their negotiators ... we can't include something the negotiating team won't accept – even if the public wants it'.[40] This reality necessarily restricted participation to elite-level negotiators, who were not necessarily interested in improving the plan.

Over the years of its involvement, however, the UN had also used its limited capacity to try to change the internal dynamics at both the grassroots and sub-elite level and create a more favourable negotiating climate. The United Nations Office for Project Services (UNOPS – now UNDP-ACT), which evolved out of the United Nations High Commission for Refugees (UNHCR)[41] has functioned since 1998 as a facilitator of bi-communal and NGO activity. It provided funding to approximately 50–80 NGOs[42] for some 150 projects between 1998 and 2004. In addition, the UN has hosted an annual 'UN Open Day' since 1998, providing an opportunity (before the checkpoint opening in April 2003) for Turkish and Greek Cypriots to intermingle and create new relationships or rekindle old ones. Consistently attracting between 6000 and 7000 people, it became a significant event on the bi-communal calendar.[43]

Conscious of its limited ability to enhance domestic incentives for resolution, the UN has also relied on American and British organisations to develop relations between Greek and Turkish Cypriots.[44] For example, the Fulbright Commission and Scholarship Program, the British Council, and USAID often worked in concert with UN agencies (particularly UNOPS, which served as a channel or facilitator) to develop citizen-level conflict resolution.[45] When asked about the UN's efforts to develop positive internal political and social incentives to end the conflict, almost all UN representatives referred the author to the work of NGOs and the US embassy.

There are hundreds of NGOs and conflict resolution agencies operating in Cyprus on separate but similar agendas. However, track-two diplomacy has largely failed to shift the entrenched positions of the Greek and Turkish Cypriot publics.[46] Since the referendums, there have been some studies of, and much reflection on, how to target social development more effectively. The general conclusion, as illustrated in the following comment from a British diplomatic source, has been that efforts need to go beyond simple inter-communal dialogue. 'I think one of the lessons we learned was that you shouldn't always see it as enough to have Greek and Turkish Cypriots around the table talking about shared problems'.[47] In light of the clear failure of peacemaking, interested parties are considering broader strategies for the resolution of this conflict.

The 2004 referendum result has prompted internal reviews in a number of key UN bodies that deal with Cyprus, resulting in some changes in focus to their programmes. They have particularly emphasised strategies to strengthen Cypriot civil society.[48] In 2004, UNOPS undertook an independent evaluation review of several focus areas, including civil society and communication. As a result of the subsequent report, UNDP-ACT has sharpened its focus on social development, cultural heritage and preservation, communication and education, and civil society strengthening. In this way, the UN is clearly developing its capacity to improve by increments the environment within which political elites function. Insofar as UNDP-ACT serves to develop social and political conditions on the island, it functions as one prong within the overall UN strategy to encourage successful adoption of a solution to the conflict. However, over the last two years, the UN also seems to be passing on responsibilities for political and social development to the European Commission, downsizing its projects in Cyprus.

Entry to the EU as a lever on Cypriot elites[49]

The EU has been a catalyst in the most recent attempt to resolve the Cyprus conflict. It was in the unique position of being both outsider and insider to Cyprus: insider because of its position as the association into which Cyprus was to be admitted and outsider because while the EU may have been the catalyst for reunification, it was rather the incentive for accession offered by the association which was the primary motivating factor for change – the EU itself played a secondary role in facilitating this change. The Union was also the main vehicle through which Greece, Turkey, and the UK – the three states directly involved in, and affected by, the conflict – interacted with it.

Commentators differ over the level of EU involvement in the Cyprus conflict over time, but the EU's attitude clearly evolved from 'detached concern'[50] in post-war Cyprus to one of increased interest and involvement in solution attempts. Hutchence and Georgiades have argued that the EU was for a long time disengaged from the Cyprus conflict.[51] However, it eventually reacted to 'the implications of the increasing institutional linkage between the EC/EU and Cyprus'.[52] Demetriou[53] directly links the major conflict-shaping changes between 2001 and 2004 to EU involvement. Müftüler-Bac and Güney have articulated four main pathways of EU involvement in the Cyprus issue. The first is through the 1973 Association Agreement linking Cyprus to the association. The second is the leverage the

EU had over Britain and Greece as members, as well as the leverage these states then had as members over EU decision making. The third has been to influence the Cypriot groups directly by providing financial aid packages and trade incentives. The fourth is, of course, through Cyprus' accession to the EU.[54] The general trend is to illustrate the relationship as one which has moved from detached concern to deep institutional involvement at multiple levels.

The EC/EU had tried quite early to implement its broad policy of 'even-handedness' regarding conflict groups within (or potentially within) its borders by facilitating a 'gentleman's agreement' on the subject of Cyprus. Among other things, this agreement accommodated 'the continuation of North Cyprus exports to the UK and Ireland'.[55] However, after 1974, the European Community ran into a number of problems with the implementation of this policy. Greek accession to the association in 1981 terminated Turkish Cypriot exports to those Community countries receiving them. Article Five of the *Cyprus Association Agreement* protecting the Turkish Cypriot economy was overruled in the European Court of Justice (ECJ) when, on 5 July 1994, the court banned the export of citrus fruit and potatoes from the TRNC to European states on the grounds that such produce had to be certified by the authorities of the Republic of Cyprus. Because that produce originated from Greek Cypriot property, the ECJ decision also had the flow-on effect of reinforcing the Greek Cypriot claim to the restitution of property rights in the TRNC. The ECJ decision took another supporting pillar from the Turkish Cypriot economy, which was already sinking under international non-recognition, sanctioned by the UN.

As a result of these and other decisions, the EU came to be seen as a significant factor in resolution efforts, with the power to alter the incentives to the parties. The EC/EU became increasingly involved in the Cyprus conflict, but its endorsement of UN resolutions regarding Republic of Cyprus sovereignty and the EC/EU's reluctance to support the *post-bellum status quo* being sought by Turkish and Turkish Cypriot governing elites meant that the EU necessarily aligned itself with the Greek Cypriot case. The EC's response to the TRNC's proclamation in 1983 is a clear example of its position:

> The ten Member States of the European Community are deeply concerned by the declaration purporting to establish a 'Turkish Republic of Northern Cyprus' as an independent State. They reject this declaration which is in disregard of successive resolutions of the United Nations. The Ten reiterate their unconditional support for the independence, sovereignty, territorial integrity and unity of the Republic of Cyprus. They continue to regard the Government of President Kyprianou as the sole legitimate Government of the Republic of Cyprus. They call upon all interested parties not to recognise this act, which creates a very serious situation in the area.[56]

In refusing to endorse the Republic's decision to apply for membership, the Turkish Cypriot leadership also refused to ally itself with the Republic's negotiating team. Correspondingly, the Turkish Cypriot community's exclusion from EU accession negotiations and preparation were to some extent beyond the EU's control as its (and Greek Cypriot) efforts to include Turkish Cypriots in the Republic of Cyprus negotiating team were made during the period of extended Turkish and Turkish Cypriot intransigence. One year after the failure of the 1992 Ghali Set of Ideas, the EC released an opinion on Cyprus which revealed a more detailed consideration of Cypriot accession in the light of the country's continued division.[57] By mid-1995, the EU had agreed to begin accession negotiations with Cyprus.[58] Subsequently, the subject of Cyprus' accession necessarily became entwined with the conflict. In the period 1994–9, the Cyprus conflict was continuously deadlocked. International perception placed primary blame for the deadlock with the Turkish and Turkish Cypriot sides, and thus progressed negotiations with the Republic of Cyprus in hope that this would create a material incentive for Turkish political compromise. The UN, particularly, recognised that the greatest resource the EU had for resolution of the Cyprus conflict was its ability to control the entry of new members.[59] Thus, the reopening of negotiations in 2002 was a direct result of Cyprus' impending accession.[60] The submission of Annan II on 10 December 2002 was purposefully designed by the UN to coincide with the European Council meeting in Copenhagen on 11–12 December 2002.[61] EU incentives were therefore becoming increasingly intertwined with UN efforts at resolution.

Until this point, two strategies were available to the EU: it could either withhold Cypriot membership until the conflict was resolved, or proceed with accession without the conflict's prior solution. Under the first scenario, significant pressure to compromise would have been placed predominantly on the Greek Cypriots, since it was they who sought accession. Under the second scenario, pressure would be placed on the Turkish government, which would not be able to advance its own EU accession course without supporting a solution in Cyprus. As it was, in 2002 the second option was chosen by the European Council. At the 2002 Copenhagen meeting, the EU announced that 'in the absence of a settlement, the application of the *acquis*[62] to the northern part of the island shall be suspended, until the Council decides unanimously otherwise, on the basis of a proposal by the Commission'.[63]

There is some evidence to suggest that the EU tried to use its 2002 Copenhagen decision as a means of supporting UN efforts, which were gearing up at the time. The conclusions of the Seville European Council meeting in June 2002 reaffirmed EU support for UN efforts by calling 'upon the leaders of the Greek Cypriot and Turkish Cypriot communities to intensify and expedite their talks in order to seize this unique window of opportunity for a comprehensive settlement, consistent with the relevant UN Security Council Resolutions'.[64]

With the conciliatory Clerides in power in south Cyprus, the EU and UN assumed that Greek Cypriot support of the Annan Plan was assured, and therefore turned their attention to exerting maximum pressure on Turkey and the Turkish Cypriot community. In this regard, the strategy worked especially well. The role of the EU as catalyst for change in Turkish, and Turkish Cypriot, politics has been acknowledged by Turkish Cypriot leader Mehmet Ali Talat:

> The remarkable success of the Justice and Development Party (AKP) in the November 2002 parliamentary elections held in Turkey and, more importantly, the defeat of the pro-status quo parties in the TRNC with the coming to power of pro-European forces in the December 2003 general elections, contributed to the beginning of a new era where concerted policies by the Turkish Cypriot leadership and the Turkish government have been decisively shaped by a vision of European Union membership.[65]

In other words, the concept of the EU and the perceived benefits of membership were primary motivators for positive political change in both north and south Cyprus, though each at different periods.

The EU's 2002 Copenhagen decision has been seen in retrospect by both UN and EU actors as giving the Greek Cypriots too much carrot and not enough stick.[66] Nevertheless, the period preceding the Republic of Cyprus' entry to the EU has been identified as the most opportune for possible reunification by a senior UN official, who observed that 'all the factors came together here in favour of a resolution. I doubt that we will be able to mobilise such a high level of international co-operation again'.[67] This position was echoed by the former EU Co-ordination Commissioner for Cyprus, Takis Hadjidemetriou, in an interview after the failed attempt at reunification: 'If I have to make an assessment, the day of the solution of the Cyprus problem was April 24 [2004]. It was the time the international conditions were suitable to support a solution, that there was a great change in the position of Cyprus in joining the EU ... [we were in a period of] rapprochement between Greece and Turkey, and the EU was willing to [work with the] UN to solve the problem'.[68] Those factors and conditions were primarily the willingness of the US, UK, Turkey, and Greece to provide incentives to the interlocutors, linked to EU accession, which were harnessed by the UN negotiating team.

As Tocci and Kovziridze have outlined, the EU through its catalytic effect played a vital, if passive, role in conflict transformation in Cyprus.[69] In Greece, the PASOK[70] government strongly supported the Secretary General's attempts at peacemaking, which culminated in its emphatic backing of the 2002 Annan Plan, as well as supporting the integration of Turkey into the EU. Greece planned Greek Cypriot accession to the EU as a means of lessening tension between itself and Turkey, and of strengthening the hand of the

Greek Cypriot negotiators, relieving the Greeks of much pressure to protect and strategise for the Greek Cypriots. In Cyprus, President Clerides' position on the conflict softened considerably, as a direct result of the increased certainty of EU membership.[71] The EU also impelled position changes in the Turkish side. The Turkish Cypriot public used the EU as an incentive to push for change within the TRNC, while the AKP's[72] rise to power on the back of EU ambitions in Turkey moderated the Turkish position and produced support for change within north Cyprus.[73] Turkey offered support to pro-reunification elites in the north as a *quid pro quo* for progress on its own accession negotiations with the EU, and as part of broader rapprochement efforts with Greece.

Britain's policy on Cyprus' accession was coloured by its conception of the EU as chiefly an arena of free trade between member states. For Britain, Cyprus' accession was therefore something to be carefully managed so as not to disrupt the expansion process, which was viewed to be of critical importance. In the words of David Hannay, 'the enlargement of the EU ... was a major objective of British foreign policy and must in no way be delayed or damaged by developments over Cyprus'.[74] However, this also means that these important differences between EU members and other states involved in the Cyprus conflict significantly limited the EU's ability to provide a clear and effective strategy to tie resolution of the Cyprus conflict with its EU accession path.

In preparing parties on the ground to accept the solution, the US and UK played a secondary role through their various subsidiaries in Cyprus. How the benefits of both reunification and EU membership were highlighted by organisations such as the British Council, the British High Commission, and the US Embassy will be discussed in the next section. But primarily through the efforts of British Special Representative for Cyprus, David Hannay, Britain was also influential in guiding EU policy on Cyprus as well as providing strategic advice to the engineers.[75] In addition, the US offered considerable resource and financial support in the event of a resolution. Hannay highlighted the importance of co-ordinated international support in improving the likelihood of the Annan Plan's adoption:

> If the United States was not fully on board, there would be no movement in Ankara; if the EU was not supportive, the Greek Cypriots were likely to focus exclusively on completing their accession negotiations before a settlement and there was also the risk of mismatch between the terms of a Cyprus settlement and those agreed for Cyprus to join the EU; if the Russians were not at least acquiescent there would be trouble every time the matter came back to the Security Council.[76]

When the EC took its 2002 Copenhagen decision to suspend the *acquis* in north Cyprus, the message was clear: north Cyprus would only enjoy the benefits of EU membership if it accepted the Annan Plan. With this assurance, Republic of Cyprus negotiators strengthened their position against the Turkish Cypriot negotiators, as the promise of EU membership without penalty removed any perceived incentive to make further significant unsavoury and unpopular compromises. This perception of strength was directed by a popular belief among sections of the public, driven by political (nongovernmental) elites that the European *acquis communautaire* held the key to the regaining of lost territories and rights.

To some extent, the support of the Greek Cypriot public for EU membership was also driven by a simplistic perception of the EU's ability to offer Cyprus security. 'Security' largely meant the protection of the EU against the Turkish army and the knowledge that a Turkish attack on an EU country would be unlikely. For Greek Cypriot elites, EU membership would protect the status of the Republic of Cyprus as the only source of sovereignty on the island, as well as providing the Greek Cypriots with another avenue for pursuing 'justice'.[77] It would also 'increase Greek Cypriot leverage on Turkey both because of an expected rise in EU pressure on Turkey and because of Turkey's own aspirations to join the Union'.[78] EU membership was perceived in the south to be a material negotiating advantage. Therefore, while Greek Cypriot negotiators spoke of the period leading up to accession as offering a 'window of opportunity' for reunification, there was simultaneously also very strong support within society for the idea that reunification on advantageous terms would be more readily gained *after* accession.[79]

Thus, not making Republic of Cyprus membership conditional upon resolution of the conflict created unequal incentives for the Cypriot parties, undermining the EU's value as a lever for the country's reunification. The decision provided motivation for resolution in the north, while prompting celebration in south Cyprus, which was no longer dependent for EU entry upon Turkish Cypriot agreement to resolve the conflict.

Failure of the EU's strategy

The EU's strategy to use accession to catalyse the Annan Plan's acceptance in both north and south Cyprus failed when in April 2004 the Greek Cypriot community voted to enter the EU without having solved the conflict. The failure can be reduced to a flawed premise: that the Greek Cypriots would accept a second-best outcome. The removal of pressure on the Greek Cypriot community, and the physical, legal, and psychological safety gained by EU membership had a two-fold effect. It has been argued that this safety freed Clerides, allowing him to make further negotiating concessions during the Annan process and to accept a solution that he might otherwise not have.[80] However, it also exposed him to a subtle domestic backlash, which resulted in his being sidelined in the 2003 elections. The EU's decision to admit Cyprus created friction within the ruling DISY party in the last years of Clerides' presidency between party members who supported Clerides' goal of bringing reunification through compromise at the negotiation table and those who believed that reunification before accession would necessarily squander Greek Cypriot advantages gained by the 1999 EC decision.[81] Domestic political pressure upon Clerides from both within and outside his party during the development of Annan I and II also played a considerable role in neutralising his ability to clearly and openly present reasons for developments and changes between plans to a confused and cautious public. Without the clear and unambiguous support of the major Greek Cypriot parties, Clerides' public responses to the plan were muted and conservative.[82] He, and the political parties surrounding him, reinforced the sense that there was still a long way to go before a solution could be reached. This may have galvanised the development of public confusion into a quiet intransigence. Ultimately, their approach allowed Greek Cypriot hawks to convince a majority of the populace at the 2004 referendum that their interests would be better served by a resolution after EU accession and may well have affected the EU's capacity to persuade the Greek Cypriots to support a solution to the conflict prior to accession.

Then-UN Special Representative to Cyprus, Alvaro de Soto, noted that '[perhaps] the reason Clerides was thrown out was that people sensed that he might be preparing to compromise and Papadopoulos didn't want to compromise'.[83] The removal of any penalty on their accession course consequently unchained Greek Cypriot nationalist elites in 2004, after the election of hard-line nationalist Tassos Papadopoulos, to spread a range of public misperceptions and fears about the consequences of reunification under the Annan Plan.

At the time, the EU was also trapped by internal divisions in the form of the divergent interests of member states, affecting its structural capacity to offer a coherent policy towards how best to approach Cyprus' accession. The accession of new states into the EU requires a consensus among all current member states, and the scope of countries acceding to the EU in 2004 had expanded to include a large number of member states whose timely accession was important to various EU member states. This enhanced Greece's power to push for Cyprus' accession, a power it had flexed on a number of occasions with reasonable success. Greece was very clear from the beginning that it would use its veto power to halt the accession of all ten acceding countries in the case that Cyprus' accession was rejected.[84]

In addition to Britain and Greece using their leverage to influence the process, there was also significant discord between member states regarding the accession of a divided polity. Many European countries, particularly France, Germany, the Netherlands, and Italy, opposed the accession of Cyprus while the conflict continued.[85] In a joint declaration at the EU General Affairs Council of 9 November 1998, they noted that

> it has not been possible to make any progress to date with regard to a political solution to the continuing division of Cyprus. The further negotiating progress will therefore also give rise to a number of problems that originate in the special situation of Cyprus. The Member States France, Germany, Italy and the Netherlands therefore consider that political solution is urgently needed as only this can ensure that these problems are resolved.[86]

This incurred a lengthy response from Greece, reminding the member states that any impediments to a solution of the conflict were due to Turkish intransigence, and that 'the actions of the European Union and its Member States must be in line with the decisions that have been taken and in no way enable third countries to stand in the way of the right of any European country fulfilling the necessary criteria to accede to the Union'.[87]

Mehmet Ali Talat has argued that 'the EU's structural inability to carry out the strategy identified at the supranational level (European Commission) to the intergovernmental level (European Council) played a pivotal role in changing the established political balance between the two sides in Cyprus'.[88] The lack of a coherent strategy on the part of the EU towards Cyprus' accession, and towards resolution of the conflict, therefore caused significant damage to prospects of resolution. At the very least, a coherent internal strategy by the EU would have facilitated a greater degree of co-operation with the UN, and may have sured-up the EU's power to transform the conflict.

The EU did, for example, have the chance to use its leverage to control the conditions of accession, so that its strategy to use Cypriot accession to ensure support of the reunification plan would not backfire once the accession matter had been decided.[89] In the December 2002 European Council meeting in Copenhagen, there was a small window of opportunity to push for the Annan Plan's acceptance:

> Turkey was asking to be pushed about the Annan Plan, and Clerides was ready to accept it. And had the EU pushed Turkey in Copenhagen, that was in December 2002, to accept it, the AK government, Erdoğan, needed the push because [Erdoğan] wasn't yet firmly enough in the saddle, he wasn't even prime minister yet, he needed to be able to come home and tell Sezer, the president, and others, 'I had to accept this plan because otherwise I wouldn't have gotten my date'. But no one pushed him, no one cared about Cyprus there. So that opportunity was lost, Clerides lost the elections, and then everything went down the drain.[90]

The failure to take up the December 2002 opportunity to pressure Turkish government elites for speedy acceptance of Annan II was a significant tactical mistake on the part of the EU. Annan III was submitted to the sides in February 2003, and in March at The Hague, negotiations on the plan again failed when Denktaş refused to submit the plan to a referendum. With that failure, the Greek Cypriot side was considered by the EU to have exhibited sufficient goodwill for resolution, and its accession path was almost complete. On 16 April 2003 the Republic of Cyprus signed the EU accession treaty, and any leverage the EU had to ensure Greek Cypriot elites continued to support the Annan Plan was removed.

At least one member of the UN core negotiating team revealed prior awareness that the EU's strategy to use Cypriot accession to ensure support of the reunification plan might backfire once the accession matter had been decided.[91] Towards the end of The Hague meeting in March 2003, it was suggested that the Annan Plan be tied to Cyprus' accession treaty. The idea was that Cyprus would be admitted to the EU on the basis of the Annan Plan. It seemed likely that Denktaş would not accept the plan, but an impending Turkish Cypriot parliamentary election in late 2003 indicated good chances that pro-reunification parties would ascend to power and be willing to endorse reunification on the basis of the plan. The Greek Cypriots, having already expressed support for the plan, would have already signed the EU accession treaty. Inserting the plan into Cyprus' accession treaty would have ensured Greek Cypriot support for the plan (they would not have had a choice), and formal acceptance of the plan by Turkish Cypriot elites would have been all that remained to be done. Thereafter, the Annan Plan would have been adopted and presumably Cyprus would have acceded to the EU united. This idea was not seriously pursued in liaison by the UN and the EU, and, as has been shown, Greek Cypriot incentives to accept the Annan Plan were dulled upon the guarantee of accession to the EU.

While other recently acceding countries went through quite a profound debate on what EU membership means in practice, this debate was lacking in south Cyprus. Because EU membership had been conceptualised as a primarily political objective, there was very little prior-accession discussion of the EU as an institution and its multiple functions and purposes. As a result, there is considerable post-accession discontent regarding the reality of living as an EU member state, and with no foreseeable compensation in the form of resolution of the conflict.

By contrast, both the concept of the EU, and the Union itself played a very different role in the perception of the conflict in the north prior to accession. In north Cyprus, the EU's influence was actively used to *develop* incentives for resolution and used by progressive Turkish Cypriot parties to craft their political strategy. The benefits of both reunification and EU membership were heavily promoted by organisations such as the British Council, the British High Commission, and the US Embassy, as subsidiary organisations of two states significantly interested in negotiations for the conflict's resolution. As such, the EU was particularly used by the British as a lever to encourage debate and political development in Turkish Cypriot society;

> [w]e decided that the best way to move forward the debate in Cyprus was to give people a better factual understanding of the EU. Together with the British Council we ran a very successful series of seminars and in particular trained on the EU ... we ran seminars on the history of EU institutions and how they work.[92]

The UBP-DP political leadership was targeted for the first of these seminars run in 2001. Mehmet Ali Talat, who was then leader of the largest opposition party, and a number of trade union representatives also attended the initial seminar. However, Denktaş soon barred government officials from attending, and as a result, Talat and the opposition of the time (today's current Turkish Cypriot government) took advantage of the seminars and training sessions to shape their vision of moving north Cyprus away from the Denktaş status quo.

> I think the fact that we were able to give these people a very clear understanding of what the EU actually was – not British propaganda, but it was probably quite seductive that it was conducted by a German – this helped quite a lot in giving a broad group of people a shared desire to be in Europe. And realise also that the only way into Europe was through a settlement. And I think, you know, it did help build a momentum which the opposition then used to their advantage to win the elections last year. So I think that is what we did in the north.[93]

The hope – but not promise – of EU accession successfully created an incentive for Turkish Cypriot public and elite support of the Annan Plan, and thus reunification. However, the guarantee of EU membership to south Cyprus gave considerable power to Greek Cypriot elites who, as will be shown in Chapter 7, convinced the Greek Cypriot public that they would receive a 'better deal' after the Republic of Cyprus became an EU member. Ultimately, the Republic of Cyprus' guaranteed EU membership created opposite effects in north and south Cyprus, which undermined the EU's value as a lever for the country's reunification. Uncoordinated and poorly planned engagement with the conflict on the part of the EU gave the protagonists the opportunity to use the Union to continue the dispute.

EU influence post-accession

Perhaps the post-accession, post-Annan period may provide the necessary balance of international pressures and capacities heretofore absent in the dynamics of the Cyprus conflict. If the UN's expertise is in high-level peacemaking and constitutional design, then the EU's ability over time to use its institutional influence over member states could facilitate the development of social, economic, and political factors which have inhibited progress to date. Further, if the suggested favourable factors are to be taken as important to the adoption of a political settlement, then the EU may be able, through its greater capacity to shape social conditions, to cultivate the required factors or conditions.

In the period leading up to Cyprus' accession, the EU was viewed as the body which could attend to the most important needs of each community. Very different views of the EU consequently developed in each community. In south Cyprus, accession to the EU was viewed as bringing justice in the face of an immoral and illegal invasion and occupation. The underlying EU principles of 'rights' and 'justice' seen to be embodied in the *acquis communautaire* would, Greek Cypriots thought, now be applied to Cyprus to correct the 'injustices' inflicted upon them by Turkey.[94] In the pre-referendum period in north Cyprus, on the other hand, the EU came to represent Turkish Cypriots' rights to freedom of speech, democratic freedoms, and political pluralism. The EU principles of 'rights', 'justice', and 'democracy' were looked to as a means of transforming Turkish Cypriot domestic politics, erasing the arbitrary and perceived undemocratic nature of TRNC politics.

The post-accession status quo has consequently led to widespread disillusionment with the realities of EU membership (or not, as the case may be) in both north and south Cyprus. In the Turkish Cypriot community the popular expectation that 'Europe' would be able to change domestic political, economic, and social conditions, and primarily to lift the community's international isolation has led in the last four years to widespread disillusionment; one sometimes hears in conversation 'Avrupalı olduk' or 'we have become European', expressed cynically. Lack of progress towards resolution of the Cyprus conflict, as well as only very slow institutional, social, and economic improvement in both societies as a result of EU accession has affected both groups' perception of the EU's usefulness. In the south, the EU's inability to provide the 'justice' Greek Cypriots seek, and the perception that the EU has taken several important decisions in Turkey's favour, has also led to growing disenchantment with the EU.[95] The uneven application of EU regulations in north and south Cyprus is also creating more bitterness both between communities and towards the EU itself. In this regard, the EU is actually damaging prospects for resolution by alienating those who could benefit directly from reunification, and who have been peace's proponents.[96]

Post-accession, the EU has been simultaneously exercising its power at a number of levels in order to manage the conflict and perhaps inch the sides closer to resolution. At one level, within the domestic Cypriot environment the post-referendum, post-accession period has seen EU officials trying to reassure Greek Cypriots about security, thus trying to provide an impetus for resolution. At a conference in Nicosia in May 2005, a member of the European Commission responsible for enlargement offered the following to his Cypriot audience:

> The current situation offers real opportunities to launch a fresh momentum. First, Cyprus has become an EU member state – an achievement that ensures that neither inter-communal violence nor military intervention should occur again. Second, the European Council decided to open accession negotiations with Turkey. And third, the Turkish Cypriot community, as shown by the latest elections, seeks the reunification of the island and its integration into the EU.[97]

Attention should be paid to the emphasis on assuaging the twin Greek Cypriot fears of threats to their physical security and Turkish Cypriot secession.

At the negotiation end, the EU has tried to use promised ratification of proposals for direct trade with north Cyprus as an incentive for return of the town of Varosha to south Cyprus in order to encourage co-operation and compromise on both sides. This has been designed particularly to break the post-Annan deadlock where the sides have avoided incremental progress for fear of it harming their respective overall goals.[98] In 2006, it was reported that '[t]he north's official line since the failed referendum on the Annan Plan two years ago has been that big issues like Varosha can only be dealt with in the context of a comprehensive solution to the Cyprus problem. However, there was deviation from this line last year when Turkish Cypriot leader Mehmet Ali Talat was seen to give support to a proposal from Luxemburg's then-presidency of the EU to swap control of Varosha for direct trade with the EU'.[99] Two countries that have subsequently held the EU presidency have devised similar exchanges in the hope of encouraging progress. In 2006, the (then) Finnish presidency attempted to broker a deal in which direct trade via the Famagusta port's opening in the Turkish Cypriot state[100] would be exchanged for the return of the uninhabited town of Varosha to the Greek Cypriot state. In early 2007, the German presidency had attempted to facilitate a similar deal. However, in an interesting reflection regarding the limitations of EU high-level power, no progress was made in any of the above mentioned attempts.

The EU's strength may, however, lie in its ability to offer incentives for resolution by influencing conditions at the non-elite level, though even here its progress is not clear. Immediately after the referendum, the EU produced a number of regulations and proposals concerning the development of the Turkish Cypriot community. On 29 April 2004, the Green Line Regulation[101] was produced, governing the establishment of 'rules concerning the crossing of goods, services, and persons'.[102] In July that year, the Commission proposed a 'comprehensive package of aid and trade measures to put an end to the isolation of the Turkish Cypriot community and to facilitate the reunification of Cyprus'.[103] Of primary importance were two draft directives: the release of €259 million to focus on the Turkish Cypriot community's development and the endorsement of direct trade between the Turkish Cypriot community and EU member states, removing the need for Turkish Cypriot goods to exit Cyprus via the Republic of Cyprus' ports. While the volume of trade has steadily increased in the four years since the Regulation's establishment, it remains low, and various complications caused by EC bureaucracy have embittered (particularly Turkish) Cypriot traders. In addition, domestic pressure against intercommunal trade remains quite high.[104]

In early 2006, the Commission released a regulation[105] establishing the EU Programme Support Office (EUPSO), supervised by the Task Force [for the] Turkish Cypriot Community seeking to make good on its April 2004 Direct Trade and Financial Aid Regulation, by distributing the promised €259 million for infrastructural development in north Cyprus. Though the Turkish Cypriot community and political leadership expressed serious frustration at the sluggish pace of EU bureaucracy (almost four years passed between the Regulation's adoption and beginning of the first projects), the EU Task Force opened EUPSO in Lefkoşa in October 2006, paving the way for the execution of a number of projects which will develop infrastructure in the north over a six-year period. In January 2007, Head of EU Taskforce for the Turkish Cypriot Community Andrew Rasbash emphasised in a press conference that 'our duty is to lessen the isolations, to help the reunification of the island and support any settlement efforts'.[106]

It is possible that post-accession, the EU will be able to use its institutional influence to level the playing field, to create new incentives for elites to compromise, to engender trust at the elite level, or even at the public level, flowing upwards to elites. But in the five short years since Cyprus' accession, clear signs of such changes cannot be expected, and certainly have not been apparent. On the contrary, the EU's approach to facilitating the Cyprus conflict has arguably increased both intra- and inter-communal tension on the island. In addition, the concept of European values and standards are also being used at the elite political level to continue battling out the Cyprus conflict. The rhetoric of the conflict, long-fought debates over Turkish migrants changing the demographic of north Cyprus, the idea of full freedom of movement, and security guarantees are now cloaked in debates about European values and rights owing to European citizens. In this respect, the conflict has merely found a new language to reinforce old positions.

What is changing, however, is a broader – and shared – understanding of the long-term bureaucratic culture of the EU. NGOs in both communities are learning about European public culture; how to apply for grants by cultivating partnerships and finding mutual benefit, to wait for results, to be responsible and accountable for projects, and to present one's organisation in a more rigorous manner. But this may not be enough.

Conclusion

In the case where there are insufficient domestic incentives for elite co-operation, external actors can play a potentially important role bringing pressure to bear on elites and creating incentives for compromise. While the UN has a long history of involvement in the Cyprus conflict as author of the major plans for political settlement, the conflicting objectives of UN agencies and its restricted ability to place real pressure on elites to co-operate have limited the UN's effectiveness. Further, recognition of the Greek Cypriots as the Republic of Cyprus' sole representatives, though necessary, has limited the UN's leverage over the Greek Cypriot elite while at the same time, *realpolitik* has limited UN leverage over Turkey. Power politics in the broader Mediterranean region has constituted a third constraint on the UN. Lastly, the UN's peacekeeping presence in Cyprus has meant that circumstances never deteriorated to a stage which impelled Cypriot elites to find a solution.

The process of admitting Cyprus to the EU formed a window of opportunity for external actors to create incentives for elite co-operation. However, those incentives were not strong enough to impel both sides' elites to support the reunification plan. The EU's impact was limited by four important dynamics: the legal facts of the Republic of Cyprus' accession (that is, EU unwillingness to penalise the Greek Cypriot community for Turkish Cypriot intransigence, resulting in the possibility of the south's accession without the north); the particular interests of member states which also had a stake in the conflict; the Union's structural limitations; and poor timing and clumsy co-ordination between the UN and EU.

This chapter showed how the Turkish Cypriot side was offered entry to the EU on the condition of Cyprus' reunification. But the turn of events meant that the Greek Cypriot side was offered EU accession without the same preconditions, giving it the potential to enter the EU and then negotiate a solution to the conflict from a position of elevated power. The incentive of EU accession was designed to overcome a history of elite intransigence and lack of co-operation, but the incentive was misapplied and caused further division. As a result, in May 2004 the Republic of Cyprus acceded to the EU, bringing with it the enduring Cyprus conflict.

7
The Politics of Adopting Consociationalism: The Referendums of 2004

Quis custodiet ipsos custodies?[1]

This book has argued that the reluctance of political elites to overcome the division of Cyprus and adopt a power-sharing solution can be attributable to a number of factors. Of primary importance has been the oppressive and divisive role of historical memory and the clear desire of elites to fulfil what they perceive to be historical legacies. Heaped on top of that baggage has been the way the 1960 state broke down, subsequently interpreted by local elites as well as some international scholars as the fault of a flawed system, that of early corporate consociationalism. In 2004, the Annan Plan engineers tried to provide a system which would meet the most significant fears and demands of both communities, but by this time, these legacies of the past had created two societies in Cyprus that would have to overcome deep mutual mistrust and almost half a century of living apart. Labouring under different imaginings of the past and the future, the actual and perceived incentives for reunification under the conditions of a power-sharing state were vastly different for both the elites and public of each group. As a result, the plan was rejected by one group and accepted by the other.

This chapter therefore examines the 2004 referendum[2] as the formal gauge of elite and public conceptions of reunification. It examines the referendum's *raison d'être*, and why the UN's strategy for adoption unravelled. The chapter will also draw upon literature on referendums to understand the events of 2004. The referendum outcome will be explained and its consequences interpreted. This is important, because understanding the referendum, its results, and its place in the political and historical geography of the Cyprus conflict is central to being able to explain where we are today, and what elites will need to wholeheartedly endorse a power-sharing Cypriot state.

The UN strategy for adoption: A case of *quis custodiet ipsos custodies?*

On 24 April 2004 Greek and Turkish Cypriots were asked to vote yes or no to the question:

> Do you approve the Foundation Agreements with all its Annexes, as well as the constitution of the Greek Cypriot/Turkish Cypriot State and the provisions as to the laws to be in force, to bring into being a new state of affairs in which Cyprus joins the European Union united?[3]

To this question, 64.90 per cent of Turkish Cypriots voted 'yes', while 75.83 per cent of Greek Cypriots voted 'no'. Without the necessary majority from both states, this most recent attempt to end the Cyprus conflict failed, and the division continued. The Greek Cypriot Republic of Cyprus acceded to the EU the following week, and the Turkish Cypriot TRNC remained an unrecognised state, albeit with increased international sympathy.

The referendum, as a mechanism for adoption of a unification plan, was introduced to Cyprus in the 1992 Set of Ideas by then-Secretary-General Boutros Boutros Ghali. In the Set of Ideas it was outlined that 'the overall framework agreement will be submitted to the two communities in separate referendums within 30 days of its completion by the two leaders at a high-level international meeting'.[4] The idea of using a referendum to approve the settlement was consistently maintained throughout the subsequent proposals for Cyprus, and was automatically absorbed into the Annan process.[5]

However, its role in the process evolved over time. In Annan I, separate referendums were to have been the second stage in the plan's adoption, scheduled for March 2003. The signing of the 'Comprehensive Settlement of the Cyprus Problem' in December 2002 by the two Cypriot leaders, binding them to the Foundation Agreement's main articles, particular annexes, and to the map which would delineate the territory of the two component states was supposed to precede this stage. At the third stage, the two Cypriot leaders would sign a treaty with guarantor powers Turkey, Greece, and the UK on 'matters related to the new state of affairs in Cyprus' on behalf of the United Cyprus Republic.[6] By Annan III, these requisites were dropped, and 'consent to submit to referendum was considered sufficient'.[7] The popular referendum therefore became an increasingly important component of the UN's strategy for adoption of the new state.

The Cyprus referendum poses a paradox. If consociational democracy is a system which contains the role of the public, concentrating political power in the elites, then why choose a mechanism associated with direct democracy to adopt that system? The answer is that the referendum was a means of resolving several problems identified by the constitutional engineers. The most important problem was that of elite intransigence. The UN was getting signals that the Cypriot public wanted reunification, but were held back by intransigent elites unendingly negotiating backroom deals, with no popular input or involvement in the decision making process.[8] This is tied into a second, legal problem: Rauf Denktaş wanted to sign the plan's acceptance as the TRNC president, an idea unacceptable to the Greek Cypriots because it would mean recognition of the TRNC as a legitimate political entity. So to overcome this impasse, the UN team came up with the idea of the 'virgin birth'. 'If there were to be no referenda, who would sign the plan? ... The only people who could create a new state of affairs were the Cypriot people'.[9] Thus, the referendum eventually came to be the only mechanism of adoption. Third, there was a frequent complaint made by commentators, politicians, and diplomats that the 1960 Republic's failure was in large part due to its lack of popular and political support; in other words, few parties were emotionally or politically invested in the Republic's creation and therefore were not tied to its success.[10] Fourth, the reunification of Cyprus was a three-fold problem of adoption, implementation, and maintenance. The focus during negotiations was not only how the plan would be implemented and how it could survive, but more immediately, how to get the plan adopted. The referendum was identified as a tool which had the most potential to overcome all these problems.

The referendum was therefore clearly seen as a device to enable the people to guard the guardians. A set of mechanisms was designed specifically to avoid elite attempts to halt the engineering process by circumventing their domination. When negotiations for the reunification of Cyprus reopened in February 2004, UN Secretary-General Kofi Annan outlined a three-fold resolution process which included a number of failsafe mechanisms in the case of deadlock between Greek and Turkish Cypriot negotiators. In the case that the Cypriot interlocutors could not agree on a reunification package, the prime ministers of Greece and Turkey would step in to continue the negotiations; and if there was still no agreement, the Secretary-General would be authorised to 'fill in the gaps' in order to complete the plan. However arrived at, the completed plan would then be submitted for endorsement to the populations of both north and south Cyprus in the form of separate, simultaneous referendums. Hence, in order to check elite intransigence, and the distinct possibility that Cypriot elites[11] would refuse to sign final documents after coming to the end of the negotiating process, the role of elite agreement in the process was whittled down.

Therefore, when negotiations to improve the Annan Plan were resumed in February 2004, all that was required of the Cypriot interlocutors was that they agree to put the plan to separate simultaneous referendums. Both communities had been locked out of the negotiating process over the years by elites doing deals behind closed doors. As a result, 'going to referenda allowed people to voice what they really wanted. It empowered them'.[12] Gone was the need for the signing of treaties to carry the Republic of Cyprus forward into the United Cyprus Republic; gone also was the need for elites to agree to anything formally.

It had been quite constantly expressed by members of the UN negotiating team that the referendum was a vital part of the reunification process; a tool which would legitimise the peace process by encouraging debate and providing public endorsement. They believed that formally including the public in any final decision would promote a more balanced, broad debate within both societies as well as simultaneously binding the Cypriot people to the resolution. In February 2004, UN Special Advisor on Cyprus Alvaro de Soto stated that 'the referendum is not only significant, it is decisive, because ultimately it is the people – it is the Cypriots themselves – who are going to decide whether this settlement is going to come about. That is how important it is'.[13]

The idea of this type of referendum addresses one of the important factors for successful consociational systems: public support of the political system. Lijphart has argued that 'approval by referendum can provide the necessary democratic legitimacy for a newly drafted constitution'.[14] McGarry and O'Leary have also noted the importance public support plays on the success of power-sharing plans.[15] For the architects of the plan, the legitimacy conveyed by a successful referendum was a key advantage of the idea.[16]

Public endorsement of the reunification plan by referendum was therefore a core part of the UN's strategy to overcome elite intransigence and defuse the powerful memories of 1960 where neither elites nor the public felt loyalty to the constitution or the state it created. Chapters 4 and 5 have shown that history and memory have played important roles in both the plan's development and its subsequent rejection by elites. Addressing the fears of history added value to the referendum as an adoption mechanism.

The UN engineers were both mindful of, and agreed with, the frequently repeated criticism that the original 1960 constitution suffered from a lack of public support and public ownership.[17] They were not alone. Almost all of the Cypriot politicians interviewed by the author listed the lack of support among elites for the 1960 constitution as a major cause of the Republic's downfall. The following comments are illustrative of the degree to which the Cypriot political class recognises the role of political support in determining the success or failure of the state: 'in my opinion the main cause [of the state's breakdown] was the fact that the ruling class of the Turkish Cypriot and Greek Cypriot community did not believe in the 1960 constitution in the first place';[18] 'the enosis and taksim campaigns took us to the 1960 state, which was everyone's second-best option. The politicians of the time were not dedicated to the success of the state; they were emotionally tied to other goals';[19] and 'in 1960, our fathers and our grandfathers were illiterate people, with no political experience. They made a lot of mistakes because of that lack of experience'.[20]

The question of using a referendum as a mechanism to register public endorsement in 1960 was apparently discussed by the parties at the time, who, for various reasons, decided against it. Interestingly though, a second, internal, decision was taken by the Greek Cypriot leadership to avoid calling a referendum because public endorsement would have made overthrowing the constitution more difficult. This was later expressed in the text of the *Akritas Plan*.[21] A perception was thus manufactured that the Greek Cypriots 'had strong feelings against the agreements and that they resented their existence, because [the agreements] barred the way to self-determination-Enosis, because they gave excessive rights to a minority ... and above all because they believed that the unfair agreements were not the result of free negotiations, but had been imposed on Makarios'.[22]

It was therefore hoped in 2004 that public loyalty to the new state would become a further incentive for elite co-operation. 'The idea [in Annan] was to promote a new state which [the public] actively created ... its purpose was to have the people of Cyprus create a new state of affairs. The referenda could help ownership',[23] a factor missing in 1960. This was considered to be a secondary benefit of the referendum mechanism; in a negotiating process which by and large excluded the public at every stage, the referendum was a useful means of provoking both public discussion and ultimately guaranteeing popular involvement in at least one stage of the process.[24]

On a more practical and immediately pressing level, the referendum was also designed to overcome certain long-standing intercommunal disputes over sovereignty and recognition. One of the plan's major hurdles was how to overcome the ideological divide between Greek and Turkish Cypriot elites. Denktaş insisted that he would sign any agreement as the president of the TRNC; the Greek Cypriots consistently refused to acknowledge the breakaway state. If Denktaş signed as president of the TRNC, the Greek Cypriot leader would not sign the agreement. But if he could not sign as president of the state, Denktaş would not sign the agreement. It also became increasingly unlikely that Denktaş would formally endorse the agreement at all. The solution was to create a referendum which leapfrogged the need for endorsement by elites. So the need for formal elite endorsement of the plan was removed by the final Annan Plan, and 'consent to submit to referenda was considered sufficient'.[25] Full responsibility for acceptance was therefore turned over to the Greek and Turkish Cypriot public. However, the responsibility was interpreted differently by each community.

Politics of referendums

As Annan's architects recognised, referendums contain significant potential to circumvent elite intransigence, by promoting the public's role in decision making. Late nineteenth-and early twentieth-century legal and political theorist A. V. Dicey wrote extensively on the strengths and weaknesses of the referendum as a political tool.[26] The referendum was valuable in representative liberal democracies for Dicey primarily because it 'may give a new freedom to all persons who take part in public life ... [and deliver voters] from bondage to the despotism of party spirit'.[27] Indeed, he envisioned the referendum as a solution to the age-old problem of *quis custodiet ipsos custodies*.

More interesting to the case of deeply divided societies were the ideas of Dicey's colleague Nathan Cree. Cree was an early American advocate of direct democracy, who promoted the idea that the referendum's value lies in its ability to

> break the crushing and stifling power of our great party machines, and give freer play to the political ideas, aspirations, opinions and feelings of the people. It will tend to relieve us from the dominance of partisan passions, and have an elevating and educative influence upon voters.[28]

The ideas expressed by Cree hold significance for societies like Cyprus, where voters have become entirely disempowered by elites who have built careers (and often livelihoods) on their involvement in the conflict. By inviting voters into the realm of decision making, elite monopolisation of political rhetoric might be dislodged. In becoming decision makers, people would be forced to examine and articulate their own 'ideas, aspirations [and] opinions'. Reflecting Dicey's idea of the referendum as democratically edifying, and Cree's observation that the referendum might serve to break party dominance, the referendum in Cyprus was constructed as a mechanism to empower an otherwise un/under-represented populace in the decision-making process by circumventing what was seen to be the problem of Rauf Denktaş' non-representation of his constituency.

These ideas are reflected in the modern work of referendum theorists like Ackerman, who argues that empowering citizens at critical periods of political change will promote responsible and measured behaviour: 'apathy will give way to concern, ignorance to information, selfishness to serious reflection on the country's future'.[29] Peacemakers and legislators clearly see value in using referendums to legitimise the establishment, or termination of states and state-boundaries. For He, popular endorsement is valuable because 'boundaries based on and legitimated by referenda secure a stable settlement and secure the long-term stability of these boundaries'.[30] He has counted '173 boundary-related referenda in the period 1791–1998'.[31] The third wave of democratisation has seen increasing use of referendums to lend democratic legitimacy to (re)unifying, seceding, and democratising states. Increasingly, it seems that without a referendum, decisions on changing a people's status in these ways can only be considered *partially* democratic.

The referendum has therefore become important to the process of democratic legitimatisation; more particularly, it has become central to the *image* of democratic legitimacy. For Butler and Ranney:

> In a system based on the principles of popular sovereignty, political equality, popular consultation, and majority rule, direct popular decisions made by referendums have a legitimacy that indirect decisions by elected representatives cannot match ... [this means] when a representative democracy wishes a particular decision to be made with maximum legitimacy, it would do well to make that decision by referendum.[32]

Major political decisions that are not endorsed by direct public approval carry less political weight than those which are. In this regard, referendums are particularly useful to legitimise or guide major political decisions in fractured societies, in which further polarisation is a constant threat.

While there is a considerable body of literature on the ability of referendums to infuse direct democracy into liberal representative systems, there has not been a similar development of work on the role of the referendum as a tool to legitimise political change in fractured societies. Yet such referendums are becoming increasingly popular, because, as Jakobsson-Hatay observes, they have

> come to play an increasingly important role in contemporary peace processes. The predominance of intrastate conflicts in the post-Cold War era has brought decisions pertaining to war and peace onto the domestic political arena. More often than not, conflict resolution ... is a matter of the parties agreeing to changing the rules of the game for their future relations: constitutional changes or amendments, or even the adoption of entirely new constitutions. Decisions of such magnitude and importance therefore call for direct involvement of 'the people.[33]

Referendums have been used widely in recent peacemaking endeavours. In Sri Lanka in 2003, civil society petitioned the government to hold a referendum to measure public support for government policy on the peace process. In South Africa in 1992, F. W. de Klerk held a referendum to give him authority to continue negotiations to end apartheid.[34] In Northern Ireland, the referendum was used as one step in the ratification of a completed peace agreement. The 1998 Belfast Agreement was approved by twin referendums in Northern Ireland and the Republic of Ireland, and formed part of a 'triple lock mechanism: first by the *political parties*, who negotiated the agreement, then by the *people* who voted in the referenda and finally by the respective *parliaments*'.[35] In Israel, Ariel Sharon held a referendum within the Likud party in 2004 to ascertain the level of endorsement of his withdrawal from the Gaza strip. On 21 May

2006 Montenegro held a referendum to decide whether to declare independence from Serbia.

But there are significant and recognised difficulties in securing a positive outcome in referendums. In societies which do not regularly use direct democracy, the referendum is a novelty about which there is often uncertainty. And, as shown in countries like Australia, the public can be conservative when asked to endorse change. Any formal change to the Australian constitution must be approved by a double majority.[36] Since 1901, only eight matters have been approved in 44 referendums. If the question is viewed as threatening or is of such profound importance as was the situation in Cyprus, 'the problem may be so complicated as to be ill-suited to a simple and satisfying "Yes" or "No" vote. The temptation, therefore, is to "play safe" and "let things be"'.[37]

Referendums may also increase tension – dangerous in already fractured polities. Butler and Ranney have argued that 'referendums by their very nature set up confrontations rather than encourage compromises'.[38] Brady and Kaplan argue that '[t]he flower, some might say weed, of nationalism grows more robustly in the referendum garden than the flower of governmental reform'.[39] Barry reasoned that collective decision making by popular vote is in fact antithetical to the spirit of consociationalism. Consociationalism depends on a group of people 'who either trust one another or do not need to because they can apply sanctions against defaulters'.[40] It necessarily involves a small number of decision makers, who are continually involved in the decision-making process, and who are authorised to make deals. This creates a culture of negotiation, concession, and reciprocal bargaining. Popular voting is the opposite of such a culture – effectively undercutting its formation.

Chambers has used Quebec's struggle for independence from Canada to highlight the way referendums can damage, rather than aid the resolution of, an issue. Her example has significant parallels with the 2004 Cypriot experience. She notes that the 1995 Quebecoise referendum campaign caused significant damage to the already fragile relationships between Anglophones and Francophones. She claims that there were few efforts to engage voters in deliberation, except during the referendum campaign, which was waged as a fierce zero-sum battle. She particularly notes, 'there was no attempt to respond to or answer minority fears about what would happen on the "Day After"'.[41] As with Cyprus, the referendum debate in Canada had the opposite effect to that which was intended: 'it moved participants further apart, heightened distrust, exacerbated misunderstanding, and left Canadians in a worse place than when they started'.[42] More concerning, perhaps, she argues that voting damages an issue irreparably because it signals closure: 'voting means taking a decision that is more or less final'.[43] Likening the referendum battle to a 'peaceful civil war', she points out that 'like civil wars they leave scars as reminders of what people will do and say when they perceive that they are involved in an all or nothing battle'.[44]

Referendum theory, both early and modern, goes some way to explain the outcome of the Cyprus referendums. In the first instance, Dicey's categorisation of the referendum as democratically edifying resonates with the intention of Annan's engineers to use the referendums to motivate the stalled discussion of the conflict in Cyprus. Formally including the public in any final decision, they believed, would promote a more balanced and intensive broad debate within both societies, as well as simultaneously linking the Cypriot people to the resolution. Cree's observation that the referendum can be used to break the power of dominant elites is useful in examining why UN engineers chose the referendum as the only formal mechanism for adoption of the consociational solution. But assisting explanation of the referendum's failure, more recent work shows that referendums can harm the resolution of difficult conflicts.

There is substantial literature to prove the influential role of elite accord on media and public opinion, particularly regarding important issues.[45] Zaller has argued that if there is elite and expert consensus on an issue, a significant portion of the media will reflect that consensus.[46] The public also tends to absorb the opinions of those elites with whom they share an ideological sympathy. But, if there is no elite and expert consensus on which the media and public can draw, then 'journalists will publicize the disagreement, often in starkly ideological terms that invoke images of good and evil ... the result will be a polarization of the general public along lines that mirror the elite ideological conflict, with the most attentive members of the public most ideologically polarized'.[47] This is called the 'polarization effect'.

A high level of political awareness in the public can enhance both the polarisation effect and elector dependence upon elites. A number of studies[48] have shown that the 'greater a person's level of political awareness, the greater the number of mainstream messages the person would internalize in the form of considerations and hence, all else equal, the greater the person's level of expressed support for the mainstream policy'.[49] Informed electors are more sensitive to cueing messages from elites and the media and to aligning themselves with those messages. The polarisation effect may also contribute to understanding the referendum results in south Cyprus.

A strategy unravelled

The UN failed in its attempt to use the referendum as the key mechanism for overcoming elite intransigence and public disengagement from the plan. Heavy reliance on the referendum meant that extraordinary pressure was placed on the Cypriot public. While the Turkish Cypriot community viewed the situation as a welcome and liberating opportunity, the Greek Cypriot community exhibited signs of unparalleled tension.

Causes of the referendum's failure

Party politics

North and south Cyprus provide contrasting case studies, where the same issues triggered divergent responses to explain the plan's ultimate rejection. Evidently, Cree's conception of the referendum as giving 'freer play to the political ideas, aspirations, opinions and feelings of the people' are pertinent in the Turkish Cypriot case. On the Turkish Cypriot side, EU accession, the TRNC's plummeting internal legitimacy, and the plan's protection of Turkish Cypriot rights were the main factors which drove the plan's acceptance.

As Chapter 5 has argued, the Turkish Cypriot community is credited with using the reunification proposal to overthrow the status quo, and elect pro-reconciliation CTP. In 2000, a number of Turkish Cypriot trade unions gathered in opposition to a Turkish economic aid package. From demonstrations against Turkish fiscal dominance and Turkish Cypriot government corruption, the movement gathered steam and developed their 'This Country is Ours' platform, organising a number of demonstrations and strikes to demand greater democratic and economic rights and supporting a European solution for Cyprus. When Annan I was first presented in November 2002, the process evolved, 'nearly every month until last February [2004] we had a general strike. Every month sixty thousand, sometimes eighty thousand people came together to demonstrate for peace. That situation supported the Annan Plan'.[50] 'This Country is Ours' claims that the result of the December 2003 parliamentary election in north Cyprus, which brought the left-wing and traditionally pro-reunification CTP into a coalition government, was directly due to the platform's concentration of pressure for change.

Over the two years between Annan I and V, Turkish Cypriot society had bitterly debated the benefits and costs of acceptance and rejection of the plan. President of the Turkish Cypriot trade union DEV-İŞ, Ali Gulle, compared the situation on the two sides in an interview after the referendum:

> In the north we have struggled for the last three years to get peace and democracy in Cyprus. ... In that three year period, everyone in the north – the workers, the teachers, every group – they really analysed their position and the Annan Plan, so they really know what was in it. That's why they've accepted the plan, with 65 percent. In the south, they didn't discuss the Annan Plan well enough.[51]

In other words, the referendum springboard was fruitfully used; the process had left the elite field and become part of the public body. In the south, on the other hand, the public was clearly trepidatious about the kind of resolution being developed. The referendum outcome was deeply influenced by long-term party politics and the conflict's history.

In both communities, party identification has become a strong linking mechanism for electors' interpretation of the conflict. In general, parties play a 'paramount role in society, as nuclei of clientelist networks and because of their capacity to mobilise large groups'.[52] Parties have tended to form the base of very strong vertical networks in both Cypriot communities. Most of the major political parties are parent organisations to trade unions, youth, women's, and senior citizens' organisations. The relationship between an elector and their party is so important because, in membership of a party, one finds not only ideology but significant employment and social networks.[53] While party membership is not necessarily inherited, it does tend to be a lifelong affiliation.[54] Contemporary party politics in the Republic of Cyprus originated in the 1981 parliamentary elections – the first elections after Archbishop Makarios' death in 1977. Since then, the Republic has become a multi-party system with a very strong left-right cleavage, and ideology has tended to mould the relationship between parties and electors.[55]

Lupia and Johnston aptly summarise the referendum result in south Cyprus when they argue that referendums 'are a story of elites who seek simplicity by attempting to narrow fundamental political issues to a single question, and of voters who seek simplicity by attempting to determine what the question means'.[56]

In Cyprus, as in other states, the attraction of political power undermines party ideological barriers. AKEL's rejection of DISY's offer for a cross-ideology presidential coalition for the sake of successfully completing Cyprus' reunification signals that there were insufficient incentives for a number of Greek Cypriot elites to support the Annan Plan's adoption. For a party with the bi-communal credentials of AKEL to support the presidential candidacy of then-DIKO leader Tassos Papadopoulos at such a critical juncture of the Cyprus conflict highlights the difficulty of placing political principle over the attainment of power. AKEL's confused official response to the final Annan Plan showed its internal fractures. Before AKEL got a chance to publicly announce its executive committee's resolution to support the plan, Papadopoulos declared his deep opposition. Purportedly shocked, and unwilling to risk any coalition fracture which might result in their loss of power, the AKEL executive chose to reconcile the two positions. In the end, General Secretary Demetris Christofias recommended that AKEL supporters vote a 'soft no', in order to support a 'hard yes' at a later, undefined, stage.[57]

AKEL's position precipitated political chaos in Greek Cypriot domestic politics among the parties that were leaning towards supporting the plan and which had all counted on the support of AKEL as a founding member of the emerging coalition in favour of the plan. It also dealt a serious blow to AKEL's reputation in the Turkish Cypriot community and to its traditional alliances with sister parties in the north.

Politics of the campaign

Unofficially, the campaign in the south against the Annan Plan began quite early. With Papadopoulos' election in February 2003, the Greek Cypriot negotiating atmosphere began to change.[58] By the Bürgenstock negotiations between Annan IV and V in March 2004, there were continuous leaks from the Greek Cypriot side in Switzerland that the plan was highly unfavourable.[59] At the same time, AKEL was advising Greek Cypriots to be 'moderate and rational', but public tension was building and there were increasing signs of political polarisation in society.[60]

Chambers maintains that 'participants in referendum debates are more likely to resort to negative and aggressive tactics in the hope, not of persuading or exercising accountability, but simply in discrediting ... [the referendum] does not give citizens strong reasons to engage in mutual accountability in the first place'.[61] Her observations resonate with the referendum campaign in the Republic of Cyprus, which was essentially a battle between those who saw incentives or benefits in a power-sharing state and those who did not. In the south, elites who found no incentive in reunification created a multifaceted campaign against the plan.

The referendum campaign officially began after Annan V's final submission on 31 March 2004. The three-week campaign was marked by 'polarisation, extremism, fanaticism and high tension'.[62] Polarisation was assisted by a number of Greek politicians, who joined one or other of the groups, by the Greek Cypriot media, and by the international players. While all parties were asserting that the 'democratic will of the Cypriot people will be respected', the UN was reminding Cypriots that it was not going to provide the island with an endless bag of solutions, the US was warning that 'things would not be the same' if the plan was rejected, and the EU was very strongly in support of the plan's approval.

Such vigorous international support of the plan increased the atmosphere of suspicion among Greek Cypriots. Annan's encouragement of Cypriots to seize the historic and unique opportunity offered to them, and EU Enlargement Commissioner (now vice-president of the European Commission) Günter Verheugen's claim that he had been 'cheated' by President Papadopoulos,[63] only contributed to Greek Cypriot suspicions and polarisation of society.

Many studies have recognised the impact of media on public opinion[64] and are increasingly coming to acknowledge the significant 'cumulative effect of many stories over a period of months or years'.[65] In such environments, elites tend to have at their control a vast array of cueing messages from which to draw, built up over a long period.[66] Therefore, the rhetoric of Papadopoulos and others, who were warning 'meddling foreigners' to stop interfering in domestic Cypriot affairs, efficiently drew upon a significant (and very long) Greek Cypriot historical memory of being the weak victim of millennia of foreign domination.[67]

Groups not directly affiliated with political parties were not stifled by the National Council's[68] policy of seeking consensus on the Cyprus conflict, and were therefore at liberty to begin their referendum campaigns before the plan had been officially completed. The Pancyprian Citizen's Movement (*Παγκύπρια Κίνηση Πολιτών*) began its advertising campaign against the plan from November 2002.[69] The Orthodox Church also contributed to the campaign against the plan, perhaps using the referendum campaign, in part, as an early platform for the 2006 Archbishropic elections.[70]

Cree's assertion that referendums may 'relieve us from the dominance of partisan passions, and have an elevating and educative influence upon voters' may have resonance with the Turkish Cypriot case, but was proven untrue in the Greek Cypriot community. Instead, Butler and Ranney's claims about referendums setting up public confrontations, and Brady and Kaplan's assertions that 'referendums are not very useful for breaking ... deadlocks because elites who are at odds have many ways to sabotage them'[71] seem more relevant. In fact, the referendum process in south Cyprus is a perfectly logical reflection of a society which has lumbered for almost two generations under the belief that a solution would bring a return to pre-1974, led by elites who had few incentives to tell them otherwise.

According to Maria Hadjipavlou, any opportunity for public engagement in the plan was lost after Annan I:

> For me one very big possibility for change was ... when we started with the submission of the Annan Plan, the first phase. The public was on board then and they were hopeful. After that when we started changing this and changing that, and not informing or educating the people, we lost the people. They were disengaged from the process because all we were hearing was the elite, governing level, and very often the information that was given out was not to educate the people but to propagandise the badness of the plan as pro-Turkish. So there was a lot of labelling of the plan, even before its rejection.[72]

For strategic reasons, political and community elites remained reserved; 'the people that were in support of the plan came in rather late because they thought that if they would come in earlier it would have undermined the position of the president in obtaining improvements in the negotiating process'.[73] Therefore, the 'yes' campaign was established quite late, in the weeks before the vote, and campaigners against the plan's acceptance had an almost free hand. In addition, the expectation that the major political parties (AKEL and DISY) would respond positively to the Annan Plan meant that no real cross-party platform was created to garner public support for the plan. Thus, the main umbrella organisation for the campaign to support the plan, the 'Yes Platform for a United European Cyprus' (*Πλατφόρμα ΝΑΙ για Ενωμένη Ευρωπαϊκή Κύπρο*), was organised only when it became clear that most parties were favouring the plan's rejection. Under the platform, a number of public and ex-political figures gathered.

The UN team consciously avoided involvement with referendum politics, drawing a very clear line between its role and that of the plan's lobbyists. Throughout the process, the UN team remained wary of promoting the plan to either side, emphasising only that the plan's development was a co-operative effort, based primarily on the many years of negotiations, agreements, and previous peace proposals.[74] While they made efforts during negotiations to point out to the negotiating teams where their major needs and fears were being addressed, and where compromises would have to be made, the UN 'had no plans to campaign',[75] and remained for the most part publicly silent. Winning acceptance of the Annan Plan was a job left to Greek and Turkish Cypriot civil society, NGOs, and political groups.

Butler and Ranney's warnings ring dangerously true in the case of Cyprus. The 2004 referendum in Cyprus set up a very damaging confrontation, and in south Cyprus at least, did not encourage compromise. The campaign, on both sides, consisted primarily of a struggle over the visual landscape. In the south, billboards, posters, stickers, and print advertisements consisted primarily of one word, 'OXI' (no), or 'NAI' (yes). The 'no' campaign, with a much better financed and structured operation, dominated important parts of the landscape, with enormous posters draped over significant monuments and buildings in town centres and billboard placements on highways. Newspaper advertisements for the 'no' campaign began after submission of the final plan and television advertisements began one week before the referendum. There is some evidence to support the claim that both the 'yes' campaign and public officials who wished to present a less negative portrayal of the plan were unable to effectively enter the television or radio media.[76] On the whole, people who tried to present the plan in a balanced way were condemned by political and public figures and sustained heavy public criticism.

Upon realising that the plan's provisions were being 'significantly misrepresented',[77] Alvaro de Soto and other members of his team attempted to present an alternative opinion. In what remains a controversial and heavily documented chapter in the referendum period, de Soto and his team were 'prevented from setting the record straight' when interviews on Greek Cypriot television programmes were mysteriously cancelled and Greek Cypriot television went into a form of 'lockdown', where non-Cypriots were cast in the role of enemies of Cyprus.[78]

Supporting Chambers' contention that referendums engender both hysteria and deep division,[79] the referendum period in south Cyprus saw very little objectivity. Political leaders against the plan could readily trigger deeply held Greek Cypriot fears that Greek Cypriots would not be safe in the new state, that the plan was 'deeply unfair', or that it would collapse as soon as it was implemented (just like 1960). Republic of Cyprus President Papadopoulos very effectively used a number of these triggers in his address to the nation on 7 April 2004, two weeks before the referendum.

My concerns focus on the uncertainty about the new Cyprus that would emerge from the Annan Plan. Whether it would be possible for the new state to be established and function properly. Whether it would be able to play its proper role in the European Union. ... Whether the new regime, on account of the deadlocks in decision taking, can have a role and a say in the United Nations and other international fora.

Some minutes later, he triggered a number of major Greek Cypriot fears by adding that

[t]he Turkish Cypriot community gains all the basic demands it made, from the first day of the implementation of the solution. To be exact, 24 hours after the holding of the referenda ...

Its entity as a 'legal constituent state' is recognised. The invasion and occupation are written off. Turkish Cypriot internal constituent state citizenship holders become accepted as legal citizens of the European Union.

Though he argues that Greek Cypriots had little to gain from the Annan Plan, the next section of his speech underlined his position as leader of that group of political elites who believed that *they* had few incentives to support the plan, because

[t]he Turkish Cypriots gain equal participation in the administration of the new Federal State, with the status of equal 'co-presidents' and equivalent and equal participation of the representatives of the Turkish Cypriot constituent state in the Council, the European Commission and all the special Committees and Institutions of the European Union.[80]

In his speech, Papadopoulos essentially used Greek Cypriot fears to assert that only the foolhardy would support the plan. He used highly emotional triggers to previous events in Greek Cypriot history and solidified a very deep partition between the plan's supporters and opponents. And because every citizen's future was tangibly affected by the referendum's outcome, the cost of being wrong was also very high. Not only did the campaign resemble Chambers' 'civil war', it was also portrayed by both sides the 'final word' on the conflict.

The issues

For both communities, four main groups of questions shaped the issues: is the plan fair (what will it give us); is it the best we can get; is it good for our future; and does it honour our past. The answer to those questions explains why elites did, or did not, support the adoption of this power-sharing solution.

For Turkish Cypriots, the plan would facilitate increased levels of democratisation and transparency, EU membership, and peace. They would come at the expense of territorial sacrifices and some physical security (with the loss of the Turkish army). For the Greek Cypriots, returns were less clear. The most significant gains were peace and territory; the Cyprus conflict would be resolved, a great percentage of the Turkish army would leave the island, and approximately 100, 000 refugees would be able to return to their properties. On the other hand, the Greek Cypriots would have lost power with acceptance of the plan. They would no longer be sole representatives of the internationally recognised state of Cyprus – in other words, they would have to *share* power with their rival group. The Greek Cypriot collective imagining is a very powerful force, and the idea that *all* of Cyprus would not return to Greek Cypriot ownership was a considerable point against the Annan Plan's value.

A significant issue was whether the plan was the best possible outcome for each community. As has been shown above, the Turkish Cypriot community was sufficiently convinced that the plan was the best of the possible outcomes. However, the Greek Cypriots were not convinced that the Annan Plan was the best possible option. Chapter 6 has argued that a number of Greek Cypriots were convinced that EU accession would bring negotiating strength and improved returns. Therefore, while the benefits of EU membership were a significant incentive for Turkish Cypriot approval of the reunification plan, EU accession became a reason for Greek Cypriots *not to* support the plan.[81] Of all the arguments against the Annan Plan, that EU membership would significantly strengthen the future Greek Cypriot negotiating position carried most weight in the referendum debate. 'It was increasingly not the EU itself, as an agglomeration of states, institutions, officials, and associated structures that impacted on the Cyprus conflict, but rather the notion of the "EU"'.[82]

The referendum's timing also clearly affected the referendum's outcome. For Turkish Cypriots, the future was expressed as 'quite dim' without resolution of the conflict; for Greek Cypriots, acceptance of the Annan Plan brought great uncertainty. Under the pressure of the 'ticking clock' of Cyprus' rapidly approaching EU membership, the referendum took on heightened importance. Accession, the single strongest means of impelling reunification, was no longer a critical factor for Greek Cypriot acceptance of the UN plan. Correspondingly, it became increasingly clear to the international community and to the engineers that the Greek Cypriot community was experiencing its first real struggles with the issues surrounding reunification. 'We were really worried about [not having enough] time [for people to think about the plan]. But we were pressed by the clock. In addition, the leadership didn't highlight the pressing of time in positive way. It was communicated to the public as something of a trap'.[83] This period of debate and turmoil climaxed at the date of the referendum. Pfirter lists the timing of the referendum as one of two factors which led to the referendum's failure in 2004,[84] and while there were other factors which played a role in the plan's rejection, the referendum's timing was certainly important.

The way the Annan Plan negotiated Cyprus' history was an important factor for both communities. The Turkish Cypriot community needed guarantees that it would not be engulfed by the larger Greek Cypriot community and the Greek Cypriot community needed guarantees that the state would not collapse again. Neither side truly seemed to believe that the Annan Plan did real justice to its past. In the Turkish Cypriot community, however, this weakness was compensated by the much more pressing desire for a stable future, providing both sufficient numbers of elites and the public to endorse the power-sharing plan.

The resentment created by the idea that the 1960 constitution was foisted upon them carried through to Greek Cypriot attitudes regarding negotiation of the Annan Plan. Thus historical memory played a significant role in the plan's rejection. Coufoudakis, opposed to the plan, argued that the 2004 referendum merely served to remove 'the stigma that the final settlement was imposed on the Cypriots by the Secretary-General's binding arbitration. Annan wanted to avoid the precedent of the 1959 Zurich and London agreements [because] Greek Cypriots had complained that these agreements were imposed under the threat of ... partition'.[85] 1960 was invoked by opponents of the plan (including Papadopoulos), who referred to foreign threats which sought to permanently divide the island.[86] For these actors, group memories were the markers of the plan's fairness.

In earlier versions of the plan, the referendum was intended to be complementary to elite development of the resolution, coming after the political elites signed the plan into law and put their political reputations behind it. The referendum was therefore meant to work on two levels: endorsing the conciliatory behaviour of the elites who would have outflanked nationalist elements in both communities; and reminding both elites and the public in the future that they had actively expressed support for the resolution. This would go some way to creating a degree of popular and elite loyalty to the new state of affairs, avoiding the lack of support which contributed to the collapse of the 1960 state. But instead, three of the major reasons Greek Cypriots voted against the 2004 plan were that the plan was unfair, had been imposed on them by international powers, and conceded too many powers to the Turkish Cypriot community. Memory, therefore, became an important determinant of the Greek Cypriot vote and also underpinned elite behaviour.

In the Greek Cypriot community in 2004, as has been shown, important elements of the political leadership exhorted the public not to support the plan. President Papadopoulos reminded Greek Cypriots that they 'would be facing history'. At the end of his first pre-referendum address, he closed with the following reminder, actively linking the Annan Plan's rejection with the protection of Cypriot Hellenism:

> I am sure that for you the moral principles and values of our people, their civilization and national historic life still mean a lot to you and you want to continue with security, justice, freedom and peace. ... I call upon you to reject the Annan Plan. I call upon you to say a resounding NO on 24 April. I call upon you to defend your dignity, your history and what is right.[87]

The clear message was thus that the plan did not honour Greek Cypriot past.

The result

Political context – so different in north and south Cyprus – plays a central role in referendum voting. In the north, broad political support of the plan aided its palatability, while in the south, the plan's bipartisan rejection, and its rejection by a figure as important as the president, can only have damaged chances of public support. As such, the Annan Plan's rejection must be situated within a network of factors and interpreted with the pressures, fears, short-term campaigns, and long-term political environment in mind. Christophorou has given the most exhaustive explanation for the referendum's failure, incorporating a vast list of factors.[88] Some of the factors he lists are also cited by most analysts trying to explain the failure.[89]

The following factors contributed to Greek Cypriot rejection of the Annan Plan. The level of public trust commanded by the position of the president meant that when he came out so emphatically against the plan, he cemented public fears about it. In his pre-referendum speech, Papadopoulos argued that the plan was 'legalising and deepening the *de facto* partition instead of ending it'.[90] The government and Papadopoulos' negotiating team also asserted that the Annan Plan would turn Cyprus into a protectorate of Turkey. As noted above, Papadopoulos invoked history, reminding the Greek Cypriot public of their proud Hellenic roots which were under threat by the Annan Plan. In addition, Papadopoulos argued that the plan depended on the 'the groundless illusion that Turkey will keep her promises'.[91] Papadopoulos' speech has also served to embed a popular assumption within the Greek Cypriot community that the Turkish Cypriots selfishly voted in favour of the plan simply because it granted them everything they desired – to the direct detriment of the Greek Cypriot community, which had been trying vainly to safeguard the rights of *all* Cypriots. Post-referendum opinion polls have shown that 80 per cent of people who voted against the Annan Plan did not believe Turkey would deliver on her commitments.[92] The president's behaviour and attitudes appear, therefore, to have influenced public attitudes, and ultimately, the result.

In the south, by the end 'the campaign took on elements of a "plebiscitarian" rather than liberal constitutionalist democracy with the role of parties and their constituent organs as formulators of comprehensive political propositions to be put before the public being pushed aside in favour of more or less charismatic direct appeals to patriotism'.[93] Jenssen and Listhaug have argued that 'during referendums voters are more likely to switch positions on an issue in order to follow a party's cue'.[94] At the same time, their study has shown that if parties are internally divided on referendum issues, party loyalty becomes a less important factor in voter decisions.[95] Exit poll results from members of the two largest parties show that the 'party machine' did not strongly control the vote: 65 per cent of DISY's electorate voted against the Annan Plan, while the party officially supported it; and 33 percent of AKEL supporters voted in favour, against AKEL's recommendation.[96] The fact that the public knew only the broad shape of what a solution would look like meant that there was an exploitable gap between public knowledge and the actual deal negotiated. In the north, NGOs and civil society groups took great pains to familiarise the public with the negotiation process. By contrast, in the south, the knowledge gap was exploited by political elites to heighten the public's sense of dissatisfaction.

Overwhelmingly, negative media portrayals of the plan painted it as unfair. Coupled with the plan's complexity, this placed the public at the mercy of experts and specialist analysts, most of whom were against the plan. The parties aided development of the polarisation effect in Greek Cypriot society. Additionally, there was significant confusion over the costs of reunification and over who would bear the brunt of those costs. Greek Cypriots believed they would bear the brunt of exorbitant reunification costs. No official cost estimates were released by the UN.[97]

The referendum's timing contributed significantly to its rejection in south Cyprus as much as to its approval in the north. EU entry was assured and Greek Cypriots could not find strong enough reasons to support a plan which would be, at best, uncertain and, at worst, turn Cyprus into a Turkish protectorate. As Crisp suggested voters are wont to do in referendum campaigns in which the issues are complex or controversial, Greek Cypriot voter conservatism prevailed. The international community's emphatic support of the UN proposal also heightened suspicion, in an already tense domestic atmosphere, that the plan was merely an 'imperialist plot to protect Turkey's EU accession course, and finish off what the invasion started'.

Finally, few of these factors would have been so effective had Greek Cypriot society not been so swayed by elites who were protecting their personal power-bases, and by an education system which instilled and perpetuated a conflict mentality among Greek Cypriots. The fact that those born *after* 1974 – who did not experience the invasion or war – were those who voted most emphatically against the plan, and who also appear in surveys and opinion polls to be most averse to a power-sharing solution. This highlights how effectively a conflict mentality has been inculcated.[98]

Interpretation of outcome

Post-Annan, the meaning of the referendum result has been heavily contested in the Cypriot discourse. In the three years between the 2004 referendum and Christofias' election to power, the battle lines were clearly drawn around the result's carcass. In the Greek Cypriot community the dispute was fierce because the definition of the result determined the path to be taken towards resolution.

The group led by Tassos Papadopoulos argued that the plan was fundamentally flawed; that it was unworkable and, most importantly, unjust.[99] Illustrative of this group are the comments of Vassos Georgiou, central committee member of AKEL, and then-director of the President of the House of Representatives' Office.[100]

Seventy-six percent [of Greek Cypriots] said no because they felt an enormous injustice. The foreigners couldn't understand why we said no. They don't understand that in Cyprus we are 82 percent Greek Cypriots and 18 percent Turkish Cypriots. We [Greek Cypriots] have made enormous concessions. The first, and most important is that we accepted a federation. Which other place in the world that has 82 percent of the population has accepted federation and not a majoritarian government? Turkey came and killed our people and took half our land, and we said ok to federation in order to fix the conflict. What else were we going to do? Federation is not a just solution. It is very unfair, in fact it's not just very unfair; to call it unfair is an understatement.[101] And the foreigners cannot understand this. In nowhere in the world has a supermajority said they would share power with a minority. But we said 'ok, we accept this federation, bi-zonal bi-communal', but for it to be a little fair! A little fair!![102]

Since the plan is said to have been so clearly unjust, the result of the referendum is also said to have been a just result, a victory for the righteous.[103] Consequently, on this view, the future must provide a solution which takes into greater consideration Greek Cypriot conceptions of retributive justice and 'fair' institutional design. Interestingly, this is still articulated as a 'bi-zonal, bi-communal solution', but one that more suitably reflects the Greek Cypriot community's numerical superiority.

On the other side of the argument are those Greek Cypriots who believe that the Annan Plan was somewhere between a necessary evil and a highly desirable initiative. For them, the plan took into account both Greek Cypriot and Turkish Cypriot concerns and needs; it was designed successfully to ensure functionality, was careful to balance the claims of Greek Cypriot numerical majority and Turkish Cypriot legislative equality, and gave both groups enough for them to begin building a common future. In this category were former presidents of the Republic of Cyprus George Vassiliou and Glafkos Clerides, former attorney general of the Republic of Cyprus Alecos Markides, former EU co-ordination commissioner Takis Hadjidimitrou, current major opposition leader Nicos Anastasiadis, and a number of academics and civil society leaders. Representative of this broad point of view is Takis Hadjidimitriou, who argues that the plan was a necessary compromise for the sake of peace:

> If someone tries to find inefficiencies [in the plan], he can find a lot. But the problem is where shall we meet the Turkish Cypriots? To meet the Turkish Cypriots, and to come to a kind of understanding with Turkey, we need to make concessions. ... We have to find a political and diplomatic solution. A diplomatic solution is not a perfect solution. It is a compromise, something which demands sacrifices and is not something which can raise public enthusiasm. The opposite, bitterness, can appear among people because they cannot recognise the fulfilment of their ambitions and what they desired the solution to include. So it is not a matter of details. For me it is a matter of where we are willing to drive Cyprus, to drive the vehicle, whether we are going to understand that in front of us is a political decision, and take the essence of the issue, and make use of the international conditions, or to start discussing details and legal points which are getting nowhere.[104]

For most of its supporters, the Annan Plan was defeated by three factors: the negative position of the Greek Cypriot president and his government; the role of political party and government partner AKEL; and the lack of realism in the Greek Cypriot community regarding a solution. The relative weight of each element changes depending on the analyst. For this group, the key to any solution is not the settlement's re-negotiation but a significant change in the Greek Cypriot political climate and a popular re-assessment of what an acceptable solution would look like.

In the period since Christofias' election, the climate has changed significantly. In September 2008, new negotiations between Talat and Christofias were opened, but the scars of 2004 were evident. The Greek Cypriot negotiators made it very clear to the UN and the international community that any resolution reached must reflect the sole efforts of the Cypriot parties; there was to be no outside mediation unless specifically requested. And while the institutional and governance aspects of any solution are likely to very closely resemble those of the Annan Plan, government soundbites for domestic consumption on the Greek Cypriot side repeatedly stress that the Annan Plan is 'dead and buried', and that they are starting from the start. The government is very clearly wary of triggering Annan-hysteria and appears unsure whether the scar from 2004 is fully healed.

On the Turkish Cypriot side, attitudes to the Greek Cypriot rejection vary quite significantly and have taken a swing towards the conservative over time. At one extreme is Gulle, whose comments that 'of course the Greek Cypriots had some worries about the Annan Plan, and we can understand their worries'[105] express understanding of the Greek Cypriot 'no'. At the other extreme sits former president of the TRNC and long-time Turkish Cypriot representative in negotiations, Rauf Denktaş, who has consistently argued that the Greek Cypriots have never truly wanted reunification. According to Denktaş, Greek Cypriots have perpetuated an illusion that they seek a compromise agreement to gain international sympathy and protection of their state, the Republic of Cyprus. 'Put them to the test', he had said, 'and they will not support reunification'.[106] So when Greek Cypriots voted against the plan in 2004, Denktaş' 'I told you so' resonated within sectors of Turkish Cypriot society.

In the years after the referendum, public sentiment had cooled into apathy and cynicism. A reactive electoral swing back to the right has been predicted, and Talat, who was elected on the basis that he could bring change to north Cyprus, seems aware of his tenuous hold on power. Both massive public discontent with the post-referendum *status quo* and the Turkish Cypriot government's continued reliance on Turkey for economic and political support has affected Talat's negotiating position, and he has appeared to have moved some steps away from the previously agreed negotiating positions.

Political consequences

The engineers' use of the referendum to elicit deep public engagement with the realistic shape of a solution was, to some extent, successful. The referendum did serve to stimulate fierce public debate; and, as Table 7.1 shows, with a voter turnout of 87 per cent[107] and 88 per cent[108] it can certainly claim public involvement – even if the public's involvement was ultimately limited to endorsement of the plan. Positives have been drawn from the referendum: it was successful in so far as it encouraged popular interaction

Table 7.1 April 2004 Cypriot referendum result

Electorate	Yes votes (per cent)	Total of yes votes	No votes (per cent)	Total of yes votes	Turnout
Greek Cypriot	24.17	99, 976	75.83	313, 704	87%
Turkish Cypriot	64.90	77, 646	35.09	41, 973	88%

Source: Republic of Cyprus Press and Information Office.

with the resolution and, importantly, public discussion. This was acknowledged by members of the UN team:

> The plan is the first time most Greek Cypriots and Turkish Cypriots really started to think about the shape of a settlement. Prior to this point, they were simply repeating the positions of their politicians. 'All refugees return, etc'. No settlement could ever look like that. [Until that point] in public discussion and political discussion people hadn't talked about the reality of a settlement.[109]

Perhaps then, one important consequence of the referendum was that it managed to encourage a genuine public debate on both sides of the divide in a way that no negotiations had previously managed. With the benefit of hindsight, a core member of the UN negotiating team reflected that the 'discussion was the key most positive moment in the history of Cyprus. People looked at it as individuals, not from partisan positions. "What would I do? What do I want?"'.[110] Continuing, the UN representative compared the responses of the two communities to the opportunity created by the referendum: 'I think the Turkish Cypriots used that much better than the Greek Cypriots did. There were real public discussions'.[111]

The political implications of the referendum results are considerable. Dynamics have been altered in relationships within and between each group. In the years since the 2004 referendum, public attitudes towards intercommunal coexistence have become steadily more conservative, and while Christofias' election in the south reflects a greater public willingness for reunification, there also seems to be an increasing sense of bitterness on both sides. This bitterness has important consequences for future reunification efforts. As indicated in Table 7.2, surveys show that as time goes by the psychological gap between Greek and Turkish Cypriots is widening. 'Most politicians agree with the assessment that the period since the April 2004 referendum has worsened the situation. Young people especially were subjected to an intensity on the Cyprus issue that they had never before encountered and had to face up to the fact that if the plan had been approved, their lives and futures would have been dramatically altered'.[112]

This sense of bitterness in the Turkish Cypriot community has stemmed from a feeling of having been rejected by the Greek Cypriots and abandoned by the international community.[113] The bitterness is directed towards both the Greek Cypriots, whom they see as blockading Turkish Cypriot society from the world, and the EU, which they see as continuing to punish the Turkish Cypriot community for a status quo, which is not their fault.

In the period since the referendum, elements within the Turkish Cypriot community have begun to redefine the burgeoning Cypriotist nationalism that was particularly evident in the year between the partial lifting of intra-island travel restrictions and the referendum. A degree of Cypriotism had

Table 7.2 Attitudes of Greek and Turkish Cypriots towards members of the other community

Question	Respondent group	2003 (%)	2004 (%)	2005 (%)	2006 (%)
In favour of both communities living together*	Greek Cypriot	67			45
Partition is 'totally unacceptable'^	Greek Cypriot		60.4		47
We have much in common with the Turkish Cypriots^	Greek Cypriot			59.6	54.2
We have much in common with the Greek Cypriots^	Turkish Cypriot			52.8	40.3
I would not mind having Turkish Cypriot neighbours^	Greek Cypriot			63.5	62
I would not mind having Greek Cypriot neighbours^	Turkish Cypriot			55.4	44.2
It is natural and acceptable for a family member to marry a Turkish Cypriot^	Greek Cypriot			22.1	18.3
It is natural and acceptable for a family member to marry a Greek Cypriot^	Turkish Cypriot			50.4	34
Greek Cypriots cannot be trusted to adhere to an agreement we might make with them^	Turkish Cypriot			60	71.3
Turkish Cypriots cannot be trusted to adhere to an agreement we might make with them^	Greek Cypriot			63.5	62

Source: * Jean Christou, 'It's nothing personal'. *Cyprus Mail*, Wednesday 12 April 2006.
^ 'Can the Cyprus Problem be Solved? Understanding the Greek Cypriot Response to the UN Peace Plan for Cyprus', *An Evidence-Based Study in Co-operation with CYMAR Market Research Ltd*, November 2004, *http://www.cypruspolls.org* (accessed 15 November, 2005). Sample size is 1000 participants from each community.

always been weakly present in both communities during the years of separation and has always been identified with the left-wing of Cypriot politics. To say one is *Cypriot* is a conscious rejection of the Greek or Turkish identities popular in each state. The term is often used in a decidedly pointed way. One is either Greek or Turkish; Greek Cypriot or Turkish Cypriot; or Cypriot. In the lead-up to the referendum, 'This Country is Ours' was a banner which clearly signified a link between the people and their land, and consequently to their identity as Cypriots. This effort was reflected (to a weaker degree) in movements on the Greek Cypriot side, and ties began to strengthen between Cypriotists on both sides of the border.

However, as a result of the referendum outcome, Cypriotism in north Cyprus is gradually taking on a decidedly *Turkish* Cypriot form, excluding Greek Cypriots from the label 'Cypriot'.[114] Interestingly, it is the inverse of the attitude that has always been prevalent within the Greek Cypriot community. Both before and after the referendum, one would frequently hear the term 'Cypriot' used to define *only* Greek Cypriots. A typical remark in conversation might be 'Cypriots shop here. Oh, and Turks also shop here sometimes'. By contrast, before the referendum the same sentence from a Turkish Cypriot would simply be that 'Cypriots shop here'. After the referendum, the statement has become 'Cypriots shop here. Oh, and Greeks also shop here sometimes'. Turkish Cypriots, on the whole, interpreted the Greek Cypriot referendum result as a very clear and decisive rejection of the Turkish Cypriot community, and this is directly reflected in their defensive reshaping of the label 'Cypriot'.

A 2007 survey commissioned by the UN showed that there were increasing levels of pessimism in both communities regarding settlement prospects, and that 'nearly 40 percent of Greek Cypriots and 31 percent of Turkish Cypriots said they did not trust the other side to adhere to an agreement'.[115] Not only are Turkish Cypriots less likely to accept any further compromises which may be necessary to entice Greek Cypriots to accept a power-sharing solution, but dissatisfaction with the status quo has also increased their ambivalence towards those sacrifices demanded of them by the Annan Plan.

The same can be said of Greek Cypriot public opinion. A 2003 report showed that 67 per cent of the Greek Cypriot population[116] were in favour of both communities living together. By 2006 that percentage had dropped to 45 per cent.[117] More disturbing was the finding that the highest percentage of respondents who had no wish to live in a reunified Cyprus was in the 18–24 and 25–34 age brackets.[118] Between 2003 and 2006 there has been a greater swing of respondents favouring partition and less willingness for coexistence, particularly by Turkish Cypriots towards Greek Cypriots. The general trend, as Table 7.2 illustrates, is a decreasing level of trust between the communities in the years since the referendum.

Thus, the referendum results have pushed the two communities further apart and tangibly increased tension and ill will. The most dangerous consequence of the referendum was the exacerbation of ill feeling at the community level. It has been many years since Turkish and Greek Cypriot people have expressed resentment of each other. This development is also reflected in, and reflective of, subtle changes in media portrayals in Greek and Turkish Cypriot news media. A very real antagonism has been created between Turkish and Greek Cypriots:

> [T]here is all this propaganda on our [Greek Cypriot] side ... that we give them [the Turkish Cypriots] and we give them, and we give them, as either services in the health sector, or work for the six or seven thousand Turkish Cypriot workers who cross and so on; so we count this in millions, and how much aid we give *them* and so on. ... So in other words we look at them as if they are parasites, and not as if they are part of us, and part also of this country. And we measure also, what we give them

by the expectation we have that they should be grateful, and that they should be really appreciative of this, and they should be saying it and so on. So we create another conflict, between the taxpayers on this side, and the others who are non-taxpayers.[119]

There is also very real policy-level aggression at the Greek Cypriot state level towards the Turkish Cypriot community, reciprocated sporadically at the Turkish Cypriot state level towards Greek Cypriots. The Republic of Cyprus has recently begun issuing Turkish Cypriots and foreign nationals residing in Greek Cypriot property in north Cyprus with eviction orders and court subpoenas, handing the orders over as individuals cross from north to south. Increasing numbers of Turkish Cypriots are complaining of harassment at the Greek Cypriot checkpoints. In addition to the harassment is a subtle racism. At the Ledra Palace checkpoints, there is a separate line for Turkish Cypriots passing south; this is regardless of whether they possess citizenship of the Republic of Cyprus. At most checkpoints, Turkish Cypriot citizens of the Republic of Cyprus are always asked for their identity cards, and the numbers always recorded, ostensibly for statistical reasons. This infrequently happens to Greek Cypriot citizens of the Republic of Cyprus, who are often simply asked upon crossing whether they are Cypriot, meaning *Greek*-Cypriot.

Recently, several Greek Cypriots have been arrested by Turkish Cypriot police. In August 2006, a journalist and his cameraman were arrested and held on charges of filming in a military zone.[120] They were released the following week, but the case added to the sense of alarm and growing bitterness felt by Greek Cypriots towards the north. It has also increased Greek Cypriot anxiety about crossing to the north. These examples highlight a very real antagonism and growing mutual mistrust between Greek and Turkish Cypriots, expressed both by officials and by ordinary members of the public.

It is important to note that this mistrust is a symptom of a clear change of intercommunal relationships at the public level. Turkish and Greek Cypriot relations at the popular level began to develop in a significant way only after the April 2003 checkpoint openings. In the year between the openings and the referendum, the relationship between the communities was exploratory but generally positive; each community was beginning to deconstruct long-held myths about the other, and media and popular sentiment was reflective of a sense of hope and timid commonality. The energy and optimism of the period between the checkpoint openings and the submission of the first Annan Plan was tangible and held considerable possibilities.[121] This growing sense of trust was destroyed by the referendum campaign in south Cyprus, the results, and their polarised interpretations.

The referendum results have also altered the Republic of Cyprus' relations with Greece, Turkey, the EU, and the UN, though this seems to be normalising after Christofias' election in 2008. Greek politicians have become sick of the Cyprus *polémique*; the Republic of Cyprus imported its dispute with Turkey into the European fold, contributing to the chaos surrounding Turkey's controversial EU accession course; and though its relationship with the EU has improved since Enlargement Commissioner Günter Verheugen publicly accused the Papadopoulos government of 'cheating' him,[122] during the Papadopoulos presidency, the UN Secretary-General warned the Cypriots 'not to take the UN for granted'. The referendum has altered the perception of the conflict at the international level, and along with that, the pendulum of international sympathy. It has caused a re-conceptualisation of the conflict by all parties and *of* the role of all parties.

Implications regarding strategies for adoption of a consociational settlement

Both the international community and the UN engineers hoped that the Cypriot experiment with direct democracy would reinforce the trend towards greater use of referendums in founding and changing regimes and become a positive example to future reunification efforts in conflict zones. The central role being played in Cyprus by direct democracy heralded great things for the world, according to the UN. In a press conference held upon the reopening of negotiations in New York in 2004, de Soto made it clear that Cyprus would be important in this regard. He continued, emphasising that 'as to whether [Cyprus] will have a snowball effect on others – I certainly hope so. Cyprus is probably, is certainly the longest peacemaking mandate that the Secretary-General of the United Nations and three or four of his predecessors – I've lost count – have had. This would obviously be an extraordinary breakthrough'.[123]

While, *prima facie*, it seems a masterstroke to remove the ultimate power of endorsement from the hands of elites with a history of thwarting peace efforts, it is still these elites who are negotiating the terms of the agreement. Bowler and Donovan stress that 'elites do not drop out of the picture because a matter is being put to a popular vote'.[124] As with Cyprus, it cannot be guaranteed that communities will have the necessary level of political independence and sophistication – or indeed the incentives – required to overcome a tradition of passive interaction with the conflict. The Cypriot case was particularly risky; the Turkish and Greek Cypriot electorates were empowered to endorse or reject a political system that had been negotiated over many years without their input and with little effort to inform them about the solution and its rationale.

Conclusion

This chapter has addressed the problem of finding a mechanism for adoption of a consociational regime, one of the most fundamental problems of the peacebuilding process in any post-conflict society. The Annan Plan's engineers believed that one method of promoting such ties was to use a tool which serves to both immediately measure popular support and strengthen elite loyalty by reminding them that their respective electorates have endorsed the solution being implemented.

In early versions of the Annan Plan, the referendum was designed to be part of a broader set of instruments which would combine elite and public support of the proposed reunification plan. However, over time, the referendum came to be seen as a means of overcoming elite intransigence, of encouraging public debate about the solution, and of creating public support. Thus in a high-risk strategy that ultimately failed, the referendum moved from being part of the adoption process to bearing the whole weight of adoption. In north Cyprus, strong elite and public support of the plan resulted in its endorsement by a 65 per cent majority. But, in the south, Greek Cypriot public support of the Annan Plan was ultimately undermined by the overwhelming hope that, as EU members, they could find a better solution than the Annan Plan which would be more reflective of their status as the dominant Cypriot community. This hope, coupled with Greek Cypriot elite manipulation of strong, real, public feelings of threat created by Turkey's continued presence on the island, ensured that 76 per cent of Greek Cypriots voted against the plan's adoption. Leapfrogging the elites simply deepened the schism because elites sought alternative methods to influence the referendum results.

The current renegotiation of another power-sharing plan for Cyprus between Greek and Turkish Cypriot political elites has grown out of the scar caused by the 2004 plan's rejection. The rejection itself was the culmination of the historical memory both carried and nurtured by Greek Cypriot political elites, the failure and perceived unjust structure of the 1960 state, insufficient internal and external incentives for key elites to compromise (or encourage it), and insufficient incentives in the plan itself to encourage elites to commit to a power-sharing state.

Conclusion

Peace is not merely a distant goal that we seek, but a means
by which we arrive at that goal.[1]

This book has sought to understand why elites in Cyprus have been
unable, or unwilling, to adopt a power-sharing solution to end the enduring Cyprus conflict. By focusing on a conflict in which elite intransigence
has been a major barrier to building peace, it has tried to throw light
on this particular aspect of adopting political settlements in divided
and post-conflict polities. The investigation of an extended period of
Cypriot history, from the beginnings of modern institution building in
1882 through to 2004 has allowed the development of impediments over
time to be shown, along with their consequences for public debate about
political solutions for Cyprus. It is also the first substantial examination of
the relationship between Cyprus and consociationalism – something long
missing in the literature.

By simultaneously drawing on an underdeveloped aspect of consociational theory – the idea of key factors – and examining the roles of historical
memory and political dynamics, the book has explained the reluctance of
political elites to overcome the division of Cyprus by adopting a power-
sharing solution. It has argued that major blockages to the conflict's resolution have come from a number of areas: specifically, elite difficulty fully
accepting the principles of power-sharing together with no tradition of elite
accommodation; historical memory into which has been built competing
ethno-nationalisms and group fears carried over from the collapse of the
1963 state and the violence between the communities which led to the 1974
war; and conflicting domestic and international incentives for elites to compromise in 2004. Together, they explain the referendum results of 2004 in
which Turkish Cypriots voted in favour, and Greek Cypriots voted against,
the ultimately stillborn Annan Plan.

Chapter 1 laid out the central tenets of consociational theory to understand whether consociational democracy is able to create a political settlement of the conflict in Cyprus. After analysing the theory and its most significant criticisms, it concluded that the theory being used for Cyprus is largely sound and is not in and of itself a major contributing factor to the inability to adopt a solution. But the absence of segmental isolation, a balance of power between the groups, a tradition of elite accommodation, and incentives from external players contribute significantly to blocking adoption.

History is one of the most significant impediments to resolution of the Cyprus conflict, because it has shaped elite and public attitudes to resolution. The historical development of ethno-nationalism in Cyprus has fed into each community's definitions and understandings of both the problem and its optimum solution. Chapter 2 traced the development of ethno-nationalism through important periods in Cypriot history, and established links between historical events, group memory, and major areas of friction which inhibit a solution to the conflict. Ultimately, the work of Chapter 2 was to show how the roots of elite attitudes to resolution are deeply planted in Cyprus' modern history. Later chapters drew a straight line between the political goals of Cypriot and external elites during this period and subsequent, especially current, obstacles to resolution.

Chapter 3 examined the first attempt to implement a consociational democratic system in Cyprus. Serious flaws in the institutions of the 1960 Republic of Cyprus were exacerbated by the absence of the key factors. The state's failure was in part a logical outcome of two national visions framed against each other by extremist elites and elements central to each of the four key factors which inflamed the institutional flaws, thereby also playing a critical role in the state's breakdown. The chapter also highlighted the role played by group memory in the state's breakdown, from the period explored in Chapter 2. In addition, its exploration of what went wrong in the 1960–3 period, at both a constitutional and political elite level, allowed us to understand why the Annan Plan was designed the way it was, and especially to understand the events which have become triggers for current elite fears of power-sharing solutions.

Chapter 4 looked at the 2004 Annan Plan as the most recent attempt to craft a comprehensive political solution to the Cyprus conflict. The Annan Plan was methodically constructed to create a state which addressed both groups' primary concerns and fears as well as their most important demands. Much of the Annan Plan was shaped by both communities' experiences of the 1960 state, and its failure, and especially by the desire of the constitutional engineers to avoid repetition of that failure.

Regardless of the plan's attempts to safeguard against a recurrence of the past's nightmares, it failed to receive support from key Greek Cypriot political leaders, including and especially the then-President of the Republic of Cyprus. Chapters 5–7, each, consequently dealt with a different aspect of elite relations to explain what has gone wrong in Cyprus. Though the constitutional engineers working in Cyprus made considerable progress towards designing a political system that would create a unified democratic country, the political conditions necessary for the plan's adoption were not met. Chapter 5 showed that in the absence of the key factor of elite trends of accommodation, and with vastly different domestic incentives for compromise in each society, political elites could not agree to support the plan. It was not a consociational lapse that led to the 2004 referendum's failure, but electoral politics, electoral outbidding, and other political dynamics which had very different effects in north and south Cyprus.

As a result of the above factors, the need for external incentives for compromise took on a heightened importance. Chapter 6 therefore examined the role of international actors in the attempt in 2004 to encourage elites to adopt the necessary compromise of this particular power-sharing solution. The UN and the EU were the primary actors which tried to change the domestic dynamics in Cyprus, but, despite the influence they (especially the EU) seemed to possess, neither actor was ultimately able to offer sufficient incentives to secure co-operation between Greek and Turkish Cypriot elites. Their success in creating incentives for compromise in one society resulted in the removal of incentives for the other.

Chapter 7 concentrated on the 2004 referendum as the mechanism for adoption of the proposed consociational state and, consequently, as the site of the Annan Plan's rejection. The attempts of the UN engineers to overcome elite intransigence by placing responsibility for adoption in the hands of the public also placed disproportionate weight on the referendum as the means of adoption. While this tactic proved successful in north Cyprus, it was simultaneously the plan's undoing; Greek Cypriots voted against the plan as a result of both a hope that as EU members a more favourable solution would be forthcoming and elite manipulation of the public's historical traumas and fears of again falling victim to Turkish violence. The rejection itself was the culmination of the historical memory both inherited by Greek Cypriot political elites and bequeathed by them onto society, memories of the failure and perceived unjust structure of the 1960 state, insufficient internal and external incentives for key elites to compromise, and insufficient incentives in the plan itself to encourage elites to commit to a power-sharing state.

Conclusions and the road from here

To begin with an obvious point, the influence of elites cannot be leapfrogged. Cyprus has shown that tools like referendums to outflank elite intransigence are easily overcome by leaders if they have either strong public support or a vulnerable populace which is presented with intimidating options. As Brady and Kaplan have said, 'elites can prune and shape public opinion in ways that make a mockery of it'.[2] Indeed, one of Lijphart's original favourable factors (strong public support for political elites) here becomes a disadvantage to a resolution where the elites themselves are the primary intransigent force. Assuming that consociational and other power-sharing or accommodationist solutions are valuable for putting post-conflict and deeply divided polities back onto the road to peace, we must appreciate that elite intransigence is a symptom of many things.

The first point is that history is important. It dictates not only the ability of elites to share power but also shapes institutional design and points of institutional conflict. A new imagining must be built for and by Cypriot society/ies to first welcome and then support the existence of the factors which must be present if peace is to be attained. Conciliatory elites must publicly extend the hand of trust to each other, and cease waiting for the moment of minimal political risk to do so. Too often, potential working relationships between like-minded Turkish and Greek Cypriot leaders are neutralised by fear of electoral backlash. At the same time, a great number of changes must take place in both Cypriot societies in order to provide realistic support for elites inclined towards conciliation. 'History' needs to be re-cast, each community's relationship with the 'Other' must be examined, and selective applications of the notions of victim and aggressor must be abandoned. In short, for a political settlement to be successfully adopted in Cyprus, both the broader society and the political environment must mature. The balance of power on the island as well as acceptance of the general segmentation of the groups into Greek and Turkish Cypriot 'states' must be embraced rather than demonised, because both aspects bring stability and facilitate the political co-operation needed for a power-sharing system to succeed. Coupled with that, much work needs to be done unpacking the concept of federalism in Cyprus.

The situation in Cyprus throws up a lesson, and a warning: in long-running, intractable conflicts, each side adopts hard positions about international laws and norms which will need to be undone at some point. This may be the process that south Cyprus is presently going through – a process north Cyprus passed in the pre-Annan period. The problem is that there is a time lag. While aspects of all conflicts (even frozen conflicts) change, public perceptions are much slower to change. This 'time-lag' can be seriously detrimental to conflict settlement. Does the 2008 election of Demetris Christofias to the Republic of Cyprus presidency mean that Greek Cypriots still seek a power-sharing solution? And will the conditions in north Cyprus hold up for long enough for the desire for a consociational, federal state to be the same on both sides of the border? Is there still time? What changes will be needed before both sides can say "yes"? Previous chapters have shown how public sentiment is drifting towards separation. At the same time, one may make tentative conclusions in the opposite direction.

Perhaps Christofias' election *is* an indication of such change, just as the election of Mehmet Ali Talat was representative of such a break in north Cyprus. If this is so, then one of the three elements outlined in Chapter 5, 'a change in the purpose of the nation', may be present. Elites like DISY's Nicos Anastassiades are rejecting the notion that co-operation is contingent upon solution of the conflict, rather than the conflict's solution being dependent upon elite co-operation. Though few, they are asking 'if we don't learn how to co-operate now, how will we learn it later?' Similarly, both sides of the Cypriot divide are beginning to confront the island's history: the examination of the way history is being told, the progress of the CMP finding of bodies of people long 'missing', talk (however quiet) about truth commissions, and a very, very slow re-examination of the concept of who has been a victim all indicate that the domestic environment is changing incrementally, subtly.

This is particularly important because on the whole, much of the technical work to build a political system for a reunited Cyprus has already been done. Forty years of negotiations, and the results of the Annan Plan, have given a very clear idea of what will be acceptable and necessary for the sides to agree to a new state. Without undervaluing the role future negotiations have left to play, it is mostly a matter now of changing public perceptions of the past, and of the future, of Cyprus.

Is there enough movement on these issues to encourage resolution? The Annan plan gave the Turkish Cypriot community security and the rights that stem from a stable democratic state. Given the instability of current internal Turkish politics, and the increasing Turkish Cypriot frustration and fears about becoming a Turkish satellite, they are likely to support future unification efforts. The Annan plan threw up a number of red-line issues in the Greek Cypriot community that will either need to be disassembled internally, or dealt with in a future plan. Similarly, international actors must be able to convince Greek Cypriots that they can guarantee the country's safety, and Greek Cypriots must believe that the international community seeks to underpin, rather than conspires to undercut, peace in Cyprus. But there are complications: for example the property issue, an important part of a resolution for both sides, is one of the few aspects of the conflict which is not waiting for a resolution to solve itself. Through courts, commissions, and private deals between people, the property aspect is rolling forward, and it cannot but complicate any future negotiated plan.

Limitations

Closely examined in this case study was the anatomy of the Cyprus conflict and its effects on efforts to design a suitable constitution and to persuade Cypriots to adopt that solution. While the four key factors proved useful in studying efforts to end the Cyprus conflict, the set of factors examined is one possible set in a group of many. A number of factors were discarded from Lijphart's various lists, and other scholars have had alternative suggestions about factors with analytic value which have been used in other case studies. Another factor for inclusion may be the significant numerical discrepancy between the Greek and Turkish Cypriot groups (approximately 75–25 per cent). While the precise set of factors utilised here may not be applicable elsewhere, the idea it has illustrated is important; that factors could have analytic value in explaining failure and success for divided societies seeking to adopt consociational solutions.

This work has limited itself to using these factors to explain why Cyprus has been unable to adopt a consociational government despite multiple attempts. It has not attempted to explain *how* to create the conditions which will facilitate the adoption of the system which has been canvassed in the book, and which does seem to be the most likely structure of governance for Cyprus. There are also a broad range of non-political conditions which would clearly improve chances of the successful adoption of a consociational solution, and which would especially improve the system's long-term survival. They have been deliberately excluded from the ambit of this work, whose goal has been to explain the political reasons for elite reluctance to adopt a power-sharing solution. An examination of societal structures and broader impediments to adopting peace would contribute another very important piece to the puzzle of why peace has not been made in Cyprus.

Scholarship on power-sharing and consociationalism in Cyprus (and other divided societies) is a burgeoning field. Until now in both Cypriot societies ideas of federalism and consociationalism have been underexplored. The official, and much of the Greek Cypriot academic, discourse denies even the *concept* of Cyprus being a divided society. Scholarship on Cyprus as a divided society is stunted,[3] primarily because the problem is articulated as one of Turkish invasion and occupation, or Greek Cypriot domination, rather than of division. While this trend is now less evident, change is slow and there is much that can contribute to understanding how to apply a political settlement to Cyprus. Much can also be learnt from comparative studies. What can the experiences of Northern Ireland and its recent success in finally creating a power-sharing government, for example, tell us about the adoption of such solutions in Cyprus? A comparison of the processes and experiences of other cases, and especially a comparison between the referendums and processes of (attempted or successful) adoption of new political institutions for Northern Ireland and Cyprus would be illuminating.

Consociationalism is a valuable system of government in polities which have deep conflicts that need to be managed. But it is also a delicate system of government. The paradox of this situation is that deeply divided societies often lack the capacity to create the conditions which will support the adoption and maintenance of a power-sharing system of government. Critics of consociational theory are therefore correct in pointing out that this is consociationalism's largest problem. Consociational theory would significantly benefit from a connection with theories that explain how positive change is created in divided societies. Much worthwhile work remains to be done in this field. If such work can be done, it promises to greatly strengthen the value and broaden the appeal of consociational democracy for deeply divided and post-conflict societies.

Appendix 1

Arend Lijphart's Schematic Presentation of Principal Propositions of Consociational Theory

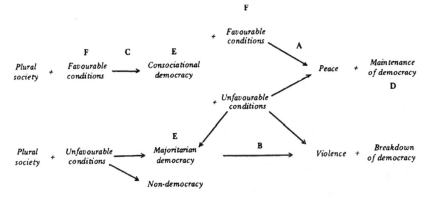

Source: Arend Lijphart, *Power-Sharing in South Africa*, policy papers in International Affairs, no. 24, Berkeley: Institute of International Studies, University of California, 1985 p. 85.

Appendix 2

Cypriot Population Distribution: 1960

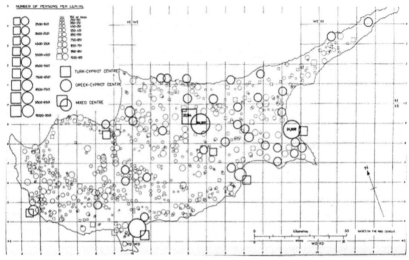

Source: Richard A. Patrick, *Political Geography and the Cyprus Conflict: 1963–1971*, Ontario, University of Waterloo, 1976 p. 10.

Appendix 3

Greek Cypriot Political Parties

Major Greek Cypriot political parties

Party	Ideology	Alliances	Recent parliamentary vote %	Foundation of party
AKEL	Communist	DIKO, EDEK	2006: 31.1% 2001: 34.7%	1926 as KKK, banned in 1931 by the British government; Re-formed 1941 as AKEL.
DISY	Centre-right	EDI, Liberal	2006: 31.4% 2001: 34.0%	1976 as a result of split with President Makarios. Traditionally houses EOKA and EOKA B supporters.
DIKO	Centre-right	AKEL, EDEK	2006: 19.9% 2001: 14.8%	1976 Founded by second president, Spyros Kyprianou.
EDEK	Social-Democrat (Centre-left)	DIKO, AKEL	2006: 8.9% 2001: 6.5%	1970 by Vassos Lyssarides, personal physician of Archbishop Makarios. Traditionally houses supporters of Makarios and Lyssarides' 1964 group of fighters against Turkish Cypriots.
EDI	Liberal	DISY	2006: 1.6% 2001: 2.6%	1993 as Movement of Free Democrats by third president Georgos Vassiliou; Later merged with ex-AKEL members ADISOK to form EDI.

Sources: Republic of Cyprus Press and Information Office; personal interviews of author.

Previous presidents of the Republic of Cyprus

President	Term of office	Party
Archbishop Makarios	1960–77	None
Spiros Kyprianou	1977–88	DIKO
George Vassiliou	1988–93	EDI
Glafkos Clerides	1993–2003	DISY
Tassos Papadopoulos	2003–8	DIKO
Demetris Christofias	2008	AKEL

Source: Republic of Cyprus Press and Information Office.

Previous presidents and prime ministers of the TRNC

Position	Name	Term of office	Party	Of Cabinet
President	Rauf Denktaş	1985–2005	UBP	
President	Mehmet Ali Talat	2005–Present	CTP	
Prime Minister	Hakki Atun	1994–6	DP	DP-CTP
Prime Minister	Derviş Eroğlu	1996–2004	UBP	UBP-DP/UBP-TKP
Prime Minister	Mehmet Ali Talat	2004–5	CTP	CTP-DP
Prime Minister	Ferdi Sabit Soyer	2005–9	CTP	CTP-DP
Prime Minister	Derviş Eroğlu	2009–Present	UBP	UBP

Source: http://www.cm.gov.nc.tr/cm/kabine/kabban.htm (accessed 27 December 2006).

Appendix 4

President Makarios' 13 Amendments to the 1960 Constitution

1. The right of veto of the president and the vice-president of the Republic to be abandoned.
2. The vice-President of the Republic to deputise for the president of the Republic in case of his temporary absence or incapacity to perform his duties.
3. The Greek president of the House of Representatives and the Turkish vice-president to be elected by the House as a whole and not as at present the president by the Greek Members of the House and the vice-president by the Turkish Members of the House.
4. The vice-president of the House of Representatives to deputise for the president of the House in case of his temporary absence or incapacity to perform his duties.
5. The constitutional provisions regarding separate majorities for enactment of certain laws by the House of Representatives to be abolished.
6. Unified municipalities to be established.
7. The administration of Justice to be unified.
8. The division of the Security Forces into Police and Gendarmerie to be abolished.
9. The numerical strength of the Security Forces and of the Defence Forces to be determined by a law.
10. The proportion of the participation of Greek and Turkish Cypriots in the composition of the Public Service and the Forces of the Republic to be modified in proportion to the ratio of the population of Greek and Turkish Cypriots.
11. The number of the members of the Public Service Commission to be reduced from ten to five.
12. All decisions of the Public Service Commission to be taken by simple majority.
13. The Greek Cypriot Communal Chamber to be abolished.

Source: Dimitris Bitsios, *Cyprus: The Vulnerable Republic*, Thessaloniki, Institute for Balkan Studies, 1975 p. 217.

Appendix 5

Alvaro de Soto's Preliminary Thoughts, 12 July 2000

1. As we are about to break until 24 July, I would like to share with you some preliminary thoughts on the way ahead. It is difficult to draw a balance sheet of a process which has not yet entered the negotiating phase as such, and that is not my purpose today. Nor has the time come for submitting proposals, let alone comprehensive proposals. I am intentionally refraining from covering the entire spectrum at this time. One step at a time. I first wish to obtain reactions to these preliminary thoughts, which contain a mixture of procedure, assumptions, emerging trends, and pending issues.
2. I am not asking for approval or concurrence with what I am about to say. My purpose is to elicit your comments, not now, but when you return from the break.
3. General points:
   - The aim is a comprehensive settlement covering all issues on the table, encompassing all legal instruments and other agreements involving non-Cypriot actors.
   - The settlement should be self-executing and provide for appropriate mechanisms for verification of compliance.
   - The settlement should leave nothing to be negotiated subsequently.
   - The settlement should include binding timetables of implementation.
   - Labels are to be avoided, at least for the present, so as to concentrate on the underlying concepts.
   - Nothing is agreed until everything is agreed.
4. General aims:
   - Political equality for Greek Cypriots and Turkish Cypriots.
   - Maximum security and institutional protection for Greek Cypriots and Turkish Cypriots to ensure that neither can dominate the other.
   - Equitable solutions for the exercise of property rights, for the right of return, and on territory.
5. Among the broad features of a potential settlement that are emerging, I see the following:
   - A common state consisting of an indissoluble partnership of politically equal, largely self-governing component states, sharing in a single international legal personality. Each component state shall have its own constitution, government, powers and distinct citizenship. The comprehensive settlement would enshrine the basic legal framework of the common state.
   - A common Cypriot nationality and government with specified powers.

- Effective participation of Greek Cypriots and Turkish Cypriots in the common government.
- Free movement throughout the island.
- An international force to be deployed under a Security Council mandate; dissolution of Greek Cypriot and Turkish Cypriot forces; prohibition of arms supplies; substantial reduction of non-Cypriot forces to equal levels. Security arrangements will have to recognise the crucial role of the Treaty of Guarantee and the Treaty of Alliance.
- The need to honour property rights. My sense is that this will require an appropriate combination of restitution, exchange and compensation. The exact make-up will be closely linked to the extent of territorial adjustment.
- The extent of territorial adjustment will require considerable further reflection. There also seems to be a correlation between territorial adjustment and the degree of integration of, or separateness between, Greek Cypriots and Turkish Cypriots in general.
- An additional factor in this equation is the powers and structures of the component states and the common state respectively.

These linkages confirm the view, which I am sure we all share, that we must advance on all issues simultaneously.

Finally, let me state my assumption that a comprehensive settlement shall commit Cyprus to EU membership while taking into account legitimate concerns in this regards.

I have attempted to share with you my impression of the state of play. The resulting snapshot is unavoidably blurry. More cannot be expected in the short time available to me because of the early break. It is obvious that considerable work remains to be done on all issues, but we must take the long view. I look forward to your comments on 24 July so as to build on what we have so far.

Source: David Hannay, *Cyprus, the Search for a Solution*, London, I. B. Taurus and Co. 2005.

Appendix 6

The 8 November 2000 Document

1. I am very glad to join you and wish to thank you for accepting my invitation to continue and intensify efforts to achieve a comprehensive settlement. I was gratified that, in New York, we saw the first signs of the real engagement and I understand that this has continued here in Geneva. I realize, of course, that there is a long way to go.

2. Since we are now seriously engaged in the substance, I wish to make a number of observations. Further to my statement of 12 September, I want to give you my thoughts, first about procedure, and then about some substantive aspects of a possible comprehensive settlement, in the hope of facilitating negotiations. However, I wish to make clear that, as with Mr de Soto's 'Preliminary Thoughts' of 12 July, and the subsequent ideas we have offered, I am not at this stage putting forward a proposal, nor am I covering all the ground. I do not intend to make these remarks public, but I will leave you with the notes of what I say just for your record.

3. On *procedure*, the first thing I wish to do is to confirm that, as concerns the United Nations, these negotiations are being conducted pursuant to Security Council Regulation 1250, which sets out four guidelines:
   - No preconditions;
   - All issues on the table;
   - Commitment in good faith to continue to negotiate until a settlement is reached; and
   - Full consideration of relevant United Nations resolutions and treaties.

4. In these negotiations, each party represents its side – and no one else – as the political equal of the other, and nothing is agreed until everything is agreed.

5. The aim is a comprehensive settlement covering all issues, encompassing all legal instruments and other agreements involving non-Cypriot actors. In other words, it should be self-implementing. To this end, it should provide for appropriate mechanisms for verification of compliance and binding timetables of implementation. It should leave nothing to be negotiated subsequently. The settlement should include the test of a 'basic law' and texts on security arrangements, territorial adjustments and the property regime, as well as the initial body of 'common state' legislation.

6. The comprehensive settlement should be submitted for approval in separate referenda so as to ensure the democratic endorsement, legitimisation, and ratification of the comprehensive settlement by each community. Unless otherwise

specified in the comprehensive settlement, subsequent changes to it could only occur by the same method.

7. Since no useful purpose would be served by myself or Mr de Soto conveying proposals from the parties back and forth, we are working towards a single negotiating text as the basis for negotiations. For this process to succeed it is essential that you provide specific comments on ideas put forward by the UN. I would ask you to give us indications of what you feel might not be fair or viable in the ideas we put to you, and why. This would be more helpful to the process than substitute proposals, position papers or suggested amendments. Without your specific comments, and those of the other side, we cannot take them on board in revising our submissions, and your participation in shaping the negotiating text will be hampered. I ask you to engage with us fully in this way so as to enable us to advance on all issues simultaneously.

8. On *substance*, as you know, we have intentionally avoided labels in these talks so as to concentrate on the underlying issues. I would like to give you a general outline of elements I believe should be a part of a comprehensive settlement. Again, I am not seeking your agreement on them at this time. Rather, I wish to indicate what I believe the parties ought to reasonably accept as a fair and viable compromise. I will now describe the elements – which, I emphasize, are not an exhaustive list.

9. The comprehensive settlement should enshrine a new partnership on which to build a better future in peace, security and prosperity on a united island. The equal status of the parties in a united Cyprus must and should be recognized explicitly in the comprehensive settlement, which will embody the results of the detailed negotiations required to translate this concept into clear and practical provisions.

10. Cyprus should have a single international legal personality. Whatever is eventually agreed regarding the status of the two 'component states', there should be one sovereign, indissoluble 'common' state. I mean that neither side could separate from the 'common state' that emerges from these negotiations, nor try to unite all or part of the island with Greece or Turkey. Nor should either side be able to dominate the 'common state' or the other 'component state'. There should be a single citizenship. Human rights and fundamental freedoms should be guaranteed.

11. The 'common state' should have what we are calling, for now, a 'common government', with a 'basic law' prescribing powers exercised by legislative, executive, and judicial branches. The 'common government' should be able to function efficiently in the modern world. This includes being able to take decisions in international bodies of which the 'common state' is a member. In the operation of the 'common government', the political equality of Greek Cypriots and Turkish Cypriots should be respected. Political equality, whilst not requiring numerical equality, must involve effective participation of Greek Cypriots and Turkish Cypriots in the 'common government', and protection of their fundamental interests.

12. There should be what we have called, for now, two 'component states' – Greek Cypriot and Turkish Cypriot – each with its own 'basic law'. The 'component states' should be largely self-governing, it being understood that they must not contravene the 'basic law' of the 'common state'. They would have power over all matters other than the essential competencies and functions that will be listed in the comprehensive settlement as being the responsibility of the 'common state'.

Neither 'component state' would be able to interfere in the governance of the other. It might be possible for the 'component states' to confer additional internal citizenship rights on persons who possess Cypriot citizenship.

13. I take it that a comprehensive settlement would commit Cyprus to EU membership. At the same time, I would hope that the EU would be prepared to address special and legitimate concerns in regard to accession. In this context, it is clearly important that the provisions of the comprehensive settlement should not represent an obstacle to such membership nor need to be renegotiated when the terms of accession are established.

14. Concerning property, we must recognize that there are considerations of international law to which we must give weight. The solution must withstand legal challenge. The legal rights which people have to their property should be respected. At the same time, I believe that a solution should carefully regulate the exercise of these rights so as to safeguard the character of the 'component states'. Meeting these principles will require an appropriate combination of reinstatement, exchange and compensation. For a period of time to be established by agreement, there may be limits on the number of Greek Cypriots establishing residence in the north and Turkish Cypriots establishing residence in the south. It is worth mentioning in this context that the criteria, form and nature of regulation of property rights will also have a bearing on the extent of territorial adjustment, and vice versa.

15. I find it hard to imagine a comprehensive settlement without a return to Greek Cypriot administration of an appreciable amount of territory. In my view, in negotiating the adjustment, a balance must be struck between a maximum return of Greek Cypriots to areas being returned to Greek Cypriot administration, and a minimum of dislocation of Turkish Cypriots. The focus should be on the number of persons affected more than the amount of territory involved. Clearly, the moment is approaching where discussions should proceed on the basis of detailed geographic data.

16. I am confident that arrangements can be made which effectively address the security concerns of each side. It is clear that one side's security must not be assured at the expense of the security of the other, and I think that both parties would be willing to come to an arrangement acceptable to all. Such an arrangement should include the continuation of the security regime established in 1960, as supplemented to reflect the comprehensive settlement; the dissolution of Greek Cypriot and Turkish Cypriot forces; a prohibition legally binding on both exporters and importers of arms supplies; agreed equal levels of Greek and Turkish troops; a United Nations mandated force and police unit that can function throughout the island; and a political mechanism which can assist in resolving security issues.

17. I am making these observations on the main issues before us after nearly a year of listening and testing ideas. My purpose is to make a further step in the direction of developing an overall picture of a comprehensive approach to a settlement. Please reflect on what I have said. I hope you will use my observations as the course to follow in the talks ahead.

18. I think it is necessary to schedule further talks in early 2001. Accordingly, I invite you to continue the proximity talks in Geneva from late January 2001. In the meantime, I am asking Mr de Soto to travel to the region and the island late this month or early next month.

19. In the time between now and the next session, I would also ask you to reflect on one final point. A strong impression that I have formed during the proximity talks is this: it is not only the sad events of the past that are the tragedy of modern Cyprus; it is also the absence of a solution. The absence of a solution prevents all Cypriots from sharing fully – and equally – in the fruits of prosperity, security and progress. A united and independent Cyprus, in which Greek Cypriots and Turkish Cypriots are equal and protected and free, as citizens of Europe, is the promise of the future. I hope that you will seize what is perhaps the best chance yet for a Cyprus settlement, in order to bequeath that promise to succeeding generations.

20. In closing, let me say again that I do not intend to make these remarks public, and I trust that you will also keep them to yourselves.

Source: David Hannay, *Cyprus, the Search for a Solution*, London, I. B. Taurus and Co. 2005.

Appendix 7

Proposals for Resolutions under United Nations Auspices

Proposal	UN Representative	Interlocutors	Date
Third Vienna Agreement		Clerides, Denktaş	August 1975
High Level Agreement (Makarios–Denktaş Accords)	Sec. Gen. Waldheim	Makarios, Denktaş	February 1977
Ten-Point Agreement (Kyprianou–Denktas Communique)	Javier Pérez de Cuéllar	Kyprianou, Denktaş	May 1979
Proximity Talks	Javier Pérez de Cuéllar	Kyprianou, Denktaş	1984–5 Summit
Draft Framework Exercise		Kyprianou, Denktaş	1985–6
Greek Cypriot Proposals (Vassiliou–Denktas Meetings)	Oscar Camillion and Gustave Feissel	Vassiliou, Denktaş	January 1989 (1988–90)
Set of Ideas on an Overall Framework on Cyprus	Sec. Gen. Boutros Ghali and Gustave Feissel	Vassiliou, Denktaş	1992
Annan Plan for Cyprus	Sec. Gen. Kofi Annan	Clerides/ Papadopoulos, Denktaş/Talat	April 2004 (2002–4)

Sources: High Level Agreement of 12 February 1977, United *Nations Document*; The Ten-Point Agreement of 19 May 1979, *United Nations Document*; 1989 Greek Cypriot Proposals, *United Nations Document*; 1992 Set of Ideas on an Overall Framework Agreement on Cyprus, *United Nations Document S/24472*; 2004 Comprehensive Settlement of the Cyprus Problem (final version) *United Nations Document*.

Appendix 8

Greek and Turkish Cypriot Attitudes Post-Referendum

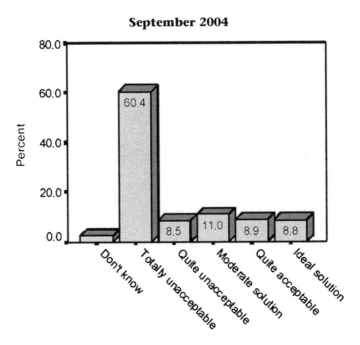

September 2004

Two-State Solution

Source: Alexandros Lordos, 'Can the Cyprus Problem be Solved? Understanding the Greek Cypriot Response to the UN Peace Plan for Cyprus', *An Evidence-Based Study in Co-operation with CYMAR Market Research Ltd*, November 2004, www.cypruspolls.org (accessed 23 March 2006).

June 2006

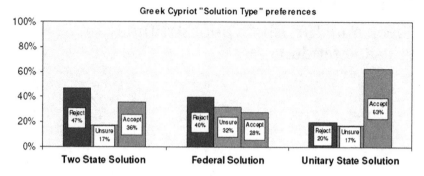

Greek Cypriot "Solution Type" preferences

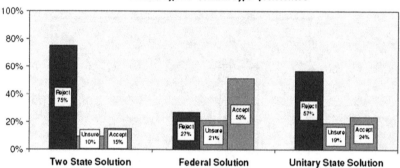

Turkish Cypriot "Solution Type" preferences

Source: Alexandros Lordos, 'Building Trust: An Inter-Communal Analysis of Public Opinion in Cyprus', *An Evidence-Based Study in Co-operation with CYMAR Market Research Ltd. and KADEM Cyprus Social Research,* June 2006, www.cypruspolls.org (accessed 13 July 2007).

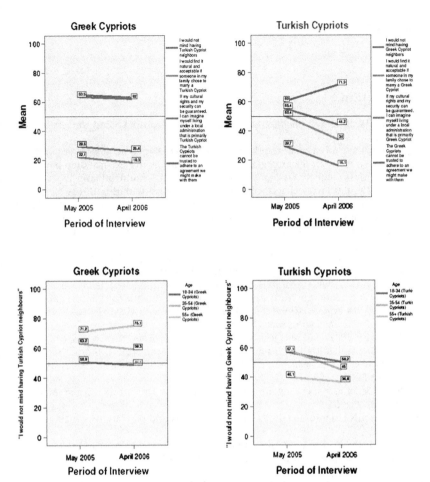

Source: Alexandros Lordos, 'Building Trust: An Inter-Communal Analysis of Public Opinion in Cyprus', *An Evidence-Based Study in Co-operation with CYMAR Market Research Ltd. and KADEM Cyprus Social Research,* June 2006, www.cypruspolls.org (accessed 13 July 2007).

Notes

Introduction

1. Stefan Wolff, *Ethnic Conflict: A Global Perspective*, Oxford, Oxford University Press 2007, p. 6.
2. National Organisation of Cypriot Fighters, Εθνική Οργάνωσις Κυπριων Αγωνιστών.
3. However, the years leading up to and succeeding Cyprus' EU accession have seen the south become increasingly – if very reluctantly – multicultural.
4. Greek Cypriot civilians and soldiers who went missing during the 1974 Turkish invasion of Cyprus are referred to in Greek as 'Οι αγνοόυμενοι'. Turkish Cypriot civilians and fighters who went missing or were killed by Greek Cypriots in the decade between 1964 and 1974 are referred to in Turkish as 'Şehitler', meaning 'the martyrs'.
5. See Alexandros Lordos, 'Rational Agent or Unthinking Follower? A Survey-Based Profile Analysis of Greek Cypriot and Turkish Cypriot Referendum Voters', March 2006, http://www.cypruspolls.org/RationalOrUnthinking.pdf (accessed 12 June 2007), and 'Building Trust: An Inter-Communal Analysis of Public Opinion in Cyprus', an evidence-based study in co-operation with CYMAR Market Research Ltd. and KADEM Cyprus Social Research, June 2006, www.cypruspolls.org (accessed 1 January 2007). See also Jean Christou, 'Poll shows two sides polarized', *Cyprus Mail*, 25 April 2007, and 'It's nothing personal', *Cyprus Mail*, 12 April 2006.
6. 'Turkish Cypriots spend as much in the south as they earn', *Cyprus Mail*, 31 August 2005.
7. Jean Christou, 'Spending up to £25 million in the north', *Cyprus Mail*, 18 December 2005.
8. The acquis communautaire is the body of laws and regulations which governs the EU.
9. Though the EU has established a number of projects which seek to improve the economic and infrastructural situation in the Turkish Cypriot state, enumerated further in Chapter 6.
10. Called the Provisional Turkish Cypriot Administration.
11. 'Η Τούρκικη Εισβολή'.
12. 'Barış harekatı'.
13. Duncan Morrow, 'Breaking Antagonism? Political Leadership in Divided Societies', in Ian O'Flynn and David Russell (eds), *Power Sharing: New Challenges for Divided Societies*, London, Pluto Press 2005 p. 45.
14. Oren Yiftachel, 'Planning as Control: Policy and Resistance in a Deeply Divided Society', *Progress in Planning*, vol. 44, 1995 p. 124.
15. Stephen Krasner, *International Regimes*, New York, Cornell University Press 1983 p. 2. Cited in B. Guy Peters, *Institutional Theory in Political Science, the 'New Institutionalism'*, London, Pinter 1999 p. 130.
16. This definition is an adaptation of Stephen Krasner's 1983 description of a regime within the field of international institutionalism.
17. Donald Rothchild, *Managing Ethnic Conflict in Africa, Pressures and Incentives for Cooperation*, Washington, Brookings Institution Press 1997 p. 34.
18. Ibid., p. 245.

1 Consociationalism in Theory and Practice

1. Brendan O'Leary in Michael Kerr, *Imposing Power-Sharing: Conflict and Coexistence in Northern Ireland and Lebanon*, Dublin, Irish Academic Press, 2005, p. xxi.
2. Sujit Choudhry, in Sujit Choudhry (ed.) *Constitutional Design for Divided Societies: Integration or Accommodation?*, Oxford, Oxford University Press, 2008, p. 13.
3. Ibid., pp. 52–3.
4. Ibid., p. 59.
5. John McGarry, Brendan O'Leary, and Richard Simeon, 'Integration or Accommodation? The Enduring Debate in Conflict Regulation', in Sujit Choudhry (ed.) *Constitutional Design for Divided Societies: Integration or Accommodation?* Oxford, Oxford University Press, 2008, p. 58.
6. Arend Lijphart, *The Politics of Accommodation: Pluralism and Democracy in the Netherlands*, Berkeley, University of California Press, 1968.
7. Ibid., p. 1.
8. Ibid., p. 103.
9. The term comes from 'Johannes Althusius's concept of *consociation* in his *Politica Methodice Digesta*, and the term 'consociational' used by David E. Apter, *The Political Kingdom in Uganda: A Study in Bureaucratic Nationalism* (Princeton 1961), 24–5 Arend Lijphart, 'Consociational Democracy', (1969) p. 211.
10. Lijphart, 'Consociational Democracy', (1969) p. 216.
11. Gerald R. McDaniel, cited in Arend Lijphart, 'Consociational Democracy', (1969) p. 225.
12. The idea of pinning consociationalism down as any kind of formal 'structure' is something which is alternately supported and rejected by both Lijphart and his successors, and will be discussed later in the chapter.
13. Ian S. Lustick, 'Lijphart, Lakatos, and Consociationalism', *World Politics*, vol. 50, no. 1, 1997, p. 96.
14. It should be noted that there is some confusion over the use of the term 'power-sharing' in the literature. Lijphart has in the past used 'power-sharing' and 'consociationalism' coterminously, however, I agree with Bogaards's point that 'the concepts of consociational and consensus democracy are best reserved to denote specific forms of power-sharing. ... In other words, consociational and consensus democracy are at least one rung lower on the ladder of generality than the concept of power-sharing'. Matthijs Bogaards, 'The Uneasy Relationship Between Empirical and Normative Types in Consociational Theory', *Journal of Theoretical Politics*, vol. 12, no. 4, 2000, pp. 416–7.
15. Milton J. Esman, 'Power-Sharing and the Constructionist Fallacy', in Markus M. L. Crepaz, Thomas A. Koelble, and David Wilsford (eds) *Democracy and Institutions: The Life Work of Arend Lijphart*, Ann Arbor, University of Michigan Press, 2000, p. 101.
16. John McGarry and Brendan O'Leary, 'Consociational Theory and Peace Agreements in Pluri-National Place, Northern Ireland and Other Cases', in Guy Ben-Porat, *Failure of the Middle East Peace Process*, London, Palgrave Macmillan, 2008, p. 9.
17. Brendan O'Leary, 'Debating Consociational Politics: Normative and Explanatory Arguments', in Sid Noel (ed.) *From Power Sharing to Democracy: Post-Conflict Institutions in Ethnically Divided Societies*, London, McGill-Queens University Press, 2005, p. 25.
18. Ibid., p. 26.

19. John McGarry and Brendan O'Leary, 'Consociational Theory, Northern Ireland's Conflict, and its Agreement 2. What Critics of Consociation Can Learn from Northern Ireland', *Government and Opposition*, vol. 41, no. 2, Spring 2006, p. 249.

20. John McGarry and Brendan O'Leary, 'Consociational Theory, Northern Ireland's Conflict, and its Agreement. Part I: What Consociationalists Can Learn from Northern Ireland', *Government and Opposition*, vol. 41, no. 1, Winter 2006, p. 45.

21. John McGarry and Brendan O'Leary, 'Consociational Theory, Northern Ireland's Conflict, and its Agreement 2. What Critics of Consociation Can Learn from Northern Ireland', p. 249.

22. In an attempt to meet critics' calls to increase the empirical testability of consociationalism, Lijphart also developed what has more recently come to be known as *consensus democracy* – a form of power-sharing which attempts to meet a broader set of criteria than consociationalism. Consensus democracy is characterised by a set of institutional devices, the most recent collection of which is executive power-sharing in coalitions, executive–legislative balance of power, multiparty system, proportional representation, interest group corporatism, federalised and decentralised government, strong bicameralism, constitutional rigidity, judicial review, and central bank independence. Arend Lijphart, *Patterns of Democracy: Government Forms and Performance in 36 Countries*, pp. 34–41. While, according to Lijphart, consociationalism is the most appropriate solution for 'deeply' or 'ethnically' divided societies, Arend Lijphart in 'Varieties of Nonmajoritarian Democracy', p. 233, he states that consensus democracy seeks to meet the needs of societies which are simply 'divided', or 'semi-plural'. He has labelled consensus democracy as a 'kinder, gentler' form of democracy, which, in contrast to consociationalism, needs to be supported by a consensual political culture. Arend Lijphart, *Patterns of Democracy: Government Forms and Performance in 36 Countries*, p. 306. Consociationalism, of course, is said to use political institutions to create that culture.

23. Ulrich Schneckener, 'Making Power-Sharing Work: Lessons from Successes and Failures in Ethnic Conflict Regulation', *Journal of Peace Research*, vol. 39, no. 2, 2002, p. 204.

24. Milton J. Esman, 'Power-Sharing and the Constructionist Fallacy', p. 101.

25. See, for example, Will Kymlicka, *Politics in the Vernacular: Nationalism, Multiculturalism and Citizenship*, Oxford, Oxford University Press, 2001; Will Kymlicka, *Multicultural Citizenship: A Liberal Theory of Minority Rights*, Oxford, Oxford University Press, 1995.

26. Arend Lijphart, 'Consociational Democracy', (1969) p. 216.

27. Ibid.

28. Ibid., pp. 216–22.

29. Arend Lijphart, 'Power-Sharing and Group Autonomy in the 1990s and the Twenty-First Century', p. 10.

30. Arend Lijphart, 'Constitutional Design for Divided Societies', *Journal of Democracy*, vol. 15, no. 2, April 2004.

31. See Arend Lijphart, 'Multiethnic Democracy', in Seymour Martin Lipset (ed.) *The Encyclopaedia of Democracy*, London, Routledge, 1995, p. 859.

32. Arend Lijphart, *Democracy in Plural Societies: A Comparative Exploration*, New Haven, Yale University Press, 1977, p. 54.

33. Arend Lijphart, 'Constitutional Design for Divided Societies', pp. 99–106.

34. Ibid., p. 100.

35. Ibid., p. 104.
36. Ibid., p. 105.
37. See the section on consociation in John McGarry et al., 'Integration or Accommodation? The Enduring Debate in Conflict Regulation', pp. 58–63.
38. Arend Lijphart, 'The Wave of Power-Sharing Democracy', in Andrew Reynolds (ed.) *The Architecture of Democracy: Constitutional Design, Conflict Management, and Democracy*, Oxford, Oxford University Press, 2002, p. 37.
39. Brendan O'Leary in Michael Kerr, *Imposing Power-Sharing: Conflict and Coexistence in Northern Ireland and Lebanon*, Dublin, Irish Academic Press, 2005, p. xxi.
40. Arend Lijphart, 'Varieties of Nonmajoritarian Democracy', p. 241.
41. For a broader survey of criticisms, see Brendan O'Leary, 'Debating Consociational Politics: Normative and Explanatory Arguments', in Sid Noel (ed.) *From Power Sharing to Democracy: Post-Conflict Institutions in Ethnically Divided Societies*, pp. 3–43.
42. Eric A. Nordlinger, *Conflict Regulation in Divided Societies*, Occasional Papers in International Affairs, no. 29, Cambridge, Harvard Centre for International Affairs, 1972.
43. Liesbet Hooghe, *A Leap in the Dark: Nationalist Conflict and Federal Reform in Belgium*, New York, Cornell University Press, 1991, p. 53; Kris Deschouwer, 'Falling Apart Together: The Changing Nature of Belgian Consociationalism, 1961–2001', *Acta Politica*, vol. 37, no. 1, 2002, pp. 68–85.
44. Kurt Richard Luther, 'Must What Goes Up Always Come Down? Of Pillars and Arches in Austria's Political Architecture', in Kurt Richard Luther and Kris Deschouwer (eds) *Party Elites in Divided Societies, Political Parties in Consociational Democracy*, London, Routledge, 1999, p. 49.
45. Ian S. Lustick, 'Lijphart, Lakatos, and Consociationalism', p. 104.
46. John McGarry and Brendan O'Leary, *Explaining Northern Ireland: Broken Images*, Oxford, Blackwell 1995 p. 339.
47. Andrew Reynolds, 'Majoritarian or Power-Sharing Government', in Markus M. L. Crepaz, Thomas A. Koelble, and David Wilsford (eds), *Democracy and Institutions: The Life Work of Arend Lijphart*, Ann Arbor, University of Michigan Press, 2000, p. 165.
48. Courtney Jung and Ian Shapiro, 'South Africa's Negotiated Transition: Democracy, Opposition, and the new Constitutional Order', *Politics and Society*, vol. 23, no. 3, 1995, pp. 269–308.
49. In reference to the South African case.
50. Andrew Reynolds, 'Majoritarian or Power-Sharing Government', in Markus M. L. Crepaz, Thomas A. Koelble, and David Wilsford (eds) *Democracy and Institutions: The Life Work of Arend Lijphart*, Ann Arbor, University of Michigan Press, 2000, p. 165.
51. For an older table of preconditions, and how they have changed over the years, see Matthijs Bogaards, 'The Favourable Factors for Consociational Democracy: A Review', *European Journal of Political Research*, vol. 33, no. 4, June 1998, p. 478.
52. Ibid., pp. 475–96.
53. He has acknowledged the cases of Cyprus and Lebanon as exceptions, but emphasises that these are exceptions which prove the rule. See Lijphart, *Democracy in Plural Societies: A Comparative Exploration*, p. 160.
54. Matthijs Bogaards, 'The Favourable Factors for Consociational Democracy: A Review', p. 475; Arend Lijphart, *Democracy in Plural Societies: A Comparative Exploration*, p. 54.
55. Lijphart, *Power-Sharing in South Africa*, p. 116.

56. Ibid., p. 490.
57. M. P. C. M van Schendelen, 'The Views of Arend Lijphart and Collected Criticisms', p. 34.
58. Although, in 1985, Lijphart created an aggregative table rating six plural societies according to a list of nine favourable factors. Each favourable factor is judged on a five-point scale, from 'very favourable' to 'very unfavourable'. See Arend Lijphart, *Power-Sharing in South Africa*, pp. 119–28.
59. Adriano Pappalardo, 'The Conditions for Consociational Democracy: A Logical and Empirical Critique', *European Journal of Political Research*, vol. 9, no. 4, 1981, p. 365.
60. Ian S. Lustick, 'Lijphart, Lakatos, and Consociationalism', p. 108.
61. Jurg Steiner, 'The Consociational Theory and Beyond', *Comparative Politics*, vol. 13, no. 3, April 1981, pp. 339–54.
62. Brian Barry, 'Political Accommodation and Consociational Democracy', *British Journal of Political Science*, vol. 5, no. 4, October 1975.
63. M. P. C. M van Schendelen, 'The Views of Arend Lijphart and Collected Criticisms', p. 30.
64. Eric A. Nordlinger, *Conflict Regulation in Divided Societies*, Occasional Papers in International Affairs, no. 29, Cambridge, Harvard Centre for International Affairs, 1972.
65. Arend Lijphart, *Power-Sharing in South Africa*, pp. 86–7.
66. While Lustick's claim is not adequately disproved by Lijphart and other consociational theorists, pursing the debate about the soundness of consociationalism's theoretical foundations is outside the scope of this work. The debate is relevant insofar as it affects the application of consociational democracy to Cyprus; that is, if it seems that Cyprus has not been able to adopt a consociational democracy *because* the theory itself is problematic.
67. Ian S. Lustick, 'Lijphart, Lakatos, and Consociationalism', p. 112.
68. Arend Lijphart, *Power-Sharing in South Africa*, p. 114.
69. Ibid., p. 115.
70. Ian S. Lustick, 'Lijphart, Lakatos, and Consociationalism', p. 108.
71. Paul R. Brass, *Ethnicity and Nationalism: Theory and Comparison*, New Delhi, Sage Publications, 1991, p. 342.
72. Andrew Reynolds, 'Building Democracy after Conflict: Constitutional Medicine', *Journal of Democracy*, vol. 16, no. 1, January 2005, p. 60.
73. Daniel P. Sullivan, 'The Missing Pillars: A Look at the Failure of Peace in Burundi Through the Lens of Arend Lijphart's Theory of Consociational Democracy', *Journal of Modern African Studies*, vol. 43, no. 1, 2005, pp. 75–95.
74. John McGarry and Brendan O'Leary, 'Consociational Theory and Peace Agreements in Pluri-National Place, Northern Ireland and Other Cases', p. 19.
75. Ibid., p. 18.
76. Excluding articles 1 and 2 (Constitution of the United Cyprus Republic, Part VI, Article 37 (2)).
77. Constitution of the United Cyprus Republic, Article 2 (4).
78. Donald L. Horowitz, *Ethnic Groups in Conflict*, Berkeley, University of California Press, 1985, fn. 26, p. 573.
79. Ibid.
80. Ibid.
81. John McGarry and Brendan O'Leary, 'Consociational Theory, Northern Ireland's Conflict, and its Agreement. Part I: What Consociationalists Can Learn from Northern Ireland', p. 47.

82. In May 2007.
83. Donald L. Horowitz, *Ethnic Groups in Conflict*, p. 572.
84. Lebanon has been alternatively classified as both a consociational paradigm state and as a state for which consociationalism is prescribed. Lijphart has used Lebanon as the non-West's foremost example of organic consociational development. However, it is not traditionally included as a consociational paradigm primarily because of its problematic history. It is frequently cited as an example of a failed consociational state.
85. John McGarry and Brendan O'Leary, 'Consociational Theory, Northern Ireland's Conflict, and its Agreement. Part I: What Consociationalists Can Learn from Northern Ireland', fn. 17, p. 47.
86. Arend Lijphart, 'The Wave of Power-Sharing Democracy', p. 45.
87. The theory primarily diverges from the consociational model in its recommendation of electoral and legislative structures which encourage cross-ethnic or inter-group collaboration. Its underlying philosophy is that a system which encourages moderation by political elites will eventually create inter-communal bonds by undercutting the political incentives for extremist behaviour.
88. Donald L. Horowitz, *A Democratic South Africa? Constitutional Engineering in a Divided Society*, p. 197.
89. Ibid., p. 139.
90. Ibid.
91. Ibid.
92. Olga Shvetsova, 'Mass-Elite Equilibrium of Federal Constitutional Legitimacy', *Constitutional Political Economy*, vol. 16, p. 125.
93. Donald Horowitz 1985; 1991; Cited in Ibid.
94. Arend Lijphart, *Democracy in Plural Societies: A Comparative Exploration*, p. 165.
95. Donald L. Horowitz, *Ethnic Groups in Conflict*, p. 573.
96. Arend Lijphart, 'Power-Sharing and Group Autonomy in the 1990s and the Twenty-First Century', pp. 6–7.
97. My thanks to John McGarry for this point.
98. Alternatively, it has also been claimed that 'once consociationalism has become part of the political culture, it tends to persist even if the objective conditions that caused its emergence have disappeared', Liesbet Hooghe, p. 33. Daalder and Lehmbruch were very early advocates of this argument. See Gerhard Lehmbruch, 'A Non-Competitive Pattern of Conflict Management in Liberal Democracies: The Case of Switzerland, Austria and Lebanon', in Kenneth D. McRae (ed.), *Consociational Democracy: Political Accommodation in Segmented Societies*, Toronto, McClelland and Stewart 1974 and Hans Daalder, 'On Building Consociational Nations: The Cases of the Netherlands and Switzerland', in Kenneth D. McRae (ed.). While, in this context, consociationalism is referred to as an 'institutional hangover', elites who find themselves empowered by a consociational political system have most likely struggled for the positions which they hold for many years and are unlikely to legislate themselves out of power. Additionally, if the society of which they are a part has a small population, then broader factors begin to play into the need to maintain the system for its own sake. Extensive social networks will have evolved in harmony with consociational democracy – making any alteration of the consociational state likely to affect much more than just the political system. Thus, as the political, socio-cultural, and economic worlds and actors become more intertwined as a result of the consociational structure, it becomes increasingly difficult for the state to disentangle itself, should it become politically obsolete.

99. Brian Barry, 'Political Accommodation and Consociational Democracy', pp. 477–505.
100. Ibid., p. 499.
101. Ronald A. Kieve, 'Pillars of Sand: A Marxist Critique of Consociational Democracy in the Netherlands', *Comparative Politics*, vol. 13, no. 3, April 1981 pp. 313–37.
102. Constitution of the United Cyprus Republic, Article 2 (1) and (2).
103. M. P. C. M van Schendelen, 'The Views of Arend Lijphart and Collected Criticisms', pp. 35–6; Jurg Steiner and Jeffrey Obler, 'Does Consociational Theory Really Hold for Switzerland?', in Milton J. Esman (ed.), *Ethnic Conflict in the Western World*, Ithaca, Cornell University Press 1977; Liesbet Hooghe, p. 33; Brian Barry, 'Political Accommodation and Consociational Democracy', p. 484.
104. Belgium's federalisation occurred quite recently, after the Second World War.
105. Robert Mnookin and Alain Verbeke, 'Bye Bye Belgium?', *International Herald Tribune*, 20 December 2006.
106. Chris Morris, 'Language Dispute Divides Belgium', *BBC News*, 13 May 2005.
107. Jurg Steiner and Jeffrey Obler, 'Does Consociational Theory Really Hold for Switzerland?', in Milton J. Esman (ed.), *Ethnic Conflict in the Western World*, Ithaca, Cornell University Press 1977.
108. Brian Barry, p. 484.
109. This claim is rooted in Barry's argument that Switzerland cannot be considered a 'pure' consociational democracy. Barry's claim, however, has been cogently contradicted by Sciarini and Hug. Pascal Sciarini and Simon Hug, 'The Odd Fellow: Parties and Consociationalism in Switzerland', in Kurt Richard Luther and Kris Deschouwer (eds), *Party Elites in Divided Societies, Political Parties in Consociational Democracy*, London, Routledge 1999.
110. Brian Barry, 'Political Accommodation and Consociational Democracy', p. 485.
111. Ibid., p. 482.
112. However, in the Swiss system, policymaking in bodies other than the federal council quite strictly follows consociational guidelines. New legislation is debated among affected parties, and a single policy is proposed for approval. But this is in addition to decision making by referenda and popular initiative.
113. Didier Pfirter, Legal Advisor to the UN Secretary General's Special Assistant. Interview with author, 6 October 2006.
114. For more details, see www.nrc.no.
115. See, for example: Arend Lijphart, *Power-Sharing in South Africa*; Val R. Lorwin, 'Segmented Pluralism: Ideological Cleavages and Political Cohesion in the Smaller European Democracies', in Kenneth D. McRae (ed.) *Consociational Democracy: Political Accommodation in Segmented Societies*, Toronto, McClelland and Stewart 1974; Brenda M. Seaver, 'The Regional Sources of Power-Sharing Failure: The Case of Lebanon', *Political Science Quarterly*, vol. 115, no. 2, Summer 2000 pp. 247–71; Jan Markusse, 'Power-Sharing and 'Consociational Democracy' in South Tyrol', *GeoJournal*, vol. 43, September 1997 pp. 77–89; Ahmet Sozen, 'A Model of Power-Sharing in Cyprus: From the 1959 London-Zurich Agreements to the Annan Plan', *Turkish Studies*, vol. 5, Spring 2004 pp. 61–77; Daniel P. Sullivan, pp. 75–95.
116. Matthijs Bogaards, 'The Favourable Factors for Consociational Democracy: A Review', pp. 475–96.
117. See for example John McGarry and Brendan O'Leary, 'Consociational Theory, Northern Ireland's Conflict, and its Agreement. Part I: What Consociationalists Can Learn from Northern Ireland', pp. 48–54; and Michael Kerr, *Imposing Power-Sharing: Conflict and Coexistence in Northern Ireland and Lebanon*, Dublin, Irish Academic Press 2005.

118. McGarry, John, and O'Leary, Brendan, 'Consociational Theory and Peace Agreements in Pluri-National Place, Northern Ireland and Other Cases', p. 7.
119. Arend Lijphart, 'Consociational Democracy', (1969) p. 219.
120. Arend Lijphart, *Democracy in Plural Societies: A Comparative Exploration.*
121. Arend Lijphart, *Power-Sharing in South Africa*, p. 119.
122. Ibid., p. 126.
123. Prior to this, crossing between north and south Cyprus was heavily constrained. For a good description of the politics and practicalities of border crossing pre-2003, see Yiannis Papadakis, *Echoes from the Dead Zone*, London, I. B. Tauris 2005. Also see N. Kliot and Y. Mansfield, 'The Political Landscape of Partition: The Case of Cyprus', *Political Geography*, vol. 16, no. 6, 1997 pp. 495–521; Costas M. Constantinou and Yiannis Papadakis, 'The Cypriot State(s) *in situ*: Cross-ethnic Contact and the Discourse of Recognition', *Global Society*, vol. 15, no. 2, 2001 pp. 125–48; Gary Gumpert and Susan J. Drucker, 'Communication Across Lands Divided: The Cypriot Communications Landscape', in Vangelis Calotychos (ed.), *Cyprus and its People: Nation, Identity and Experience in an Unimaginable Community, 1955–1997*, Colorado, Westview Press 1998; Maria Hadjipavlou-Trigeorgis, 'Unofficial Inter-Communal Contacts and their Contribution to Peace-building in Conflict Societies: The Case of Cyprus', *The Cyprus Review*, vol. 5, no. 2, Fall 1993.
124. It was only after Annan III that the constituent states were labelled 'Greek' and 'Turkish' Cypriot.
125. Information obtained by the author in a number of private conversations.
126. Electoral separation was not particular to the Annan Plan. The 1960 Republic of Cyprus used separate electoral lists for each community.
127. Primarily because it necessitates the legalisation of the loss of a significant amount of territory that was owned by Greek Cypriots prior to the 1974 Turkish occupation.
128. Arend Lijphart, *The Politics of Accommodation: Pluralism and Democracy in the Netherlands*, p. 102; Arend Lijphart, 'Consociational Democracy', (1969), p. 217; Arend Lijphart, *Democracy in Plural Societies: A Comparative Exploration*, p. 56.
129. Arend Lijphart, *Democracy in Plural Societies: A Comparative Exploration*, p. 56.
130. Matthijs Bogaards, 'The Favourable Factors for Consociational Democracy: A Review', p. 478.
131. Arend Lijphart, 'Multiethnic Democracy', p. 859.
132. Arend Lijphart, *Power-Sharing in South Africa*, p. 123.
133. Arend Lijphart, 'Consociational Democracy', (1969) p. 217.
134. Ibid.
135. Arend Lijphart, *Democracy in Plural Societies: A Comparative Exploration*, pp. 99–103; Arend Lijphart, *Power-Sharing in South Africa*, p. 127; Arend Lijphart, 'Multiethnic Democracy', p. 859.

2 Cypriot History(ies) as the Foundation of Modern Reunification Politics

1. Aristotle, *Politics.*
2. B. Guy Peters, p. 63.
3. David Marsh and Gerry Stoker (eds), *Theory and Methods in Political Science*, Hampshire, Palgrave Macmillan, 2002, p. 296.
4. B. Guy Peters, p. 63.

5. Brendan O'Leary, 'Debating Consociational Politics: Normative and Explanatory Arguments', p. 25.
6. Oren Yiftachel, 'The Homeland and Nationalism', *Encyclopedia of Nationalism*, vol. 1, 2000, p. 383.
7. Walker Connor, 'A Few Cautionary Notes on the History and Future of Ethnonational Conflicts', in Andreas Wimmer et al. (eds), *Facing Ethnic Conflicts, Towards a New Realism*, Oxford: Rowman and Littlefield Publishers Inc. 2004, p. 23.
8. Peter Alter, *Nationalism*, London: Edward Arnold, 1994, p. 8.
9. Rebecca Bryant, 'The Purity of Spirit and the Power of Blood: A Comparative Perspective on Nation, Gender and Kinship in Cyprus', *Journal of the Royal Anthropological Institute*, vol. 8, no. 3, September 2002 pp. 509–30.
10. Yiannis Papadakis, 'Nationalist Imaginings of War in Cyprus', http://www.cyprus-conflict.net/Papadakis%20-%20nationalism.htm (accessed 16 November 2005).
11. At this time, Cypriots were 'Christians' and 'Muslims', rather than 'Greek' and 'Turkish'. The latter terms were not used either in the original source literature or in the Cypriot vernacular, until after the turn of the century – and even then were not used uniformly until much later. In this chapter, I have largely chosen to use the terms 'Greek Cypriot' and 'Turkish Cypriot' (except where a point is to be made) for the sake of simplicity and clarity.
12. 'The Great Idea'.
13. '*Enosis*' (Ένωση) is Greek for 'union', and became a byword for the union of Cyprus with Greece. Historically, it is linked with the Μεγάλη Ιδέα (or Great Idea) of unifying all the historic Hellenic lands under a modern Greek state.
14. Turkish for partition or division.
15. Nazım Beratlı, *Kıbrıslı Türk Kimliği'nin Oluşması*. Lefkoşa, Işık Kitabevi Yayınları 1999, cited in Altay Nevzat, *Nationalism Amongst the Turks of Cyprus: The First Wave*, Oulu: Oulu University Press 2005 p. 51.
16. Cengiz Orhonlu, in Halil İnalcık (ed.), 'The Ottoman Turks Settle in Cyprus', *The First International Congress of Cypriot Studies: Presentations of the Turkish Delegation*, Ankara: Institute for the Study of Turkish Culture 1971 pp. 76–7.
17. Altay Nevzat, pp. 51–2.
18. Orhonlu places their number at approximately 4000.
19. Name referring especially to non-Muslim ethnic or community groups in the Ottoman Empire. Each millet typically had a degree of internal autonomy, and members were generally subject to laws which governed their particular group.
20. Roderic H. Davison, 'Turkish Attitudes Concerning Christian – Muslim Equality in the Nineteenth Century', *The American Historical Review*, vol. 59, no. 4, July 1954. Cited in Altay Nevzat, p. 87.
21. Ibid., p. 88.
22. Altay Nevzat, p. 151.
23. Nevzat points to an increased popularity in Cyprus of literature about the developments in Ottoman and other Turkic regions. Ibid., p. 155.
24. In October 1906 Ali Sıdkı, İsmail Zeki, Ahmed Rüşdi, and Edhem Safi were asked to set up an İttihat ve Terakki Cemiyeti (Committee of Union and Progress, CUP) branch in Cyprus. The Lefkoşa branch was duly established early in 1907. A Larnaca office was later established, and became a central port for the dissemination of propaganda to other Ottoman provinces. Ibid., pp. 156–7.
25. Ibid., p. 156.
26. Rebecca Bryant, *Imagining the Modern: The Cultures of Nationalism in Cyprus*, London, I. B. Tauris and Co 2004.

27. Rolandos Katsiaounis, *Labor, Society and Politics in Cyprus During the Second Half of the Nineteenth Century*, Nicosia, Cyprus Research Centre 1996.

28. Although according to some authors, the first signs of anti-Muslim 'rabble-rousing' were recorded in 1895; however, Turkish Cypriot concern has been recorded as early as 1882, when community leaders complained to the Earl of Kimberly about *enotist* agitation among the Greek Cypriots. See Altay Nevzat, p. 130.

29. Rebecca Bryant, *Imagining the Modern: The Cultures of Nationalism in Cyprus*, p. 97.

30. Ibid., p. 98.

31. Ibid.

32. Rolandos Katsiaounis, p. 232.

33. Rebecca Bryant, *Imagining the Modern: The Cultures of Nationalism in Cyprus*, p. 100.

34. Altay Nevzat, p. 138.

35. Ibid., p. 139.

36. The Pious Foundation in Cyprus, a statutory body which administers properties accrued for charitable use.

37. This control increased after 1914, when the British began appointing both delegates to the Evkaf, one of whom had been previously appointed by Istanbul.

38. Altay Nevzat, p. 168.

39. Rebecca Bryant, *Imagining the Modern: The Cultures of Nationalism in Cyprus*, p. 236.

40. President Makarios, Speech at Yialousa village, 14 March 1971, cited in Stanley Mayes, *Makarios: A Biography*, London, Macmillan Press 1981 p. 212. Given the fertile history of misquoting in texts regarding Cyprus, I am hesitant to utilise direct quotes from secondary source material. However, Mayes has a record of closely examining his source material. In this case, he notes in a footnote on page 284 that his efforts to acquire a copy of the speech were 'met with coy evasiveness'.

41. Peter Loizos, *Unofficial Views, Cyprus: Society and Politics*, Nicosia, Intercollege Press, 2001, p. 84.

42. The underlying theme during and after the battle between the Bishops of Kyrenia and Kition for the Archbishopric in 1900 was the division between the old and new guard of the Church in Cyprus. As primary privilege-holder during Ottoman times, the church was a bastion of conservatism. However, as the British began stripping the church of its powers, a schism grew between the groups which favoured attempting during the British period the continuation of the clientelism established during Ottoman times, and the group which pursued a 'hellenistic' vision of Cyprus. As the years wore on, the nationalist group, wrapped within a modernising exterior, both shaped ethnic discourse within Cyprus and gained increasing power, thus coming to a position where (along with the nationalist intelligentsia) they formed the *enotist* and nationalist elite.

43. Rebecca Bryant, *Imagining the Modern: The Cultures of Nationalism in Cyprus*, p. 223.

44. They rejected the 1948 Winster constitution, the 1952 Hopkinson plan, as well as the 1956 Radcliffe proposals. (I include here only plans rejected exclusively by the Greek Cypriot side).

45. Oliver P. Richmond, 'Ethnonationalist Debates and International Peacemaking: The Case of Cyprus', *Nationalism and Ethnic Politics*, vol. 5, no. 2, Summer 1999 p. 37.

46. Rebecca Bryant, 'Justice or Respect? A Comparative Perspective on Politics in Cyprus', *Ethnic and Racial Studies*, vol. 24, no. 6, November 2001 p. 907.

47. 682 men, according to the records of the Greek consul in Cyprus at the time. See Rolandos Katsiaounis, p. 211.
48. Ibid., p. 213.
49. Ibid., p. 213.
50. It has frequently been argued by partisans of both sides that Greek Cypriots sought *enosis* from the first days of British administration. They argue that such requests were dealt with ambiguously by the British, who verbally supported the ideal of a greater Hellenic nation, without actually committing to it. However, recent research has shown these arguments to be inaccurate. Such assertions, due primarily to misinterpretation of historical events, have been popular because they provide a simple and effective link between Greek Cypriot applications for unification with Greece and British subterfuge, thus creating a consequent thesis that the Cyprus conflict is a simple act of divide and conquer, and the Cypriots are but hapless victims of Britain's colonial interests. It is true of later times that applications for *enosis* were always followed by equally impassioned Turkish Cypriot requests for the maintenance of the *status quo*, or, failing that, the re-establishment of Turkish rule. On the whole, the requests of both groups were handled with equal ambiguity.
51. Rebecca Bryant, *Imagining the Modern: The Cultures of Nationalism in Cyprus*, p. 187.
52. In support of this argument, Hadjipavlou has written that

> being the victim is often a psychological comforting position. Victims are absolved from the need to accept responsibility for their role in the conflict. They are, furthermore, preoccupied with the distant and recent past of the conflict and cannot attend to the possibility of a future co-existence. Victims are conscious exclusively of their own pain and cannot empathize with the suffering of the other party.

Maria Hadjipavlou, 'Multiple Stories: The "Crossings" as Part of Citizens' Reconciliation Efforts in Cyprus?', *Innovation*, vol. 20, no. 1, 2007 p. 58.
53. Rebecca Bryant, *Imagining the Modern: The Cultures of Nationalism in Cyprus*.
54. See, for example, Ibid.; Rolandos Katsiaounis, p. 25; Yiannis Papadakis, *Echoes from the Dead Zone*, London, I. B. Tauris 2005; Diana Weston Markides, *Cyprus 1957–1963 From Colonial Conflict to Constitutional Crisis: The Key Role of the Municipal Issue*, Minnesota, University of Minnesota 2001; Altay Nevzat; Andrekos Varnava, *The Cyprus Problem and the Defence of the Middle-East, 1945–1960: Britain's Reluctant Relinquishment of a Place d' Armes*, Melbourne, published by author (publication of Honours dissertation) 2001.
55. *Ethniki Organosis Kypriou Agoniston: National Organisation of Cypriot Fighters*. The 'EOKA period' is the time between 1955 and 1959, when this Greek Cypriot guerrilla organisation began an insurrection against the British occupation of Cyprus, and in the name of union with Greece.
56. The British, on their arrival in Cyprus, viewed the Cypriots with an ethnic lens, and their attitude, as well as the bureaucratic mechanisms of the colonial machine, promoted the division of groups along linguistic lines. Thus the Cypriots were both viewed and disciplined 'as members of his or her ethnic group', Rebecca Bryant, *Imagining the Modern: The Cultures of Nationalism in Cyprus*, pp. 51–2. The British legal system and its ideals of 'liberalism and equality under the law' resulted in 'a disintegration of traditional structures of authority and to new legal-political structures in which "equal" subjects were represented as "naturally" members of communities', Rebecca Bryant, *Imagining the Modern: The Cultures of Nationalism in Cyprus*, p. 70.

57. Ibid., p. 187.
58. Altay Nevzat, p. 336.
59. Ibid.
60. Evanthis Hatzivassiliou, *The Cyprus Question, 1878–1960: The Constitutional Aspect*, Minnesota, Minnesota Mediterranean and East European Monographs 2002 p. 1. Economic qualifications were attached to voting rights, as was gender qualification. This remained the case until the last elections before political liberties were frozen in 1930.
61. R. Hamilton Lang, *Cyprus: Its History, Its Present Resources, and Future Prospects*, London, Macmillan and Co. 1878 p. 270.
62. Ibid., p. 271.
63. Ibid.
64. Peter Loizos, 'Cyprus, part two: An Alternative Analysis. Minority Rights Group Report no 30, 1976', *Unofficial Views, Cyprus: Society and Politics*, Nicosia, Intercollege Press 2001 p. 82.
65. For support and a meticulous study of the period, see Altay Nevzat, pp. 120–9.
66. Ibid., p. 125.
67. Peter Loizos, 'Cyprus, part two: An Alternative Analysis. Minority Rights Group Report no 30, 1976', p. 82.
68. Altay Nevzat, p. 127.
69. Ibid.
70. Federal electoral lists in the Annan Plan were based on whether one was a citizen of the Greek or Turkish Cypriot constituent state. While voting rights were therefore allocated on the basis of internal state citizenship, one's internal citizenship was determined by their mother tongue. Therefore, the determinate factor of electoral eligibility was one's ethnic grouping.
71. For example see Neophytos Loizides and Eser Keskiner, 'The Aftermath of the Annan Plan Referendums: Cross-Voting Moderation for Cyprus?', *Southeast European Politics*, vol. 5, no. 2–3, December 2004 pp. 158–71; Anna Jarstad, *Changing the Game: Consociational Theory and Ethnic Quotas in Cyprus and New Zealand*, Report No. 58, Department of Peace and Conflict Research, Sweden, Uppsala University 2001.
72. In exceptional circumstances, the British government could use its imperial Orders-in-Council to enforce laws. See Altay Nevzat, p. 121.
73. Altay Nevzat, p. 120.
74. Minutes of the Legislative Council, 25 April 1907, cited in Altay Nevzat, p. 165.
75. Altay Nevzat, p. 127.
76. In the week before the 2004 referendum, the Bishop of Paphos stated 'that which we failed to achieve in 1955–1959, namely *enosis* with the motherland Greece, we shall achieve through EU membership ... we shall ... celebrate Cyprus' *enosis* with Greece'. Denktaş replied that the comment was proof that Cyprus' EU accession process was merely 'backdoor *enosis*'. See 'Bishop warns "yes" voters will go to hell', *Cyprus Mail*, 20 April 2004.
77. A recent example can be found in a speech given by president of the Republic of Cyprus Tassos Papadopoulos in Greece to the Greek head of state in July 2006. Papadopoulos reminded the Greeks that 'we ... want our Greek brothers to realise that we in Cyprus, as we resist Turkish expansionism and fight for the national and physical survival of Greek Hellenism, are forward defenders of Hellenism in its widest meaning and dimension'. In a written response, the editor of Toplum Postası (the London Turkish Cypriot community's newspaper)

warned that Papadopoulos would be 'remembered for entrenching partition and his messages of defending Hellenism will be construed by the entire world to mean that the Republic of Cyprus is nothing more than a Greek Republic of Cyprus'. Alkan Chaglar, 'Papadopoulos' talk of defending Hellenism is alienating Turkish Cypriots', *Sunday Mail*, 22 April 2007.

78. For a definition of the term 'deeply divided', see 'definitions' section of Introduction.

79. The Greek language was formerly divided into two categories, *katharevousa* and *demotiki*. *Katharevousa* is the more formal (and complex) version of Greek, which was used after Greece gained independence from the Ottoman Empire, while *demotiki* was the language of daily use. Knowledge of *katharevousa* was frequently used to indicate status. It was replaced by *demotiki* in 1976 as the official language of Greece.

80. By contrast, a 1949 report on the state of education in Turkish Cypriot schools comments, 'the present system of teaching without books should be discontinued, and books used in Turkish Schools in Turkey should be accepted as text books in the Turkish elementary schools', *An Investigation into Matters Concerning and Affecting the Turkish Community in Cyprus: Interim Report of the Committee on Turkish Affairs 1949*, Nicosia, Cyprus Government Printing Office 1949 p. 46. That this should be formally recommended as late as 1949 indicates a gap between the organized nationalisation of identity in Greek and Turkish Cypriot cultures of education.

81. Altay Nevzat, p. 299.

82. Rebecca Bryant, *Imagining the Modern: The Cultures of Nationalism in Cyprus*, p. 37.

83. The word itself comes from a combination of two Greek words, lino (linen) and bambaki (cotton). The connotation is that these people are both fabrics sewn together, although there is an alternative story that Christians who converted to Islam (or Muslims who converted to Christianity, depending on who tells the story) used to wear a small square of fabric, which indicated faith secretly. This does, however, seem an unlikely story considering that in Ottoman times co-villagers would have known quite clearly the religious affiliations and family history of the people they lived with, including their *linobambaki* neighbours, and such secret symbols and deceptions would have seemed unnecessary. Bryant maintains that the element of 'secrecy' in the conversions and dual worship was merely theoretical, and in fact the *linobambaki* were quite open about their duality.

84. Traditionalist Greek Cypriot historians particularly argue that they converted to avoid exorbitant taxation rates and persecution based on religion. This is listed as part of the official history of Cyprus on the Republic of Cyprus' website – see http://www.cyprus.gov.cy/cyphome/govhome.nsf/0/7164EC79564ABEF4C2256B6B003B1395?OpenDocument&languageNo=1 (accessed 15 November 2005).

85. Rebecca Bryant, *Imagining the Modern The Cultures of Nationalism in Cyprus*, p. 65.

86. Ibid., p. 66.

87. For support see Altay Nevzat, p. 271.

88. Although criticisms were cautious. İnönü was also heavily criticised at the time by Turkish nationalists for his decision to 'abandon' Cyprus.

89. G. S. Georghallides, cited in Altay Nevzat, p. 401.

90. Ibid., p. 402.

91. Ibid., p. 416.
92. The Greek Cypriots used Greece to make their initial lobbies to the United Nations. The issue was first raised at the Assembly's fifth session in 1950, then again in the sixth, seventh, and eighth assemblies. The Cypriots recoursed to the ninth Assembly in 1954.
93. The first recorded murder of a Turkish Cypriot by EOKA was in January 1956. However much it is said that this battle had Turkish Cypriots as neutral non-combatants, EOKA battles did spill over into the Turkish Cypriot world; if only (at the beginning) by the fact of its exclusionary ethno-nationalist rhetoric, which rendered the Turkish Cypriot community (at best) invisible, causing increased insecurity and fear for both the future of Cyprus, and the Turkish Cypriot community's place in it.
94. I am grateful to Andrekos Varnavas for this point. For further exploration of this argument, see Andrekos Varnava, *The Cyprus Problem and the Defence of the Middle-East, 1945–1960: Britain's Reluctant Relinquishment of a Place d' Armes*.
95. This was British policy during the various United Nations Assembly discussions, and until Britain organised the 1955 London Conference, to which were invited Greek and Turkish government representatives.
96. Xydis reports that the main purpose of the London Conference was to 'demonstrate the intense interest of Turkish decision-makers in the Cyprus question'. Stephen G. Xydis, *Cyprus, Reluctant Republic*, The Hague, Mouton and Co. 1973 p. 43. Ankara's attitude in the early fifties was that Cyprus should remain a British colony, but the Turkish ambassador to Greece informed the Greek Foreign Ministry in 1954 that if any changes in Cyprus' status were to be proposed, Turkey would need to be involved in the decision. See Stephen G. Xydis, fn. 31 p. 43.
97. Peter Loizos, 'Aspects of Pluralism in Cyprus', *Unofficial Views, Cyprus: Society and Politics*, Nicosia, Intercollege Press 2001 p. 17.
98. There are two main arguments in the literature on this subject. The first maintains that it was the British who were responsible for encouraging Turkish involvement in Cyprus. The second is that Turkey had consistently pressured the British government to either partition Cyprus and divide it between Greece and Turkey or to deliver Cyprus back to Turkey in the event of their quitting the island. The key difference here is that it is traditionally held that the British were manoeuvring towards the division of Cyprus for their own benefit, and strategically brought Turkey into negotiations in order to weaken the position of both Greece and the Greek Cypriots. Revisionist scholars, however, maintain that British policy was consistently driven by pressure from, and fear of Turkey, as well as weakened by divisions between the Colonial Office and Foreign Ministry. In the first case, see for example Diana Weston Markides. In the second, see Christopher Hitchens, *Hostage to History: Cyprus from the Ottomans to Kissinger*, London, Verso 1997; Peter Loizos, *Unofficial Views, Cyprus: Society and Politics*, Nicosia, Intercollege Press 2001.
99. Oliver P. Richmond, 'Ethnonationalist Debates and International Peacemaking: The Case of Cyprus', p. 48.
100. *Türk Mukavemet Teşkilatı, Turkish Resistance Organisation*. The most significant difference between *Volkan* and TMT was Turkey's covert but systematic support of TMT. TMT appears to have been established without the knowledge of Dr. Küçük, who was more closely involved with *Volkan*. It seems that Küçük was later convinced to support TMT. I am grateful to Altay Nevzat for these points.

101. Robert McDonald, *The Problem of Cyprus*, Adelphi Papers no. 234, International Institute for Strategic Studies, Winter 1988/9, London, Brassey's 1989 p. 9.
102. Christopher Hitchens, *Hostage to History: Cyprus from the Ottomans to Kissinger*, p. 53.
103. Andrekos Varnava, *The Cyprus Problem and the Defence of the Middle-East, 1945–1960: Britain's Reluctant Relinquishment of a Place d' Armes*, pp. 64–5.
104. Rebecca Bryant, *Imagining the Modern: The Cultures of Nationalism in Cyprus*, p. 223.
105. Ibid.
106. Isaiah Berlin, *Liberty*, Oxford, Oxford University Press 2002 p. 31.
107. Rebecca Bryant, *Imagining the Modern: The Cultures of Nationalism in Cyprus*, p. 222.
108. Ibid., p. 223.
109. In the first decade of Ottoman rule, some 8000 Anatolian families settled in Cyprus, and over subsequent years, settlement continued sporadically. According to Attalides, 'Muslim peasants were settled on the lands of the dispossessed Venetian aristocracy ... [and] by this way, villages and village-quarters of Turkish-speaking Muslim peasants came to be interspersed over the whole of the island with the Greek ones'. Michael Attalides, Cyprus, *Nationalism and International Politics*, Edinburgh, Q Press 1979 p. 1.
110. For a map of Cypriot population distribution in 1960 see Appendix 2.
111. Northern Ireland and Lebanon are perhaps the most immediately relevant examples of this approach.
112. Either through fear or genuine support.

3   The First Consociational State: Why Did it Fail?

1. Glafkos Clerides, former president of the Republic of Cyprus.
2. The Zurich Agreement was signed on 11 February 1959 and the London Agreement was signed on 19 February 1959.
3. 1965 Galo Plaza Report on Cyprus, *United Nations Document* section B.22.
4. Ibid.
5. Ibid.
6. Hubert Faustmann, 'Independence Postponed: Cyprus 1959–1960', Hubert Faustmann and Nicos Peristianis (eds) *Britain in Cyprus: Colonialism and Post-Colonialism 1878–2006*, Berlin, Bibliopolis 2006 p. 420.
7. Andrekos Varnava, *The Cyprus Problem and the Defence of the Middle-East, 1945–1960: Britain's Reluctant Relinquishment of a Place d' Armes*.
8. Robert McDonald, p. 10.
9. I have noted in Chapter 1 that in his categorisation of executive designs, Lijphart maintains a preference for parliamentary systems over presidential. In this element, the 1960 design deviates from the 'ideal type'. However, Lijphart also makes it clear that this does not discount its 'consociationality'.
10. Stanley Kyriakides, *Cyprus: Constitutionalism and Crisis Government*, Philadelphia, University of Philadelphia Press 1968 p. 63.
11. Constitution of the Republic of Cyprus, Article 50, Article 57.
12. Ibid., Article 47.
13. Ibid., Article 36, paragraph 2.
14. Ibid., Article 39, Article 43.
15. Ibid., Article 59, paragraph 3.

16. S. A de Smith, *The New Commonwealth and its Constitutions*, London, Stevens and Sons 1964 p. 288.
17. Stanley Kyriakides, p. 62 (Articles 46 and 57 of the constitution).
18. Constitution of the Republic of Cyprus, Article 61.
19. 35 Greek Cypriot and 15 Turkish Cypriot Representatives. Constitution of the Republic of Cyprus, Article 62 paragraph 2.
20. Bi-communalism was further reinforced by the necessity of citizens nominating themselves as members of either the Greek Cypriot or Turkish Cypriot community in order to be eligible for election. Constitution of the Republic of Cyprus, Article 2.
21. Ibid., Article 78, paragraph 1.
22. Ibid., Article 78, paragraph 2.
23. Ibid., Article 67.
24. Ibid., Article 87 paragraph 1.
25. Ibid., Article 87, paragraph 1.
26. Robert McDonald, p. 11.
27. Stanley Kyriakides, p. 69.
28. Constitution of the Republic of Cyprus, Article 133, paragraph 2.
29. Ibid., Article 137.
30. Ibid., Article 143.
31. Ibid., Article 151.
32. Ibid., Article 149.
33. Ibid., Article 156 (b).
34. Ibid., Article 156.
35. Ibid., Article 153, paragraph 1 (1).
36. Ibid., Article 153, paragraph 1 (2).
37. Article 159 of the Constitution:

   1. A court exercising civil jurisdiction in cases where the plaintiff and the defendant belong to the same Community shall be composed solely of a judge or judges belonging to that Community.
   2. A court exercising jurisdiction in a case where the accused and the person injured belong to the same Community, or where there is no person injured, shall be composed of a judge or judges belonging to that Community.

38. Stanley Kyriakides, p. 71. Regarding the inalienable nature of the treaties, see Constitution of the Republic of Cyprus, Article 182, paragraph 1.
39. Evanthis Hatzivassiliou, p. 27.
40. The British subsequently governed Cyprus by decree until independence in 1960.
41. Evanthis Hatzivassiliou, p. 36.
42. Eighteen representatives were elected on the 'general roll' and four representatives were elected on the Turkish Cypriot roll.
43. There were also five official representatives of the governor in the council, appointed by the British government. The governor was to hold ultimate veto rights over all decisions. In addition, there was to be an Executive Council to advise the governor, composed of three Greek Cypriots and one Turkish Cypriot appointed from the Legislative Council, each of whom was to head a government department.
44. Anna Jarstad, p. 95.
45. Evanthis Hatzivassiliou, p. 46.
46. Ibid., p. 52.

47. The assembly was to be composed of 13 elected Greek Cypriot and eight elected Turkish Cypriot representatives, as well as three official and four appointed representatives.
48. Stephen G. Xydis, p. 44.
49. Ibid.
50. Evanthis Hatzivassiliou, p. 56.
51. Responsible for religious and educational matters.
52. Hatzivassilou argues that Greece rejected the plan primarily because of the accompanying statements of the Colonial Secretary Lennox-Boyd in December 1956 which intimated British acceptance of partition. Hatzivassiliou also argues that subsequent Turkish proposals for Cypriot constitutions were emboldened by, and based upon, that initial 1956 British statement. Evanthis Hatzivassiliou, p. 64.
53. Anna Jarstad, pp. 94–110.
54. Tozun Bahchelli, *Greek-Turkish Relations Since 1955*, Colorado, Westview Press 1990 p. 43.
55. The official name later given to the negotiated agreements in Zurich and London.
56. Also sometimes referred to as the 'Joint Commission'.
57. Along with the strategic requirements of (primarily) Greece and Turkey, and (secondly) Britain, which were reinforced by the treaties of Guarantee, Alliance, and Establishment, explained in the section above.
58. Dimitris Bitsios, *Cyprus: The Vulnerable Republic*, Thessaloniki, Institute for Balkan Studies, 1975 pp. 98–9.
59. Ibid., p. 109.
60. Evangelos Averoff-Tossizza, *Lost Opportunities: The Cyprus Question, 1950–1963*, Athens, Aristide D. Caratzas 1986.
61. Oliver P. Richmond, 'Ethnonationalist Debates and International Peacemaking: The Case of Cyprus', *Nationalism and Ethnic Politics*, vol. 5, no. 2, Summer 1999 p. 42.
62. Ibid.
63. Ibid., p. 43.
64. Ibid., p. 48.
65. Ibid.; Stanley Kyriakides, p. 76.
66. Oliver P. Richmond, 'Ethnonationalist Debates and International Peacemaking: The Case of Cyprus', p. 42.
67. Stanley Kyriakides.
68. Robert McDonald, *The Problem of Cyprus*, Adelphi Papers no. 234, International Institute for Strategic Studies Winter 1988/9, London, Brassey's 1989 p. 11.
69. See for example Brendan O'Malley and Ian Craig, *The Cyprus Conspiracy*, London, Tauris Publishers 1999; Andreas Theophanous, 'Prospects for Solving the Cyprus Problem and the Role of the European Union', *Publius*, vol. 30, no. 1–2, 2000 pp. 217–41; Christopher Hitchens, *Hostage to History: Cyprus from the Ottomans to Kissinger*, London, Verso 1997.
70. S. A de Smith, *The New Commonwealth and its Constitutions*, London, Stevens and Sons 1964 p. 296, italics added.
71. Bitsios headed the Greek delegation to the UN between 1961 and 1965 and was Greek Foreign Minister from 1974–7.
72. See Dimitris Bitsios, *Cyprus: The Vulnerable Republic*, pp. 98–9; Glafcos Clerides, *Cyprus: My Deposition*, Nicosia, Alithia Publishing Co. 1990 vol. 1 pp. 76–7; and Stephen G. Xydis, *Cyprus, Reluctant Republic*, The Hague, Mouton and Co. 1973 pp. 365–75.

73. This was legislated as the 'Turkish Cypriot Municipal Committees (Temporary Provision) Law, No. 33/1959'.
74. CAP 240.
75. Alecos Markides, Former Attorney General of the Republic of Cyprus. Interview with author, 2 July 2004.
76. Richard A. Patrick, *Political Geography and the Cyprus Conflict: 1963–1971*, Ontario, University of Waterloo 1976 p. 39.
77. See for example Diana Weston Markides.
78. Called the 'Turkish Communal Chamber Turkish Municipal Corporations Law'.
79. Called the 'Village Administration and Improvement Law', CAP 243.
80. See Appendix 2.
81. Arend Lijphart, *Power-Sharing in South Africa*, p. 126.
82. Late 1963 and 1964.
83. Late 1964 to pre-invasion 1974.
84. Steiner and a number of others have identified the risk of establishing a consociational system in societies where there were only two significant groups. Steiner argued that zero-sum battles for power were more likely to occur in these societies because gains for one group were easily perceived as coming at the expense of the other group. Jürg Steiner, *Amicable Agreement versus Majority Rule: Conflict Resolution in Switzerland*, Chapel Hill, University of North Carolina Press 1974 p. 268.
85. Arend Lijphart, *Democracy in Plural Societies: A Comparative Exploration*, p. 56.
86. Ibid., p. 160.
87. Evanthis Hatzivassiliou.
88. Article 78 (2) cited in Stanley Kyriakides, p. 83.
89. Alecos Markides, Former Attorney General of Republic of Cyprus. Interview with author, 2 July 2004.
90. For Makarios' 13 amendments, see Appendix 4.
91. Stanley Kyriakides, p. 76.
92. Robert McDonald, p. 9.
93. Peter Loizos, 'Cyprus Part Two: An Alternative Analysis', p. 77.
94. Ibid.
95. Brendan O'Malley and Ian Craig, pp. 90–1.
96. Peter Loizos, 'Cyprus Part Two: An Alternative Analysis'.
97. Nevertheless several authors maintain that Greek and Turkish Cypriot political leaders 'initially cooperated in launching the new government, pledging to support and implement the treaties and new constitution'. Richard A. Patrick, p. 35. Contradictory evidence exists on this point, however. Clerides, for example maintains that, in the Republic's first stages, the representatives voted on ideological rather than ethnic grounds, Glafkos Clerides, *Cyprus: My Deposition*. On the other hand, Clerides' attorney general, Alekos Markides, argued that goodwill between elites in the early years was entirely non-existent, Alecos Markides, Former Attorney General of Republic of Cyprus. Interview with author, 2 July 2004.
98. Incidentally, Articles 59 and 70 of the 1960 constitution states that a Turkish Cypriot may *not* be elected to the House of Representatives if he is a religious functionary.
99. While the Turkish Cypriots were extensively consulted by the Turkish negotiators.
100. According to this argument, it was only *after* the Zurich meeting that Prime Minister Karamanlis showed Archbishop Makarios the full text and asked for his support. Makarios initially approved the document, upon the condition of some minor negotiated changes, but later showed an increased concern, especially about the Treaty of Guarantee.

101. Member of Makarios' negotiating team and legal advisor to the Greek Cypriot side. Later president of the Republic of Cyprus from 1991–2001.
102. Legal advisor and member of the Turkish Cypriot negotiating team. President of the Turkish Republic of Northern Cyprus from 1983 to 2004. Rauf R. Denktaş, *The Cyprus Triangle*, London, George Allen and Unwin 1982 p. 25.
103. Evangelos Averoff-Tossizza.
104. Stephen G. Xydis, pp. 365–75.
105. See for support Glafkos Clerides, *Cyprus: My Deposition*, Nicosia, Alithia Publishing Co. 1990 vol. 1 pp. 74–7; Rauf R. Denktaş, *The Cyprus Triangle*, p. 25.
106. Glafcos Clerides, *Cyprus: My Deposition*, p. 71.
107. For a cogent summary of Makarios' actions during the London Conference, see Kudret Özersay, 'The Validity and Scope of the 1959–1960 Cyprus Treaties', in Resat Arim (ed.), *Cyprus and International Law*, Ankara, Foreign Policy Institute 2002 pp. 24–6.
108. See, for example, Alan James, 'The Making of the Cyprus Settlement, 1958–1960', *The Cyprus Review*, vol. 10, no. 2 1998 pp. 18–19; Stephen G. Xydis, pp. 437–9.
109. Stephen G. Xydis.
110. Diana Weston Markides, p. 72.
111. Stanley Kyriakides, p. 68.
112. Brendan O'Malley and Ian Craig, *The Cyprus Conspiracy*, London, Tauris Publishers 1999 p. 83.
113. CO 926/977, 12/06/57.
114. EOKA leaders for Makarios and Denktaş and TMT for Küçük.

4 Getting the Institutions Right: Making Plans for Cyprus

1. Kofi Annan, 'Report of Kofi Annan on Good Offices in Cyprus', *United Nations Document*, 1 April 2003 UN doc S/2003/398; Kofi Annan, 'Report of the Secretary-General on Cyprus', *United Nations Document*, 16 April 2004 UN doc S/2004/302; Kofi Annan, 'Report of the Secretary-General on his Mission of Good Offices in Cyprus', United Nations Document, 28 May 2004 UN doc S/2004/437.
2. Kofi Annan, 'Report of Kofi Annan on Good Offices in Cyprus', *United Nations Document*, 1 April 2003 UN doc S/2003/398 paragraph 77.
3. 'The Greek Cypriot side could take comfort in the fact that Switzerland was clearly a sovereign State and its cantons did not enjoy a right to secede. The Turkish Cypriots could take comfort in the fact that the Swiss model, which they had regularly cited as their inspiration, was the model to be applied'. Ibid.
4. Information for this section was drawn from interviews with members of the UN negotiating team, and from David Hannay, *Cyprus, the Search for a Solution*.
5. See Appendix 5 for details of the Preliminary Thoughts.
6. See Appendix 6 for details of this document.
7. However, in the face of Denktaş' reluctance to engage with the UN engineers, Talat became unofficially involved in the plan's development after the submission of Annan I. The negotiating dynamics therefore had been subtly changing for some time previous to his election as prime minister. This information is based on interviews with members of the UN core negotiating team in 2005 and 2006.
8. Constitution of the United Cyprus Republic, Article 22 (3).
9. Constitution of the United Cyprus Republic, Article 25 (2).
10. Constitution of the United Cyprus Republic, Article 5 (1) a.

11. Only four of the six Greek Cypriot members and two of the three Turkish Cypriot members will have full voting rights.
12. Kofi Annan, 'Report of the Secretary-General on his Mission of Good Offices in Cyprus', United Nations Document, 28 May 2004 UN doc S/2004/437 paragraph 44, p. 11.
13. Constitution of the United Cyprus Republic, Article 42.
14. With the safeguard that at least one-third of every level of the public service must be staffed by members of each constituent state.
15. Constitution of the United Cyprus Republic, Article 6 (2).
16. Both Cypriot and foreign.
17. This provision was added into the third version of the plan.
18. Constitution of the United Cyprus Republic, Article 36 (2).
19. Constitution of the United Cyprus Republic, Article 36 (6).
20. Population resettlement and the issue of property are very important aspects of the Cypriot reunification juggernaut, but outside the scope of this thesis. There have been a number of recent publications on this issue. For an outline of the issue, see Gürel, Ayla and Özersay, Kudret, *The Politics of Property in Cyprus: Conflicting Appeals to 'Bizonality' and 'Human Rights' by the Two Cypriot Communities*, PRIO Report 3/2006 http://www.prio.no/files/manualimport/cyprus/documents/Cyprus%20Property%20Report.pdf (accessed 12 July 2007).
21. Constitution of the Turkish Cypriot State, Article 107 (3).
22. Ibid., Article 107 (4).
23. Ibid., Article 111 (1).
24. Broadly based upon the Belgian design of a *formateur*-cum prime minister and drawing upon the same philosophy of a prime minister who can create cross-party alliances.
25. Constitution of the Turkish Cypriot State, Article 112 (3).
26. Ibid., Articles 5, 83, 84.
27. Ibid., Article 89.
28. The powers of the president of the Greek Cypriot constituent state are laid out in Articles 47 and 56 of the Greek Cypriot constituent state constitution.
29. Constitution of the Greek Cypriot State, Article 65 (1).
30. Ibid., Article 65 (2).
31. Three of whom must be elected representatives of the Latin, Armenian, and Maronite communities.
32. John McGarry et al., 'Integration or Accommodation? The Enduring Debate in Conflict Regulation', in Sujit Choudhry, ed., *Constitutional Design for Divided Societies: Integration or Accommodation?* Oxford, Oxford University Press, 2008 p. 53.
33. Kofi Annan, 'Report of Kofi Annan on Good Offices in Cyprus' (S/2003/398), paragraph 85.
34. Including international agreements which fall within the legislative competence of the constituent states; ratification of treaties and adoption of laws regulating airspace, continental shelf, and territorial waters; adoption of laws and regulations regarding citizenship, immigration, taxation, and water resources; election of the Presidential Council; approval of the federal budget. Constitution of the United Cyprus Republic, Article 25 (2).
35. Alecos Markides, Former Attorney General of Republic of Cyprus. Interview with author, 2 July 2004.

36. Keith Kyle, 'A British View of the Annan Plan', *Cyprus Review*, vol. 16, no. 1, Spring 2004, p. 17.
37. Member of UN core negotiating team in Cyprus. Confidential interview with the author.
38. Ibid.
39. Remarks by US Ambassador Michael Klosson at the Turkish Cypriot Nicosia Bar Association: Tuesday, 30 September 2003.
40. Kofi Annan, 'Report of the Secretary-General on his Mission of Good Offices in Cyprus', 28 May 2004, p. 17. This purpose was reiterated in a personal interview to the author by a member of the UN negotiating team.
41. Kofi Annan, 'Report of Kofi Annan on Good Offices in Cyprus', 1 April 2003, paragraph 82.
42. Didier Pfirter, Legal Advisor to the UN Secretary General's Special Assistant. Interview with author, 6 October 2006.
43. A number of these points were reiterated separately by different members of the UN's negotiating team in Cyprus in interviews with the author.
44. Member of UN core negotiating team. Interview with the author.
45. Alecos Markides, interview with the author, 2 July 2004.
46. Ibid.
47. Didier Pfirter, Legal Advisor to the UN Secretary General's Special Assistant. Interview with the author, 6 October 2006.
48. Ibid.
49. Opening Statement and Press Conference by Secretary General's Special Advisor on Cyprus, Alvaro de Soto, Ledra Palace, Nicosia, 20 April 2004.
50. Alecos Markides, interview with the author, 2 July 2004.
51. Member of UN core negotiating team in Cyprus. Confidential interview with the author.
52. Kofi Annan, 'Report of the Secretary-General on his Mission of Good Offices in Cyprus', 28 May 2004, paragraph 57.
53. However, a significant reason the Annan Plan was rejected by the Greek Cypriot community was because it was perceived as being 'unbalanced' and 'favoured' the Turkish Cypriot community.
54. Kyriakides cites three examples given by Vice President Küçük of Turkish Cypriot experiences of executive domination. The first regarded the taxation crisis, the second concerned the composition of the units of the Cyprus Army, and the third was the municipality issue. It is worth quoting Küçük's interpretation of the crises:

> When in April 1961 the Greeks and Turks in the House of Representatives could not agree whether the Colonial taxation legislation should be extended for a further period of three months or two months, Government was faced with a serious situation ... the Turkish Ministers hoped that ... it would be possible to settle the dispute within constitutional provisions but the President categorically refused even to discuss the matter and, by assuming he had supra-constitutional powers, directed personally that Law or no Law taxes shall be collected. ...
> When in October 1961, there was a difference of opinion between myself and the President and Greek Members of the Council, on the composition of the units of the Cyprus Army, I had to rely on my power of veto, in order to prevent the Council from taking an administrative decision which would not work. ...

The President's handling of the question of municipalities is another example of the Greek attitude and determination not to implement constitutional provisions relating to Turkish rights. The President clearly stated that he would not allow any legislation providing for the creation of separate municipalities. Later, after he had tried his hand to set up un-constitutional Government agencies instead of municipalities and the matter was referred by us to the Supreme Constitutional Court, he clearly stated that he would not listen to any judgement of the Constitutional Court.

Stanley Kyriakides, pp. 108–9, fn. 10.

55. Kofi Annan, 'Report of Kofi Annan on Good Offices in Cyprus', 1 April 2003, paragraph 81.
56. Ibid., emphasis added.
57. Didier Pfirter, Legal Advisor to the UN Secretary General's Special Assistant. Interview with the author, 6 October 2006.
58. Denktaş had a significant aversion to any form of cross-voting, because, to his mind, it would inhibit the election of 'pure Turks'. The implication was that any Turkish Cypriot voted into power because s/he was acceptable to the Greek Cypriot community was a sort of quisling. This was a significant disappointment to some of the UN engineering team, who would have liked to implement mixed electorates for executive elections.
59. Article 26 (2) of the UCR constitution states that

All members of the Presidential Council shall be elected by Parliament for a fixed five-year term on a single list by special majority. The list shall specify the voting members.

60. Kofi Annan, 'Report of Kofi Annan on Good Offices in Cyprus', 1 April 2003, paragraph 84.
61. Alecos Markides, interview with the author, 2 July 2004.
62. Şener Levent, editor Afrika Newspaper. Interview with the author, 17 June 2004.
63. Didier Pfirter, Legal Advisor to the UN Secretary General's Special Assistant. Interview with the author, 6 October 2006.
64. So long as the majority included one member from each constituent state. Constitution of the United Cyprus Republic, Article 5 (2) (b).
65. Alecos Markides, interview with the author, 2 July 2004.
66. Representative of the Diplomatic Office of the President of the Republic of Cyprus. Confidential interview with the author.
67. Didier Pfirter, legal advisor to UN Secretary General. Television interview on Mega TV, 29 February 2004.
68. Interview with Greek Cypriot member of the committee on laws, 2006, name withheld.
69. Kofi Annan, 'Report of Kofi Annan on Good Offices in Cyprus', 1 April 2003, paragraph 93.
70. 'The idea about the three neutral judges intervening ... where disagreement paralyses a function of the state ... came from Greece'. Alecos Markides, interview with the author, 2 July 2004.
71. This was one element of several which was promoted as being both gravely unjust, insulting and illogical by a large number of Greek Cypriot politicians and public figures, and thus caused great consternation among the Greek Cypriot public, who cited it as one of the main reasons for voting against the plan in April 2004.
72. Alecos Markides, interview with author, 2 July 2004.

73. UN Resolution 541 (1983) (S/RES/541 (1983)) and subsequent resolutions.
74. Previous president of the Republic of Cyprus Glafkos Clerides was the first Greek Cypriot politician to support this solution. In a 1975 speech at Argo Gallery in Lefkosia, he suggested a federal solution as a settlement. Being the first time such a solution was proposed, he received much criticism from within the Greek Cypriot community.
75. David Hannay, *Cyprus, the Search for a Solution*, London: I. B. Taurus and Co. 2005 p. 128.
76. Cited in David Hannay, ibid., p. 143.
77. Ibid., p. 142.
78. For details of the constitutional changes made, see Stanley Kyriakides, pp. 114–9.
79. For support see Stanley Kyriakides, p. 115.
80. Kofi Annan, 'Report of Kofi Annan on Good Offices in Cyprus', 1 April 2003, especially paragraphs 73–7; and Kofi Annan, 'Report of the Secretary General on his Mission of Good Offices in Cyprus', *United Nations Document*, 28 May 2004.
81. Member of the UN core negotiating team. Confidential interview with the author.
82. Costas M. Constantinou and Yiannis Papadakis, pp. 141.
83. Ian Brownlie, *Principles of Public International Law*, Oxford, Clarendon Press, 1990, p. 88; T. D. Grant, *The Recognition of States: Law and Practice in Debate and Evolution*, Westport, Praeger Publishers, 1999; Warbrick, Colin, 'Recognition of States', *International and Comparative Law Quarterly*, no. 41, 1992, pp. 473–82.
84. Kofi Annan, 'Report of Kofi Annan on Good Offices in Cyprus', 1 April 2003, paragraphs 74 and 75.
85. Ibid., paragraph 76.
86. Ibid.
87. Ibid.
88. Constitution of the United Cyprus Republic, Article 22 (3).
89. Kofi Annan, 'Report of the Secretary-General on his Mission of Good Offices in Cyprus', 28 May 2004, paragraph 52.
90. However, it also dates back to historical Greek Cypriot perceptions of a Hellenic Cyprus, which needed to be protected from foreign 'contamination'.
91. Kofi Annan, 'Report of Kofi Annan on Good Offices in Cyprus', 1 April 2003, paragraph 102.
92. Kofi Annan, 'Report of Kofi Annan on Good Offices in Cyprus', 1 April 2003, paragraphs 102 and 103.
93. Serhan Peksoylu, columnist with *Afrika* newspaper. Correspondence with the author.
94. This concern was particularly articulated to the author by Alpay Durduran, Mehmet Cakici, Izzet Iskan, and Ali Seylani in interviews in 2004 both before and after the referendums.
95. In a strange twist which shows political adaptability to ideology, the traditional Greek Cypriot argument that 'all refugees must return home' was reversed in September 2004 when Arif Mustafa, a Turkish Cypriot refugee from Episkopi went to the Republic of Cyprus' Supreme Court in order to reclaim his land. Testing the sincerity of this claim, Mustafa sought and was granted the right to return to the home he fled after the 1974 war, which was currently occupied by a Greek Cypriot refugee from the north. Immediately after the results of the case were known, widespread panic engulfed the Greek Cypriot refugee community, concerned that it would be 'overrun' by Turkish Cypriots reclaiming lost property. The immediate Greek Cypriot response was that 'we will be made refugees for a second time'. The official response by the Republic of Cyprus was to launch an appeal to the court,

contesting Mustafa's right to return by arguing that the people who lived in his house also had rights and needed protection. Interestingly, this has been the traditional Turkish Cypriot response to the Greek Cypriot 'all refugees must return' argument. At the same time, the Greek Cypriot government supported the case of Titina Loizidou, a Greek Cypriot refugee from Kyrenia who took the Republic of Turkey to the European Court of Human Rights (Case of Loizidou v. Turkey. Case no. 40/1993/435/514) for denying her the right to enjoy her property.

96. Information for the following paragraphs is based on confidential interviews with a member of the UN core negotiating team, and from David Hannay.

97. For further details on the negotiation of this issue, see David Hannay, p. 127.

98. The original 30,000 migrants were the third category.

99. And the number had expanded to approximately 50,000. Both sides by this time preferred to have a total number of migrants specified clearly under a single category, rather than separated into three groups, as with Annan I.

100. Preference was given to people born and raised in Cyprus and to those who had married Turkish Cypriots.

101. For a transitional period of 19 years or until Turkey's accession to the EU, whichever came first. Constitution of the United Cyprus Republic, Article 3 (5).

102. Interestingly, the Turkish and Greek Cypriot negotiators changed their positions very late in the negotiations regarding the distribution of power between the state and federal governments. As the wealthier state, the Greek Cypriots would have no real need or incentive for strong co-operation with the Turkish Cypriot state. They realised therefore that it would be to their advantage to *not* have to apply the cumbersome process of gaining Turkish Cypriot agreement. Likewise, the Turkish Cypriot negotiators began to see that there may be significant financial advantage to ceding certain powers to the federal government. They also realised that in a more centralised state, the federal government would absorb and redistribute a greater proportion of state-raised revenue. Because the Greek Cypriot state would have been more populous and also wealthier, much of the income would have been redistributed from the Greek Cypriot constituent state to the Turkish Cypriot constituent state.

103. Didier Pfirter, Legal Advisor to the UN Secretary General's Special Assistant. Interview with the author, 6 October 2006.

104. Excluding articles 1 and 2 (Constitution of the United Cyprus Republic, Part VI, Article 37 (2)).

105. Constitution of the United Cyprus Republic, Article 25 (1).

106. Ibid., Article 37 (3).

5 How Close Were They, Really? Elite Support of a Power-Sharing Solution

1. Thucydides, *History of the Peloponnesian War*, London, Penguin, 1972, Book One, p. 107.

2. Oliver P. Richmond, 'Ethnonationalist Debates and International Peacemaking: The Case of Cyprus', p. 41.

3. Clerides and Denktaş are also perfect examples of how Cypriot political elites become vehicles of historical memory. Both men are second-generation ethnic-leaders. The fathers of both men were central political figures in Cypriot colonial politics, and so in a very literal sense, Glafkos Clerides and Rauf Denktaş represent the way elites carry and are guided by communal historical memory.

4. Denktaş was famous for walking out during negotiations, to the point where his withdrawal was a predictable safety net for Greek Cypriots, who could continue negotiations knowing that should progress become uncomfortable, they could rely on Turkish Cypriot withdrawal from inter-communal talks without losing any diplomatic face themselves.

5. Hannes Lacher and Erol Kaymak, 'Transforming Identities: Beyond the Politics of Non-Settlement in North Cyprus', *Mediterranean Politics*, vol. 10, no. 2, July 2005, pp. 147–66.

6. Ibid., p. 153.

7. Ibid., p. 154.

8. Many left-wing politicians, union leaders, and community elites place responsibility for the strong public support of the Annan Plan with NGO and political groups who held extended campaigns explaining the plan to the public. The alternative opinion is that the Turkish Cypriot population was so exhausted with the state of affairs that the increased democratisation and economic and societal independence offered by the resolution ensured their support. In this view, while elite support did assist public confidence, it was not the main, driving force behind the plan's acceptance.

9. Hannes Lacher and Erol Kaymak, p. 155.

10. The following paragraphs are based on information from interviews with Turkish Cypriot politicians who are listed in the bibliography.

11. For example, left-wing newspaper *Avrupa* (later *Afrika*) was sued for defamation by Rauf Denktaş in 1998. On 29 December 1999 the court ruled in favour of the prosecution and ordered the newspaper to pay costs of US$200, 000. When the paper was unable to pay, police seized all assets, effectively closing it down. The editor of *Afrika*, Şener Levent, has more than a hundred cases pending against him in court, including charges of spying for the Greek Cypriot government.

    Past leader of the opposition Alpay Durduran maintains that in his years as opposition leader, he saw no bills or legislation before they were passed, had no role in any debates, and no functional role in the parliament. He asserts that there is no functional opposition in northern Cyprus politics, and speaks of being frustrated at the complete lack of information available to opposition.

    Ali Gulle, president of DEV-İŞ, says that 'all these left wing trade unions which have been cooperating with the Greek Cypriot trade unions have always been pushed aside, and even now, it's getting worse. ... In the TRNC, the members of our trade unions have been thrown out of their jobs, because of their membership. They are always being frightened, and threatened that they should either get into a right wing trade union, or they'll be out of a job. This is one of the worst. As a trade unionist I have been arrested because I voted for the Annan Plan, and because I support the referendum, I have been arrested many times'. Interview with the author, 17 April 2004.

12. Mehmet Cakici, member of the TRNC Legislative Assembly (Peace and Democracy Movement – Barış ve Demokrasi Hareketi). Interview with the author, March 2004.

13. Ibid.

14. These events are also referred to in passing by David Hannay, p. 171.

15. British diplomatic source. Confidential interview with the author, 2004.

16. Ibid.

17. Information for the following paragraphs is from interviews with Turkish Cypriot politicians, academics, and journalists listed in the bibliography.

18. Hannes Lacher and Erol Kaymak.
19. The division separating the Greek and Turkish Cypriot areas is called the Green Line.
20. Under the Green Line Regulation (8208/04) adopted on 4 May 2004, the value of goods traded across the line is approximately €100,000 per month. However, obstacles such as no telecom interconnection, limited free movement of buses and trucks, and low inter-group trust between businesspeople remain significant barriers to increasing intra-island trade. See, for further discussion, Christalla Yakinthou, 'The European Union's Management of the Cyprus Conflict: System Failure or Structural Metamorphosis?', *Ethnopolitics*, vol VII, no. 3, 2009.
21. Hannes Lacher and Erol Kaymak, p. 157.
22. While the UK does not officially recognise the Turkish Cypriot passport, a visa or entry stamp is frequently attached to a separate piece of paper and then placed within the Turkish Cypriot passport. This avoids the problem of recognition while also making travel for Turkish Cypriots less difficult.
23. Vamik D. Volkan, *Cyprus – War and Adaptation: A Psychoanalytic History of the Two Ethnic Groups in Conflict*, Charlottesville, University Press of Virginia 1979; Vamik D. Volkan, 'Turks and Greeks of Cyprus: Psychopolitical Considerations', in Vangelis Calotychos (ed.), *Cyprus and its People: Nation, Identity and Experience in an Unimaginable Community, 1955–1997*, Colorado, Westview Press 1998; Vamik Volkan, *Killing in the Name of Identity, a Study of Bloody Conflicts*, Virginia, Pitchstone Publishing 2006.
24. Hannes Lacher and Erol Kaymak.
25. As Chapter 4 has argued, the Turkish Cypriot community has linked acceptance of the Annan Plan with stemming the loss of Turkish Cypriot identity through emigration and the altering demographic pattern. According to the Annan Plan, approximately 50,000 Turkish immigrants would stay in Cyprus, with the rest to return to Turkey. A further (temporary) cap of 5 per cent on the population of Turkish nationals living in the north of Cyprus would prevent the continuous flow of Turkish labour into Cyprus, meeting a serious Greek and Turkish Cypriot concern. In addition, reunification of Cyprus would stimulate the economy, boosting employment in many sectors. Moreover, the proposed federal level of government would create opportunities for public employment. For these reasons, many Turkish Cypriots viewed the Annan Plan as a means of rejuvenating their society.
26. It also seems that public trust is continuing to plummet in the post-Annan environment, where international promises to assist the Turkish Cypriot community in the wake of the Greek Cypriot rejection of reunification have, on the whole, not been implemented. Blame for this failure is placed at the feet of the international community, the Turkish Cypriot government, and the Greek Cypriot people. Some signs show that in order to deflect pressure for the lack of progress, the Turkish Cypriot government may be encouraging inter-communal resentment.
27. With the single exception of George Vassiliou, who ran as an independent and was a businessman prior to his political life.
28. David Hannay, *Cyprus, the Search for a Solution*, p. 13.
29. Christophorou Christophorous, 'An Old Cleavage Causes New Divisions: Parliamentary Elections in the Republic of Cyprus, 21 May 2006', *South European Society and Politics*, vol. 12, no. 1, 2007 p. 113.
30. The major Greek Cypriot political parties are outlined in Appendix 3.

31. Christophorou Christophorous, 'An Old Cleavage Causes New Divisions: Parliamentary Elections in the Republic of Cyprus, 21 May 2006', p. 113.
32. AKEL's refusal to ally with DISY is due to DISY's historical connection with EOKA, and particularly EOKA B. AKEL claims that DISY gave refuge to a number of EOKA B terrorists, and particularly those who were guilty of killing left-wing Greek and Turkish Cypriots. It is also, therefore, quite poignantly paradoxical that DISY was the only significant Greek Cypriot political party to officially support the 2004 Annan Plan, and that AKEL, with the most pro-reconciliation record, officially rejected the plan.
33. Information for the remainder of this section is based on interviews with representatives of AKEL, academics, and core members of the UN negotiating team, listed in the bibliography.
34. In a 2007 television interview with Yiannis Kareklas, AKEL General Secretary Demetris Christofias was asked whether there had been an agreement with Papadopoulos about who would be the three-party alliance 2008 presidential candidate. He initially refused to answer the question and then stated that 'there was no written agreement'. Papadopoulos has publicly denied the claims.
35. The *Akritas Plan* was an instructional text written in 1963 as a tactical guideline for pursuing *enosis* and escaping the Republic of Cyprus. While a highly secret document, its presence was eventually discovered and published by the Greek language newspaper *Politis* on 21 April 1966. When challenged, President Makarios neither confirmed nor denied its existence, and there is evidence to support the claim that it was written with his approval.
36. These three elements are adaptations drawn from the work of Duncan Morrow, 'Breaking Antagonism? Political Leadership in Divided Societies', in Ian O'Flynn and David Russell (eds), *Power Sharing: New Challenges for Divided Societies*, London: Pluto Press 2005.
37. Peter A. Hall, and Rosemary C. R. Taylor, 'Political Science and the Three New Institutionalisms', *Political Studies*, vol. 44, no. 4, December 1996, pp. 936–57.
38. Duncan Morrow, p. 55.
39. Ibid.
40. Ibid.
41. The first set of inter-communal agreements or guidelines after the coup and invasion were the 1977 Makarios-Denktaş Accords, which outlined the basic foundation of an agreement. After Makarios' death in August 1977, incoming President Spiros Kyprianou found very little leeway for political manoeuvring, partly as a result of the growing power of the refugee movement in the south. Kyprianou harnessed these groups to stay in power and adopted their demands for a maximalist resolution. Since then, political parties have been very wary of the influence of refugee groups and have often competed for their votes. This has created a circularity where refugee groups have become more powerful and politicians have felt it more politically expedient to pander to these pressure groups, while within closed circles acknowledging an alternate political reality.
42. Kyrenia forms one of the island's northernmost geographical boundaries. As a result of the *de facto* partition, the Republic of Cyprus' northernmost border is now in Lefkosia, however, upon approaching the southern dividing line between northern and southern Lefkosia/Lefkoşa, one is greeted with a large banner reading 'τα σύορα μας δεν είαι εδώ. Είναι στην Κερνεια'. (These are not our borders. Our borders are in Kyrenia). Effectively, it is a protest against the claim that the areas north of Lefkosia form part of the TRNC.

43. At a meeting of the DISY executive to explain the party's position on the Annan Plan to DISY members in early April 2004, many members articulated a sense of deep betrayal by their leaders, who had 'told us for thirty years that we would go back to our homes, and now tell us that we won't'. (Meeting attended by the author).

44. In Greek Cypriot society, the people displaced as a result of the 1947 war are referred to as 'refugees'. It is a label to which is attached a high degree of emotionality. When Alvaro de Soto suggested in a press conference that the 'refugees' were in actuality 'internally displaced persons', he was met with public hysteria and accusations that he sought to downplay the Greek Cypriot community's suffering. The term 'refugee' is perceived in south Cyprus as giving a higher value and legitimacy than the clinical term 'internally displaced' to the community's distress regarding the ongoing status of the large group. Ironically, the term refugee also carries another important connotation which is not acknowledged by the Greek Cypriot community. Under international law, 'refugee' is the term given to a person who has fled persecution and resides *outside the borders of their country*. It would seem that the term therefore carries within it an acknowledgement of the Turkish Cypriot claim that in Cyprus there are *two* sovereign nations. This is a direct contradiction of the claim that 'our borders are in Kyrenia' (see previous footnote). This example is interesting for its suggestion that a society is able to simultaneously hold mutually contradictory 'truths', remarkable because *both* these truths form the foundation of the Greek Cypriot conflict imagining.

45. The refugee issue in the Greek Cypriot community is deeply complex and has been articulated by a number of authors. See particularly: Peter Loizos, 'Ottoman Half-Lives: Long-term Perspectives on Particular Forced Migrations', *Journal of Refugee Studies*, vol. 12, no. 3, 1999; Roger Zetter, 'Reconceptualizing the Myth of Return: Continuity and Transition Amongst the Greek Cypriot Refugees of 1974' *Journal of Refugee Studies*, vol. 12, no. 1, 1999; Roger Zetter, 'Rehousing the Greek Cypriot Refugees from 1974: Dependency, Assimilation, Politicisation', in John Koumoulides (ed.), *Cyprus in Transition 1960–1985*, London, Trigraph 1986.

46. Newsletter circulated electronically by *Nepomak* (World Organisation for Young Overseas Cypriots) regarding protest against anniversary of establishment of the Turkish Republic of Northern Cyprus. Circulated on 15 November 2005 and received by email on the same date.

47. http://kypros.org/Occupied_Cyprus/bellapais/ (accessed 4 June 2007). Emphasis in the original.

48. http://www.lobbyforcyprus.org/statements/millennium/Millennium.htm (accessed 4 June 2007).

49. Donald L. Horowitz, 'Constitutional Design: An Oxymoron?', *Nomos*, vol. 42, 2000, pp. 253–84.

50. Member of UN core negotiating team in Cyprus. Private interview with the author, 2006.

51. The information for the following two paragraphs is based on information from interviews with a number of Turkish and Greek Cypriot left-wing politicians, interviews with Katie Clerides and Maria Hadjipavlou, and interviews with NGO and UNOPS/UNDP staff who facilitated bi-communal projects. All sources are cited in the bibliography.

52. Information for this paragraph is drawn from interviews with Turkish and Greek Cypriot trade union and youth board representatives, who are listed in the bibliography.

53. Ali Gulle, President of the Revolutionary Trade Unions Movement (DEV-İŞ), interview with author, 20 May 2004.
54. For CTP.
55. Ali Seylani, Member of Parliament for CTP in the TRNC and president of the TRNC Civil Servants Trade Union. Interview with the author 17 June 2004.
56. Jean Christou, 'A question of education', *Cyprus Mail*, 12 April 2006.
57. Ibid.
58. See UN Document S/26026.
59. The most important of the CBMs were the provisions to reopen Nicosia Airport (closed since 1974) and the vacant town of Varosha (fenced off since 1974). In both cases, elites were unable to agree on elements like the displaying of flags, the nationality of security personnel, and the distribution of power within the newly opened areas. Underlying these disagreements was a struggle for domestic legitimacy, exhibited through the display of national or ethnic symbols.
60. Interview with Alpay Durduran, 23 March 2004.
61. 'Public enemy number one', *Cyprus Mail*, 22 January 2006.
62. Information for this paragraph is drawn from confidential interviews with party members of DISY and CTP.
63. When Denktaş was asked why he did not consult the Greek Cypriot leadership about his decision to open the checkpoints, he replied that 'if I had to talk to the Greeks about it, the borders would never have been opened. There would have been endless negotiations about it'. Confidential interview with member of core UN negotiating team, 2004.
64. See Simon Bahçeli, 'Studies under way to open new crossing at Zodia', *Cyprus Mail*, 22 July 2004; Jean Christou, 'The mines are gone, but where's the checkpoint?', *Cyprus Mail*, 29 April 2005; Photini Philippidou, 'UN: Zodhia will not open until both sides are ready', *Cyprus Mail*, 20 August 2005; Elias Hazou, 'Confusion over Zodhia checkpoint', *Cyprus Mail*, 30 August 2005; Elias Hazou, 'Zodhia checkpoint to open today', *Cyprus Mail*, 31 August 2005; Markides, Constantine, 'Zodhia crossing opens – finger-pointing between both sides continues ahead of pilgrimage', *Cyprus Mail*, 1 September 2005.
65. See 'President stays firm on Ledra opening', *Cyprus Mail*, 4 December 2005.
66. Information for the role of the Education Commission is based on an interview with Gül Barcay, former member of the TRNC Education Commission on the Revision of History Textbooks.
67. Gül Barcay, former member of the TRNC Education Commission on the Revision of History Textbooks. Interview with the author, 11 October 2006.
68. My thanks to Rebecca Bryant for the point.
69. See Christalla Yakinthou, 'The European Union's Management of the Cyprus Conflict: System Failure or Structural Metamorphosis?'.
70. There were 1493 Greek Cypriot, and 502 Turkish Cypriot people listed as missing as a result of fighting between 1963 and 1974. The Greek Cypriots who went missing after 1974 are referred to in Greek as 'οι αγνοόυμενοι' or 'the missing'.
71. Quoted in Nassos Stylianou, 'We Need to Write Our Own History Books', *Cyprus Mail*, 10 February 2007.
72. Olga Demetriou, 'The EU and the Cyprus Conflict: The Perceptions of the Border and Europe in the Cyprus Conflict', *Working Papers Series in EU Border Conflicts Studies*, no. 18, June 2005, p. 23.
73. For a more detailed analysis, see Christalla Yakinthou, 'The Quiet Deflation of Den Xehno? Changes in the Greek Cypriot Communal Narrative on the Missing Persons in Cyprus', *Cyprus Review*, vol. 20, no. 1, Spring 2008 pp. 15–33.

74. This is not to say that the issue has not been politicised in north Cyprus. On the contrary, the 'families of the martyrs' associations have frequently been used to remind the domestic and international community of Greek Cypriot (and Greek) barbarities. There are particular cases where all the men and boys of particular villages were taken by Greek Cypriots and slaughtered. The women remain in these villages to the present and function in a gruesome kind of 'tourist guide' role, reminding visitors and journalists of Greek atrocities. In these cases, women serve the role of a physical living memory, a link to, and reminder of a past where Greek Cypriots cannot be trusted.

75. This has created a number of complications. Because the Greek Cypriot missing people have not been declared dead, their estates are not inheritable by law, and their widows have been unable to remarry. Effectively, the lives of their families have been frozen in time.

76. Old wounds are opened from time to time, bringing with them a bitter reminder to Greek Cypriots of their victimhood and the danger that still emanates from Turkey. In 2007, for example, a story was circulated by a Greek Cypriot journalist based in the United States that there was evidence to support an old claim that a young boy listed as injured in 1974 was taken to Adana, Turkey after treatment in Cyprus. It was speculated that the boy was raised, unknowingly, as a Turk. Hopes of the boy's family were raised and then dashed when nothing came of the assertion, but it was enough to rekindle Greek Cypriot public anxiety about the conflict. Shortly after, a similar story arose from a Greek Cypriot mother who had heard that her missing son might have been raised by a Turkish Cypriot woman whose husband was a Turkish army officer. For further details see Elias Hazou, 'I know my son is alive', *Cyprus Mail*, 20 March 2007; Alexia Saoulli, 'Clerides: Denktaş never told me the child was dead', *Cyprus Mail*, 7 March 2007.

77. At the time of writing, November 2008. For current details, see www. cmp-cyprus.org

78. Confidential interview with UN official (2006).

79. Sporting and cultural contact with the Turkish Cypriot community is also blocked at the international level. Several attempts to set up football matches in north Cyprus have been blocked. In July 2007 a friendly match to be played in north Cyprus between English club Luton Town and Turkish Cypriot club Cetinkaya was cancelled after protests from Cypriot FA Cup officials. The cancellation had political ramifications. The first scheduled meeting in more than a year between Greek and Turkish Cypriot Presidents Papadopoulos and Talat was cancelled, reportedly in protest against the decision to stop the soccer match. For support and details, see Jean Christou, 'Peace talks halted by football match', *Cyprus Mail*, 13 July 2007.

80. 'Annual report on the implementation of Council Regulation (EC) 866/2004 of 29 April 2004 and the situation resulting from its application', *Communication from the European Commission*, COM (2006) 551, 25 September 2006.

81. 'The Cyprus problem', where the adjective 'problem' is not articulated but left assumed.

82. Also 'the Cyprus problem'.

83. Particularly during the Denktaş government, Turkish Cypriot political elites contributed to this Greek Cypriot fear by heavily pressing the idea that acknowledgement on the part of Greek Cypriot citizens of the TRNC would contribute to recognition of the state's sovereignty. This is especially the case for Greek Cypriots who would cross to north Cyprus before checkpoint control

was relaxed. The focus in the text above is on Greek Cypriot manipulation of the legal implications of sovereignty in Cyprus because during the 'Annan period' it was Greek Cypriot concepts of sovereignty which affected public attitudes to reunification. It was also a disproportionate focus of attention by diplomats whom I interviewed in the immediate post-Annan environment. During this period, criticisms of the Republic of Cyprus government were more freely expressed than had previously been the case, when Turkish Cypriot elite intransigence would have been the focus for diplomats regarding the cause of the conflict's perpetuation.

84. Costas M. Constantinou and Yiannis Papadakis, 'The Cypriot State(s) *in situ*: Cross-ethnic Contact and the Discourse of Recognition', *Global Society*, vol. 15, no. 2, 2001 p. 126.
85. Ibid., p. 129.
86. Based on personal observations of author.
87. The Greek Cypriot government's behaviour is partly attributable to the fact that Denktaş unilaterally opened the checkpoints. The move was largely unexpected, and therefore threw a number of Republic of Cyprus policies into chaos. Because there was such an overwhelming response by the Greek Cypriot public to cross north, the Papadopoulos government seemed unsure about how to align its strategy regarding protecting the Republic of Cyprus' sovereignty with immediate public sentiment.
88. Assuming that the Papadopoulos government was pursuing a policy of a unitary Cyprus formed (or, more accurately, *resumed*) under the Republic of Cyprus umbrella, then its reaction to the checkpoint openings is strategically puzzling. It is commonly assumed that Denktaş opened the checkpoints as a result of Turkish pressure to appear more conciliatory (after he abandoned the negotiations for Annan III) and to relieve domestic pressure placed on him by increasingly discontented Turkish Cypriots who were becoming threatening in their unity against his leadership. One would imagine that this would have been a perfect opportunity for the Greek Cypriot government to simultaneously harness Turkish Cypriot discontent and increase Greek Cypriot negotiating power by reminding Turkish Cypriots that they can resume citizenship of the Republic of Cyprus. To absorb Turkish Cypriots into the Republic of Cyprus would be an ultimate Greek Cypriot nationalist ideal because it would enable the abandonment of the 'federal compromise'. Therefore, it seems, in the Greek Cypriot government's panic over its initial loss of power over the Greek Cypriot community, it also lost an important strategic opportunity to change the dynamics of the Cyprus conflict to its favour.
89. 'Cyprus Government Cautious on Turkish Cypriot Plan for Green Line Crossings', *Voice of America Press Releases and Documents*, 22 April 2003.
90. Cited in 'Free movement of people is not basic solution to Cyprus problem – official', *Xinhua News Agency*, 23 April 2003.
91. 'Cyprus spokesman says no change in Turkish Cypriot policy', *BBC Monitoring European*, 30 April 2003.
92. G. Leonidas, 'The dynamic created by the spontaneous public – response to the lifting', *Athens News Agency*, 29 April 2003.
93. 'President shows interest in arrests of Greek Cypriots in north', *BBC Monitoring European*, 2 May 2003. This statement was in response to the arrest of a number of Greek Cypriots by Turkish Cypriot police, for attempting to steal a church bell from a church in north Cyprus.

94. 'Greek Cypriot press pays tribute to people power in landmark Green Line crossings', *Agence France-Presse*, 24 April 2003.
95. Ibid.
96. 'Church angry at Greek Cypriots who travel north only for pleasure', *Agence France-Presse*, 13 May 2003.
97. The Cypriot Orthodox Church subsequently played an important role in the 2004 campaign against the Annan Plan. The Bishop of Kyrenia went so far as to damn the souls of Greek Cypriots who would vote in favour of the plan at the referendum. His comment was, 'those who [vote] yes will lose their homeland and the kingdom of heaven'. Demetra Molyva, 'Synod calls for rejection', *Cyprus Weekly*, 23–29 April 2004.
98. Jean Christou, 'Poll shows two sides polarized', *Cyprus Mail*, 25 April 2007.
99. Jean Christou, 'Poll shows two sides polarized', *Cyprus Mail*, 25 April 2007.
100. On 28 October 1940 the then Greek Prime Minister Metaxas was issued an ultimatum by Mussolini to allow the Axis powers to continue their war from within Greek borders, or face war. Metaxas was supposed to have famously replied a single word, 'ochi' (no) which was picked up by the Greek public and chanted as a protest by thousands who took to the streets some hours later.
101. Though the occasions themselves are areas of dispute between left- and right-wing Greek and Turkish Cypriots. Traditionally, these commemorations have been more enthusiastically supported by the right-wing. See Yiannis Papadakis, 'Nation, Narrative and Commemoration: Political Ritual in Divided Cyprus', *History and Anthropology*, vol. 14, no. 3, 2003 pp. 253–70.
102. It has been argued that Turkish Cypriot elites would not have been able to facilitate such changes to the textbooks had there not been extensive public support for the move. Even if this is so, elite endorsement of such changes provides a powerful social signal that times have moved on, and the conflict is ending.
103. Tassos Papadopoulos, *Address to the Nation by the President of the Republic of Cyprus*, 7 April 2004. Transcript available at http://www.cyprus-conflict.net/Tassos-Annan.htm (accessed 22 May 2005).
104. Interview with Vassos Georgiou, then-Director of the Office of the President of the House of Representatives, 8 September 2006.
105. With the exception of President Rauf Denktaş, who has been a constant opponent of reunification unless on a very loose confederal basis. I would argue that the 'Denktaş element' was rendered rather impotent by the time he chose not to attend the second round of negotiations in Lucerne (2004).
106. Confirmed in interviews with a number of Turkish Cypriot politicians who have been listed in the bibliography.
107. 'Turkish Cypriot umbrella organisations. "This Country is Ours" encompassed some 41 political parties, trade unions, NGOs, and other bodies which banded together to form an effective opposition to the Denktaş regime. They organised a number of discussions about the Annan Plan and claim to be a driving force behind Turkish Cypriot support for reunification on the basis of the plan "Common Vision" incorporated some 90 civil society organisations from very different ideological backgrounds.'
108. Ali Gulle, president of the Revolutionary Trade Unions Movement (DEV-İŞ), interview with the author, 17 April 2004.
109. George Vassiliou, 'EU Enlargement: Implications for Europe, Cyprus and the Eastern Mediterranean', *Mediterranean Quarterly*, vol. 13, no. 1, 2002 p. 17.
110. See Alexandros Lordos, 'Can the Cyprus Problem be Solved? Understanding the Greek Cypriot Response to the UN Peace Plan for Cyprus', *An Evidence-Based*

Study in Co-operation with CYMAR Market Research Ltd, November 2004, www.cypruspolls.org (accessed 15 November 2005).

111. I contest the assertions made by Alexander Lordos that 'on the whole, Greek Cypriots understood the provisions of the [Annan] plan' on the grounds that his questions were pre-disposed to receiving a particular answer and not to delve into issues with sufficient depth. See Alexandros Lordos, 'Can the Cyprus Problem be Solved? Understanding the Greek Cypriot Response to the UN Peace Plan for Cyprus'.

112. Much of the following section is based upon the author's personal observations of events in Cyprus during the period in question, as well as upon interviews with Greek Cypriot politicians and NGO representatives involved in the 2004 referendum campaigns.

113. There were two primary explanations of the Annan Plan produced in booklet form, the first by the newspaper Phileleftheros on 15 February 2004 and the second by the International Peace Research Institute Oslo (PRIO), also in February 2004.

114. For example, when DISY leader Nicos Anastasiades publicly conceded that the Greek Cypriot public had been given an 'idealised version' of a resolution for 30 years, he faced an enormous public backlash, which included at its most extreme point, a bombing of his residence by Greek Cypriot extremists Chrysi Avgi (Golden Dawn).

115. Michael Attalides, 'The Political Process in Cyprus and the Day After the Referendum', *The Cyprus Review*, vol. 16, no. 1, Spring 2004 p. 146.

6   UN and EU: Offering Incentives for Resolution

1. American diplomat Professor Chester Crocker. Cited in Donald Rothchild, p. 249.

2. This statement is made on the assumption that the relevant international actors seek a peaceful resolution of the conflict in question.

3. Chantal de Jonge Oudraat, 'A Larger European Union: A More Effective Actor in the United Nations?', in Esther Brimmer and Stefan Frohlich (eds), *The Strategic Implications of European Union Enlargement*, Washington, Centre for Transatlantic Relations 2005 p. 249.

4. Hans Köchler, 'Quo Vadis, United Nations?', *I. P. O Research Papers*, June 2004, http://hanskoechler.com/koechler-quo-vadis-UN.htm#(III) (accessed 20 December 2006).

5. A/Res/55/2.

6. Such as the US coalition decision to invade Iraq in March 2003 without the relevant UN Security Council support, and the UN's failures in Kosovo, Bosnia (1992–5), and Rwanda (1994).

7. Donald Rothchild, p. 253.

8. Ibid., p. 254.

9. Ibid., p. 249.

10. It has been heavily involved as the primary organ of institutional development, political reform, and the maintenance of negative peace since the breakdown of the Republic of Cyprus in late 1963. The UN's involvement in Cyprus predates the state's breakdown. In February 1960 the Republic of Cyprus requested technical assistance from UNEPTA (later UNDP), to ascertain its economic possibilities, and aid economic acceleration.

11. Resolution of 4 March 1964, UN Document S/5575.

12. Oliver Richmond, 'UN Mediation in Cyprus, 1964–65: Setting a Precedent for Peace-making?', in James Ker-Lindsay and Oliver Richmond (eds) *The Work of the UN in Cyprus: Promoting Peace and Development*, Hampshire, Palgrave Macmillan, 2001 p. 102.
13. See Appendix 7. Richmond has catalogued UN attempts to resolve the Cyprus conflict into several periods: the immediate post-breakdown period, where the UN was established as mediator and peacekeeper between the combatant sides; a subsequent and more robust peacemaking period, where broader ranging peacemaking techniques were tried; the 'good offices' phase, which marked the failure of those mid-1960s peacemaking efforts and the consequent end of direct peacemaking; and the post-1974 broadening of responsibility and reshaping of the role of 'good offices' in Cyprus. Oliver Richmond, 'UN Mediation in Cyprus, 1964–65: Setting a Precedent for Peace-making?', p. 103. During these years, UN mediation efforts have been varied and have included initial attempts at power mediation, the role of good offices, and the development of various settlement plans.
14. Special Representative of UN Secretary General in Cyprus Alvaro de Soto, correspondence with author, 2 August 2006.
15. UN Resolution 186. Italics added.
16. Resolution 186 (1964):

> The Security Council ... recommends further that the Secretary General designate ... a mediator who shall use his best endeavours with the representatives of the communities and also with the aforesaid four governments, for the purpose of promoting a peaceful solution and an agreed settlement of the problem confronting Cyprus.

The implication for a *re*negotiation of the situation was perceived by the Greek Cypriots to justify their complaints and demands.

17.
> The Security Council ... recommends that the function of the Force [UNFICYP] should be in the interest of preserving international peace and security, to use its best efforts to prevent a recurrence of fighting and, as necessary, to contribute to the maintenance and restoration of law and order and a return to normal conditions.

The mandate of the Force was perceived by the Turkish Cypriots to be supporting their requests for a return to the 1960 constitution, rather than the Greek Cypriot requests for a modified constitutional order.
18. Oliver Richmond, 'UN Mediation in Cyprus, 1964–65: Setting a Precedent for Peace-making?', p. 102.
19. Analyses of the UN's role generally falls into two camps. Representing these divisions are Richmond and James, who have led analyses of the UN's role in Cyprus, focusing particularly on the problem's continuation. While Richmond maintains that UNFICYP has become a 'mechanism for the consolidation of the status quo' (p. 102), James argues that it can count Cyprus among its victories. For James, UNFICYP has been integral in the maintenance of peace on the ground, as well as providing the resources and manpower to keep channels of communication open between the disputants over a very long period. Supporting James' position is the fact that the most feasible option for the comprehensive resolution of this conflict lies in the top desk drawer

of the UN Secretary General, awaiting approval by both sides; supporting Richmond's analysis is the fact that the document remains unsigned. See for example, Oliver P. Richmond, *Mediating in Cyprus: The Cypriot Communities and the United Nations*, London, Frank Cass Publishers, 1998; and Alan James, 'The UN Force in Cyprus', in Ramesh Thayer and Carlyle A. Thayer (eds) *A Crisis of Expectation: UN Peacekeeping in the 1990s*, Colorado, Westview Press, 1995.

20. Oliver P. Richmond, *Mediating in Cyprus: The Cypriot Communities and the United Nations*, p. 124.

21. Ibid., pp. 215–8.

22. Alan James, *Keeping the Peace in the Cyprus Crisis of 1963–64*, Hampshire, Palgrave Macmillan 2002 p. 99.
    The Republic of Cyprus was initially recognised by the UN as the sovereign body for two key reasons: firstly, international dislike of secession; secondly, the UNFICYP needed to be invited by the sovereign body. So if the UN was to recognise two sovereign bodies, it would necessarily reduce the Greek Cypriots to the status of a 'community', which would not put them in a frame of mind conducive to signing the invitation; there was, and continues to be a general international predisposition to see the Republic of Cyprus as a legal political authority. That is, nation states prefer to recognise other nation states. The sovereign entity which the UN and the international community chose to work with was therefore the Republic of Cyprus under the control of the Greek Cypriot community. It must be made clear, however, that the UN Council did not create the authority of the Greek Cypriot regime. Alan James maintains that 'rather, what it did, was to make an influential proclamation of a position which had already been adopted in very significant quarters. There was never much likelihood that the Council would do otherwise'. Alan James, *Keeping the Peace in the Cyprus Crisis of 1963–64*, loc. cit.

23. Oliver Richmond, 'UN Mediation in Cyprus, 1964–65: Setting a Precedent for Peace-making?', p. 105.

24. 1965 Galo Plaza Report on Cyprus, *United Nations Document S/6253-A/6017*.

25. Oliver Richmond, 'UN Mediation in Cyprus, 1964–65: Setting a Precedent for Peace-making?', p. 114.

26. Ibid., p. 116.

27. For an explanation of international pressures on the UN, see David Hannay; Oliver Richmond, 'Peacekeeping and Peacemaking in Cyprus 1974–1994', *Cyprus Review*, vol. 6, no. 2, 1994 pp. 7–42; Edward Newman, 'The Most Impossible Job in the World: The Secretary-General and Cyprus', in James Ker-Lindsay and Oliver Richmond (eds) *The Work of the UN in Cyprus: Promoting Peace and Development*, Hampshire, Palgrave Macmillan 2001.

28. For discussion of these regional power shifts, see Tozun Bahcheli, *Greek-Turkish Relations Since 1955*.

29. Oliver P. Richmond, *Mediating in Cyprus: The Cypriot Communities and the United Nations*, p. 200.

30. Oliver Richmond, 'UN Mediation in Cyprus, 1964–65: Setting a Precedent for Peace-making?', p. 119.

31. Two uninhabited islands in the Aegean which were the object of a military crisis and sovereignty dispute between Turkey and Greece.

32. Between June and August 1996 three Greek Cypriots were killed: A Greek Cypriot soldier was shot in the buffer zone on 3 June 1996; on 11 August, Tassos Isaac was killed during a demonstration protesting the 1974 Turkish incursion;

four days later, his cousin, Solomos Solomou, was shot while trying to remove a Turkish flag from a flagpole in the buffer zone.

33. Republic of Cyprus president Glafkos Clerides ordered a number of Russian S-300 land-to-air missiles; there was a strong diplomatic response from Turkey, which made threats against the deployment. The missiles were subsequently deployed to Crete. Clerides' decision to purchase the missiles is commonly seen as a provocative move made just before an election to heighten the threat perception among Greek Cypriots voters in order to galvanise Clerides' public support.

34. Core member of UN negotiating team in private interview with author.

35. Ibid.

36. Ibid.

37. David Hannay, *Cyprus, the Search for a Solution*, pp. 88–91; Core member of UN negotiating team in private interview with author.

38. In a confidential interview with the author in 2006.

39. Core member of UN negotiating team in private interview with author.

40. Ibid.

41. UNHCR was established in the post-war period to provide assistance to refugees. In 1998, it was replaced with UNOPS, whose main role was that of facilitator of bi-communal and NGO peace-directed activity. In 2005, UNOPS was replaced by UNDP-ACT.

42. Statistics provided by Marina Vassilara, UNOPS Project Officer, March 2004.

43. With the establishment of EU financial support for project work in societal development, UNDP-ACT split into two branches: one funded by USAID and the other funded by the EU.

44. Information based on interviews with: Marina Vassilara, UNOPS Project Officer, 24 March 2004 and 24 October 2006; American diplomatic source, 2004; and Peter Skelton, Director of the British Council in Cyprus, 22 June 2004.

45. It is significant that until the rejection of the Annan Plan, very little focus was directed on the development of social conditions favourable to resolution separate to intercommunal relations. The development of social conditions was defined by almost all groups as the development of relations between Turkish and Greek Cypriots. Before the checkpoints opened, the deconstruction of mutually antagonistic mythologies was the main focus of NGO work. A significant portion of this work was established by Ghali's CBMs, and carried out between 1993 and 1997. This was done by gathering small groups of targeted individuals who then received intensive conflict resolution training. The idea was for them to become leaders who would then train other members of their community. After the checkpoints opened, inter-group interaction was much easier, and NGOs focused on network building. To the best of my knowledge, no NGO had focused extensively on identifying and altering other conditions that would be negative factors for a resolution. There was some work done on the altering of school textbooks to present a more balanced historical view of Cyprus. However, the project was abandoned after fierce public criticism.

46. While discussion is beyond the boundaries of this work, there is a vast literature on track-two diplomacy in Cyprus and its effectiveness. For example, see: Kerstin Wittig, *People United in a Country Divided, Bi-Communal Activities in Cyprus*, Unpublished Master of Arts thesis, Tübingen University, 2005; Maria Hadjipavlou-Trigeorgis, 'Unofficial Inter-Communal Contacts and their Contribution to Peace-building in Conflict Societies: The Case of Cyprus', *The Cyprus Review*, vol. 5, no. 2, Fall 1993; Maria Hadjipavlou-Trigeorgis, 'Little Confidence in Confidence Building? Conflict Resolution in the Context of the United Nations', *Cyprus and*

the *European Union*, Sudostevropa, Gersdelchaft, 1997; Maria Hadjipavlou-Trigeorgis, 'The Role of Joint Narrative in Conflict Resolution: The Case of Cyprus', in Mehmet Yashin (ed.), *Step-mothertongue, From Nationalism to Multiculturalism: Literatures of Cyprus, Greece and Turkey*, London, Middlesex University Press 2000; Benjamin J. Broome, 'Overview of Conflict Resolution Activities in Cyprus: Their Contribution to the Peace Process', *The Cyprus Review*, vol. 10, no. 1, Spring 1998 pp. 47–67; Benjamin J. Broome, 'Participatory Planning and Design in a Protracted Conflict Situation: Applications with Citizen Peace-Building Groups in Cyprus', *Systems Research and Behavioural Science*, vol. 19, no. 4, 2002 pp. 313–21; Christodoulos Pelayias, 'Across the Cyprus Ethnic Divide: Conflict Resolution or Conflict Management?', *Cyprus Review*, vol. 7, no. 1, 1995 pp. 114–22; Leonard W. Doob, 'A Cyprus Workshop: An Exercise in Intervention Methodology', *The Journal of Social Psychology*, vol. 94, December 1974 pp. 161–78; Leonard W. Doob, 'A Cyprus Workshop: Exercise in Intervention Methodology During a Continuing Crisis', *The Journal of Social Psychology*, vol. 98, December 1976 pp. 143–4; Clem McCartney, 'Civil Society in Divided Societies', *Civil Society Making a Difference*, paper presented at discussion panel organised by UNOPS-University of Cyprus 7 February 2005.

47. Senior British High Commission source, confidential interview with author.
48. Information for this paragraph is derived from interviews with Marina Vassilara, UNOPS Project Officer, and Pembe Menteş, Programme Analyst, UNDP-ACT, 24 October 2006.
49. A version of this section appears in Christalla Yakinthou, 'The EU's Management of the Cyprus Conflict: System Failure or Structural Metamorphosis?', *Ethnopolitics*, September 2009.
50. Justin Hutchence and Harris Georgiades, 'The European Union and the Cyprus Problem: Powerless to Help?', *The Cyprus Review*, vol. 11, no. 1, 1999 p. 87.
51. Ibid., p. 89.
52. Ibid.
53. Olga Demetriou, 'The EU and the Cyprus Conflict: The Perceptions of the Border and Europe in the Cyprus conflict', *Working Papers Series in EU Border Conflicts Studies*, no. 18, June 2005.
54. Meltem Müftüler-Bac and Aylin Güney, 'The European Union and the Cyprus Problem 1961–2003', *Middle Eastern Studies*, vol. 41, no. 2, March 2005 p. 281.
55. Ibid., p. 285.
56. EC declaration of 17 November 1983, EC-Bulletin 1983/11, point 2.4.1, p. 68. Cited in Frank Hoffmeister, *Legal Aspects of the Cyprus Problem*, Leiden, Martinus Nijhoff Publishers 2006 p. 84.
57. Commission Opinion (93) 313, EC Bulletin, Supplement 5/93, Luxemburg 1993. For details of the opinion, see Alecos Markides, *Cyprus and European Union Membership: Important Legal Documents*, Nicosia 2002.
58. Although there were a series of decisions and small tussles between the European Council and European Commission between the June 1994 Corfu European Council decision to extend enlargement to Cyprus and Malta and the March 1995 General Affairs Council agreement to begin negotiations for accession with Cyprus.
59. Core member of the UN negotiating team, private interview with author.
60. Harriet Martin, *Kings of Peace, Pawns of War: the Untold Story of Peace-Making*, London, Continuum 2006 p. 50; Core member of the UN negotiating team, private interview with author.

61. Frank Hoffmeister, *Legal Aspects of the Cyprus Problem*, Leiden, Martinus Nijhoff Publishers 2006 p. 121; confirmation by member of core UN negotiating team in private interview with author.
62. The *acquis communautaire* is the body of laws and regulations which governs the EU.
63. Council of the European Union, Copenhagen European Council Presidency Conclusions 12 and 13 December 2002, pt 12 p. 4. http://ue.eu.int/ueDocs/cms_Data/docs/pressData/en/ec/73842.pdf (accessed 25 February 2009).
64. Council of the European Union, Seville European Council Presidency Conclusions 21 and 22 June 2002, pt. 24 p. 7. http://ue.eu.int/ueDocs/cms_Data/docs/pressdata/en/ec/72638.pdf (accessed 25 February 2009).
65. Mehmet Ali Talat, 'Turkish Cypriots' Expectations from the European Union', http://www.esiweb.org/pdf/esi_turkey_tpq_id_41.pdf (accessed 21 April 2007) pp. 3–4.
66. Articulated by a number of UN high-level representatives in interviews with the author.
67. Senior UN official. Confidential interview with author.
68. Former EU Co-ordination Commissioner Takis Hadjidemetriou. Interview with author, 22 June 2004.
69. Nathalie Tocci and Tamara Kovziridze, p. 24.
70. Πανελλήνιο Σοσιαλιστικό Κίνημα, Panhellenic Socialist Movement.
71. David Hannay, p. 46.
72. Adalet ve Kalkınma Partisi, Justice and Development Party.
73. Nathalie Tocci and Tamara Kovziridze, loc. cit.
74. David Hannay, p. 50.
75. Core member of the UN negotiating team. Confidential interview with author.
76. David Hannay, pp. 63–4.
77. Nathalie Tocci and Tamara Kovziridze, p. 26.
78. Ibid.
79. Greek Cypriot diplomatic source in confidential interview with author, 2004. Also based on the author's private conversations with the leaders of a number of Greek Cypriot lobby groups situated in Greece, the US, the UK, and Australia.
80. Nathalie Tocci and Tamara Kovziridze, p. 26.
81. Evidenced by the creation of the political party EURO-KO in 2004 just prior to the referendum. The party was founded by breakaway members of DISY, who promptly joined the anti-Annan campaign.
82. Interview with Maria Hadjipavlou, Director of Cyprus Peace Centre, Lecturer UCY, 28 October 2006.
83. Alvaro de Soto, quoted in Harriet Martin, p. 61.
84. Then-Greek foreign minister Theodoros Pangalos stated publicly at a seminar 'Cyprus, the European Union, and Greece's Role' in November 1996 that: 'If Cyprus is not admitted, then there will be no enlargement of the Community, and if there is no enlargement there will be no end to the negotiations now going on for the revision of the treaties, and the Community will thus enter into an unprecedented crisis'. *Cyprus News Agency*, 22 November 1996.
85. Former EU Co-ordination Commissioner Takis Hadjidemetriou. Interview with author, 2 October 2006.
86. Cited in Frank Hoffmeister, p. 100.
87. Ibid., p. 101.

88. Mehmet Ali Talat, 'Turkish Cypriots' Expectations from the European Union', http://www.esiweb.org/pdf/esi_turkey_tpq_id_41.pdf (accessed 21 April 2007) p. 3.
89. Member of core UN negotiating team in confidential interview with author (2006).
90. Core member of the UN negotiating team in private interview with the author.
91. Member of core UN negotiating team in confidential interview with author.
92. Ibid.
93. British diplomatic source. Interview with author.
94. Olga Demetriou, 'The EU and the Cyprus Conflict: The Perceptions of the Border and Europe in the Cyprus conflict', p. 17.
95. In 2005 the 'North Cyprus Immovable Property Commission' (IPC) was set up to rule on restitution, exchange of properties, or compensation to Greek Cypriots with land in the north. In an ambiguous ruling in 2006, the European Court of Human Rights (European Court of Human Rights) tentatively ruled that the IPC provided adequate domestic recourse to justice. The opening of the EU Programme Support Office in north Cyprus in late 2006 was also viewed with significant concern in the south, as a sign that the EU was edging towards recognition of the TRNC.
96. For further elaboration on this point, see Mete Hatay, Fiona Mullen, and Julia Kalimeri, 'Intra-island trade in Cyprus: Obstacles, oppositions, and psychological barriers', *PRIO Cyprus Centre Paper*, 2/2008. Does Mete's report support this point?
97. Olli Rehn, 'Cyprus: One Year After Accession', speech given at the Cyprus International Conference Centre, 13 May 2005, Nicosia.
98. This is not a recent development. There has been an unwritten law in the politics of the Cyprus problem in which both sides have agreed that 'nothing is agreed on until everything is agreed on'.
99. Simon Bahçeli, 'Turks could consider piecemeal deals on Cyprus problem', *Cyprus Mail*, Wednesday 12 April 2006.
100. The opening of Famagusta port in north Cyprus for international trade with the Turkish Cypriot community has long been a negotiation point between the communities.
101. Council Regulation no. 866/2004 of 29 April 2004. Available at http://ec.europa.eu/enlargement/key_documents/turkish_cypriot_community_en.htm.
102. Green Line Regulation (Council Regulation no. 866/2004 of 29 April 2004) p1 (4).
103. 'Commission proposes comprehensive measures to end isolation of Turkish Cypriot community', Brussels, 7 July 2004, *European Union Press Release*, IP/04/857. Available at http://ec.europa.eu/enlargement/key_documents/turkish_cypriot_community_en.htm.
104. See Mete Hatay, Fiona Mullen, and Julia Kalimeri, 'Intra-island trade in Cyprus: Obstacles, oppositions, and psychological barriers', *PRIO Cyprus Centre Paper*, 2/2008.
105. Council Regulation (EC) No. 389/2006 of 27 February 2006 establishing an instrument of financial support for encouraging the economic development of the Turkish Cypriot community. Available at http://ec.europa.eu/enlargement/key_documents/turkish_cypriot_community_en.htm.
106. 'The EU is working for Financial Aid', *Cyprus Observer*, 19 January 2007.

7 The Politics of Adopting Consociationalism: The Referendums of 2004

1. 'Who will guard the guards?', Juvenal, *Satires*, VI, 347.
2. Regarding use of the term 'referendum', the plural is used when particular emphasis is placed upon there being two separate referendums in 2004. Otherwise, when addressing the general phenomenon of the 2004 vote in Cyprus, the singular 'referendum' will be used.
3. The Comprehensive Settlement of the Cyprus Problem, version V, Annex IX (1).
4. 1992 Set of Ideas on an Overall Framework Agreement on Cyprus, *United Nations Document S/24472*, paragraph 1, p. 9.
5. Didier Pfirter, Legal Advisor to the UN Secretary General's Special Assistant. Interview with author, 6 October 2006.
6. The Comprehensive Settlement of the Cyprus Problem, version I.
7. Kudret Özersay, 'Separate Simultaneous Referenda in Cyprus: Was it a "Fact" or an "Illusion"?', *Turkish Studies*, vol. 6, no. 3, September 2005 p. 384.
8. Interviews with members of core UN negotiating team between 2004 and 2006.
9. Lisa Jones, UN Political Affairs Officer. Interview with author, 15 September 2005.
10. See for example Diana Weston Markides; Stephen G. Xydis; Evanthis Hatzivassiliou; Prodromos Panayiotopoulos, 'The Emergent Post-Colonial State in Cyprus', *Commonwealth and Comparative Politics*, vol. 37, no. 1, March 1999 pp. 31–55. The opinions of Cypriot politicians and diplomats based in Cyprus were obtained in interviews with the author.
11. At the time, the UN's concern was primarily Turkish Cypriot elites; specifically then-TRNC President Rauf Denktaş. '[The referendum idea] was clearly designed to work around Denktaş because it had become quite clear that the Turkish Cypriots wanted the Annan Plan, and Denktaş didn't want it, so at some point we told him, "well you're preventing your people from getting what they want". And at some point he said that he would have a referendum [so] ... we took him at his word'. Core member of UN negotiating team. Confidential interview with author.
12. Lisa Jones, UN Political Affairs Officer. Interview with author, 15 September 2005.
13. Press Conference of the Secretary General of the UN and his Special Advisor on Cyprus, UN Headquarters, New York, 13 February 2004.
14. Arend Lijphart, 'Constitutional Design for Divided Societies', p. 106.
15. John McGarry et al., 'Integration or Accommodation? The Enduring Debate in Conflict Regulation', p. 84.
16. Didier Pfirter, Legal Advisor to the UN Secretary General's Special Assistant. Correspondence with author, March 2007.
17. Expressed in interviews and correspondence with the author between 2004 (prior to referendum) and 2006.
18. Representative of the diplomatic office of the president of the Republic of Cyprus. Private interview with author, 2004.
19. Mehmet Cakici, member of the TRNC Legislative Assembly (Peace and Democracy Movement – Bariş ve Demokrasi Hareketi). Interview with author, March 2004.
20. Nicos Koutsou, (then) president of New Horizons. Interview with author, 2 March 2004.

21. See text of the Akritas Plan, quoted in Glafkos Clerides, *Cyprus: My Deposition*, Nicosia, Alithia Publishing Co. 1990 vol. 1, p. 213.
22. Glafkos Clerides, *Cyprus: My Deposition*, Nicosia, Alithia Publishing Co. 1990 vol. 1, p. 210.
23. Lisa Jones, UN Political Affairs Officer. Interview with author, 15 September 2005.
24. An interesting comparison can be made with the process held to endorse the Belfast Agreement in Northern Ireland, which more consciously and concertedly involved the public in the adoption process by using information sessions, public hearings, videos, workshops and seminars.
25. Kudret Özersay, 'Separate Simultaneous Referenda in Cyprus: Was it a "Fact" or an "Illusion"?', p. 384.
26. Albert Venn Dicey, 'Ought the Referendum to be Introduced?', *Contemporary Review*, LVII, April 1890; Albert Venn Dicey, 'The Referendum', *National Review*, vol. 23, March 1894 pp. 65–72; Albert Venn Dicey, 'The Referendum and its Critics', *Quarterly Review*, vol. 212, 1910; Albert Venn Dicey, 'A Leap in the Dark: A Criticism of the Principles of Home Rule as Illustrated by the Bill of 1893', London, John Murray, Albemarle Street, W. 1912.
27. Albert Venn Dicey, 'The Referendum and its Critics', p. 559.
28. Nathan Cree, *Direct Legislation by the People*, Chicago, A. C. McClurg & Company, 1892 p. 16.
29. Bruce Ackerman, *We the People: Foundations*, Cambridge, Harvard University Press 1993 p. 54.
30. Baogang He, 'Referenda as a Solution to the National Identity/Boundary Question: An Empirical Critique of the Theoretical Literature', *Alternatives*, vol. 27, no. 1, Jan–March 2002 p. 76.
31. Ibid., p. 68.
32. David Butler and Austin Ranney in David Butler and Austin Ranney (eds), *Referendums Around the World: The Growing Use of Direct Democracy*, Hampshire, Palgrave Macmillan 1994 p. 11.
33. Ann-Sofi Jakobsson Hatay, 'Popular Referenda and Peace Processes: The Twin Referenda on the Annan Plan for a Reunited Cyprus Put In Perspective', *Turkish Daily News*, 5/6 May 2004.
34. Ibid.
35. Ibid.
36. A majority of voters in a majority of states, and a nationwide majority of voters.
37. L. F. Crisp, *Australian National Government*, Melbourne, Longman Cheshire 1983 p. 59.
38. David Butler and Austin Ranney, in David Butler and Austin Ranney (eds), *Referendums: A Comparative Study of Practice and Theory*, Washington, American Enterprise Institute for Public Policy Research 1978 p. 19.
39. Henry E. Brady and Cynthia S. Kaplan, 'Eastern Europe and the Former Soviet Union', in David Butler and Austin Ranney (eds) *Referendums Around the World: The Growing Use of Direct Democracy*, p. 16.
40. Brian Barry, p. 485.
41. Simone Chambers, 'Constitutional Referendums and Democratic Deliberation', in Matthew Mendelson and Andrew Parkin (eds), *Referendum Democracy: Citizens, Elites and Deliberation in Referendum Campaigns*, Hampshire, Palgrave Macmillan 2001 p. 243.
42. Ibid., p. 246.

43. Ibid., p. 245.
44. Ibid., p. 247.
45. For a summary of the literature, see Wayne Errington and Narelle Miragliotta, *Media and Politics: An Introduction*, Melbourne, Oxford University Press 2008. Also see, for example, Shanto Iyengar, 'Shortcuts to Political Knowledge: Selective Attention and the Accessibility Bias', in John Ferejohn and James Kuklinski (eds), *Information and the Democratic Process*, Urbana, University of Illinois Press 1990; David Fan, *Predictions of Public Opinion from the Mass Media*, New York, Greenwood 1988; Benjamin Page, Robert Shapiro, and Glenn Dempsey, 'Television News and Changes in Americans' Policy Preferences', *American Political Science Review*, vol. 83, 1987 pp. 23–44.
46. John R. Zaller, *The Nature and Origins of Mass Opinion*, especially Chapter 12; John R. Zaller, 'Political Awareness, Elite Opinion Leadership, and the Mass Survey Response', *Social Cognition*, vol. 8, 1990 pp. 125–53.
47. John R. Zaller, *The Nature and Origins of Mass Opinion*, p. 327.
48. Summarised in John R. Zaller, *The Nature and Origins of Mass Opinion*, Cambridge, Cambridge University Press 1992.
49. John R. Zaller, *The Nature and Origins of Mass Opinion*, Cambridge, Cambridge University Press 1992 p. 98.
50. Ali Seylani, Member of Parliament for CTP in the TRNC and president of the TRNC Civil Servants Trade Union. Interview with author 17 June 2004.
51. Ali Gulle, President of the Revolutionary Trade Unions Movement (DEV-İŞ), interview with author, 20 May 2004.
52. Christophorou Christophorous, 'An Old Cleavage Causes New Divisions: Parliamentary Elections in the Republic of Cyprus, 21 May 2006', *South European Society and Politics*, vol. 12, no. 1, 2007 p. 113.
53. To understand the depth of clientelistic networks in Cyprus, one can observe parties' frequent campaign promises at election time to 'stamp out' nepotism and cronyism. President Papadopoulos, in his July 2007 announcement to open his re-election campaign, even made a point of highlighting his 'lack of discrimination for people with different political ideologies'. Alexia Saoulli, 'Tassos Officially in the Running', *Cyprus Mail*, 24 July 2007.
54. Katie Clerides, Member of Parliament, Democratic Rally. Interview with author, 6 July 2004.
55. Christophorou Christophorous, 'Party Change and Development in Cyprus (1995–2005)', *South European Society and Politics*, vol. 11, no. 3, 2006 p. 521.
56. Arthur Lupia and Richard Johnston, 'Are Voters to Blame? Voter Competence and Elite Manoeuvres in Referendums', in Matthew Mendelson and Andrew Parkin (eds), p. 207.
57. In Greek his statement was «εμείς δεν θέλουμε ηχηρό όχι».
58. Alvaro de Soto in Harriet Martin, *Kings of Peace, Pawns of War: The Untold Story of Peace-Making*, London, Continuum 2006 p. 43.
59. Before the Bürgenstock negotiations, the Republic of Cyprus' chief negotiator Tassos Tzionis stated in a television interview that the Annan Plan was inadequate and unfair. He also maintained that this was his personal, not professional, opinion.
60. Craig Webster and Alexandros Lordos, 'Who Supported the Annan Plan? An Exploratory Statistical Analysis of the Demographic, Political, and Attitudinal Correlates', *The Cyprus Review*, vol. 18, no. 1, pp. 13–35.
61. Simone Chambers, p. 242.

62. Christophorou Christophorous, 'The Vote for a United Cyprus Deepens Divisions: The 24 April 2004 Referenda in Cyprus', *South European Society and Politics*, vol. 10, no. 1, 2005 p. 76.
63. Verheugen claimed he had been cheated by Papadopoulos, because the latter had continually asked for the support of the EU to reunify Cyprus under the Annan Plan, and had given his word that the Greek Cypriot side would not avert a settlement. Verheugen also criticised the government for running an unfair and unbalanced information campaign about the Annan Plan's objectives and contents.
64. There is a very large body of research on the topic, which falls outside the boundaries of this work. Key works include: John Street, *Mass Media, Politics and Democracy*, Hampshire, Palgrave Macmillan 2001, especially Chapter 4; Ciaran McCullagh, *Media Power: A Sociological Introduction*, Basingstoke, Palgrave Macmillan 2002, especially Chapter 7; Denis McQuail, *McQuail's Reader in Mass Communication Theory*, London, Sage Publications 2002, especially part 17.
65. John R. Zaller, *The Nature and Origins of Mass Opinion*, p. 311.
66. Shaun Bowler and Todd Donovan, 'Popular Control of Referendum Agendas: Implications for Democratic Outcomes and Minority Rights', in Matthew Mendelson and Andrew Parkin (eds), p. 131.
67. During the referendum campaign, a number of people supporting the 'yes' campaign were publicly accused of being foreign agents, paid off by imperialist powers. A journalist printed a list of public figures alleged to be in the employ of the imperialists, via the UN. Some time after the referendum, a parliamentary enquiry was called to examine the finances of those people. It amounted to a very public, government-supported witch-hunt, and further contributed to the atmosphere of fear and suspicion of Greek Cypriot society.
68. As highlighted in Chapter 5, the National Council plays an important strategic role in Greek Cypriot politics of the Cyprus conflict. The relationship between the president and the National Council is important in this regard, but is beyond the scope of this work. For further discussion, see Stelios Stavridis, 'The International Relations of the Cypriot Parliament', *Journal of Southern Europe and the Balkans*, vol. 5, no. 3, December 2003 pp. 337–54.
69. It was a very well funded, and highly professional campaign which was run by the advertising agency owned by the then-government spokesman's wife.
70. Christophorou Christophorous, 'The Vote for a United Cyprus Deepens Divisions: The 24 April 2004 Referenda in Cyprus', pp. 85–104.
71. Henry E. Brady and Cynthia S. Kaplan, p. 215.
72. Maria Hadjipavlou, Associate Professor, University of Cyprus. Interview with author, 28 October 2006.
73. Alecos Markides, former Attorney General of the Republic of Cyprus. Interview with author, 2 July 2004.
74. The point was stressed both publicly and privately. It was raised independently by each of the UN officials interviewed by the author.
75. Senior UN Advisor. Confidential interview with author.
76. The method and nature of advertising and campaigning during the referendum campaign is examined in a forthcoming report by Index, Cyprus. It has also been commented on by Amnesty International. See 'Europe and Central Asia: Summary of Amnesty International's Concerns in the Region, January–June 2004', *Amnesty International*, AI Index: EUR 01/005/2004, http://web.amnesty.org/library/Index/ENGEUR010052004?open&of=ENG-CYP (accessed 12 July 2006).

77. Senior UN Advisor. Confidential interview with author.

78. For support see 'Europe and Central Asia: Summary of Amnesty International's Concerns in the Region, January–June 2004', *Amnesty International*.

79. Simone Chambers.

80. Tassos Papadopoulos, *Address to the Nation by the President of the Republic of Cyprus*, 7 April 2004. Transcript available at http://www.cyprus-conflict.net/ Tassos-Annan.htm (accessed 22 May 2005).

81. See for support Makarios Drousiotis, 'The collapse of the illusions', *Cyprus Mail*, 10 December 2006.

82. Olga Demetriou, 'The EU and the Cyprus Conflict: Review of the Literature', *Working Papers Series in EU Border Conflicts Studies*, no. 5, January 2004 p. 15.

83. Member of core UN negotiating team. Confidential interview with author.

84. Didier Pfirter, 'Cyprus – A UN Peace Effort Under Conditions of ECHR Applicability', in Stephan Breitenmoser et al. (eds), *Human Rights, Democracy and the Rule of Law, Liber Amicorum Luzius Wildhaber*, Zurich, Nomos, 2007, p. 6, fn. 35.

85. Van Coufoudakis, 'Cyprus – the Referendum and its Aftermath', *The Cyprus Review*, vol. 16, no. 2, Fall 2004 p. 73.

86. Most of these claims were made in pamphlets, political speeches, and media interviews. Representative of these opinions is the work of Claire Palley, who was an employee of the Greek Cypriot government, and clear opponent of the Annan Plan. See Claire Palley, *An International Relations Debacle – The UN Secretary-General's Mission of Good Offices in Cyprus 1999–2004*, Portland, Hart Publishing 2005.

87. Tassos Papadopoulos, *Address to the Nation by the President of the Republic of Cyprus*, 7 April 2004.

88. Christophorou Christophorous, 'The Vote for a United Cyprus Deepens Divisions: The 24 April 2004 Referenda in Cyprus', pp. 85–104.

89. For example see Michael Attalides, 'The Political Process in Cyprus and the Day After the Referendum', *The Cyprus Review*, vol. 16, no. 1, Spring 2004 pp. 137–46; Tozun Bahcheli, 'Saying Yes to EU Accession: Explaining the Turkish Cypriot Referendum and its Aftermath', *The Cyprus Review*, vol. 16, no. 2, Fall 2004 pp. 55–66; Van Coufoudakis, 'Cyprus – the Referendum and its Aftermath', pp. 67–82; Viola Drath, 'The Cyprus Referendum: An Island Divided by Mutual Mistrust', *American Foreign Policy Interests*, vol. 26, 2004 pp. 341–51; Ann-Sofi Jakobsson Hatay, 'Popular Referenda and Peace Processes: The Twin Referenda on the Annan Plan for a Reunited Cyprus Put In Perspective'; Neophytos Loizides and Eser Keskiner, 'The Aftermath of the Annan Plan Referendums: Cross-Voting Moderation for Cyprus?', *Southeast European Politics*, vol.5, no. 2–3, December 2004 pp. 158–71; Kudret Özersay, 'Separate Simultaneous Referenda in Cyprus: Was it a "Fact" or an "Illusion"?'.

90. Tassos Papadopoulos, *Address to the Nation by the President of the Republic of Cyprus*.

91. Ibid.

92. Presentation by George Vassiliou at the Fourth Annual EU-Turkey Conference, Barcelona, June 2004.

93. Michael Attalides, 'The Political Process in Cyprus and the Day After the Referendum', p. 138.

94. Anders Todal Jenssen and Ola Listhaug, 'Voters' Decisions in the Nordic EU Referendums of 1994: The Importance of Party Cues', in Matthew Mendelson and Andrew Parkin (eds), p. 190.

95. Ibid., p. 188.
96. Christophorou Christophorous, 'The Vote for a United Cyprus Deepens Divisions: The 24 April 2004 Referenda in Cyprus', p. 82.
97. Ibid., pp. 85–104. Although there were three estimates released, with wildly different estimates. The first was conducted by Symeon Matsis, the second conducted by ex-president of the Republic, George Vassiliou, and the third by Eichengreen. All were based on Annan III.
98. See Appendix 8. Please note that the 2004 poll captures a very specific period in Cypriot history and should not be extrapolated beyond 2004. For the relationship between age and preference for resolution, and for a more current analysis, please see Alexandros Lordos, Erol Kaymak, and Nathalie Tocci, 'A People's Peace in Cyprus: Testing Public Opinion on the Options for a Comprehensive Settlement', April 2009.
99. The main parties include government partners DIKO and EDEK, as well as EURO.KO, and independents.
100. Though one suspect's Georgiou's position is likely to have changed, given that he now works in close affiliation with the president of the republic. The president of the House of Representatives at the time, for whom he worked, was now-president Dimitris Christofias.
101. The untranslated version is 'είναι τζαι τζαμέ τζε τζιε που το very unfair'.
102. Interview with Vassos Georgiou, Director of the Office of the President of the House of Representatives, 8 September 2006.
103. There is a strong reductionism apparent when the debate turns to why the Turkish Cypriots voted in favour of resolution. On the whole, it is perceived in the Greek Cypriot community that the Turkish Cypriots voted yes because the plan made them immediate members of the EU at zero accession cost; because it gave them international recognition; and because it gave them everything they wanted: 'that's why the Turks said yes. Since it was all in their favour, they said yes. That's why'. Interview with Vassos Georgiou. It is interesting to note that of the reasons listed above, the first and second are also cited by Greek Cypriot supporters of the Annan Plan. There is so little credit given in either community to the idea that voters might have supported the plan simply for the sake of the country's reunification that it is very infrequently listed as a reason for voting yes.
104. Former EU Co-ordination Commissioner Takis Hadjidemetriou, interview with author 22 June 2004.
105. Ali Gulle, President of the Revolutionary Trade Unions Movement (DEV-İŞ), interview with author, 20 May 2004.
106. Harriet Martin, p. 44.
107. In the Greek Cypriot community.
108. In the Turkish Cypriot community.
109. Member of the UN core negotiating team. Confidential interview with author.
110. Ibid.
111. Ibid.
112. Jean Christou, 'It's nothing personal', *Cyprus Mail*, Wednesday 12 April 2006.
113. Simon Bahçeli, 'A lover spurned: Will the Turkish Cypriots now turn away?', *Cyprus Mail*, 12 April 2006; Jean Christou, 'It's nothing personal', *Cyprus Mail*, 12 April 2006; Jean Christou, 'Poll shows two sides polarized', *Cyprus Mail*, 25 April 2007. See also Mehmet Ali Talat, 'Turkish Cypriots' Expectations from the European Union', http://www.esiweb.org/pdf/esi_turkey_tpq_id_41.pdf

(accessed 21 April 2007). Information for this section is also based the author's personal interviews with representatives of NGOs in north Cyprus.

114. Information for this section is based on the author's personal observations from fieldwork in 2006, and on interviews with Turkish Cypriot academics and representatives of NGOs.

115. Jean Christou, 'Poll shows two sides polarized', *Cyprus Mail*, 25 April 2007.

116. Jean Christou, 'It's nothing personal'.

117. Ibid.

118. 18–24 years: 63per cent was not in favour of living together; 25–34 years: 59per cent was not in favour of living together. 35–55 years: almost even split; 55+ years: majority in favour of living together. Survey published in Jean Christou, 'It's nothing personal'.

119. Maria Hadjipavlou, Associate Professor, University of Cyprus. Interview with author, 28 October 2006.

120. Jean Christou, 'Journalists freed but two more held', *Cyprus Mail*, 29 August 2006.

121. Some of that energy is captured by Maria Hadjipavlou: 'Wednesday I was in my office, and I get this call 'they opened it' [the first checkpoint], so I rushed immediately to experience it. And in no time, I mean, as soon as it became known, thousands of people started really pouring in, and when I crossed I didn't show anything, I just walked through; the police on both sides couldn't control the people. So for me, that was a real revolution from below'. Maria Hadjipavlou, Associate Professor, University of Cyprus. Interview with author, 28 October 2006.

122. By assuring the EU that the Greek Cypriot government would continue to support the Annan Plan's adoption before its entry into the EU.

123. Press Conference of the Secretary General of the UN and his Special Advisor on Cyprus, UN Headquarters, New York, 13 February 2004, http://www.un.int/cyprus/pressconf13.2.04.htm (accessed 26 June 2006).

124. In Matthew Mendelson and Andrew Parkin (eds), *Referendum Democracy: Citizens, Elites and Deliberation in Referendum Campaigns*, Hampshire, Palgrave Macmillan 2001 p. 14.

Conclusion

1. Martin Luther King Jr.

2. Henry E. Brady and Cynthia S. Kaplan, 'Eastern Europe and the Former Soviet Union', in David Butler and Austin Ranney (eds), p. 216.

3. There have been some notable exceptions, though they have not yet succeeded in opening up a strong academic debate. See: Tozun Bahcheli's articles, 'Searching for a Cyprus Settlement: Considering Options for Creating a Federation, a Confederation, or Two Independent States', *Publius*, vol. 30, no. 1–2, 2000, pp. 203–16; Tozun Bahcheli and Sid Noel, 'Power-Sharing for Cyprus (again)? EU Accession and the Prospects for Reunification Under a Belgian Model of Multi-level Governance'; and Andreas Panayiotou's 'Models of Compromise and "Power Sharing" in the Experience of Cypriot Modernity', *The Cyprus Review*, vol. 18, no. 2, Fall 2006 pp. 75–103.

Glossary

Acquis Communautaire	The European Union's body of laws and regulations.
Akritas Plan	A Greek Cypriot instructional text written in 1963 as a tactical guideline for pursuing *enosis* and escaping the Republic of Cyprus.
Avrupalı olduk	We have become European.
Βόρεια Κύπρος	North Cyprus.
Bu Memleket Bizimdir Platformu	'This Country is Ours' Platform.
Η Μεγάλη Ιδέα	The Great Idea (the historical 're-joining' of the Hellenic world).
Εθνικό Συμβούλιο	National Council (Republic of Cyprus).
Ένωση/enosis	Union (with Greece).
Επέτειος του ΟΧΙ	'The day of No', symbolising Greece's refusal to join the Axis powers on 28 October 1940, consequently sending Greece to war to defend its border against Italy.
Evkaf	The Pious Foundation in Cyprus. A statutory body which administers properties accrued for charitable use. In Ottoman and British times, it was the source of significant communal wealth.
Kanlı Noel	Bloody Christmas.
Linobambaki	Cypriots who practised both Christian Orthodox and Islamic rituals.
Υποστηρικτής του ψευδοκράτους	Supporter of the pseudo-state.
Millet	Name referring especially to non-Muslim ethnic or community groups in the Ottoman Empire. Each millet typically had a degree of internal autonomy, and members were generally subject to laws which governed their particular group.
Müftü	Communal leader of the Muslims with responsibility for interpreting religious laws and issuing appropriate fatwas.
Muhtar	Elected head of a village.

Οι αγνοούμενοι	The Missing (collective term for the Greek Cypriots who went missing as a result of the 1974 Turkish incursion).
Taksim	Partition.
Τα κατεχόμενα/ Οι κατεχομενες περιοχές	The occupied (territories).
Şehitler	The Martyrs (collective term for Turkish Cypriots who went missing or were killed as a result of Greek Cypriot attacks in the decade between 1964 and 1974).
Συμπατριώτες	Compatriots.
Παγκύπρια Κίνηση Πολιτών	Pancyprian Citizen's Movement.
Πλατφόρμα ΝΑΙ για Ενωμένη Ευρωπαϊκή Κύπρο	Yes Platform for a United European Cyprus.
Ψευδό	False/pseudo.

Bibliography

Primary sources

Personal interviews*

2004

Kemal Ataken, Teacher, Near East Junior College, 19 June 2004.

Philip Barton, British Deputy High Commissioner to Cyprus, 14 June 2004.

Mehmet Çakici, Member of Parliament Turkish Republic of Northern Cyprus, Peace and Democracy Movement, 23 March 2004 and 17 June 2004.

Wlodek Cibor, Senior Advisor to United Nations Special Representative to Cyprus, 24 June 2004.

Katie Clerides, Member of Parliament, Democratic Rally, 8 March 2004 and 6 July 2004.

Marios Constantinou, Lecturer of Political Science, University of Cyprus, continuous correspondence, 2004.

Mrs Dogruer, Former Department of Refugee Relocation, Turkish Republic of Northern Cyprus, 16 June 2004.

Alpay Durduran, President of Patriotic Union Party, Former Leader of Opposition, Turkish Republic of Northern Cyprus, 23 March 2004.

Ali Gulle, President of Turkish Cypriot trade union DEV-İŞ, 17 April 2004 and 20 May 2004.

Takis Hadjidemetriou, Former European Union Coordination Commissioner, Republic of Cyprus, 22 June 2004.

Izzet Izcan, Former General Secretary of Peace and Democracy Movement, Turkish Republic of Northern Cyprus, 23 March 2004.

Erol Kaymak, Lecturer, Eastern Mediterranean University, 28 February 2004 and 12 June 2004.

Andreas Koukoumas, Secretary Of Education Department, Pancyprian Federation of Labour, 16 March 2004.

Nicos Koutsou, President New Horizons, 2 March 2004.

Şener Levent, Editor Afrika Newspaper, 17 June 2004.

Alecos Markides, Former Attorney General of Republic of Cyprus, 2 July 2004.

Menelaos Menelaou, Diplomatic Office of the President of the Republic of Cyprus, 25 February 2004.

Filiz Naldoven, Poet, Artists and Artists, continuous correspondence, 2004–8.

Elia Petridou, Tech4Peace, 14 June 2004.

Hans-Christian von Reibritz, Deputy Head of Mission of German Embassy in Cyprus, 15 June 2004.

Ali Seylani, Member of Parliament Turkish Republic of Northern Cyprus, CTP, President of KAMU-SEN trade union, 17 June 2004.

Peter Skelton, Director British Council in Cyprus, 22 June 2004.

John Swift, Ambassador of Ireland to Cyprus, 17 May 2004.

* The names of additional UN and Greek Cypriot diplomatic sources have been suppressed for reasons of confidentiality.

Yiouli Taki, International Peace Research Institute Oslo (Cyprus Branch), 30 June 2004.
Jan Varso, Slovak Ambassador to Cyprus, 9 June 2004.
Marina Vassilara, Project Officer, UNOPS, 24 March 2004.

2005
Lisa Jones, Political Affairs Officer, United Nations, 15 September 2005.
Serhan Peksoylu, Columnist, Afrika Newspaper, continuous correspondence, 2004–6.

2006
Gül Barcay, Lecturer EMU, Former member of TRNC Education Commission, 11 October 2006.
Wlodeck Cibor, Chief of Mission UN in Cyprus, 19 September 2006.
Katie Clerides, Executive Committee DISY, 31 August 2006.
Hubert Faustmann, Lecturer, Intercollege, 28 September 2006.
Vassos Georgiou, Director of Office of President of House of Representatives, AKEL Central Committee, 8 September 2006.
Christophe Girod, UN, Third Member of the Committee on Missing Persons, 11 October 2006.
Ayla Gürel, Researcher PRIO, 8 September 2006.
Takis Hadjidemetriou, Former EU Co-ordination Commissioner, 2 October 2006.
Michalis Hadjimichael, Lecturer Intercollege, 15 September 2006.
Maria Hadjipavlou, Director of Cyprus Peace Centre, Lecturer UCY, 28 October 2006.
Constantinos Likourgos, Greek Cypriot Technical Committee, 20 October 2006.
Alecos Markides, Former Attorney General of the Republic of Cyprus, correspondence November 2006.
Pembe Menteş, Programme Analyst, UNDP-ACT, 24 October 2006.
Altay Nevzat, Lecturer EMU, 31 August 2006.
Kudret Özersay, Lecturer EMU/Turkish Cypriot Technical Committee, 4 September 2006.
Dider Pfirter, Swiss Ambassador at Large, former Legal Advisor to the Special Representative of the Secretary General of the United Nations, 6 October 2006.
Ahmet Sözen, Director of Cyprus Policy Center/Lecturer EMU, 27 September 2006.
Yiouli Taki, Researcher INDEX, 20 September 2006.
Marina Vassilara, Project Officer, UNDP-ACT, 24 October 2006.
Kemal Zihni, Youth Board AKEL, 31 August 2006.

Constitutions and draft constitutions

1960 Constitution of the Republic of Cyprus http://www.servat.unibe.ch/law/icl/cy00000.html (accessed 12 July 2006).
2002 Basis for a Comprehensive Settlement of the Cyprus Problem (version one), *United Nations Document.*
2003 Revised Basis for a Comprehensive Settlement of the Cyprus Problem (second revised version) *United Nations Document.*
2004 Comprehensive Settlement of the Cyprus Problem (final version) *United Nations Document.*
United Cyprus Republic, Constitution of the Greek Cypriot State, Appendix B, Annex I (final version) *United Nations Document.*
United Cyprus Republic, Constitution of the Turkish Cypriot State (final version) *United Nations Document.*

United Nations documents

13 Points Proposed by President Makarios to United Nations Security Council, 30 November 1963, *United Nations Document.*

1965 Galo Plaza Report on Cyprus, *United Nations Document.*

High Level Agreement of 12 February 1977, *United Nations Document.*

The Ten-Point Agreement of 19 May 1979, *United Nations Document.*

1989 Greek Cypriot Proposals, *United Nations Document.*

1992 Set of Ideas on an Overall Framework Agreement on Cyprus, *United Nations Document S/24472.*

Communication by the Secretary General and the Deputy Secretary General to the 824th meeting of the Ministers' Deputies, *United Nations Information Documents,* 15 January 2003, SG/Comm(2003)824 (restricted).

Opening Statement and Press Conference by Secretary General's Special Advisor on Cyprus, Alvaro de Soto, Ledra Palace, Nicosia: 20 April 2004.

Kofi Annan, 'Report of Kofi Annan on Good Offices in Cyprus', *United Nations Document,* 01 April 2003 UN doc S/2003/398.

Kofi Annan, 'Report of the Secretary General on Cyprus', *United Nations Document,* 16 April 2004 UN doc S/2004/302.

Kofi Annan, 'Report of the Secretary General on his Mission of Good Offices in Cyprus', *United Nations Document,* 28 May 2004 UN doc S/2004/437.

Kofi Annan, 'Report of the Secretary General on the United Nations Operation in Cyprus', *United Nations Document,* 24 September 2004 UN doc S/2004/756.

Under-Secretary-General for Political Affairs Sir Kieran Prendergast Briefing to the Security Council on the Secretary General's Mission of Good Offices in Cyprus, 22 June 2005 www.moi.gov.cy/moi/pio/pio.nsf (accessed 25 June 2005).

European Union documents

Green Line Regulation (Council Regulation no. 866/2004 of 29 April 2004), *European Union Document.*

'Proposal for a COUNCIL REGULATION Establishing an Instrument of Financial Support for Encouraging the Economic Development of the Turkish Cypriot Community', *European Union Document,* July 2004.

'Commission proposes comprehensive measures to end isolation of Turkish Cypriot community', Brussels, 7 July 2004, *European Union Press Release,* IP/04/857.

Media sources

Bahçeli, Simon, 'Studies under way to open new crossing at Zodia', *Cyprus Mail,* 22 July 2004.

Bahçeli, Simon, 'Turks could consider piecemeal deals on Cyprus problem', *Cyprus Mail,* 12 April 2006.

Bahçeli, Simon, 'A lover spurned: Will the Turkish Cypriots now turn away?', *Cyprus Mail,* 12 April 2006.

Bahçeli, Simon, 'Turks bury Alaminos missing with full military honours', *Cyprus Mail,* 13 July 2007.

Drousiotis, Makarios, 'The collapse of the illusions', *Cyprus Mail,* 10 December 2006.

Chaglar, Alkan, 'Papadopoulos' talk of defending Hellenism is alienating Turkish Cypriots', *Sunday Mail,* 22 April 2007.

Christou, Jean, 'Papadopoulos trashes plan', *Cyprus Mail,* 8 April 2004.

Christou, Jean, 'The mines are gone, but where's the checkpoint?', *Cyprus Mail,* 29 April 2005.

Christou, Jean, 'Spending up to £25 million in the north', *Cyprus Mail*, 18 December 2005.

Christou, Jean, 'It's nothing personal', *Cyprus Mail*, 12 April 2006.

Christou, Jean, 'A question of education', *Cyprus Mail*, 12 April 2006.

Christou, Jean, 'Journalists freed but two more held', *Cyprus Mail*, 29 August 2006.

Christou, Jean, 'Poll shows two sides polarized', *Cyprus Mail*, 25 April 2007.

Christou, Jean, 'Peace talks halted by football match', *Cyprus Mail*, 13 July 2007.

Fallaci, Oriana, 'Interview with Archbishop Makarios III', November 1974, http://www.cyprus-conflict.net/makarios%20-%20interview%20with%20fallaci.htm (accessed 10 January 2007).

Hazou, Elias, 'Confusion over Zodhia checkpoint', *Cyprus Mail*, 30 August 2005.

Hazou, Elias, 'Zodhia checkpoint to open today', *Cyprus Mail*, 31 August 2005.

Hazou, Elias, 'I know my son is alive', *Cyprus Mail*, 20 March 2007.

Ickes, William, 'Hundreds of Greek, Turkish Cypriots cross reopened border on second day', *Agence France-Presse*, 24 April 2003.

Leonidas, G., 'The dynamic created by the spontaneous public – response to the lifting ...', *Athens News Agency*, 29 April 2003.

Markides, Constantine, 'Zodhia crossing opens – finger-pointing between both sides continues ahead of pilgrimage', *Cyprus Mail*, 1 September 2005.

Mnookin, Robert and Verbeke, Alain, 'Bye Bye Belgium?', *International Herald Tribune*, 20 December 2006.

Molyva, Demetra, 'Synod calls for rejection', *Cyprus Weekly*, 23–29 April 2004.

Morris, Chris, 'Language dispute divides Belgium', *BBC News*, 13 May 2005.

Philippidou, Photini, 'UN: Zodhia will not open until both sides are ready', *Cyprus Mail*, 20 August 2005.

Saoulli, Alexia, 'Clerides: Denktaş never told me the child was dead', *Cyprus Mail*, 7 March 2007.

Saoulli, Alexia, 'Tassos officially in the running', *Cyprus Mail*, 24 July 2007.

Stylianou, Nassos, 'We need to write our own history books', *Cyprus Mail*, 10 February 2007.

Uludag, Sevgul, Interview with the Bishop of Morphou, *Yeniduzen*, 17 April 2003.

'Bishop warns 'yes' voters will go to hell', *Cyprus Mail*, 20 April 2004.

'Church angry at Greek Cypriots who travel north only for pleasure', *Agence France-Presse*, 13 May 2003.

'Cyprus government cautious on Turkish Cypriot plan for green line crossings', *Voice of America Press Releases and Documents*, 22 April 2003.

'Cyprus spokesman says no change in Turkish Cypriot policy', *BBC Monitoring European*, 30 April 2003.

'Free movement of people is not basic solution to Cyprus problem – official', *Xinhua News Agency*, 23 April 2003.

'Greek Cypriot press pays tribute to people power in landmark Green Line crossings', *Agence France-Presse*, 24 April 2003.

'Low-key funerals for Greek Cypriot missing', *Cyprus Mail*, 13 July 2007.

'President shows interest in arrests of Greek Cypriots in north', *BBC Monitoring European*, 2 May 2003.

'President stays firm on Ledra opening', *Cyprus Mail*, 4 December 2005.

'Public enemy number one', *Cyprus Mail*, 22 January 2006.

'Swiss expert to advise sides in Cyprus', *Dunya*, 26 February 2004.

'The EU is working for financial aid', *Cyprus Observer*, 19 January 2007.

'Turkish Cypriots spend as much in the south as they earn', *Cyprus Mail*, 31 August 2005.

'US sees Annan Plan as fair, balanced, urges "yes" vote – April 8 background briefing by senior state department official', *State Department Press Releases and Documents*, 12 April 2004.

'UN Swiss diplomat on Cyprus issue', *Athens News Agency*, 4 April 2004.

'Viewers fooled by Belgium split', *BBC News*, 14 December 2006.

Interview given by Didier Pfirter, Legal Advisor, Secretary-General's Mission of Good Offices, to Lefteris Adenlinis, Politis newspaper 'Didier Pfirter interview on property issue', 4 April 2004.

Interview given by Didier Pfirter, Legal Advisor, Secretary-General's Mission of Good Offices, to KIBRIS TV, 20 March 2003.

Interview given by Didier Pfirter, Legal Adviser, Secretary-General's Mission of Good Offices, to MEGA TV, 29 February 2004.

Speeches, transcripts and lectures

Alvaro de Soto, keynote address 'The Accession of Cyprus to the EU: Challenges and Opportunities', Conference at Columbia University, May 4 2003.

Alexander Downer MP, Address by the Minister for Foreign Affairs to open the Annual Conference of the Federation of Cypriot Communities, Adelaide, 22 January 1999, www.dfat.gov.au/media/speeches/foreign/1999/990122_cypriot_comm.html (accessed 19 February 2003).

Petro Georgiou, MP, 'Australian Foreign Policy and Europe: Old Friends, New Challenges', *Department of Foreign Affairs and Trade*, Speech to the Second Hellenic Council Conference, Canberra, 22 June 1996.

Tassos Papadopoulos, *Address by the President of the Republic of Cyprus at the 13th World Congress of Overseas Cypriots*, 25 August 2003, Private collection of author.

Tassos Papadopoulos, *Address to the Nation by the President of the Republic of Cyprus*, 7 April 2004, Transcript available at http://www.cyprus-conflict.net/Tassos-Annan.htm (accessed 22 May 2005).

Press Conference of Secretary General of UN and his Special Advisor on Cyprus, UN Headquarters, New York, 13 February 2004, http://www.un.int/cyprus/pressconf13.2.04.htm (accessed 26 June 2006).

Remarks by US Ambassador Michael Klosson at the Turkish Cypriot Nicosia Bar Association, Tuesday, 30 September 2003, www.americanembassy.org.cy/AnnanPlanRemarksSept30_03.htm (accessed 23 August 2004).

Transcript of United States Under-Secretary Mark Grossman's Question and Answer session with Greek Cypriot and Turkish Cypriot journalists via digital video conference, US Embassy, Nicosia, Friday 24 January 2003, www.americanembassy.org.cy/dvcgrossman.htm (accessed 25 March 2004).

Other primary documents

An Investigation into Matters Concerning and Affecting the Turkish Community in Cyprus: Interim Report of the Committee on Turkish Affairs 1949, Nicosia, Cyprus Government Printing Office 1949.

'Europe and Central Asia: Summary of Amnesty International's Concerns in the Region, January-June 2004', *Amnesty International*, AI Index: EUR 01/005/2004 http://web.amnesty.org/library/Index/ENGEUR010052004?open&of=ENG-CYP (accessed 12 July 2006).

'Joint Statement by Academics of Cyprus on the Proposed Plan for a Solution', Hamamboculeri.org: Alternatif Haber, 23 November 2002, (accessed 15 May 2006).

Newsletter circulated electronically by *Nepomak* (World Organisation for Young Overseas Cypriots) regarding protest against anniversary of establishment of the Turkish Republic of Northern Cyprus. Circulated on 15 November 2005. (Received by email on the same date.)

US Department of State Foreign Relations, 1964–1968, Volume XVI, Cyprus; Greece; Turkey, Documents 156–75, Office of the Historian, US Department of State.

US Department of State Foreign Relations, 1964–1968, Volume XVI, Cyprus; Greece; Turkey, Documents 176–93, Office of the Historian, US Department of State.

US Department of State Foreign Relations, 1964–1968, Volume XVI, Cyprus; Greece; Turkey, Documents 194–217, Office of the Historian, US Department of State.

Secondary sources

Ackerman, Bruce, *We the People: Foundations*, Cambridge, Harvard University Press, 1993.

Alexiou, Alexis, Gurel, Ayla, Hatay, Mete, and Taki, Yiouli, *The Annan Plan for Cyprus: A Citizen's Guide*, Oslo, International Peace Research Institute, 2003.

Almond, Gabriel, 'Comparative Political Systems', *Journal of Politics*, vol. 18, no. 3, August 1956, pp. 391–409.

Alter, Peter, *Nationalism*, London, Edward Arnold, 1994.

Anastasiou, Harry, 'Conflict, Alienation, and the Hope of Peace: The Struggle for Peace in Militarised Cyprus', *The Cyprus Review*, vol. 8, no. 2, Fall 1996, pp. 79–96.

Apeyitou, Eleni, 'Turkish-Cypriot Nationalism: Its History and Development (1571–1960)', *The Cyprus Review*, vol. 15, no. 1, Spring 2003, pp. 67–98.

Argerious III, John Louis, 'The Annan Plan for Cyprus: Why the Neutral Voter Said "No"', *Florida State University D-Scholarship Repository*, Article 46, 21 June 2005, http://dscholarship.lib.fsu.edu/undergrad/46/ (accessed 10 March 2006).

Asmussen, Jan, 'Life and Strife in Mixed Villages: Some Aspects of Inter-Ethnic Relations in Cyprus Under British Rule', *The Cyprus Review*, vol. 8, no. 1, 1996, pp. 101–10.

Atlas, Pierre M. and Licklider, Roy, 'Conflict Among Former Allies After Civil War Settlement: Sudan, Zimbabwe, Chad, and Lebanon', *Journal of Peace Research*, vol. 36, no. 1, 1999, pp. 35–54.

Attalides, Michael, *Cyprus, Nationalism and International Politics*, Edinburgh, Q Press, 1979.

Attalides, Michael, 'The Political Process in Cyprus and the Day After the Referendum', *The Cyprus Review*, vol. 16, no. 1, Spring 2004, pp. 137–46.

Averoff-Tossizza, Evangelos, *Lost Opportunities: The Cyprus Question, 1950–1963*, Athens, Aristide D. Caratzas, 1986.

Ayres, Ron, 'European Integration: The Case of Cyprus', *The Cyprus Review*, vol. 8 no. 1, 1996, pp. 39–62.

Baier-Allen, Susanne M., 'So Near and Yet So Far: Elusive Settlement in Cyprus', *Hellenic Studies*, vol. 11, no. 2, 2003, pp. 105–18.

Bahcheli, Tozun, *Greek-Turkish Relations Since 1955*, Colorado, Westview Press, 1990.

Bahcheli, Tozun, 'Cyprus in the Post-Cold War Environment: Moving Towards a Settlement?', in Vangelis Calotychos (ed.) *Cyprus and its People: Nation, Identity and Experience in an Unimaginable Community, 1955–1997*, Colorado, Westview Press, 1998.

Bahcheli, Tozun, 'Turkish Cypriots, the EU Option, and Resolving Ethnic Conflict in Cyprus', in Andreas Theophanous, Nicos Peristianis, and Andreas Ioannou (eds) *Cyprus and the European Union*, Nicosia, Intercollege Press, 1999.

Bahcheli, Tozun, 'Searching for a Cyprus Settlement: Considering Options for Creating a Federation, a Confederation, or Two Independent States', *Publius*, vol. 30, no. 1–2, 2000, pp. 203–16.

Bahcheli, Tozun, 'Saying Yes to EU Accession: Explaining the Turkish Cypriot Referendum and its Aftermath', *The Cyprus Review*, vol. 16, no. 2, Fall 2004, pp. 55–66.

Bahcheli, Tozun and Noel, Sid, 'Power-Sharing for Cyprus (again)? EU Accession and the Prospects for Reunification Under a Belgian Model of Multi-level Governance', in Sid Noel (ed.) *From Power Sharing to Democracy: Post-Conflict Institutions in Ethnically Divided Societies*, London, McGill-Queens University Press, 2005.

Barkey, Henri J. and Gordon, Philip H., 'Cyprus: The Predictable Crisis', *The National Interest*, vol. 66, Winter 2001/2002, pp. 83–93.

Barkey, Henri J., 'Cyprus: Between Ankara and a Hard Place', *Brown Journal of World Affairs*, vol. 10, no. 1, 2003, pp. 229–40.

Barry, Brian, 'Political Accommodation and Consociational Democracy', *British Journal of Political Science*, vol. 5, no. 4, October 1975, pp. 477–505.

Bartkus, Viva Ona, *The Dynamic of Secession*, Cambridge, Cambridge University Press, 1999.

Bellaigue, Christopher de, 'Conciliation in Cyprus?', *The Washington Quarterly*, vol. 22, no. 2, Spring 1999, pp. 183–93.

Bellamy, Richard, 'Dealing With Difference: Four Models of Pluralist Politics', *Parliamentary Affairs*, vol. 53, no. 1, January 2000, pp. 198–217.

Berlin, Isaiah, *Liberty*, Oxford, Oxford University Press, 2002.

Bertrand, Gilles, 'Turkish Cypriot's Exit, Voice and Loyalty', EuroFor Conference paper, Austria, 4–7 April 2002.

Bially Mattern, Janice, 'Taking Identity Seriously', *Cooperation and Conflict*, vol. 35, no. 3, September 2000, pp. 299–308.

Birand, Mehmet Ali, 'Papadopoulos Has Saved Us From Our Complex', *The Cyprus Review*, vol. 16, no. 2, Fall 2004, pp. 105–8.

Bitsios, Dimitris, *Cyprus: The Vulnerable Republic*, Thessaloniki, Institute for Balkan Studies, 1975.

Bogaards, Matthijs, 'The Favourable Factors for Consociational Democracy: A Review', *European Journal of Political Research*, vol. 33, no. 4, June 1998, pp. 475–96.

Bogaards, Matthijs, 'The Uneasy Relationship Between Empirical and Normative Types in Consociational Theory', *Journal of Theoretical Politics*, vol. 12, no. 4, 2000, pp. 395–423.

Bohn, David Earle, 'Consociationalism and Accommodation in Switzerland', *The Journal of Politics*, vol. 43, no. 4, Nov 1981, pp. 1236–40.

Bolukbasi, Suha, 'Boutros-Ghali's Cyprus Initiative in 1992: Why Did it Fail?', *Middle Eastern Studies*, vol. 31, no. 3, 1995, pp. 460–77.

Bostock, William W., 'Language Grief: A "Raw Material" of Ethnic Conflict', *Nationalism and Ethnic Politics*, vol. 3, no. 4, Winter 1997, pp. 94–112.

Bowler, Shaun and Donovan, Todd, 'Popular Control of Referendum Agendas: Implications for Democratic Outcomes and Minority Rights', in Matthew Mendelson and Andrew Parkin (eds) *Referendum Democracy: Citizens, Elites and Deliberation in Referendum Campaigns*, Hampshire, Palgrave Macmillan, 2001.

Boyle, Kevin and Hadden, Tom 'The Peace Process in Northern Ireland', *International Affairs*, vol. 71, no. 2, April 1995, pp. 269–83.

Brady, Henry E. and Kaplan, Cynthia S., 'Eastern Europe and the Former Soviet Union', in David Butler and Austin Ranney (eds) *Referendums Around the World: The Growing Use of Direct Democracy*, Hampshire, Palgrave Macmillan, 1994.

Brass, Paul R., *Ethnicity and Nationalism: Theory and Comparison*, New Delhi, Sage Publications, 1991.

Brewin, Christopher, 'Reluctant Commitment: Past Aloofness and Present Problems in European Attitudes to Cyprus', in Andreas Theophanous, Nicos Peristianis, and Andreas Ioannou (eds) *Cyprus and the European Union*, Nicosia, Intercollege Press, 1999.

Brito, Alexandra Barahona de, Enriquez, Carmen Gonzalez, and Aguilar, Paloma (eds) *The Politics of Memory and Democratization: Transitional Justice in Democratizing Societies*, Oxford, Oxford University Press, 2001.

Brodie, Ian, 'The Market for Political Status', *Comparative Politics*, vol. 28, no. 3, April 1996, pp. 253–71.

Broome, Benjamin J., 'Overview of Conflict Resolution Activities in Cyprus: Their Contribution to the Peace Process', *The Cyprus Review*, vol. 10, no. 1, Spring 1998, pp. 47–67.

Broome, Benjamin J., 'Participatory Planning and Design in a Protracted Conflict Situation: Applications with Citizen Peace-Building Groups in Cyprus', *Systems Research and Behavioural Science*, vol. 19, no. 4, 2002, pp. 313–21.

Brown, David, 'Why is the Nation-State so Vulnerable to Ethnic Nationalism?', *Nations and Nationalism*, vol. 4, no. 1, 1998, pp. 1–15.

Brownlie, Ian, *Principles of Public International Law*, Oxford, Clarendon Press, 1990.

Bryant, Rebecca, 'An Education in Honor: Patriotism and Rebellion in Greek Cypriot Schools', in Vangelis Calotychos (ed.) *Cyprus and its People: Nation, Identity and Experience in an Unimaginable Community, 1955–1997*, Colorado, Westview Press, 1998.

Bryant, Rebecca, 'An Aesthetics of Self: Moral Remaking and Cypriot Education', *Comparative Studies in Society and History*, vol. 43, no. 3, July 2001, pp. 583–614.

Bryant, Rebecca, 'Justice or Respect? A Comparative Perspective on Politics in Cyprus', *Ethnic and Racial Studies*, vol. 24, no. 6, November 2001, pp. 892–924.

Bryant, Rebecca, 'The Purity of Spirit and the Power of Blood: A Comparative Perspective on Nation, Gender and Kinship in Cyprus', *Journal of the Royal Anthropological Institute*, vol. 8, no. 3, Sept 2002, pp. 509–30.

Bryant, Rebecca, 'Bandits and "Bad Characters": Law as Anthropological Practice in Cyprus, c. 1900', *Law and History Review*, vol. 21, no. 2, Summer 2003, pp. 243–69.

Bryant, Rebecca, *Imagining the Modern: The Cultures of Nationalism in Cyprus*, London, I. B. Tauris and Co, 2004.

Bryant, Rebecca, 'An Ironic Result in Cyprus', *Middle East Report Online*, May 12 2004.

Bryant, Rebecca, 'A Dangerous Trend in Cyprus' *Middle East Report Online*, vol. 235, Summer 2005 www.merip.org/mer/mer235/bryant.html (accessed 7 February 2006).

Burnham, Peter, Gilland, Karin, Grant, Wyn, and Layton-Henry, Zig, *Research Methods in Politics*, Hampshire, Palgrave Macmillan, 2004.

Butler, David and Ranney, Austin (eds) *Referendums: A Comparative Study of Practice and Theory*, Washington, American Enterprise Institute for Public Policy Research, 1978.

Butler, David and Ranney, Austin (eds) *Referendums Around the World: The Growing Use of Direct Democracy*, Hampshire, Palgrave Macmillan, 1994.

Byrne, Sean 'Power Politics as Usual in Cyprus and Northern Ireland: Divided Islands and the Roles of External Ethno-guarantors', *Nationalism and Ethnic Politics*, vol. 6, no. 1, Spring 2000, pp. 1–23.

Calotychos, Vangelis, 'Interdisciplinary Perspectives: Difference at the Heart of Cypriot Identity and its Study', in Vangelis Calotychos (ed.) *Cyprus and its People: Nation, Identity and Experience in an Unimaginable Community, 1955–1997*, Colorado, Westview Press, 1998.

Camp, Glen D., 'Cyprus and East Mediterranean Security Problems: New Developments–Old Problems', *The Cyprus Review*, vol. 16, no. 2, Fall 2004, pp. 13–36.

Camp, Glen D., 'Island Impasse: Peacemaking on Cyprus, 1980–1994', in Vangelis Calotychos (ed.) *Cyprus and its People: Nation, Identity and Experience in an Unimaginable Community, 1955–1997*, Colorado, Westview Press, 1998.

Camp, Glen D., 'Policy Implications of the East Mediterranean Security Situation', *The Cyprus Review*, vol. 14, no. 1, Spring 2002, pp. 29–54.

Campbell, Colm, Aoláin, Fionnuala Ní and Harvey, Colin. 'The Frontiers of Legal Analysis: Reframing the Transition in Northern Ireland', *The Modern Law Review*, vol. 66, no. 3, May 2003, pp. 317–45.

Çarkoğlu, Ali and Sozen, Ahmet, 'The Turkish Cypriot General Elections of December 2003: Setting the Stage for Resolving the Cyprus Conflict?', *South European Society and Politics*, vol. 9, no. 3, Winter 2004, pp. 122–36.

Carras, Costa, 'Greek-Turkish Forum – First Public Event, March 2002 – Cyprus: Year of Decision', *The Cyprus Review*, vol. 14, no. 1, Spring 2002, pp. 87–100.

Carver, Field Marshal Lord 'Peacekeeping in Cyprus', in John Koumoulides (ed.) *Cyprus in Transition 1960–1985*, London, Trigraph, 1986.

Cavit, Ahmet, 'The British Rule in Turkish Cypriot Text-Books and Turkish Cypriot Text-Books in Cyprus', *The Cyprus Review*, vol. 6, no. 1, 1994, pp. 65–80.

Cemil, Huseyin, *The Truth is Sour*, Melbourne, published by the author, 2005.

Chadjipadelis, Th. and Andreadis, I., 'Analysis of the Cyprus Referendum on the Annan Plan', 2007, published online by http://www.psa.ac.uk/2007/pps/Chadjipadelis.pdf (accessed 22 July 2007).

Chambers, Simone, 'Constitutional Referendums and Democratic Deliberation', in Matthew Mendelson and Andrew Parkin (eds) *Referendum Democracy: Citizens, Elites and Deliberation in Referendum Campaigns*, Hampshire, Palgrave Macmillan, 2001.

Christophorous, Christophorou, 'The Vote for a United Cyprus Deepens Divisions: The 24 April 2004 Referenda in Cyprus', *South European Society and Politics*, vol. 10, no. 1, 2005, pp. 85–104.

Christophorous, Christophorou, 'Party Change and Development in Cyprus (1995–2005)', *South European Society and Politics*, vol. 11, no. 3, 2006, pp. 513–42.

Christophorous, Christophorou, 'An Old Cleavage Causes New Divisions: Parliamentary Elections in the Republic of Cyprus, 21 May 2006', *South European Society and Politics*, vol. 12, no. 1, 2007, pp. 111–28.

Clerides, Glafkos, *Cyprus: My Deposition*, Nicosia, Alithia Publishing Co., 1990.

Connor, Walker, 'A Few Cautionary Notes on the History and Future of Ethnonational Conflicts', in Andreas Wimmer, Richard J. Goldstone, Donald L. Horowitz, Ulrike Joras, and Conrad Schetter (eds) *Facing Ethnic Conflicts, Towards a New Realism*, Oxford, Rowman and Littlefield Publishers Inc., 2004.

Constantinou, Marios, 'Constitutional Learning for Cypriots in the Light of the Swiss and EU Experience: A Sociological Perspective', *The Cyprus Review*, vol. 14, no. 2, Fall 2002, pp. 13–44.

Constantinou, Marios, 'Constitutional Learning for Cypriots in the Light of the Swiss and EU Experience: A Sociological Perspective. Part II: Theoretical and Practical Stakes of Federalism', *The Cyprus Review*, vol. 15, no. 1, Spring 2003, pp. 13–66.

Constantinou, Marios, 'The Cavafian Poetics of Diasporic Constitutionalism: Towards a Neo-Hellenistic Decentering of the Kyp(riot)ic Experience', reference unknown.

Constantinou, Costas M. and Papadakis, Yiannis, 'The Cypriot State(s) *in situ*: Cross-ethnic Contact and the Discourse of Recognition', *Global Society*, vol. 15, no. 2, 2001, pp. 125–48.

Constantinou, Costas M. and Richmond, Oliver P., 'The Long Mile of Empire: Power, Legitimation and the UK Bases in Cyprus', *Mediterranean Politics*, vol. 10, no. 1, March 2005, pp. 65–84.

Coufoudakis, Van, 'The Dynamics of Political Partition and Division in Multiethnic and Multireligious Societies – the Cyprus Case', in Van Coufoudakis (ed.) *Essays on the Cyprus Conflict*, New York, Pella Publishing, 1976.

Coufoudakis, Van, 'Cyprus: Domestic Politics and Recent UN Proposals', in Christos Ioannides ed. *Cyprus: Domestic Dynamics, External Constraints*, New York, Aristide D. Caratzas, 1992.

Coufoudakis, Van, 'Cyprus – the Referendum and its Aftermath', *The Cyprus Review*, vol. 16, no. 2, Fall 2004, pp. 67–82.

Couloumbis, Theodore A. and Klarevas, Louis J., 'An Outline of a Plan Toward a Comprehensive Settlement of the Greek-Turkish Dispute', in Vangelis Calotychos (ed.) *Cyprus and its People: Nation, Identity and Experience in an Unimaginable Community, 1955–1997*, Colorado, Westview Press, 1998.

Crawshaw, Nancy, *The Cyprus Revolt: An Account of the Struggle for Union with Greece*, London, George Allen and Unwin, 1978.

Cree, Nathan, *Direct Legislation by the People*, Chicago, A. C. McClurg and Company, 1892.

Crisp, L. F., *Australian National Government*, Melbourne, Longman Cheshire, 1983.

Daalder, Hans, 'On Building Consociational Nations: The Cases of the Netherlands and Switzerland', in Kenneth D. McRae (ed.) *Consociational Democracy: Political Accommodation in Segmented Societies*, Toronto, McClelland and Stewart, 1974.

Dahl, Robert A., *Polyarchy: Participation and Opposition*, New Haven, Yale University Press, 1971.

Demetriou, Olga, 'The EU and the Cyprus Conflict: Review of the Literature', *Working Papers Series in EU Border Conflicts Studies*, no. 5, January 2004.

Demetriou, Olga, 'The EU and the Cyprus Conflict: The View of Political Actors in Cyprus', *Working Papers Series in EU Border Conflicts Studies*, no. 9, July 2004.

Demetriou, Olga, 'The EU and the Cyprus Conflict: The Perceptions of the Border and Europe in the Cyprus conflict', *Working Papers Series in EU Border Conflicts Studies*, no. 18, June 2005.

Denktaş, Rauf R., *The Cyprus Problem in a Nutshell*, Lefkoşa, Public Information Office, Turkish Cypriot Administration, 1974.

Denktaş, Rauf R., *The Cyprus Triangle*, London, George Allen and Unwin, 1982.

Dent, Martin, 'Cyprus: A new and more hopeful step in the struggle to free the tempting morsel from the net of entanglement in the rivals' aspirations of its neighbours to dominate and devour', *Journal of Southern Europe and the Balkans*, vol. 5, no. 2, August 2003, pp. 241–5.

Deschouwer, Kris, 'Falling Apart Together: The Changing Nature of Belgian Consociationalism, 1961–2001', *Acta Politica*, vol. 37, no. 1, 2002, pp. 68–85.

de Smith, S. A., *The New Commonwealth and its Constitutions*, London, Stevens and Sons, 1964.

Dewachter, Wilfried, 'Changes in a Particratie: The Belgian Party System from 1944–1986', in Hans Daalder (ed.) *Party Systems in Denmark, Austria, Switzerland, the Netherlands, and Belgium*, London, Frances Pinter Publishers, 1987.

Diamond, Louise and Fisher, Ronald J., 'Integrating Conflict Resolution Training and Consultation: A Cyprus Example', *Negotiation Journal*, vol. 11, no. 3, July 1995, pp. 287–301.

Dicey, Albert Venn, 'Ought the Referendum to be Introduced?', *Contemporary Review*, LVII, April 1890.

Dicey, Albert Venn, 'The Referendum', *National Review*, vol. 23, March 1894, pp. 65–72.

Dicey, Albert Venn, 'The Referendum and its Critics', *Quarterly Review*, vol. 212, 1910.

Dicey, Albert Venn, *A Leap in the Dark: A Criticism of the Principles of Home Rule as Illustrated by the Bill of 1893*, London, John Murray, Albemarle Street, W. 1912.

Dicey, Albert Venn, *Introduction to the Study of the Law of the Constitution*, London, Macmillan, 1915.

Dodd, Clement, 'Constitutional Features of the UN Plan for Cyprus and its Antecedents', *Turkish Studies*, vol. 6, no. 1, March 2005, pp. 39–51.

Doob, Leonard W., 'Cypriot Patriotism and Nationalism', *Journal of Conflict Resolution*, vol. 30, no. 2, 1986, pp. 383–96.

Doob, Leonard W., 'A Cyprus Workshop: An Exercise in Intervention Methodology', *The Journal of Social Psychology*, vol. 94, December 1974, pp. 161–78.

Doob, Leonard W., 'A Cyprus Workshop: An Exercise in Intervention Methodology During a Continuing Crisis', *The Journal of Social Psychology*, vol. 98, December 1976, pp. 143–44.

Douglas, Neville, 'The Politics of Accommodation, Social Change and Conflict Resolution in Northern Ireland', *Political Geography*, vol. 17, no. 2, 1998, pp. 209–29.

Drath, Viola, 'The Cyprus Referendum: An Island Divided by Mutual Mistrust', *American Foreign Policy Interests*, vol. 26, 2004, pp. 341–51.

Drousiotis, Makarios, 'The Construction of Reality and the Mass Media in Cyprus', Nicosia, October 2005, http://www.makarios.ws/cgibin/hweb?-A=980&-V=perireousa (accessed 12 November 2005).

Drousiotis, Makarios, 'The Greco-Turkish "Para-State" and Cyprus 1947–1958', in Hubert Faustmann and Nicos Peristianis (eds) *Britain in Cyprus: Colonialism and Post-Colonialism 1878–2006*, Berlin, Bibliopolis, 2006.

Druckman, Daniel and Broome, Benjamin J., 'Value Differences and Conflict Resolution: Familiarity or Liking?', *The Journal of Conflict Resolution*, vol. 35, no. 4, December 1991, pp. 571–93.

Dundas, Guy, 'Cyprus from 1960 to EU Accession: The Case for Non-Territorial Autonomy, *Australian Journal of Politics and History*, vol. 50, no. 1, 2004, pp. 86–94.

Dunér, Bertil, 'Cyprus: North is North, and South is South', *Security Dialogue*, vol. 30, no. 4, December 1999, pp. 485–96.

Elazar, Daniel, 'Form of State: Federal, Unitary or ...', Jerusalem Center for Public Affairs, 1994, www.jcpa.org/dje/index-fs.htm (accessed 12 November 2003).

Elazar, Daniel, 'The Significance of Federalism in Redesigning Consititutional Systems', Jerusalem Center for Public Affairs, 1994, www.jcpa.org/dje/index-fs.htm (accessed 12 November 2003).

Elazar, Daniel, 'Constitutionalizing Globalisation: The Postmodern Revival of Confederal Arrangements', Jerusalem Center for Public Affairs, 1997, www.jcpa.org/dje/index-fs.htm (accessed 12 November 2003).

Elazar, Daniel, 'Federalism and Peace-Making', Jerusalem Center for Public Affairs, 1998, www.jcpa.org/dje/index-fs.htm (accessed 12 November 2003).

Elazar, Daniel, 'What are Federal Solutions?', *Two Peoples, One Land: Federal Solutions for Israel, the Palestinians and Jordan*, Jerusalem Center for Public Affairs, www.jcpa.org/dje/index-fs.htm (accessed 12 November 2003).

Errington, Wayne and Miragliotta, Narelle, *Media and Politics: An Introduction*, Melbourne, Oxford University Press, 2008.

Esman, Milton J., 'Power Sharing and the Constructionist Fallacy', in Markus M. L. Crepaz, Thomas A. Koelble, and David Wilsford (eds) *Democracy and Institutions: The Life Work of Arend Lijphart*, Ann Arbor, University of Michigan Press, 2000.

Evriviades, Marios and Bourantonis, Dimitris, 'Peacekeeping and Peacemaking: Some Lessons from Cyprus', *International Peacekeeping*, vol. 1, no. 4, Winter 1994, pp. 394–412.

Fan, David, *Predictions of Public Opinion from the Mass Media*, New York, Greenwood, 1988.

Farr, Thomas F., 'Overcoming the Cyprus Tragedy: Let Cypriots be Cypriot', *Mediterranean Quarterly*, vol. 8, Fall 1997, pp. 32–62.

Faustmann, Hubert, 'Independence Postponed: Cyprus 1959–1960', *The Cyprus Review*, vol. 14, no. 2, Fall 2002, pp. 99–119.

Faustmann, Hubert, 'The Cyprus Question Still Unresolved: Security Concerns and the Failure of the Annan Plan', *Suedost Europa-Mitteilungen*, June 2004, pp. 44–68.

Faustmann, Hubert, 'The Reunification Process in Germany: Similarities and Differences with regard to Cyprus', *Symposium on Aspects of the Reunification in Germany and Cyprus*, paper presented at Goethe Zentrum, Nicosia, 28 February 2004.

Faustmann, Hubert, 'Independence Postponed: Cyprus 1959–1960', Hubert Faustmann and Nicos Peristianis (eds) *Britain in Cyprus: Colonialism and Post-Colonialism 1878–2006*, Berlin, Bibliopolis, 2006.

Fisher, Ronald J., 'The Potential Complementarity of Mediation and Consultation within a Contingency Model of Third Party Intervention', *Journal of Peace Research*, vol. 28, no. 1, 1991, pp. 29–42.

Fisher, Ronald J., 'Cyprus: The Failure of Mediation and the Escalation of an Identity-Based Conflict to an Adversarial Impasse', *Journal of Peace Research*, vol. 38, no. 3, 2001, pp. 307–26.

Fox, Jonathan, 'The Salience of Religious Issues in Ethnic Conflicts: A Large-N Study', *Nationalism and Ethnic Politics*, vol. 3, no. 3, Autumn 1997, pp. 1–19.

Frognier, Andre-Paul, 'The Mixed Nature of Belgian Cabinets between Majority Rule and Consociationalism', *European Journal of Political Research*, vol. 16, no. 2, March 1988, pp. 207–28.

Galanos, Alexis M. P., 'The Presidency Path, A Constitution Imposed from the Outside', *Parliamentarian*, vol. 74, issue 3, July 1993, pp. 3–10.

Ganev, Venelin I., 'History, Politics, and the Constitution: Ethnic Conflict and Constitutional Adjudication in Postcommunist Bulgaria', *Slavic Review*, vol. 63, no. 1, Spring 2004, pp. 66–89.

Gibran, Kahlil, *The Garden of the Prophet*, London, Heinemann, 1954.

Gorvett, Jon, 'Vote on Annan Plan Results in Reversal of Fortue for Turkish, Greek Cypriots', *The Washington Report on Middle East Affairs*, vol. 23, no. 5, June 2004, pp. 40–2.

Grant, T. D., *The Recognition of States: Law and Practice in Debate and Evolution*, Westport, Praeger Publishers, 1999.

Grofman, Bernard, 'Arend Lijphart and the "New Institutionalism"', in Markus M. L. Crepaz, Thomas A. Koelble, and David Wilsford (eds) *Democracy and Institutions: The Life Work of Arend Lijphart*, Ann Arbor, University of Michigan Press, 2000.

Groom, A. J. R, 'Cyprus, Greece and Turkey: A Treadmill for Diplomacy', in John Koumoulides (ed.) *Cyprus in Transition 1960–1985*, London, Trigraph, 1986.

Guelke, Adrian, 'Ethnic Rights and Majority Rule: The Case of South Africa', *International Political Science Review*, vol. 13, no. 4, 1992, pp. 415–32.

Gumpert, Gary and Drucker, Susan J., 'Communication Across Lands Divided: The Cypriot Communications Landscape', in Vangelis Calotychos (ed.) *Cyprus and its People: Nation, Identity and Experience in an Unimaginable Community, 1955–1997*, Colorado, Westview Press, 1998.

Gürel, Ayla and Özersay, Kudret, *The Politics of Property in Cyprus: Conflicting Appeals to 'Bizonality' and 'Human Rights' by the Two Cypriot Communities*, PRIO Report 3/2006 http://www.prio.no/files/manualimport/cyprus/documents/Cyprus%20Property%20Report.pdf (accessed 12 July 2007).

Hadenius, Axel and Karvonen, Lauri, 'The Paradox of Integration in Intra-State Conflicts', *Journal of Theoretical Politics*, vol. 13, no. 1, 2001, pp. 35–51.

Hadjipavlou-Trigeorgis, Maria, 'Cyprus and Lebanon: A Historical Comparative Study in Ethnic Conflict and Outside Interference', *The Cyprus Review*, vol. 2, no. 1, Spring 1990, pp. 97–129.

Hadjipavlou-Trigeorgis, Maria, 'Unofficial Inter-Communal Contacts and their Contribution to Peace-building in Conflict Societies: The Case of Cyprus', *The Cyprus Review*, vol. 5, no. 2, Fall 1993.

Hadjipavlou-Trigeorgis, Maria and Trigeorgis, Lenos, 'Cyprus: An Evolutionary Approach to Conflict Resolution', *Journal of Conflict Resolution*, vol. 37, no. 2, June 1993, pp. 340–60.

Hadjipavlou-Trigeorgis, Maria, 'Little Confidence in Confidence Building? Conflict Resolution in the Context of the United Nations', *Cyprus and the European Union*, Sudostevropa, Gersdelchaft, 1997.

Hadjipavlou-Trigeorgis, Maria, 'Different Relationships to the Land: Personal Narratives, Political Implications and Future Possibilities in Cyprus', in Vangelis Calotychos (ed.) *Cyprus and Its People*, Westview Press, 1998.

Hadjipavlou-Trigeorgis, Maria, 'The Role of Joint Narrative in Conflict Resolution: The Case of Cyprus', in Mehmet Yashin (ed.) *Step-mothertongue, From Nationalism to Multiculturalism: Literatures of Cyprus, Greece and Turkey*, London, Middlesex University Press, 2000.

Hadjipavlou, Maria, 'Multiple Stories: The "Crossings" as Part of Citizens' Reconciliation Efforts in Cyprus?', *Innovation*, vol. 20, no. 1, 2007, pp. 53–73.

Hague, Rod, Harrop, Martin and Breslin, Shaun, *Comparative Government and Politics: An Introduction*, London, Macmillan Press, 1998.

Hall, Peter A. and Taylor, Rosemary C. R., 'Political Science and the Three New Institutionalisms', *Political Studies*, vol. 44, no. 4, December 1996, pp. 936–57.

Hamill, James, 'A Disguised Surrender? South Africa's Negotiated Settlement and the Politics of Conflict Resolution', *Diplomacy and Statecraft*, vol. 14, no. 3, September 2003, pp. 1–30.

Hannay, David, 'Cyprus: Missed Opportunities and the Way Ahead', *The Wyndham Place Charlemagne Trust 27th Corbishley Memorial Lecture*, September 22, 2003.

Hannay, David, *Cyprus, the Search for a Solution*, London, I. B. Taurus and Co., 2005.

Harbottle, Michael, *The Impartial Soldier*, London, Oxford University Press, 1970.

Harris, Peter and Reilly, Ben (eds) *Democracy and Deep-Rooted Conflict: Options for Negotiators*, Stockholm, International Institute for Democracy and Electoral Assistance, 1998.

Hatzivassiliou, Evanthis, *The Cyprus Question, 1878–1960: The Constitutional Aspect*, Minnesota, Minnesota Mediterranean and East European Monographs, 2002.

Hatzivassiliou, Evanthis, 'British Strategic Priorities and the Cyprus Question, 1954–1958', in Hubert Faustmann and Nicos Peristianis (eds) *Britain in Cyprus: Colonialism and Post-Colonialism 1878–2006*, Berlin, Bibliopolis, 2006.

He, Baogang, 'Referenda as a Solution to the National Identity/Boundary Question: An Empirical Critique of the Theoretical Literature', *Alternatives*, vol. 27, no. 1, Jan–March 2002, pp. 67–97.

Henn, Francis, 'The Nicosia Airport Incident of 1974: A Peacekeeping Gamble', *International Peacekeeping*, vol. 1, no. 1, Spring 1994, pp. 80–99.

Heraclides, Alexis, *The Self-Determination of Minorities in International Politics*, London, Frank Cass and Co., 1991.

Heraclides, Alexis, 'The 55 Year Cyprus Debacle: A Bird's Eye View', *The Cyprus Review*, vol. 15, no. 2, Fall 2003, pp. 64–80.

Heraclides, Alexis, 'The Cyprus Problem: An Open and Shut Case? Probing the Greek Cypriot Rejection of the Annan Plan', *The Cyprus Review*, vol. 16, no. 2, Fall 2004, pp. 37–54.

Hitchens, Christopher, 'Uncorking the Genie: The Cyprus Question and Turkey's Military Rule', *MERIP Reports*, no. 122, March–April 1984, pp. 25–7.

Hitchens, Christopher, *Hostage to History: Cyprus from the Ottomans to Kissinger*, London, Verso, 1997.

Hitchens, Christopher, 'The Perils of Partition', *The Atlantic Monthly*, March 2003.

Hocknell, Peter, 'Contested "Development": A Retrospective of the UN Development Programme in Cyprus', in James Ker-Lindsay and Oliver Richmond (eds) *The Work of the UN in Cyprus: Promoting Peace and Development*, Hampshire, Palgrave Macmillan, 2001.

Hoffmeister, Frank, 'Cyprus v Turkey: App. No. 25781/94', *The American Journal of International Law*, vol. 96, no. 2, April 2002, pp. 445–52.

Hoffmeister, Frank, *Legal Aspects of the Cyprus Problem*, Leiden, Martinus Nijhoff Publishers, 2006.

Hooghe, Liesbet, *A Leap in the Dark: Nationalist Conflict and Federal Reform in Belgium*, New York, Cornell University Press, 1991.

Horowitz, Donald L., 'Three Dimensions of Ethnic Politics', *World Politics*, vol. 23, no. 2, Jan 1971, pp. 232–44.

Horowitz, Donald L., *Ethnic Groups in Conflict*, Berkeley, University of California Press, 1985.

Horowitz, Donald L., *A Democratic South Africa? Constitutional Engineering in a Divided Society*, Berkeley, University of California Press, 1991.

Horowitz, Donald L., 'Constitutional Design: An Oxymoron?', *Nomos*, vol. 42, 2000, pp. 253–84.

Horowitz, Donald L., 'Constitutional Design: Proposals Versus Processes', in Andrew Reynolds (ed.) *The Architecture of Democracy: Constitutional Design, Conflict Management, and Democracy*, Oxford, Oxford University Press, 2002.

Horowitz, Donald L., 'Explaining the Northern Ireland Agreement: The Sources of an Unlikely Constitutional Consensus', *British Journal of Political Science*, vol. 32 April 2002, pp. 193–220 Part 2.

Horowitz, Donald L., 'Some Realism about Constitutional Engineering', in Andreas Wimmer, Richard J. Goldstone, Donald L. Horowitz, Ulrike Joras, and Conrad Schetter (eds) *Facing Ethnic Conflicts, Towards a New Realism*, Oxford, Rowman and Littlefield Publishers Inc., 2004.

Hudson, Michael C., 'Trying Again: Power-Sharing in Post-Civil War Lebanon', *International Negotiation*, vol. 2, 1997, pp. 103–22.

Hunt, David, 'Three Greek Islands and the Development of International Law', in John Koumoulides (ed.) *Cyprus in Transition 1960–1985*, London, Trigraph, 1986.

Hutchence, Justin and Georgiades, Harris, 'The European Union and the Cyprus Problem: Powerless to Help?', *The Cyprus Review*, vol. 11, no. 1, 1999, pp. 83–96.

Hylland Eriksen, Thomas, 'Formal and Informal Nationalism', *Ethnic and Racial Studies*, vol. 16, no. 1, January 1993, pp. 1–25.

Ioannides, Christos P., 'Changing the Demography of Cyprus: Anatolian Settlers in the Turkish-Occupied North', in Christos P. Ioannides ed. *Cyprus: Domestic Dynamics, External Constraints*, New York, Aristide D. Caratzas, 1992.

Ioannou, Yiannis E., 'Language, Politics and Identity: An Analysis of the Cypriot Dilemma', *The Cyprus Review*, vol. 3, no. 1, Spring 1991, pp. 15–41.

İslamoğlu, Mahmut, 'Turkish Cypriot Folklore: An Individual's Perspective', in Emel Doğramacı, William Haney, and Güray König (eds) *First International Congress on Cypriot Studies*, Gazimağusa, Eastern Mediterranean University Press, 1997.

Itzkowitz, Norman and Volkan, Vamik, 'Turkish and Greek Identities and a Comparison Between Them', in Emel Dogramaci, William Haney, and Güray König (eds) *First International Congress on Cypriot Studies*, Gazimagusa, Eastern Mediterranean University Press, 1997.

Iyengar, Shanto, 'Shortcuts to Political Knowledge: Selective Attention and the Accessibility Bias', in John Ferejohn and James Kuklinski (eds) *Information and the Democratic Process*, Urbana, University of Illinois Press, 1990.

Jackman, Robert W., 'Political Elites, Mass Publics, and Support for Democratic Principles', *The Journal of Politics*, vol. 34, no. 3, August 1972, pp. 753–73.

Jakobsson Hatay, Ann-Sofi, 'The Orphan Peace Plan: Kofi Annan's Proposal for a Reunited Cyprus', *Weltpolitik Policy Forum*, www.weltpolitik.net (accessed 21 July 2003).

Jakobsson Hatay, Ann-Sofi, 'Popular Referenda and Peace Processes: The Twin Referenda on the Annan Plan for a Reunited Cyprus Put In Perspective', *Turkish Daily News*, 5/6 May 2004.

James, Alan, 'The UN Force in Cyprus', in Ramesh Thayer and Carlyle A. Thayer (eds) *A Crisis of Expectation: UN Peacekeeping in the 1990s*, Colorado, Westview Press, 1995.

James, Alan, 'The Making of the Cyprus Settlement, 1958–1960', *The Cyprus Review*, vol. 10, no. 2, 1998.

James, Alan, *Keeping the Peace in the Cyprus Crisis of 1963–64*, Hampshire, Palgrave Macmillan, 2002.

Jarstad, Anna, *Changing the Game: Consociational Theory and Ethnic Quotas in Cyprus and New Zealand*, Report No. 58, Department of Peace and Conflict Research, Sweden, Uppsala University, 2001.

Jensen, Lloyd, 'Negotiations and Power Asymmetries: The Cases of Bosnia, Northern Ireland and Sri Lanka', *International Negotiation*, vol. 2, 1997, pp. 21–41.

Jenssen, Anders Todal and Listhaug, Ola, 'Voters' Decisions in the Nordic EU Referendums of 1994: the Importance of Party Cues', in Matthew Mendelson and Andrew Parkin (eds) *Referendum Democracy: Citizens, Elites and Deliberation in Referendum Campaigns*, Hampshire, Palgrave Macmillan, 2001.

Johnson, Carter, 'Democratic Transition in the Balkans: Romania's Hungarian and Bulgaria's Turkish Minority (1989–99)', *Nationalism and Ethnic Politics*, vol. 8, no. 1 Spring 2002, pp. 1–28.

Joseph, Joseph S., *Cyprus: Ethnic Conflict and International Politics*, London, Macmillan Press, 1997.

Jung, Courtney and Shapiro, Ian, 'South Africa's Negotiated Transition: Democracy, Opposition, and the new Constitutional Order', *Politics and Society*, vol. 23, no. 3, 1995, pp. 269–308.

Kadioglu, Ayse, 'The Paradox of Turkish Nationalism and the Construction of Official Identity', *Middle Eastern Studies*, vol. 32, no. 2, April 1996.

Kaiser, André, 'Types of Democracy: From Classical to New Institutionalism', *Journal of Theoretical Politics*, vol. 9, no. 4, 2000, pp. 419–44.

Karoulla-Vrikkis, Dimitra, 'The Language of the Greek Cypriots Today: A Revelation of an Identity Crisis?', *The Cyprus Review*, vol. 3, no. 1, Spring 1991, pp. 42–58.

Karp, Jeffrey A., 'The Influence of Elite Endorsements in Initiative Campaigns', in Shaun Bowler, Todd Donovan, and Caroline J. Tolbert (eds) *Citizens as Legislators: Direct Democracy in the United States*, Columbus, Ohio State University Press, 1998.

Katsiaounis, Rolandos, *Labor, Society and Politics in Cyprus During the Second Half of the Nineteenth Century*, Nicosia, Cyprus Research Centre, 1996.

Kedar, Alexandre and Yiftachel, Oren, 'Land Regime and Social Relations in Israel', in H. de Soto and F. Cheneval (eds) *Realizing Property Rights*, Zurich, Ruffer and Rub Publishing House, 2006.

Keman, Hans, 'Political Stability in Divided Societies: A Rational-Institutional Explanation', *Australian Journal of Political Science*, vol. 34, no. 2, July 1999, pp. 34–50.

Kentas, Giorgos I., 'A Realist Evaluation of Cyprus' Survival Dilemma as a Result of the Annan Plan', *The Cyprus Review*, vol. 15, no. 2, Fall 2003, pp. 13–64.

Ker-Lindsay, James, 'The Origins of the UN Presence in Cyprus', in James Ker-Lindsay and Oliver Richmond (eds) *The Work of the UN in Cyprus: Promoting Peace and Development*, Hampshire, Palgrave Macmillan, 2001.

Ker-Lindsay, James and Webb, Keith, 'Cyprus', *European Journal of Political Research*, vol. 44, 2005, pp. 975–982.

Kerr, Michael, *Imposing Power-Sharing: Conflict and Coexistence in Northern Ireland and Lebanon*, Dublin, Irish Academic Press, 2005.

Kieve, Ronald A., 'Pillars of Sand: A Marxist Critique of Consociational Democracy in the Netherlands', *Comparative Politics*, vol. 13, no. 3, April 1981, pp. 313–37.

Killoran, Moira, 'Nationalism and Embodied Memory in Northern Cyprus', in Vangelis Calotychos (ed.) *Cyprus and its People: Nation, Identity and Experience in an Unimaginable Community, 1955–1997*, Colorado, Westview Press, 1998.

Killoran, Moira, 'Time, Space and National Identities in Cyprus', in Mehmet Yashin (ed.) *Step-mothertongue, From Nationalism to Multiculturalism: Literatures of Cyprus, Greece and Turkey*, London, Middlesex University Press, 2000.

Kizikyurek, Niyazi, 'From Traditionalism to Nationalism and Beyond', *The Cyprus Review*, vol. 5, no. 2, 1992, pp. 58–67.

Kliot, N. and Mansfield, Y., 'The Political Landscape of Partition: The Case of Cyprus', *Political Geography*, vol. 16, no. 6, 1997, pp. 495–521.

Köchler, Hans, 'Quo Vadis, United Nations?', *I. P. O Research Papers*, June 2004, http://hanskoechler.com/koechler-quo-vadis-UN.htm#(III) (accessed 20 December 2006).

Koole, Ruud and Daalder, Hans, 'The Consociational Democracy Model and the Netherlands: Ambivalent Allies?', *Acta Politica*, vol. 37, 2002, pp. 23–43.

Koulish, Robert E., 'Opportunity Lost? The Social (Dis)Integration of Roma Minority Rights in Post-Transition Hungary', *Nationalism and Ethnic Politics*, vol. 8, no. 1, Spring 2002, pp. 81–104.

Kumar, Radha, 'The Troubled History of Partition', *Foreign Affairs*, vol. 76, no. 1, January 1997, pp. 22–34.

Kushner, David, 'Self-Perception and Identity in Contemporary Turkey', *Journal of Contemporary History*, vol. 32, no. 2, 1997, pp. 219–33.

Kyle, Keith, 'British Policy on Cyprus 1974–2002', *The Cyprus Review*, vol. 14, no. 1, Spring 2002, pp. 101–10.

Kyle, Keith, 'A British View of the Annan Plan', *The Cyprus Review*, vol. 16, no. 1, Spring 2004, pp. 13–28.

Kyle, Keith, 'Twenty-one Years With Cyprus', *The Cyprus Review*, vol. 16, no. 2, Fall 2004, pp. 109–12.

Kymlicka, Will, *Multicultural Citizenship: A Liberal Theory of Minority Rights*, Oxford, Oxford University Press, 1995.

Kymlicka, Will, *Politics in the Vernacular: Nationalism, Multiculturalism and Citizenship*, Oxford, Oxford University Press, 2001.

Kyriacou, Andreas P., 'An Ethnically Based Federal and Bicameral System: The Case of Cyprus', *International Review of Law and Economics*, vol. 20, no. 2, 2000, pp. 251–68.

Kyriakides, Stanley, *Cyprus: Constitutionalism and Crisis Government*, Philadelphia, University of Philadelphia Press, 1968.

Lacher, Hannes and Kaymak, Erol, 'Transforming Identities: Beyond the Politics of Non-Settlement in North Cyprus', *Mediterranean Politics*, vol. 10, no. 2, July 2005, pp. 147–66.

Ladbury, Sarah, 'The Turkish Cypriots: Ethnic Relations in London and Cyprus', in James L. Watson (ed.) *Between Two Cultures: Migrants and Minorities in Britain*, Oxford, Basil Blackwell, 1997.

Laipson, Ellen B., 'Cyprus: A Quarter Century of US Diplomacy', in John Koumoulides (ed.) *Cyprus in Transition 1960–1985*, London, Trigraph, 1986.

Lang, R. Hamilton, *Cyprus: Its History, Its Present Resources, and Future Prospects*, London, Macmillan and Co., 1878.

Laouris, Yiannis, 'Information Technology in the Service of Peacebuilding: The Case of Cyprus', *World Futures*, vol. 60, 2004, pp. 67–79.

Lapidoth, Ruth, *Autonomy: Flexible Solutions to Ethnic Conflicts*, Washington, United States Institute of Peace Press, 1996.

Lee, Dwight E., *Great Britain and the Cyprus Convention Policy of 1878*, Cambridge, Harvard University Press, 1934.

Lehmbruch, Gerhard, 'A Non-Competitive Pattern of Conflict Management in Liberal Democracies: The Case of Switzerland, Austria and Lebanon', in Kenneth D. McRae, *Consociational Democracy: Political Accommodation in Segmented Societies*, Toronto, McClelland and Stewart, 1974.

Lijphart, Arend, *The Politics of Accommodation: Pluralism and Democracy in the Netherlands*, Berkeley, University of California Press, 1968.

Lijphart, Arend, 'Consociational Democracy', *World Politics*, vol. 21, no. 2, January 1969, pp. 207–25.

Lijphart, Arend, 'Consociational Democracy', in Kenneth D. McRae (ed.) *Consociational Democracy: Political Accommodation in Segmented Societies*, Toronto, McClelland and Stewart, 1974.

Lijphart, Arend, *Democracy in Plural Societies: A Comparative Exploration*, New Haven, Yale University Press, 1977.

Lijphart, Arend, 'Consociational Theory: Problems and Prospects. A Reply', *Comparative Politics*, vol. 13, no. 3, April 1981, pp. 355–60.

Lijphart, Arend, *Power-Sharing in South Africa*, Policy Papers in International Affairs, no. 24, Berkeley, Institute of International Studies, University of California, 1985.

Lijphart, Arend, 'Multiethnic Democracy', in Seymour Martin Lipset (ed.) *The Encyclopedia of Democracy*, London, Routledge, 1995.

Lijphart, Arend, *Patterns of Democracy: Government Forms and Performance in 36 Countries*, New Haven, Yale University Press, 1999.

Lijphart, Arend, 'Power-Sharing and Group Autonomy in the 1990s and the Twenty-First Century', paper prepared for delivery at the Kellogg Institute Conference, *Constitutional Design 2000: Institutional Design, Conflict Management, and Democracy in the Late Twentieth Century*, Univeristy of Notre Dame, December 1999.

Lijphart, Arend, 'Definitions, Evidence, and Policy: A Response to Matthijs Bogaards' Critique', *Journal of Theoretical Politics*, vol. 12, no. 4, 2000, pp. 425–31.

Lijphart, Arend, 'Varieties of Nonmajoritarian Democracy', in Markus M. L. Crepaz, Thomas A. Koelble, and David Wilsford (eds) *Democracy and Institutions: The Life Work of Arend Lijphart*, Ann Arbor, University of Michigan Press, 2000.

Lijphart, Arend, 'Negotiation Democracy versus Consensus Democracy: Parallel Conclusions and Recommendations', *European Journal of Political Research*, vol. 41, no. 1, 2002, pp. 107–13.

Lijphart, Arend, 'The Wave of Power-Sharing Democracy', in Andrew Reynolds (ed.) *The Architecture of Democracy: Constitutional Design, Conflict Management, and Democracy*, Oxford, Oxford University Press, 2002.

Lijphart, Arend, 'Constitutional Design for Divided Societies', *Journal of Democracy*, vol. 15, no. 2, April 2004, pp. 96–109.

Loizides, Neophytos and Keskiner, Eser, 'The Aftermath of the Annan Plan Referendums: Cross-Voting Moderation for Cyprus?', *Southeast European Politics*, vol. 5, no. 2–3, December 2004, pp. 158–71.

Loizos, Peter 'How Might Turkish and Greek Cypriots See Each Other More Clearly?', in Vangelis Calotychos (ed.) *Cyprus and its People: Nation, Identity and Experience in an Unimaginable Community, 1955–1997*, Colorado, Westview Press, 1998.

Loizos, Peter, 'Intercommunal Killings in Cyprus', *Man*, vol. 23, no. 4, December 1988, pp. 639–53.

Loizos, Peter, 'Ottoman Half-Lives: Long-term Perspectives on Particular Forced Migrations', *Journal of Refugee Studies*, vol. 12, no. 3, 1999.

Loizos, Peter, *Unofficial Views, Cyprus: Society and Politics*, Nicosia, Intercollege Press, 2001.

Lordos, Alexander, 'Rational Agent or Unthinking Follower? A Survey-Based Profile Analysis of Greek Cypriot and Turkish Cypriot Referendum Voters', March 2006, http://www.cypruspolls.org/RationalOrUnthinking.pdf (accessed 12 June 2007).

Lordos, Alexandros, 'Can the Cyprus Problem be Solved? Understanding the Greek Cypriot Response to the UN Peace Plan for Cyprus', *An Evidence-Based Study in Co-operation with CYMAR Market Research Ltd*, November 2004, www.cypruspolls.org (accessed 15 November 2005).

Lordos, Alexandros, 'Civil Society Diplomacy: A New Approach for Cyprus?', *An Evidence-Based Study in Co-operation with CYMAR Market Research Ltd. and KADEM Cyprus Social Research*, February 2005, www.cypruspolls.org (accessed 15 November 2005).

Lordos, Alexandros, 'Building Trust: An Inter-Communal Analysis of Public Opinion in Cyprus', *An Evidence-Based Study in Co-operation with CYMAR Market Research Ltd. and KADEM Cyprus Social Research*, June 2006, www.cypruspolls.org (accessed 1 January 2007).

Lordos, Alexandros, Kaymak, Erol, and Tocci, Nathalie. 'A People's Peace in Cyprus: Testing Public Opinion on the Options for a Comprehensive Settlement', CEPS Paperbacks, Brussels, April 2009.

Lorwin, Val R., 'Belgium: Conflict and Compromise', in Kenneth D. McRae (ed.) *Consociational Democracy: Political Accommodation in Segmented Societies*, Toronto, McClelland and Stewart, 1974.

Lupia, Arthur and Johnston, Richard, 'Are Voters to Blame? Voter Competence and Elite Manoeuvres in Referendums', in Matthew Mendelson and Andrew Parkin (eds) *Referendum Democracy: Citizens, Elites and Deliberation in Referendum Campaigns*, Hampshire, Palgrave Macmillan, 2001.

Lustick, Ian S., 'Stability in Deeply Divided Societies: Consociationalism versus Control', *World Politics*, vol. 31, no. 3, April 1979, pp. 325–344.

Lustick, Ian S., 'Lijphart, Lakatos, and Consociationalism', *World Politics*, vol. 50, no. 1, 1997, pp. 88–117.

Luther, Kurt Richard, 'Must What Goes Up Always Come Down? Of Pillars and Arches in Austria's Political Architecture', in Kurt Richard Luther and Kris Deschouwer (eds) *Party Elites in Divided Societies, Political Parties in Consociational Democracy*, London, Routledge, 1999.

Macdonald, Michael, 'The Siren's Song: the Political Logic of Power-Sharing in South Africa', *Journal of Southern African Studies*, vol. 18, no. 4, 1992, pp. 709–25.

MacGinty, Roger, 'Constitutional Referendums and Ethnonational Conflict: The Case of Northern Ireland', *Nationalism and Ethnic Politics*, vol. 9, no. 2, 2003, pp. 1–22.

Malloy, Tove H. and Soykan, Tankut, 'Addressing the Settlement of Self-Determination Conflicts Through Complex Power-Sharing: The Case of Cyprus', ECMI Report no. 52, *European Centre for Minority Issues*, October 2004.

Maoz, Ifat, Ward, Andrew, Katz, Michael, and Ross, Lee, 'Reactive Devaluation of an "Israeli" vs "Palestinian" Peace Proposal', *Journal of Conflict Resolution*, vol. 46, no. 4, August 2002, pp. 515–46.

Markides, Alecos, *Cyprus and European Union Membership: Important Legal Documents*, Nicosia, 2002.

Markides, Diana and Georghallides, G. S., 'British Attitudes to Constitution-Making in Post-1931 Cyprus', *Journal of Modern Greek Studies*, vol. 13, no. 1, May 1995, pp. 63–81.

Markusse, Jan, 'Power-Sharing and "Consociational Democracy" in South Tyrol', *GeoJournal*, vol. 43, September 1997, pp. 77–89.

Marsh, David and Stoker, Gerry (eds) *Theory and Methods in Political Science*, Hampshire, Palgrave Macmillan, 2002.

Martin, Harriet, *Kings of Peace, Pawns of War: The Untold Story of Peace-Making*, London, Continuum, 2006.

Mavratsas, Ceasar V. and Demetriou, Kyriacos N., 'Paschalis Kitromilides on the Ideological Origins of Greek Enlightenment, Orthodoxy and Nationalism', *Canadian Review of Studies in Nationalism*, vol. 24, no. 1–2, 1997.

Mavratsas, Caesar V., 'The Ideological Contest Between Greek-Cypriot Nationalism and Cypriotism 1974–1995: Politics, Social Memory and Identity', *Ethnic and Racial Studies*, vol. 20, no. 4, October 1997, pp. 717–37.

Mavratsas, Caesar V., 'Greek Cypriot Economic and Political Culture: The Effects of 1974', in Vangelis Calotychos (ed.) *Cyprus and its People: Nation, Identity and Experience in an Unimaginable Community, 1955–1997*, Colorado, Westview Press, 1998.

Mavratsas, Caesar V., 'National Identity and Consciousness in Everyday Life: Towards a Sociology of Knowledge of Greek-Cypriot Nationalism', *Nations and Nationalism*, vol. 5, no. 1, January 1999, pp. 91–104.

Mayes, Stanley, *Makarios: A Biography*, London, Macmillan Press, 1981.

McAdams, A. James, *Judging the Past in Unified Germany*, Cambridge, Cambridge University Press, 2001.

McCartney, Clem, 'Civil Society in Divided Societies', *Civil Society Making a Difference*, paper presented at discussion panel organised by UNOPS-University of Cyprus, 7 February 2005.

McCullagh, Ciaran, *Media Power: A Sociological Introduction*, Basingstoke, Palgrave Macmillan, 2002.

McDonald, Robert, *The Problem of Cyprus*, Adelphi Papers no. 234, International Institute for Strategic Studies, Winter 1988/9, London, Brassey's, 1989.

McDonald, Robert, 'Cyprus: a Peacekeeping Paradigm', *World Today*, vol. 49, no. 10, October 1993, pp. 182–4.

McGarry, John, O'Leary, Brendan, and Simeon, Richard, 'Integration or Accommodation? The Enduring Debate in Conflict Regulation', in Sujit Choudhry, (ed.) *Constitutional Design for Divided Societies: Integration or Accommodation?*, Oxford, Oxford University Press, 2008.

McGarry, John, and O'Leary, Brendan, 'Consociational Theory and Peace Agreements in Pluri-National Place, Northern Ireland and Other Cases', in Guy Ben-Porat, *Failure of the Middle East Peace Process*, London, Palgrave Macmillan, 2008.

McGarry, John and O'Leary, Brendan, 'Consociational Theory, Northern Ireland's Conflict, and its Agreement. Part I: What Consociationalists Can Learn from Northern Ireland', *Government and Opposition*, vol. 41, no. 1, Winter 2006, pp. 43–63.

McGarry, John and O'Leary, Brendan, 'Consociational Theory, Northern Ireland's Conflict, and its Agreement 2. What Critics of Consociation Can Learn from Northern Ireland', *Government and Opposition*, vol. 41, no. 2, Spring 2006, pp. 249–77.

McLaren, Lauren M., 'Turkey's Eventual Membership of the EU: Turkish Elite Perspectives on the Issue', *Journal of Common Market Studies*, vol. 38, no. 1, March 2000, pp. 117–29.

McQuail, Denis, *McQuail's Reader in Mass Communication Theory*, London, Sage Publications, 2002.

Meier, Benjamin M., 'Reunification of Cyprus: The Possibility of Peace in the Wake of Past Failure', *Cornell International Law Journal*, vol. 34, no. 2, 2001, pp. 455–80.

Mendelsohn, Matthew, 'Public Brokerage: Constitutional Reform and the Accommodation of Mass Publics', *Canadian Journal of Political Science*, vol. 33, no. 2, June 2000, pp. 245–72.

Mendelson, Matthew and Parkin, Andrew (eds), *Referendum Democracy: Citizens, Elites and Deliberation in Referendum Campaigns*, Hampshire, Palgrave Macmillan, 2001.

Michaelides, Alecos P., 'Cyprus Accession to the European Union: A Vision and a Challenge for Today', public lecture given at the London School of Economics and Political Science, 30 October 1996.

Milburn, Tom W., 'What Can We Learn From Comparing Mediation Across Levels', http://www.gmu.edu/academic/pcs/milburn.htm (accessed 10 July 2006).

Milne, David, 'One State or Two? Political Realism on the Cyprus Question', *The Round Table*, vol. 92, January 2003.

Morag, Nadav, 'Cyprus and the Clash of Greek and Turkish Nationalisms', *Nationalism and Ethnic Politics*, vol. 10, no. 4, 2004, pp. 595–624.

Morrow, Duncan, 'Breaking Antagonism? Political Leadership in Divided Societies', in Ian O'Flynn and David Russell (eds) *Power Sharing: New Challenges for Divided Societies*, London, Pluto Press, 2005.

Mount, Gavin, 'A "World of Tribes?"', in Greg Fry and Jacinta O'Hagan (eds) *Contesting Images of World Politics*, London, Macmillan Press, 2000.

Müftüler-Bac, Meltem, 'The Cyprus Debacle: What the Future holds', *Futures*, vol. 31, no. 6, 1999, pp. 559–75.

Müftüler-Bac, Meltem and Güney, Aylin, 'The European Union and the Cyprus Problem 1961–2003', *Middle Eastern Studies*, vol. 41, no. 2, March 2005, pp. 281–93.

Nagal, C., 'Reconstructing Space, Re-Creating Memory: Sectarian Politics and Urban Development in Post-War Beirut', *Political Geography*, vol. 21, no. 5, June 2002, pp. 717–25.

Neack, Laura and Knudson, Roger M., 'The Multiple Meanings and Purposes of Peacekeeping in Cyprus', *International Politics*, vol. 36, December 1999, pp. 465–502.

Necatigil, Zaim M., *The Cyprus Question and the Turkish Position in International Law*, Oxford, Oxford University Press, 1989.

Neophytou, Christos A., 'A Critical Analysis of the Proposed UN Annan Plan for the Settlement of the Cyprus Problem and the Importance of International and European Law in the Shaping of the New Proposed Constitution for Cyprus', *CPE PgDL Dissertation*, London Metropolitan University, May 2003.

Nevzat, Altay, *Nationalism Amongst the Turks of Cyprus: The First Wave*, Oulu, Oulu University Press, 2005.

Newman, Edward, 'The Most Impossible Job in the World: The Secretary-General and Cyprus', in James Ker-Lindsay and Oliver Richmond (eds) *The Work of the UN in Cyprus: Promoting Peace and Development*, Hampshire, Palgrave Macmillan, 2001.

Nicolet, Claude, *United States Policy Towards Cyprus, 1954–1974*, Zurich, Bibliopolis, 2001.

Nordlinger, Eric A., *Conflict Regulation in Divided Societies*, Occasional Papers in International Affairs, no. 29, Cambridge, Harvard Centre for International Affairs, 1972.

Norris, Pippa, 'Stable Democracy and Good Governance in Divided Societies: Do Power-Sharing Institutions Work?', paper for presentation at the International Studies Association 46th Annual Convention, March 2005, 7 February 2005.

Nugent, Neill, 'EU Enlargement and "the Cyprus Problem"', *Journal of Common Market Studies*, vol. 38, no. 1, March 2000, pp. 131–50.

Nugent, Neill (ed.) *European Union Enlargement*, Hampshire, Palgrave Macmillan, 2004.

Nugent, Neill, 'Cyprus and the European Union: The Significance of its Smallness, Both as an Applicant and a Member', *European Integration*, vol. 28, no. 1, March 2006, pp. 51–71.

O'Duffy, Brendan, 'Exchange Theory and Conflict Regulation: Cyprus Through the British-Irish (Northern Ireland) Prism', *EPCR Conference Working Paper*, 23–6 March 2002.

Oguzlu, Tarik, 'Is the Latest Turkish-Greek Détente Promising for the Future?', *European Security*, vol. 12, no. 2, Summer 2003, pp. 45–62.

O'Hagan, Jacinta, 'A "Clash of Civilizations?"', in Greg Fry and Jacinta O'Hagan (eds) *Contesting Images of World Politics*, London, Macmillan Press, 2000.

O'Leary, Brendan, 'An Iron Law of Nationalism and Federation? A (Neo-Diceyian) Theory of the Necessity of a Federal *Staatsvolk*, and of Consociational Rescue', *Nations and Nationalism*, vol. 7, no. 3, 2001, pp. 273–96.

O'Leary, Brendan, 'Debating Consociational Politics: Normative and Explanatory Arguments', in Sid Noel (ed.) *From Power Sharing to Democracy: Post-Conflict Institutions in Ethnically Divided Societies*, London, McGill-Queens University Press, 2005.

O'Malley, Brendan and Craig, Ian, *The Cyprus Conspiracy*, London, Tauris Publishers, 1999.

O'Malley, Brendan, 'Origins of the Cyprus Problem', in *Cyprus: History, Present and the Future Series*, Lecture at Massachusetts Institute of Technology, Cambridge, United States, 16 January 2001.

Orhonlu, Cengiz, 'The Ottoman Turks Settle in Cyprus', in Halil İnalcık (ed.) *The First International Congress of Cypriot Studies: Presentations of the Turkish Delegation*, Ankara, Institute for the Study of Turkish Culture, 1971.

Orwell, George 'Notes on Nationalism', 1945, http://www.george-orwell.org/Notes_on_Nationalism/0.html (accessed 1 May 2006).

Oudraat, Chantal de Jonge, 'A Larger European Union: A More Effective Actor in the United Nations?', in Esther Brimmer and Stefan Frohlich (eds) *The Strategic Implications of European Union Enlargement*, Washington, Center for Transatlantic Relations, 2005.

Özerk, Kamil Z., 'Reciprocal Bilingualism as a Challenge and Opportunity: The Case of Cyprus', *International Review of Education*, vol. 47, no. 3–4, 2001, pp. 253–65.

Özersay, Kudret, 'The Validity and Scope of the 1959–1960 Cyprus Treaties', in Resat Arim (ed.) *Cyprus and International Law*, Ankara, Foreign Policy Institute, 2002.

Özersay, Kudret, 'Separate Simultaneous Referenda in Cyprus: Was it a "Fact" or an "Illusion?"', *Turkish Studies*, vol. 6, no. 3, September 2005, pp. 379–99.

Ozgur, Ozdermir A., *Cyprus in my Life*, Zurich, Bibiliopolis, 2001.

Oztoprak, Canan, 'The Experience of Bi-communal Contacts Through the Eyes of a Turkish-Cypriot', conference paper, www.cyprus-conflict.net/oztoprak.htm (accessed 12 July 2004).

Pace, Roderick, 'Enlargement and the Mediterranean Dimension of the European Union: The Role of Cyprus', in Andreas Theophanous, Nicos Peristianis, and Andreas Ioannou (eds) *Cyprus and the European Union*, Nicosia, Intercollege Press, 1999.

Packard, Martin, 'Cyprus 1964: Subversion of a Mission', www.cyprus-conflict.net/packard.htm (accessed 20 August 2003).

Page, Benjamin, Shapiro, Robert and Dempsey, Glenn, 'Television News and Changes in Americans' Policy Preferences', *American Political Science Review*, vol. 83, 1987, pp. 23–44.

Palley, Claire 'Ways Forward: The Constitutional Options', in David Watt (ed.) *The Constitution of Northern Ireland: Problems and Prospects*, London, Heinemann Ltd., 1981.

Palley, Claire, *An International Relations Debacle – The UN Secretary-General's Mission of Good Offices in Cyprus 1999–2004*, Portland, Hart Publishing, 2005.

Panayiotopoulos, Prodromos, 'The Emergent Post-Colonial State in Cyprus', *Commonwealth and Comparative Politics*, vol. 37, no. 1, March 1999, pp. 31–55.

Panayiotou, Andreas, 'Models of Compromise and "Power Sharing" in the Experience of Cypriot Modernity', *The Cyprus Review*, vol. 18, no. 2, Fall 2006, pp. 75–103.

Papadakis, Yiannis, 'The National Struggle Museums of a Divided City', *Ethnic and Racial Studies*, vol. 17, no. 3, July 1994, pp. 400–19.

Papadakis, Yiannis, '*Enosis* and Turkish Expansionism: Real Myths or Mythical Realities?', in Vangelis Calotychos (ed.) *Cyprus and its People: Nation, Identity and Experience in an Unimaginable Community, 1955–1997*, Colorado, Westview Press, 1998.

Papadakis, Yiannis, 'Nation, Narrative and Commemoration: Political Ritual in Divided Cyprus', *History and Anthropology*, vol. 14, no. 3, 2003, pp. 253–70.

Papadakis, Yiannis, 'Discourses of "the Balkans" in Cyprus: Tactics, Strategies and Constructions of "Others"', *History and Anthropology*, vol. 15, no. 1, March 2004, pp. 15–27.

Papadakis, Yiannis, 'Nationalist Imaginings of War in Cyprus', http://www.cyprus-conflict.net/Papadakis%20-%20nationalism.htm (accessed 16 November 2005).

Papadakis, Yiannis, *Echoes from the Dead Zone*, London, I. B. Tauris, 2005.

Pappalardo, Adriano, 'The Conditions for Consociational Democracy: A Logical and Empirical Critique', *European Journal of Political Research*, vol. 9, no. 4, 1981, pp. 365–90.

Patrick, Richard A., *Political Geography and the Cyprus Conflict: 1963–1971*, Ontario, University of Waterloo, 1976.

Pelayias, Christodoulos, 'Across the Cyprus Ethnic Divide: Conflict Resolution or Conflict Management?', *The Cyprus Review*, vol. 7, no. 1, 1995, pp. 114–22.

Peristianis, Nicos, 'A Federal Cyprus in a Federal Europe', in Andreas Theophanous, Nicos Peristianis, and Andreas Ioannou (eds) *Cyprus and the European Union*, Nicosia, Intercollege Press, 1999.

Peters, B. Guy, *Institutional Theory in Political Science, the 'New Institutionalism'*, London, Pinter, 1999.

Pfirter, Didier, 'Cyprus – A UN Peace Effort Under Conditions of ECHR Applicability', in Stephan Breitenmoser, Bernhard Ehrenzeller, Marco Sassoli, and Walter Stoffel (eds) *Human Rights, Democracy and the Rule of Law, Liber Amicorum Luzius Wildhaber*, Zurich, Nomos, 2007.

Picard, Elizabeth, *Lebanon, A Shattered Country: Myths and Realities of the Wars in Lebanon*, New York, Holmes and Meier Publishers, 1996.

Polyviou, Polyvios G., *The Problem of Cyprus: Constitutional and Political Aspects*, Nicosia, 1974.

Putnam, Robert D., *Making Democracy Work: Civic Traditions in Modern Italy*, New Jersey, Princeton University Press, 1993.

Qvortrup, Matt, 'Fair Voting? The Regulation of Referendums in Cyprus in Comparative Perspective', *The Cyprus Review*, vol. 17, no. 2, Fall 2005, pp. 13–25.

Qvortrup, Mads, *A Comparative Study of Referendums: Government by the People*, Manchester, Manchester University Press, 2002.

Qvortrup, Mads, 'A. V. Dicey: The Referendum as the People's Veto', *History of Political Thought*, vol. 20, no. 3, August 1999, pp. 532–46.

Rehn, Olli, 'Cyprus: One Year After Accession', speech given at the Cyprus International Conference Centre, 13 May 2005, Nicosia.

Reiterer, Albert, 'Managing Ethnic Conflicts in Western Europe', *Peace and Security*, vol. 30, 1998, pp. 23–35.

Reynolds, Andrew, 'Majoritarian or Power-Sharing Government', in Markus M. L. Crepaz, Thomas A. Koelble, and David Wilsford (eds) *Democracy and Institutions: The Life Work of Arend Lijphart*, Ann Arbor, University of Michigan Press, 2000.

Reynolds, Andrew, 'Building Democracy after Conflict: Constitutional Medicine', *Journal of Democracy*, vol. 16, no. 1, January 2005, pp. 54–68.

Richards, Michael, 'National Identity, Cyprus and Global Contexts', *The Cyprus Review*, vol. 12, no. 2, Fall 2000, pp. 27–44.

Richmond, Oliver, 'Peacekeeping and Peacemaking in Cyprus 1974–1994', *The Cyprus Review*, vol. 6, no. 2, 1994, pp. 7–42.

Richmond, Oliver P., *Mediating in Cyprus: The Cypriot Communities and the United Nations*, London, Frank Cass Publishers, 1998.

Richmond, Oliver P., 'Ethnonationalist Debates and International Peacemaking: The Case of Cyprus', *Nationalism and Ethnic Politics*, vol. 5, no. 2, Summer 1999, pp. 36–61.

Richmond, Oliver P., 'Ethno-nationalism, Sovereignty and Negotiating Positions in the Cyprus Conflict: Obstacles to a Settlement', *Middle Eastern Studies*, vol. 35, no. 3, 1999, pp. 42–63.

Richmond, Oliver, 'UN Mediation in Cyprus, 1964–65: Setting a Precedent for Peacemaking?', in James Ker-Lindsay and Oliver Richmond (eds) *The Work of the UN in Cyprus: Promoting Peace and Development*, Hampshire, Palgrave Macmillan, 2001.

Richmond, Oliver, 'A Perilous Catalyst? EU Accession and the Cyprus Problem', *The Cyprus Review*, vol. 13, no. 2, 2001, pp. 125–31.

Richmond, Oliver, 'Shared Sovereignty and the Politics of Peace: Evaluating the EU's "Catalytic" Framework in the Eastern Mediterranean', *International Affairs*, vol. 82, no. 1, 2005, pp. 149–76.

Rizvi, Gowher, 'Ethnic Conflict and Political Accommodation in Plural Societies: Cyprus and Other Cases', *The Journal of Commonwealth and Comparative Politics*, vol. 31, no. 1, March 1993, pp. 57–83.

Rotberg, Robert I., 'Cyprus After Annan: Next Steps Towards a Solution', *World Peace Foundation Reports*, no. 37, 2003.

Rotberg, Robert, 'The Cyprus Crucible: The Importance of Good Timing', *Leadership*, vol. 25, no. 3, Fall 2003.

Rothchild, Donald, *Managing Ethnic Conflict in Africa, Pressures and Incentives for Cooperation*, Washington, Brookings Institution Press, 1997.

Sajo, Andras, *Limiting Government: An Introduction to Constitutionalism*, Budapest, Central European University Press, 1999.

Salih, H. Ibrahim, *Cyprus: Ethnic Political Counterpoints*, Maryland, University Press of America, 2004.

Sambanis, Nicholas, 'Ancient Affections: Standing in the Way of Resolution in Cyprus?', *SAIS Review*, vol. 14, no. 2, 1994, pp. 125–39.

Sambanis, Nicholas, 'The United Nations Operation in Cyprus: A New Look at the Peacekeeping-Peacemaking Relationship', *International Peacekeeping*, vol. 6, no. 1, Spring 1999, pp. 79–108.

Sanders, Elizabeth, 'Historical Institutionalism', in R. A. W. Rhodes, Sarah A. Binder, and Bert A. Rockman (eds) *The Oxford Handbook of Political Institutions*, Oxford, Oxford University Press, 2006.

Saner, Raymond and Yiu, Lichia, 'External Stakeholder Impacts on Third-Party Interventions in Resolving Malignant Conflicts: The Case of a Failed Third-Party Intervention in Cyprus', *International Negotiation*, vol. 6, 2001, pp. 387–416.

Sant Cassia, Paul, 'The Archbishop in the Beleaguered City: An Analysis of the Conflicting Roles and Political Oratory of Makarios', *Byzantine and Modern Greek Studies*, vol. 8, 1982–3, pp. 191–212.

Savvides, Philippos K., 'Cyprus: The Dynamics of Partition', unpublished paper, University of Utah.

Schechla, Joseph, 'Ideological Roots of Population Transfer', *Third World Quarterly*, vol. 14, no. 2, 1993, pp. 239–75.

Schimmelfennig, Frank, 'The Community Trap: Liberal Norms, Rhetorical Action, and the Eastern Enlargement of the European Union', *International Organisation*, vol. 55, no. 1, Winter 2001, pp. 47–80.

Schneckener, Ulrich, 'Making Power-Sharing Work: Lessons from Successes and Failures in Ethnic Conflict Regulation', *Journal of Peace Research*, vol. 39, no. 2, 2002, pp. 203–28.

Sciarini, Pascal and Hug, Simon, 'The Odd Fellow: Parties and Consociationalism in Switzerland', in Kurt Richard Luther and Kris Deschouwer (eds) *Party Elites in Divided Societies, Political Parties in Consociational Democracy*, London, Routledge, 1999.

Seaver, Brenda M., 'The Regional Sources of Power-Sharing Failure: The Case of Lebanon', *Political Science Quarterly*, vol. 115, no. 2, Summer 2000, pp. 247–71.

Seraphim-Loizou, Elenitsa, *The Cyprus Liberation Struggle 1955–1959 Through the Eyes of a Woman*, Nicosla, Epiphaniou Publications, 2000.

Shain, Yossi and Sherman, Martin, 'Dynamics of Disintegration: Diaspora, Secession and the Paradox of Nation-States', *Nations and Nationalism*, vol. 4, no. 3, 1998, pp. 321–46.

Shvetsova, Olga, 'Mass-Elite Equilibrium of Federal Constitutional Legitimacy', *Constitutional Political Economy*, vol. 16, 2005, pp. 125–41.

Siegfried, Andre, *Switzerland: A Democratic Way of Life*, London, Jonathan Cape, 1950.

Smith, Anthony D., *The Nation in History: Historiographical Debates about Ethnicity and Nationalism*, Hanover, University Press of New England, 2000.

Smith, Anthony D., *Nationalism: Theory, Ideology, History*, London, Polity Press, 2001.

Smooha, Sammy, 'Types of Democracy and Modes of Conflict Management in Ethnically Divided Societies', *Nations and Nationalism*, vol. 8, no. 4, 2002, pp. 423–31.

Sommer, Jerry, 'Security in Cyprus: Threat Perceptions, Possible Compromises and the Role of the EU', *Bonn International Center for Conversion Paper 44*, Bonn, BICC Bonn, 2005.

Sozen, Ahmet, 'A Model of Power-Sharing in Cyprus: From the 1959 London-Zurich Agreements to the Annan Plan', *Turkish Studies*, vol. 5, Spring 2004, pp. 61–77.

Spyrou, Spyros, 'Education, Ideology, and the National Self: The Social Practice of Identity Construction in the Classroom', *The Cyprus Review*, vol. 12, no. 1, Spring 2000, pp. 61–81.

Stamatakis, Nikos A., 'History and Nationalism: The Cultural Reconstruction of the Modern Greek Cypriot Identity', *The Cyprus Review*, vol. 3, no. 1, Spring 1991, pp. 59–86.

Stanovcic, Vojislav, 'Problems and Options in Institutionalizing Ethnic Relations', *International Political Science Review*, vol. 13, no. 4, 1992, pp. 359–79.

Stavridis, Stelios, 'The International Relations of the Cypriot Parliament', *Journal of Southern Europe and the Balkans*, vol. 5, no. 3, December 2003, pp. 337–54.

Stavridis, Stelios, 'The European Union's Contribution to Peace and Stability in the Eastern Mediterranean (the So-Called Athens-Nicosia-Ankara Triangle): A Critique', *Fundación SIP Zaragoza*, Working Paper, November 2005.

Steiner, Jürg, *Amicable Agreement versus Majority Rule: Conflict Resolution in Switzerland*, Chapel Hill, University of North Carolina Press, 1974.

Steiner, Jürg, 'The Principles of Majority and Proportionality', in Kenneth D. McRae (ed.) *Consociational Democracy: Political Accommodation in Segmented Societies*, Toronto, McClelland and Stewart, 1974.

Steiner, Jürg and Obler, Jeffrey, 'Does Consociational Theory Really Hold for Switzerland?', in Milton J. Esman (ed.) *Ethnic Conflict in the Western World*, Ithaca, Cornell University Press, 1977.

Steiner, Jürg, 'The Consociational Theory and Beyond', *Comparative Politics*, vol. 13, no. 3, April 1981, pp. 339–54.

Steiner, Jürg, 'Research Strategies Beyond Consociational Theory', *The Journal of Politics*, vol. 43, no. 4, November 1981, pp. 1241–50.

Street, John, *Mass Media, Politics and Democracy*, Hampshire, Palgrave Macmillan, 2001.

Sullivan, Daniel P., 'The Missing Pillars: A Look at the Failure of Peace in Burundi Through the Lens of Arend Lijphart's Theory of Consociational Democracy', *Journal of Modern African Studies*, vol. 43, no. 1, 2005, pp. 75–95.

Syrigos, Angelos M., 'Cyprus and the EU: Sovereign State, Negotiations and Objections from an International Law Point of View', Andreas Theophanous, Nicos Peristianis, and Andreas Ioannou (eds) *Cyprus and the European Union*, Nicosia, Intercollege Press, 1999.

Szczerbiak, Aleks and Taggart, Paul, 'The Politics of European Referendum Outcomes and Turnout: Two Models', *West European Politics*, vol. 27, no. 4, September 2004, pp. 557–83.

Talat, Mehmet Ali, 'Turkish Cypriots' Expectations from the European Union', http://www.esiweb.org/pdf/esi_turkey_tpq_id_41.pdf (accessed 21 April 2007).

Taki, Yiouli, Outline of Presentation, *Civil Society Making a Difference*, discussion panel organised by UNOPS-University of Cyprus, 7 February 2005.

Theodoulou, Mike, 'Pipeline Politics', *Cyprus Diplomatist*, Jan 1990, pp. 43–5.

Theodoracopoulos, Panayotis, 'Speaking on a Bi-Communal and Bi-Zonal Federation in Cyprus', *A Journal of Foreign Policy Issues*, www.hri.org/MFA/thesis/autumn98/bicommunal.html (accessed 28 May 2004).

Theophanous, Andreas, 'Prospects for Solving the Cyprus Problem and the Role of the European Union', *Publius*, vol. 30, no. 1–2, 2000, pp. 217–41.

Thompson, Brian, 'Transcending Territory: Towards an Agreed Northern Ireland?', *International Journal on Minority and Group Rights*, vol. 6, 1999, pp. 235–66.

Thompson, Spurgeon, St. Karayanni, Stavros, and Vassiliadou, Myria 'Cyprus After History', *Interventions*, vol. 6, no. 2, pp. 282–99.

Thucydides, *History of the Peloponnesian War*, London, Penguin, 1972.

Tocci, Nathalie, 'Towards Peace in Cyprus: Incentives and Disincentives', *Brown Journal of World Affairs*, vol. 10, no. 1, 2003, pp. 199–212.

Tocci, Nathalie and Kovziridze, Tamara, 'Cyprus', in Bruno Coppieters ed. *Europeanization and Conflict Resolution: Case Studies from the European Periphery*, Ghent, Ghent Academia Press, 2004.

Tocci, Nathalie, 'Reflections on Post-Referendum Cyprus', *The International Spectator*, vol. xxxix, no. 3, July–September 2004.

Toonen, Theo A. J., 'Governing a Consensus Democracy: The Interplay of Pillarisation and Administration', *West European Politics*, vol. 23, no. 3, July 2000, pp. 165–78.

Trimikliniotis, Nicos, 'A Communist's Post-Modern Power Dilemma: One Step Back, Two Steps Forward, "Soft No" and Hard Choices', *The Cyprus Review*, vol. 18, no.1, Spring 2006, pp. 37–86.

'United Nations Peace-keeping Force in Cyprus', *The Blue Helmets: A Review of United Nations Peace-keeping* (3rd edn), New York, United Nations Department of Public Information, 1996.

van Schendelen, M. P. C. M., 'The Views of Arend Lijphart and Collected Criticisms', *Acta Politica*, vol. 19, January 1984, pp. 19–56.

Van Parijs, Phillipe, 'Power-Sharing Versus Border-Crossing in Ethnically Divided Societies', *Nomos*, vol. 42, 2000, pp. 296–320.

Varnavas, Andreas, *A Brief History of the Liberation Struggle of EOKA (1955–1959)*, Nicosia, 2001.

Varnava, Andrekos, *The Cyprus Problem and the Defence of the Middle-East, 1945–1960: Britain's Reluctant Relinquishment of a Place d' Armes*, Melbourne, published by author (publication of Honours dissertation), 2001.

Varnava, Andrekos, '*Punch* and the British Occupation of Cyprus in 1878', *Byzantine and Modern Greek Studies*, vol. 29, no. 2, 2005, pp. 167–86.

Vassiliou, George, 'EU Enlargement: Implications for Europe, Cyprus and the Eastern Mediterranean', *Mediterranean Quarterly*, vol. 13, no.1, 2002, pp. 12–20.

Vassiliou, George, 'The Cyprus Problem and the European Union', *The Cyprus Review*, vol. 16, no. 2, Fall 2004, pp. 95–102.

Vayrynen, Tarja, 'Ethnic Communality and Conflict Resolution', *Cooperation and Conflict*, vol. 33, no. 1, 1998, pp. 59–80.

Veremis, Thanos and Savvides, Philippos, 'Cyprus After the Referenda of April 24: What Next?', *The Cyprus Review*, vol. 16, no. 2, Fall 2004, pp. 83–94.

Volkan, Vamik D., *Cyprus – War and Adaptation: A Psychoanalytic History of the Two Ethnic Groups in Conflict*, Charlottesville, University Press of Virginia, 1979.

Volkan, Vamik D., 'Turks and Greeks of Cyprus: Psychopolitical Considerations', in Vangelis Calotychos (ed.) *Cyprus and its People: Nation, Identity and Experience in an Unimaginable Community, 1955–1997*, Colorado, Westview Press, 1998.

Volkan, Vamik D., interview by Yael Navaro-Yashin, 'Layers Upon Layers: Politics, Psychology and Language in a Changing World', in Mehmet Yashin (ed.) *Stepmothertongue, From Nationalism to Multiculturalism: Literatures of Cyprus, Greece and Turkey*, London, Middlesex University Press, 2000.

Volkan, Vamik D., *Killing in the Name of Identity, a Study of Bloody Conflicts*, Virginia, Pitchstone Publishing, 2006.

Warbrick, Colin, 'Recognition of States', *International and Comparative Law Quarterly*, no. 41, 1992, pp. 473–82.

Ward, Alan J., 'Northern Ireland: A Constitutional Postscript, 1972–1992', in Alan J. Ward, *The Irish Constitutional Tradition: Responsible Government and Modern Ireland 1782–1992*, Washington, The Catholic University of America Press, 1994.

Webster, Craig, 'Division or Unification in Cyprus? The Role of Demographics, Attitudes and Party Inclination on Greek Cypriot Preferences for a Solution to the Cyprus Problem', *Ethnopolitics*, vol. 4, no. 3, September 2005, pp. 299–309.

Webster, Craig, 'Commonwealth Diplomatic Missions: A Comparative Empirical Investigation of the Foreign Policy of Five Commonwealth Members', *The Round Table*, vol. 361, 2001, pp. 529–39.

Webster, Craig, and Lordos, Alexandros, 'Who Supported the Annan Plan? An Exploratory Statistical Analysis of the Demographic, Political, and Attitudinal Correlates', *The Cyprus Review*, vol. 18, no. 1, pp. 13–35.

Weeping Island, A Collection of Cypriot Literature, The United Cypriots Friendship Association, 2001.

Weston Markides, Diana, *Cyprus 1957–1963 From Colonial Conflict to Constitutional Crisis: The Key Role of the Municipal Issue*, Minnesota, University of Minnesota, 2001.

Wilford, R. A., 'Inverting Consociationalism? Policy, Pluralism and the Post-Modern', in Brigid Hadfield (ed.) *Northern Ireland: Politics and the Constitution*, Buckingham, Open University Press, 1992.

Wilkinson, Steven Ian, 'India, Consociational Theory, and Ethnic Violence', *Asian Survey*, vol. 40, no. 5, September–October 2000, pp. 767–91.

Wimmer, Andreas, *Nationalist Exclusion and Ethnic Conflict: Shadows of Modernity*, Cambridge, Cambridge University Press, 2002.

Wintle, Michael, 'Pillarisation, Consociation and Vertical Pluralism in the Netherlands Revisited: A European View', *West European Politics*, vol. 23, no. 3, July 2000, pp. 139–52.

Wittig, Kerstin, *People United in a Country Divided, Bi-Communal Activities in Cyprus*, unpublished Master of Arts thesis, Tübingen University, 2005.

Wolff, Stefan, *Ethnic Conflict: A Global Perspective*, Oxford, Oxford University Press, 2007.

Wolleh, Oliver, 'Local Peace Constituencies in Cyprus: Citizens' Rapprochement by the Bi-Communal Conflict Resolution Trainer Group', *Berghof Report Nr. 8*, Berghof Research Centre for Constructive Conflict Management, March 2001, http://www.berghof-center.org/publications/reports/complete/br8e.pdf (accessed 26 July 2004).

Wolleh, Oliver, 'Cyprus: A Civil Society Caught Up in the Issue of Recognition', *Searching for Peace in Europe and Eurasia 2002*, www.euconflict.org (accessed 23 August 2004).

Woodhouse, C. M., 'Cyprus: The British Point of View', in John Koumoulides (ed.) *Cyprus in Transition 1960–1985*, London, Trigraph, 1986.

Xydis, Stephen G., *Cyprus, Reluctant Republic*, The Hague, Mouton and Co., 1973.

Yakinthou, Christalla, 'The Quiet Deflation of Den Xehno? Changes in the Greek Cypriot Communal Narrative on the Missing Persons in Cyprus', *Cyprus Review*, vol. 20, no. 1, Spring 2008, pp. 15–33.

Yakinthou, Christalla, 'The House that Annan Built?', in A. Varnavas and H. Faustmann (eds) *Reunifying Cyprus: The Annan Plan and Beyond*, London, I. B. Tauris and Co., 2009.

Yakinthou, Christalla, 'The European Union's Management of the Cyprus Conflict: System Failure or Structural Metamorphosis?', *Ethnopolitics*, vol. VII, no. 3, 2009.

Yaşın, Mehmet, *Don't go Back to Kyrenia*, London, Middlesex University Press, 2001.

Yennari, Katerina, 'Building Bridges in Cyprus: the Role of the European Union in the Reconciliation of the Two Communities', *The Cyprus Review*, vol. 15, no. 2, Fall 2003, pp. 81–102.

Yiangou, George S., 'A Critical Evaluation of the Applicability of the Aland Model into the Conflict Situation in Cyprus with a View to Achieving Peaceful Governance', *The Cyprus Review*, vol. 14, no. 1, Spring 2002, pp. 13–28.

Yiftachel, Oren, *State Policy and Political Stability in a Biethnic Democracy: The Influence of Israel's Land Use Planning on Arab-Jewish Relations in the Galilee*, Perth, University of Western Australia, 1990 unpublished PhD thesis.

Yiftachel, Oren, 'Planning as Control: Policy and Resistance in a Deeply Divided Society', *Progress in Planning*, vol. 44, 1995, pp. 115–84.

Yiftachel, Oren, 'The Homeland and Nationalism', *Encyclopedia of Nationalism*, vol. 1, 2000, pp. 359–83.

Yiftachel, Oren, *Ethnocracy, Land and Identity Politics in Israel/Palestine*, Pennsylvania, University of Pennsylvania Press, 2006.

Yıldız, Netice, 'Turkish Culture within the Context of the Cypriot Cultural Heritage', in Emel Doğramacı, William Haney, and Güray König (eds) *First International Congress on Cypriot Studies*, Gazimağusa, Eastern Mediterranean University Press, 1997.

Yesilada, Birol Ali, 'Social Progress and Political Development in the Turkish Republic of Northern Cyprus', *The Cyprus Review*, vol. 1, no. 2, Fall 1989, pp. 91–112.

Zaller, John R., 'Political Awareness, Elite Opinion Leadership, and the Mass Survey Response', *Social Cognition*, vol. 8, 1990, pp. 125–53.

Zaller, John R., *The Nature and Origins of Mass Opinion*, Cambridge, Cambridge University Press, 1992.

Zembylas, Michalinos and Karahasan, Hakan, 'The Politics of Memory and Forgetting in Pedagogical Practices: Towards Pedagogies of Reconciliation and Peace in Divided Cyprus', *The Cyprus Review*, vol. 18, no. 2, Fall 2006, pp. 15–35.

Zetter, Roger, 'Reconceptualizing the Myth of Return: Continuity and Transition Amongst the Greek Cypriot Refugees of 1974', *Journal of Refugee Studies*, vol. 12, no. 1, 1999.

Zetter, Roger, 'Rehousing the Greek Cypriot Refugees from 1974: Dependency, Assimilation, Politicisation', in John Koumoulides (ed.) *Cyprus in Transition 1960–1985*, London, Trigraph, 1986.

Zetter, Roger, '"We are Strangers Here": Continuity and Transition: The Impact of Displacement and Protracted Exile on the Greek Cypriot "Refugees"', in Vangelis Calotychos (ed.) *Cyprus and its People: Nation, Identity and Experience in an Unimaginable Community, 1955–1997*, Colorado, Westview Press, 1998.

Γλαύκου Κληρίδη, Ντοκουμέντα Μιας Εποχής 1993–2003, Λευκοσία, Πολιτεία 2007.

Index

Accommodationism, 11–12
Afrika newspaper, 216
AKEL, 74, 100,
  and DIKO, 101–2, 152
  and DISY, 100, 152, 219
  and CTP, 106
  election of, 101–2
  position on Annan Plan, 107, 152–4,
    160–2,
Akritas Plan, 102, 146, 219, 232
Anastasiadis, Nicos, 162, 174, 225
Annan Plan
  I, 74, 86, 92, 105, 134, 143, 151, 154,
    211, 216
  II, 74, 130, 136
  III, 74, 143, 223, 236
  IV, 74, 105, 153
  V, 9, 75, 92, 105, 119, 151–3
  and 2004 referendum, 118–19, 143–69
  and consociationalism, 11, 13, 78–80
  and EU, 128–37
  and Switzerland, 24–6, 74, 84
  and refugee return, 30, 157, 164
  conspiracy regarding, 108
  constituent states, 77–8
  development of, 80–92
  federal state, 75–7
  Greek Cypriot support of, 120, 161–3
  Greek Cypriot rejection of, 96, 100–3,
    119–20, 157–61
  influence of 1960 constitution on,
    81–7
  influence of 1960 state's breakdown
    on, 87–92
  involvement of Cypriot actors in
    development of, 80–93
  Turkish Cypriot opposition to, 96, 98,
    126, 136–7
  Turkish Cypriot support of, 97–9,
    118–9, 151–2
  UN development of, 73–94, 131–3
Annan, Kofi, 81, 125, 144
anniversaries, national
  commemorated by Greek Cypriots, 2,
    117–8

commemorated by Turkish Cypriots,
  2, 117–8
autonomy
  and Annan Plan, 30, 43, 85, 94
  in colonial Cyprus, 40–1, 56–9,
  in Cyprus 29–31, 48–9, 52–3, 62–4
  principle of and consociationalism,
    14–16, 29

balance of power
  in Annan Plan, 81
  in consociational theory, 17–18, 29,
    30–1, 171
  in Cyprus, 31–2
  in 1960 Republic of Cyprus, 61,
    64–7, 71
Belgium
  and Annan Plan, 74, 90, 212
  and consociationalism, 12, 24–7
  applicability to Cyprus, 24–6, 74,
  criticisms of model, 17, 24–7
  partition of, 25
blood
  -bond and ethno-nationalism, 36
  political metaphor of, 36
Britain
  administration of Cyprus, 36, 39–51
  and Cypriot independence, 46, 51–2,
    56–9, 65
  and Cyprus' accession to EU, 98, 129,
    132, 136–7
  and EOKA/TMT, 1, 46–8
  Imperialism/anticolonialism in
    Cyprus, 1, 39–48, 56, 70
  postcolonial military presence in
    Cyprus, 53, 70–1
  role in Annan Plan's development,
    126–7
Bryant, Rebecca, 38–41, 45

centrifugal forces, 23
checkpoints at borders, 2, 8, 105, 108–9,
  113–16, 127, 167,
Christofias, Demetris, 105–8, 152,
  161–2, 164, 168, 173–4, 218

268